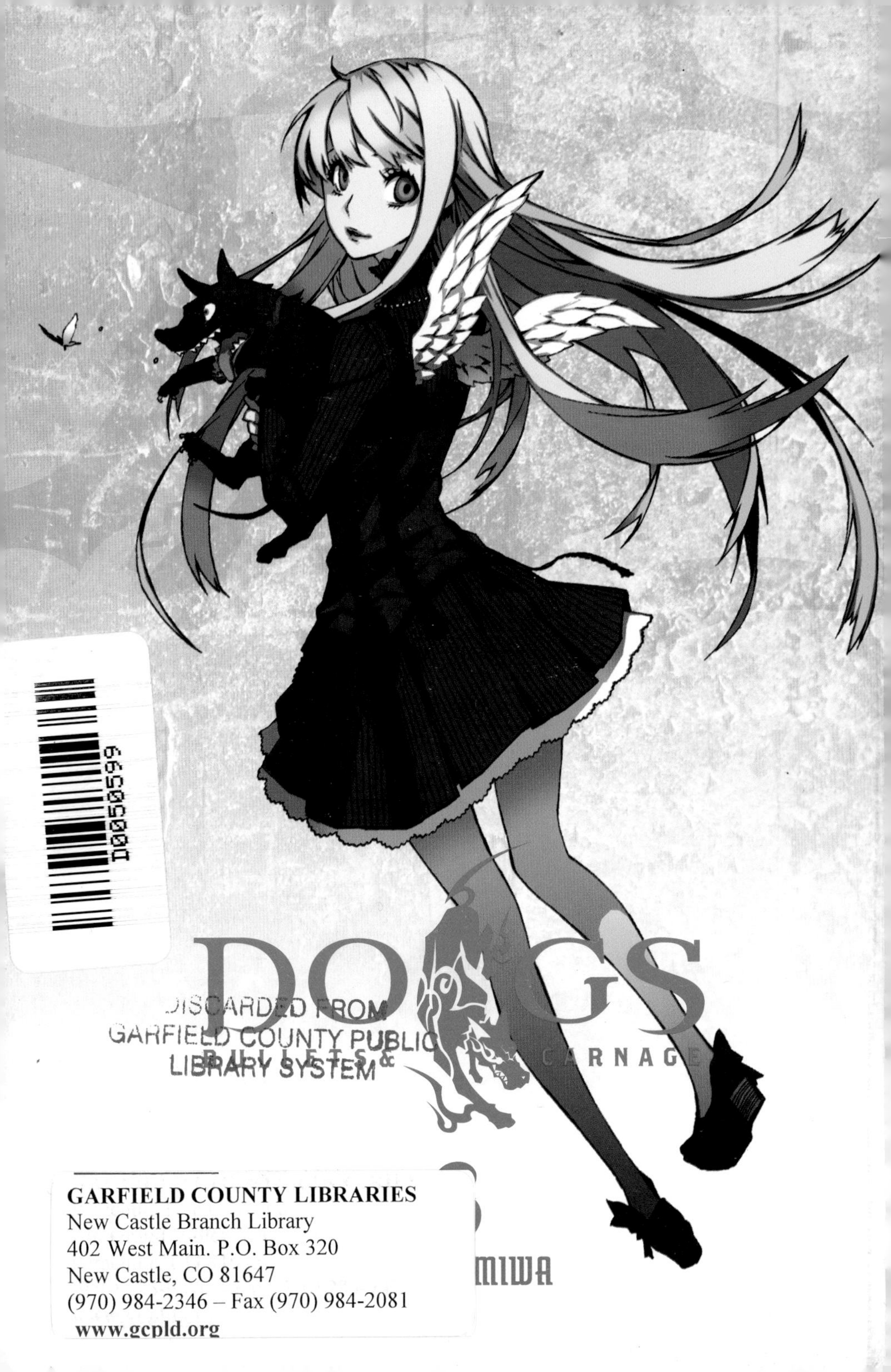
DOGS
BULLETS & CARNAGE
MIWA

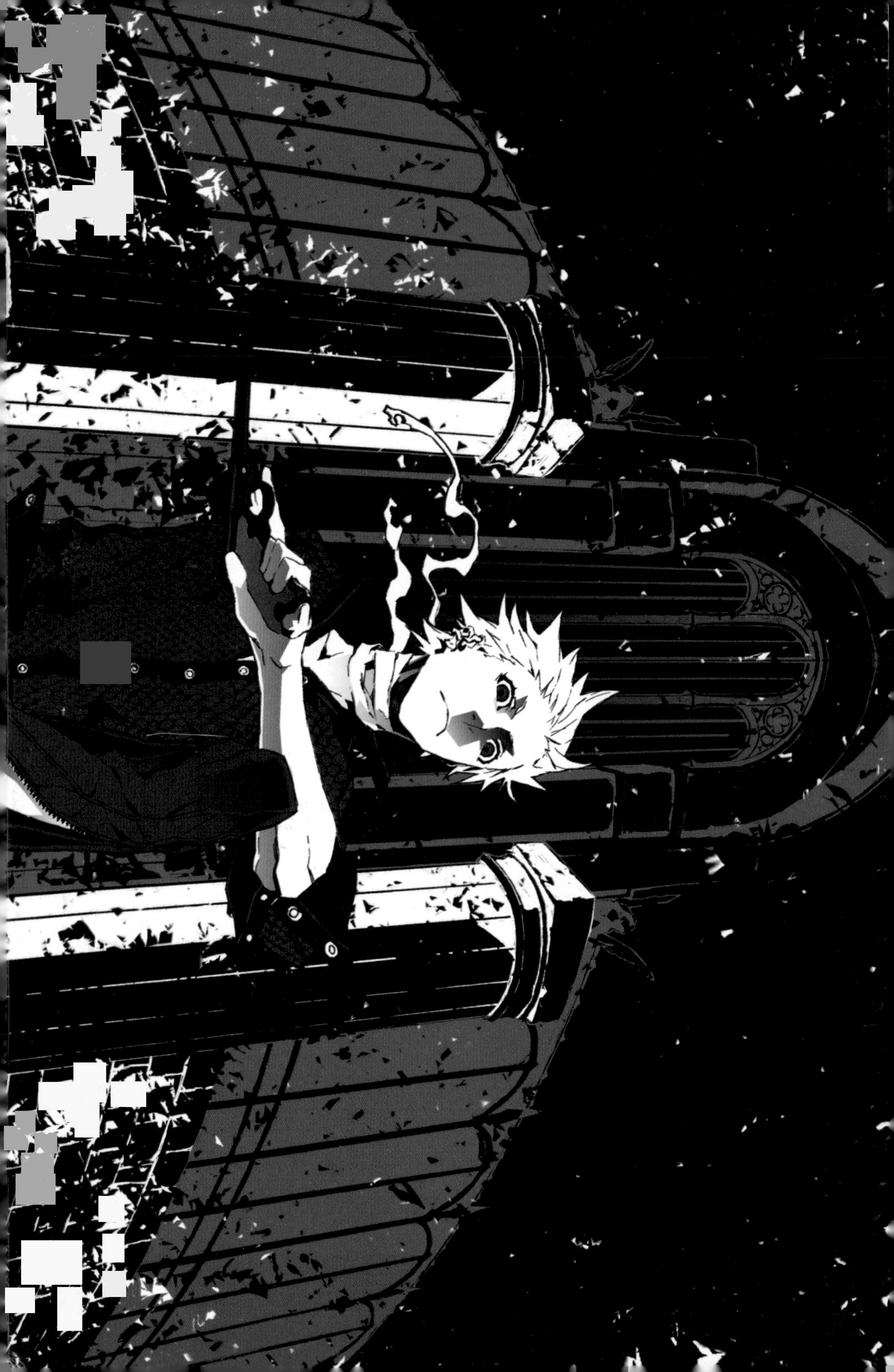

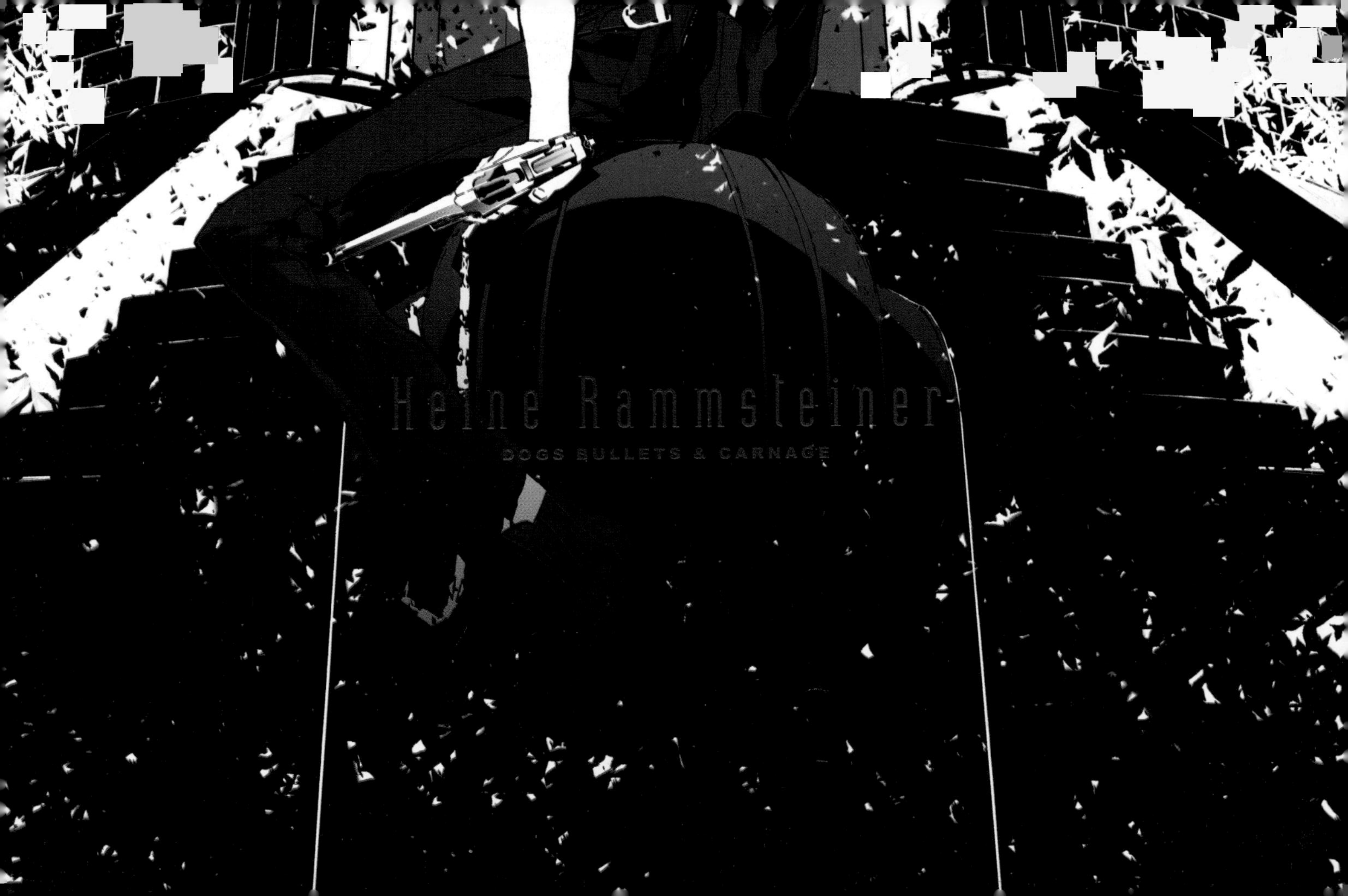
Heine Rammsteiner
DOGS BULLETS & CARNAGE

DOGS

BULLETS & CARNAGE

3 CONTENTS

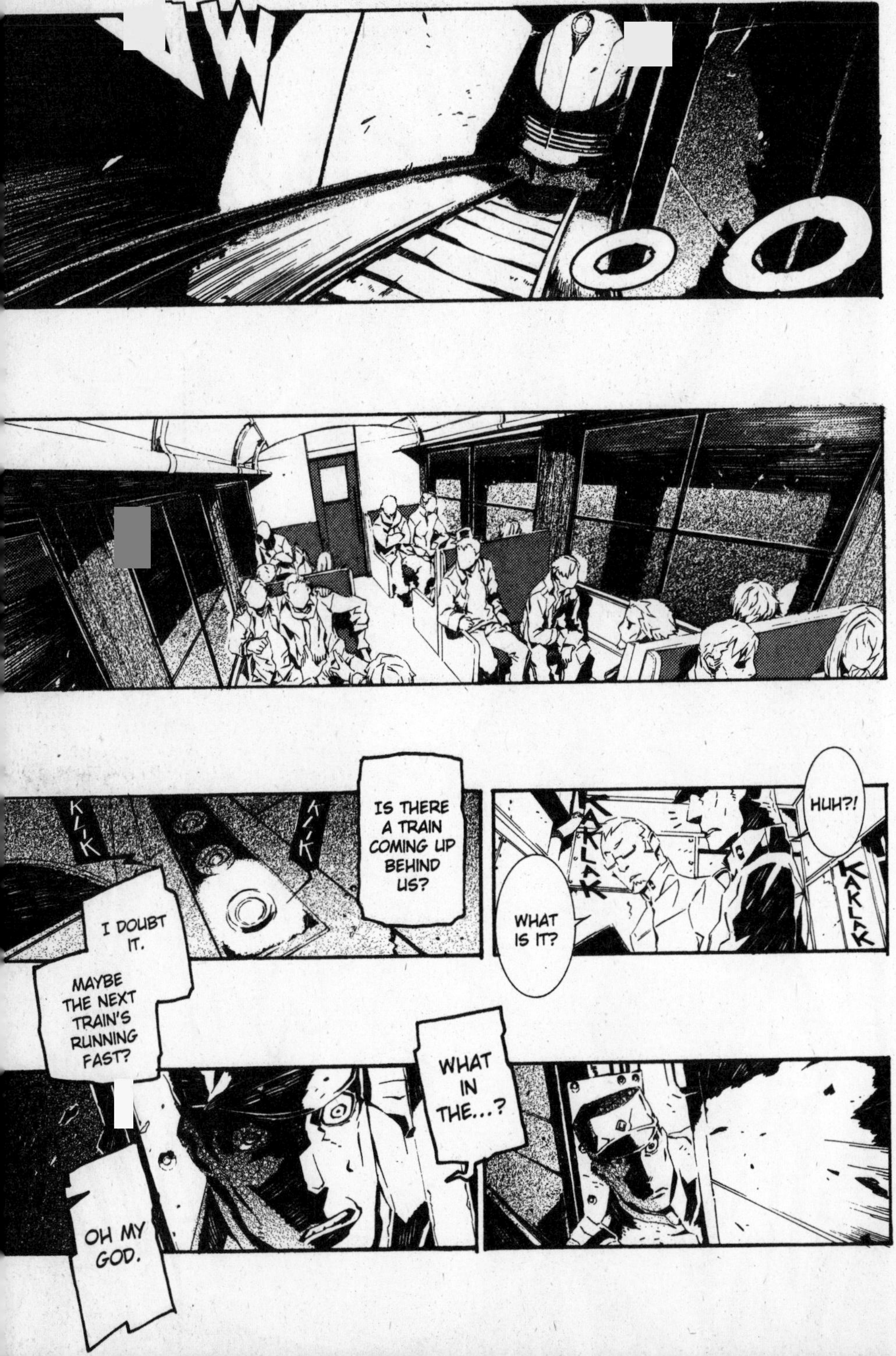
HUH?!
KAKLAK
KAKLAK
WHAT IS IT?
IS THERE A TRAIN COMING UP BEHIND US?
KLIK
KLIK
I DOUBT IT.
MAYBE THE NEXT TRAIN'S RUNNING FAST?
WHAT IN THE...?
OH MY GOD.

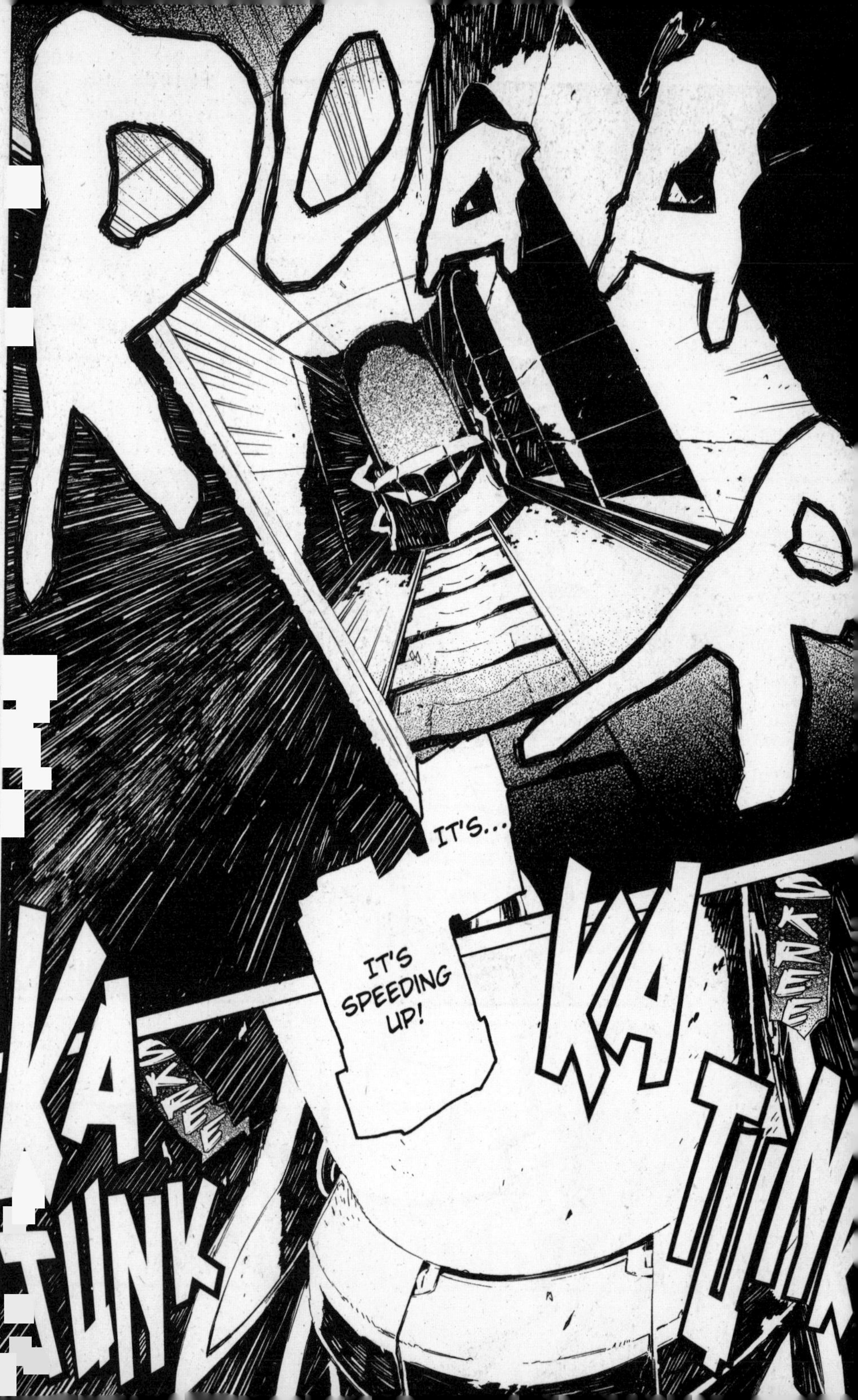
IT'S...
IT'S SPEEDING UP!
SKREE
KA TUNK
KA TUNK
SKREE

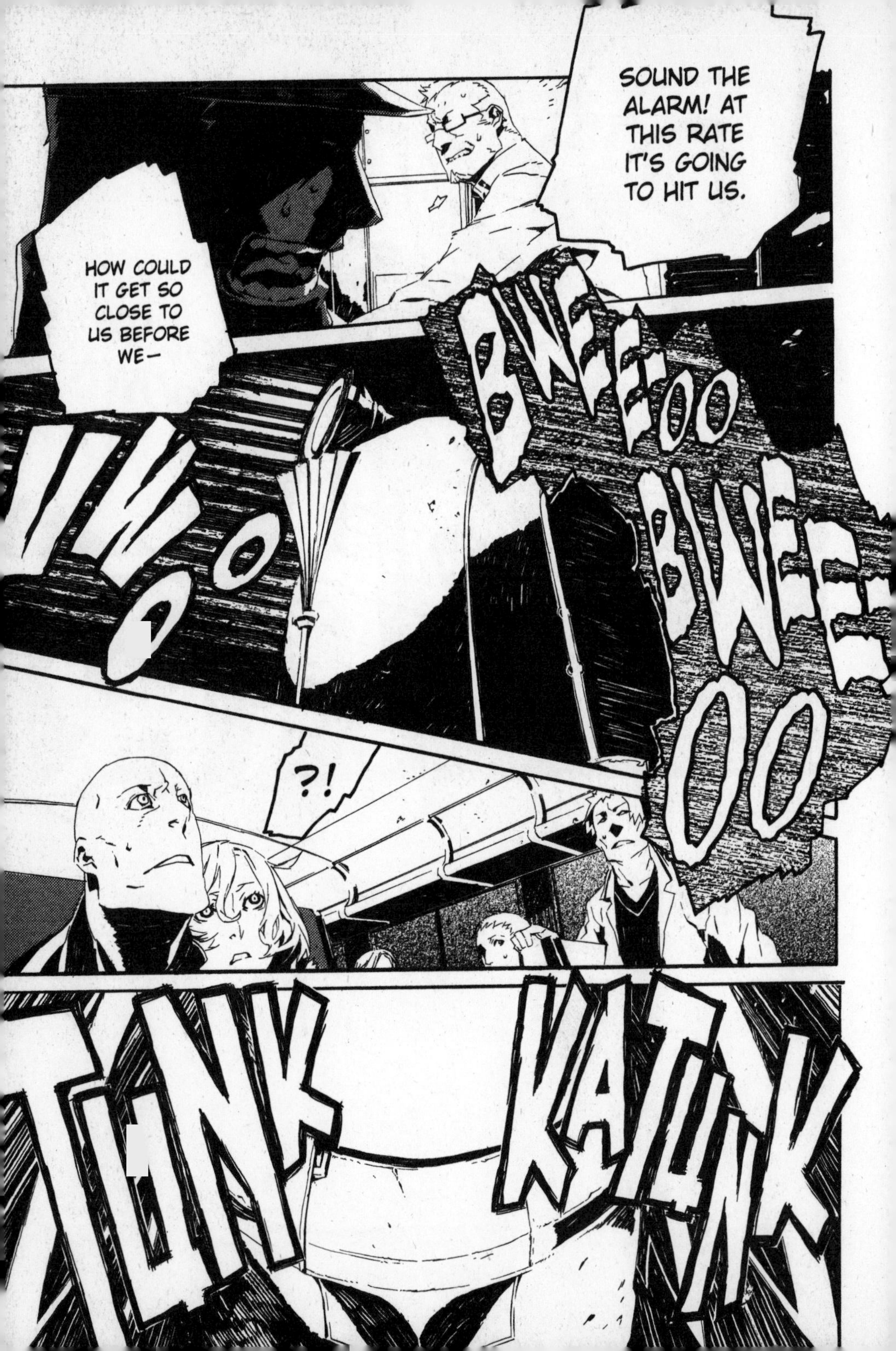
SOUND THE ALARM! AT THIS RATE IT'S GOING TO HIT US.
HOW COULD IT GET SO CLOSE TO US BEFORE WE—
BWEE-OO
BWEE-OO
WHOO
?!
KATONK
TONK

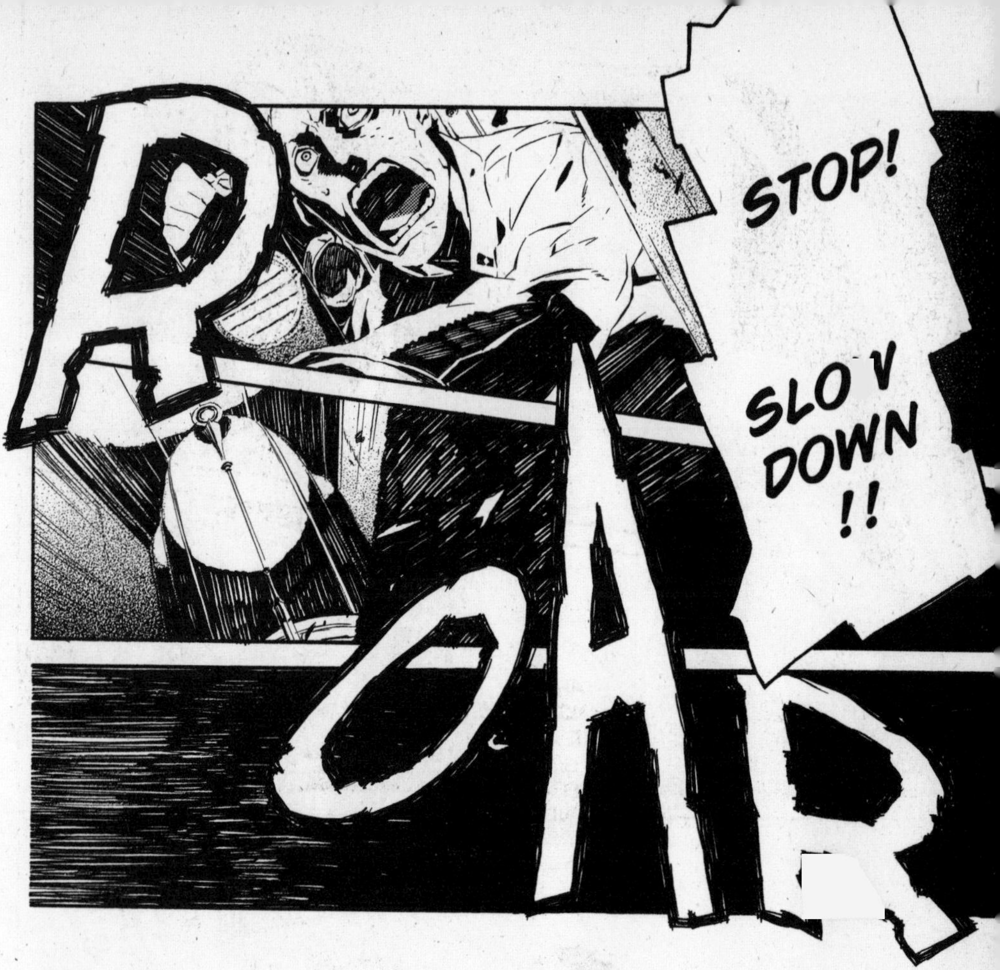
STOP!
SLOW DOWN!!
ROAR

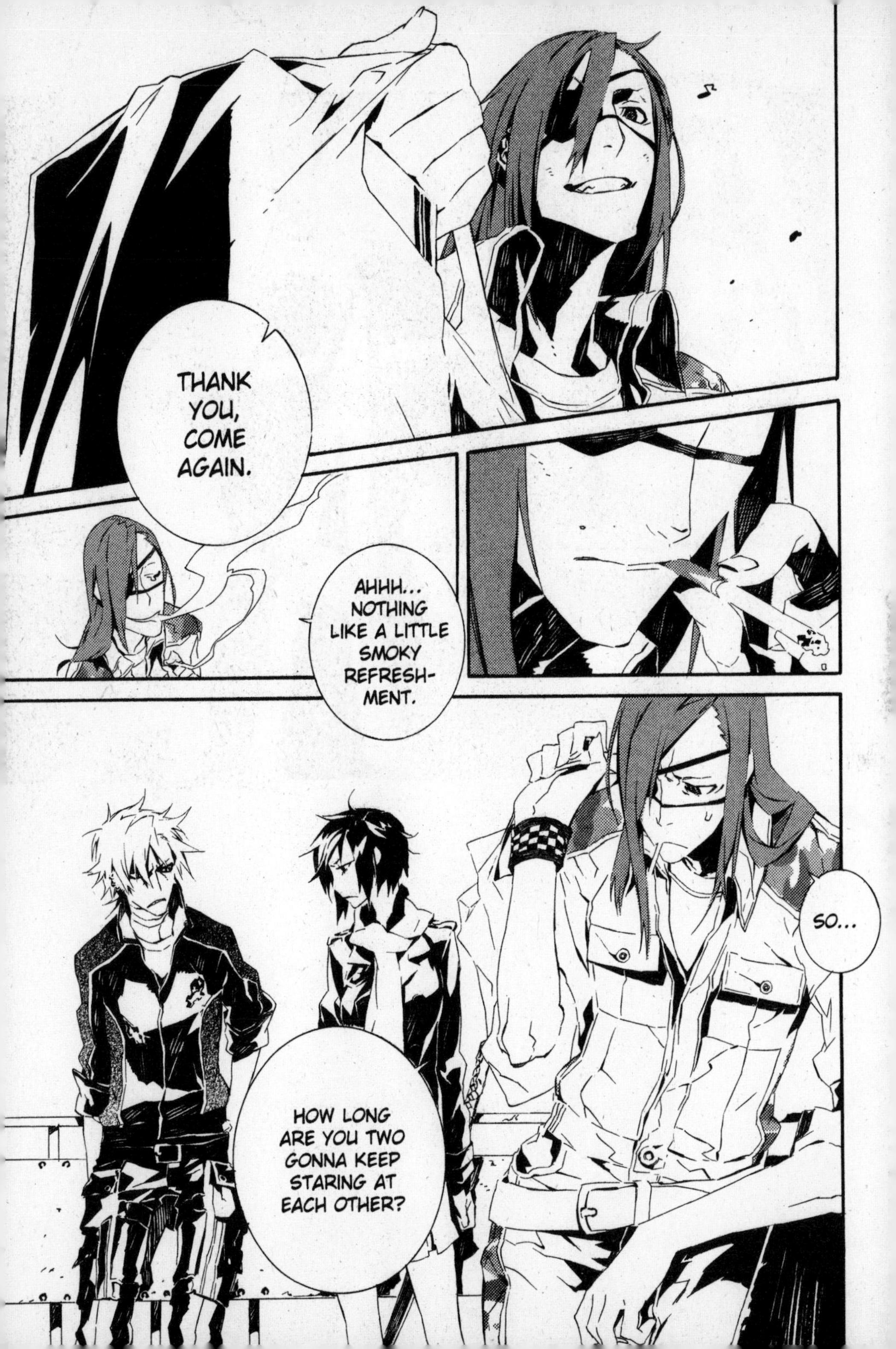
THANK YOU, COME AGAIN.
AHHH... NOTHING LIKE A LITTLE SMOKY REFRESH-MENT.
SO...
HOW LONG ARE YOU TWO GONNA KEEP STARING AT EACH OTHER?

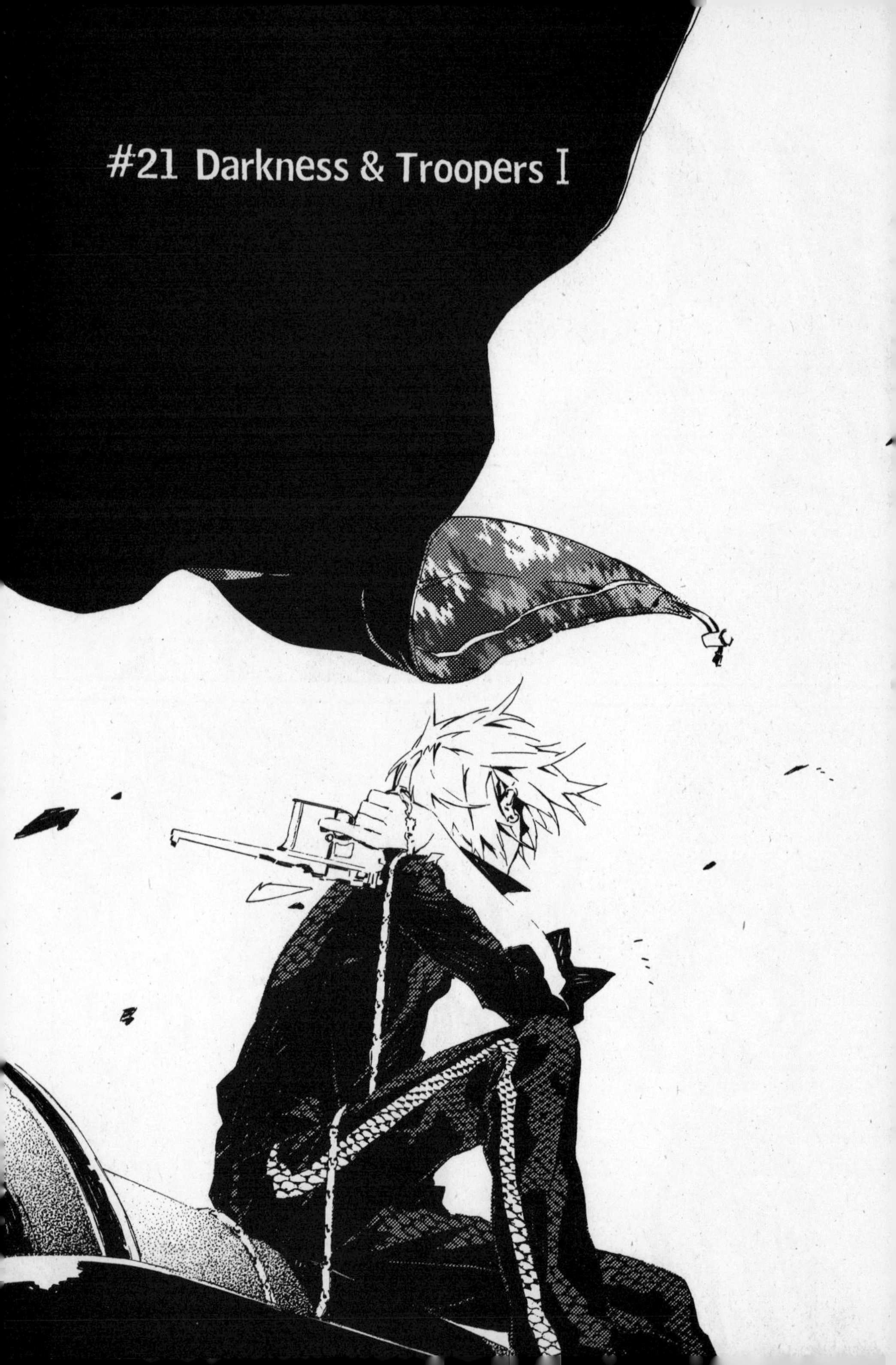
#21 Darkness & Troopers I

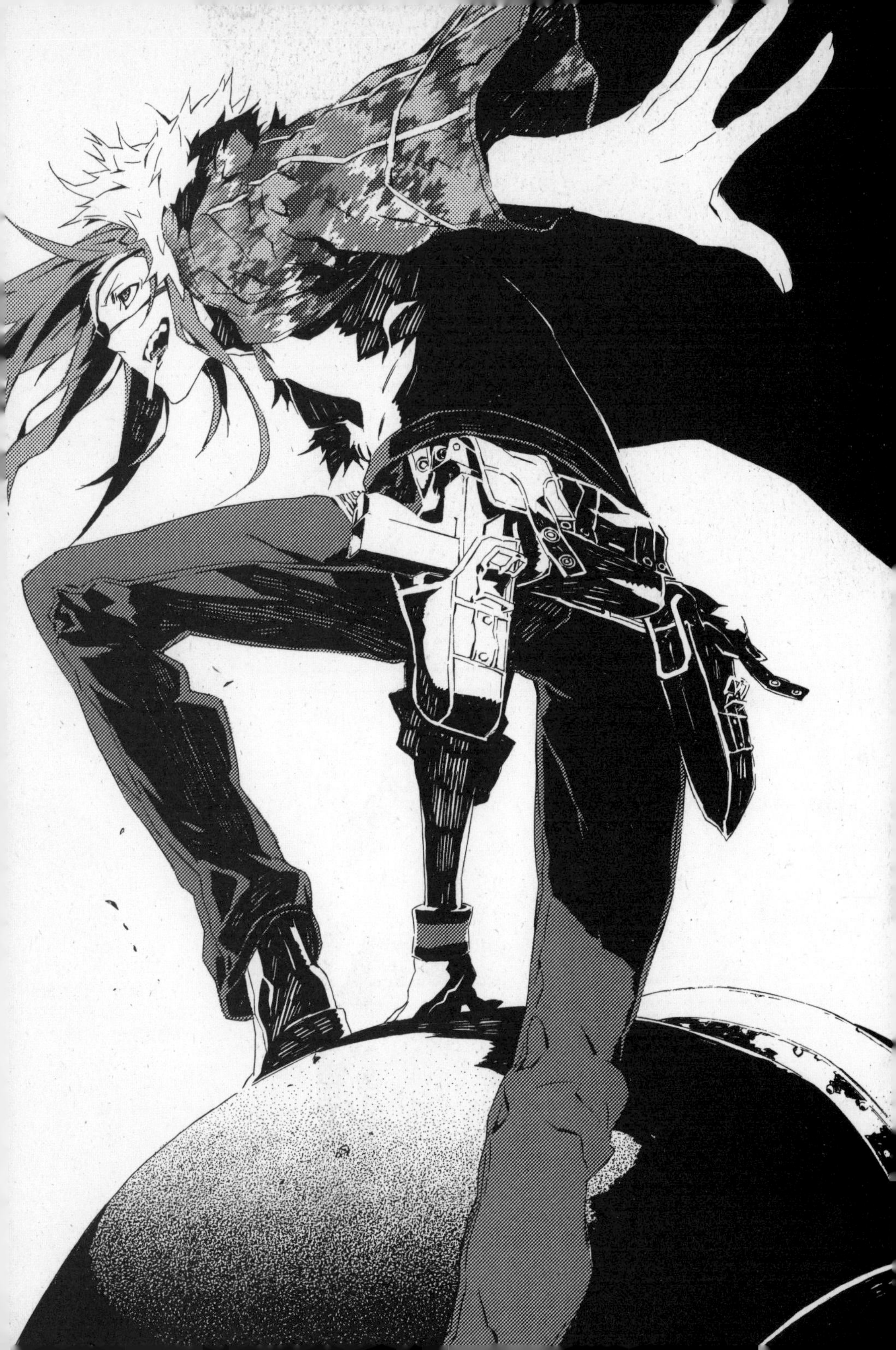

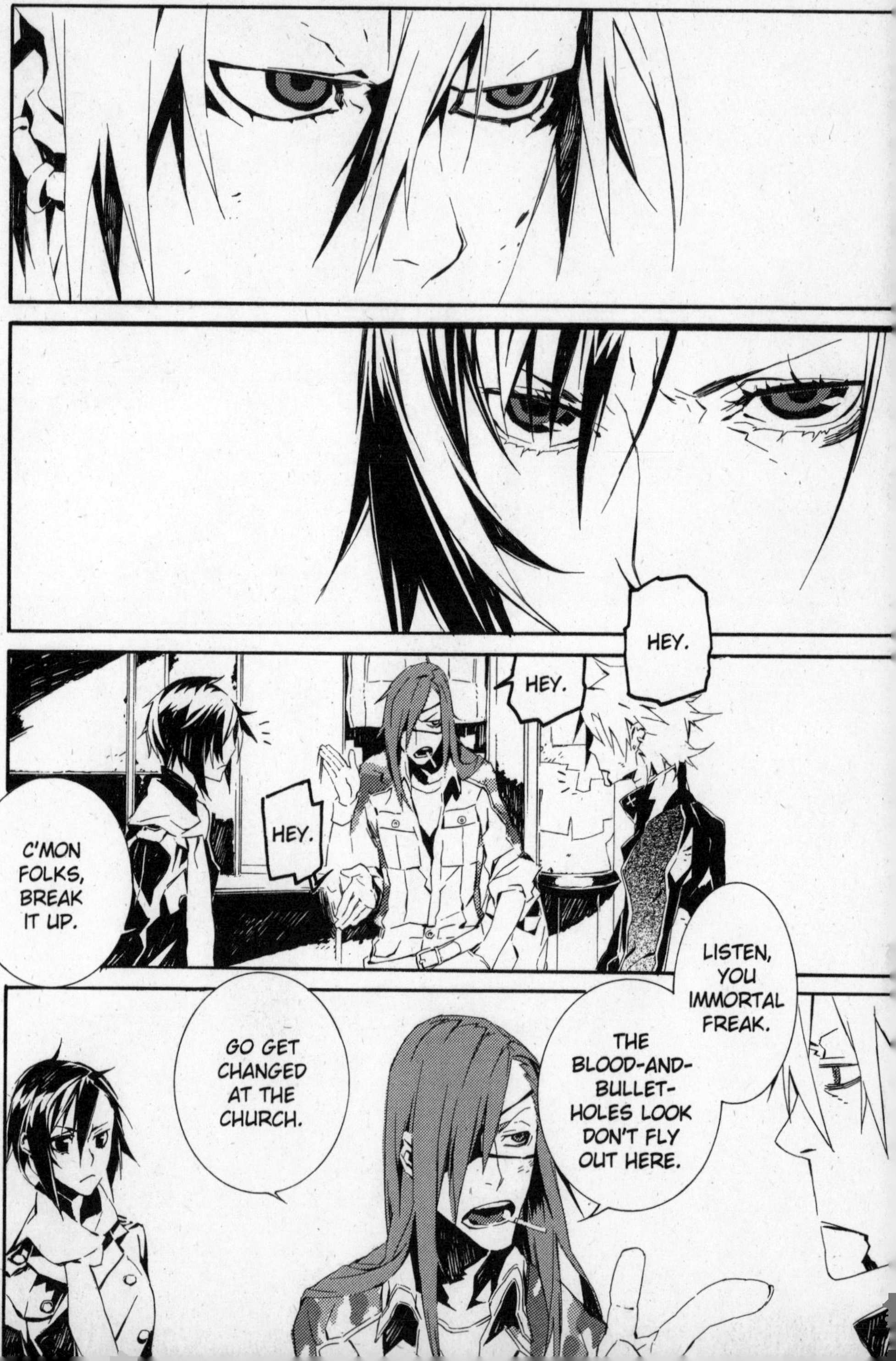
HEY.
HEY.
HEY.
C'MON FOLKS, BREAK IT UP.
LISTEN, YOU IMMORTAL FREAK.
THE BLOOD-AND-BULLET-HOLES LOOK DON'T FLY OUT HERE.
GO GET CHANGED AT THE CHURCH.

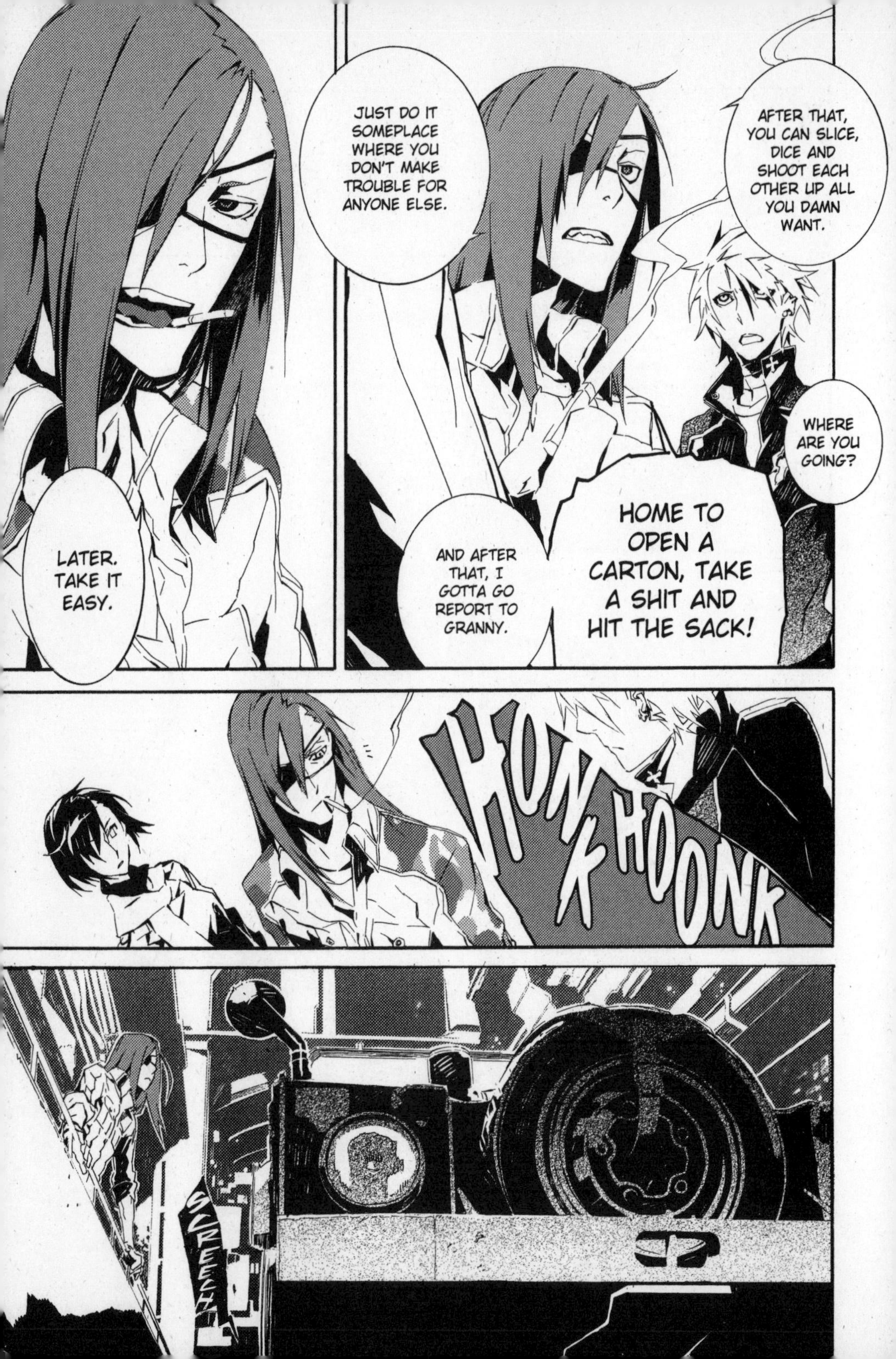
JUST DO IT SOMEPLACE WHERE YOU DON'T MAKE TROUBLE FOR ANYONE ELSE.
AFTER THAT, YOU CAN SLICE, DICE AND SHOOT EACH OTHER UP ALL YOU DAMN WANT.
WHERE ARE YOU GOING?
HOME TO OPEN A CARTON, TAKE A SHIT AND HIT THE SACK!
AND AFTER THAT, I GOTTA GO REPORT TO GRANNY.
LATER. TAKE IT EASY.
HONK
HOONK
SCREECH

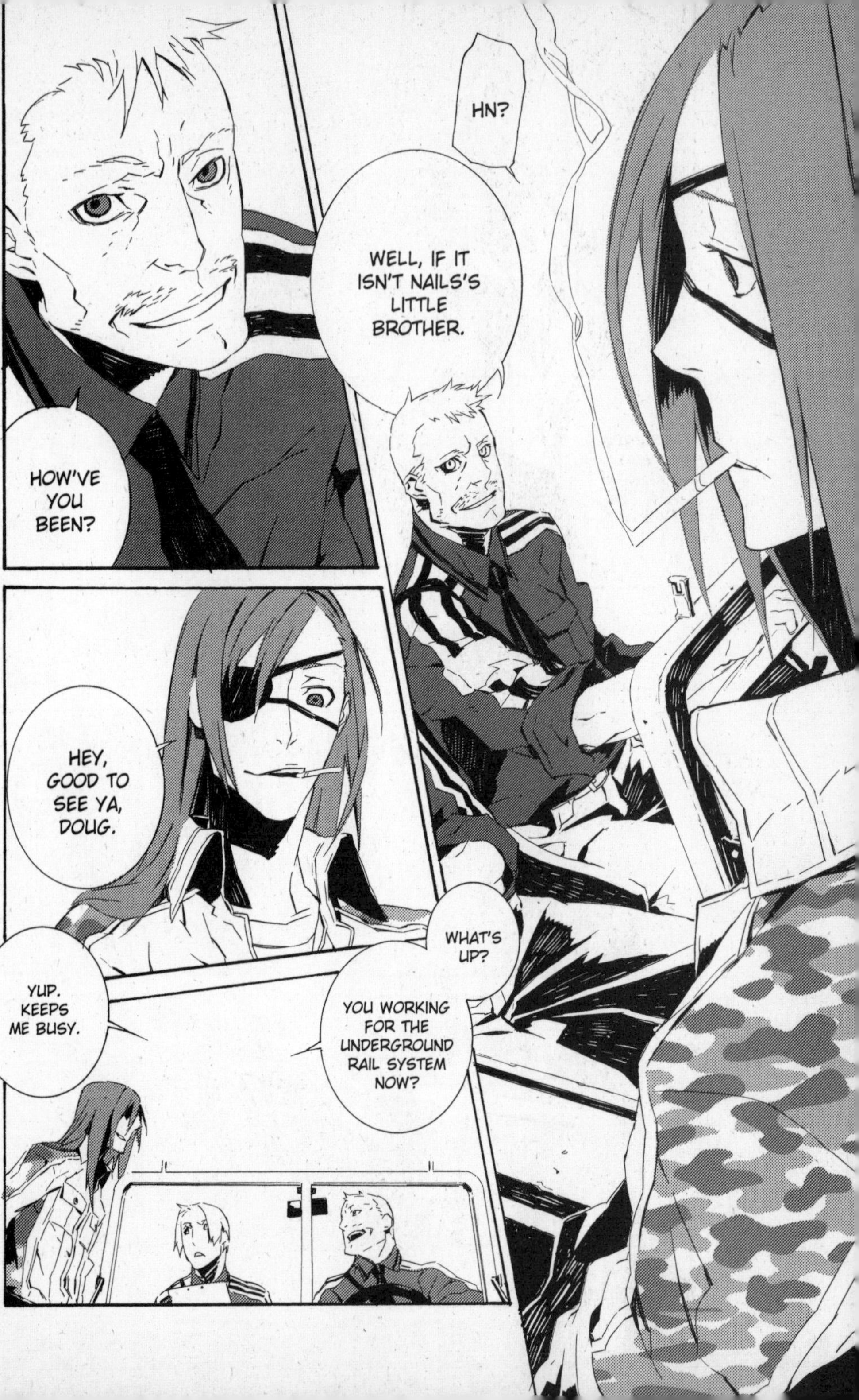
HN?
WELL, IF IT ISN'T NAILS'S LITTLE BROTHER.
HOW'VE YOU BEEN?
HEY, GOOD TO SEE YA, DOUG.
WHAT'S UP?
YOU WORKING FOR THE UNDERGROUND RAIL SYSTEM NOW?
YUP. KEEPS ME BUSY.

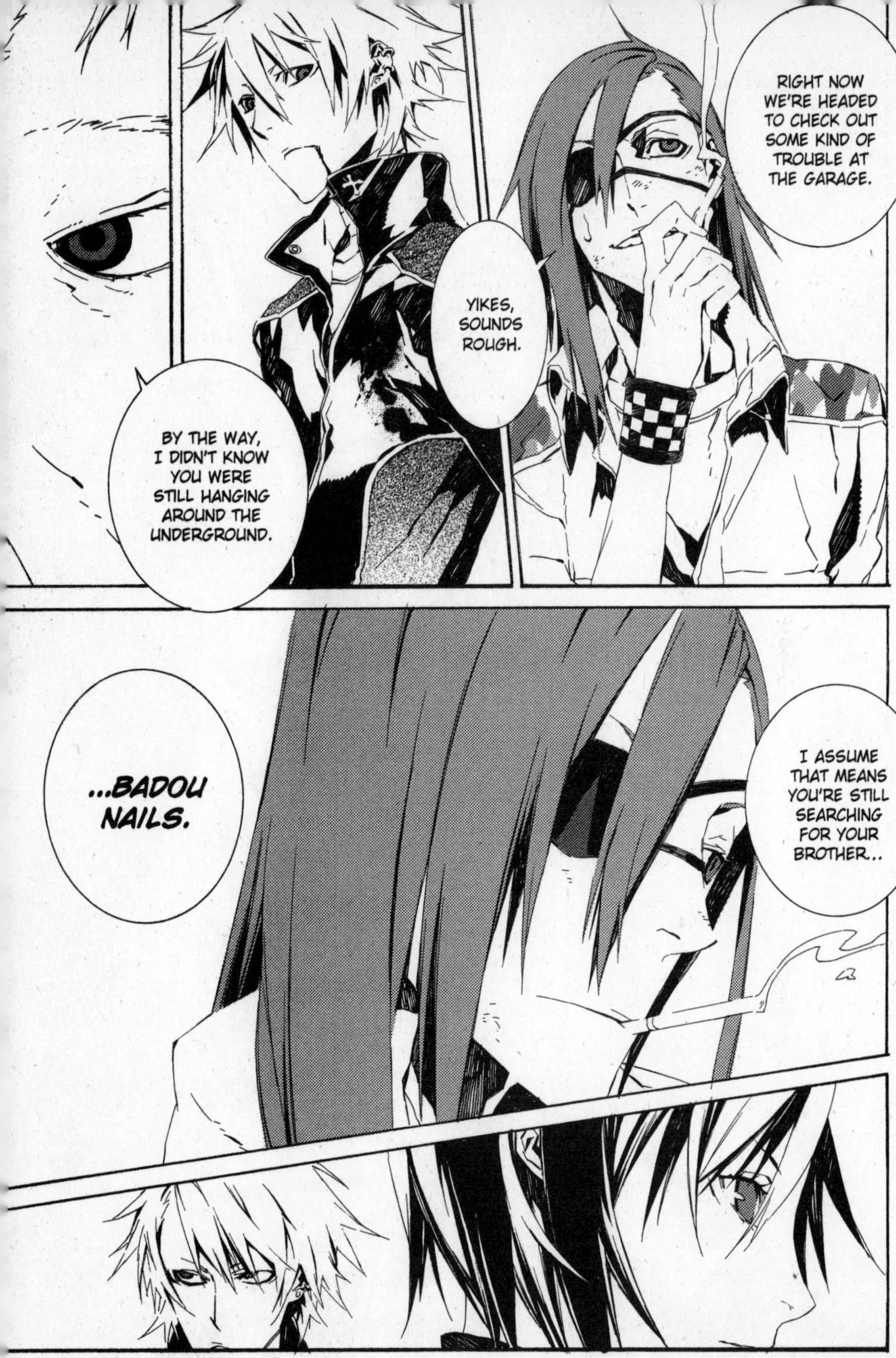
RIGHT NOW WE'RE HEADED TO CHECK OUT SOME KIND OF TROUBLE AT THE GARAGE.
YIKES, SOUNDS ROUGH.
BY THE WAY, I DIDN'T KNOW YOU WERE STILL HANGING AROUND THE UNDERGROUND.
I ASSUME THAT MEANS YOU'RE STILL SEARCHING FOR YOUR BROTHER...
...BADOU NAILS.

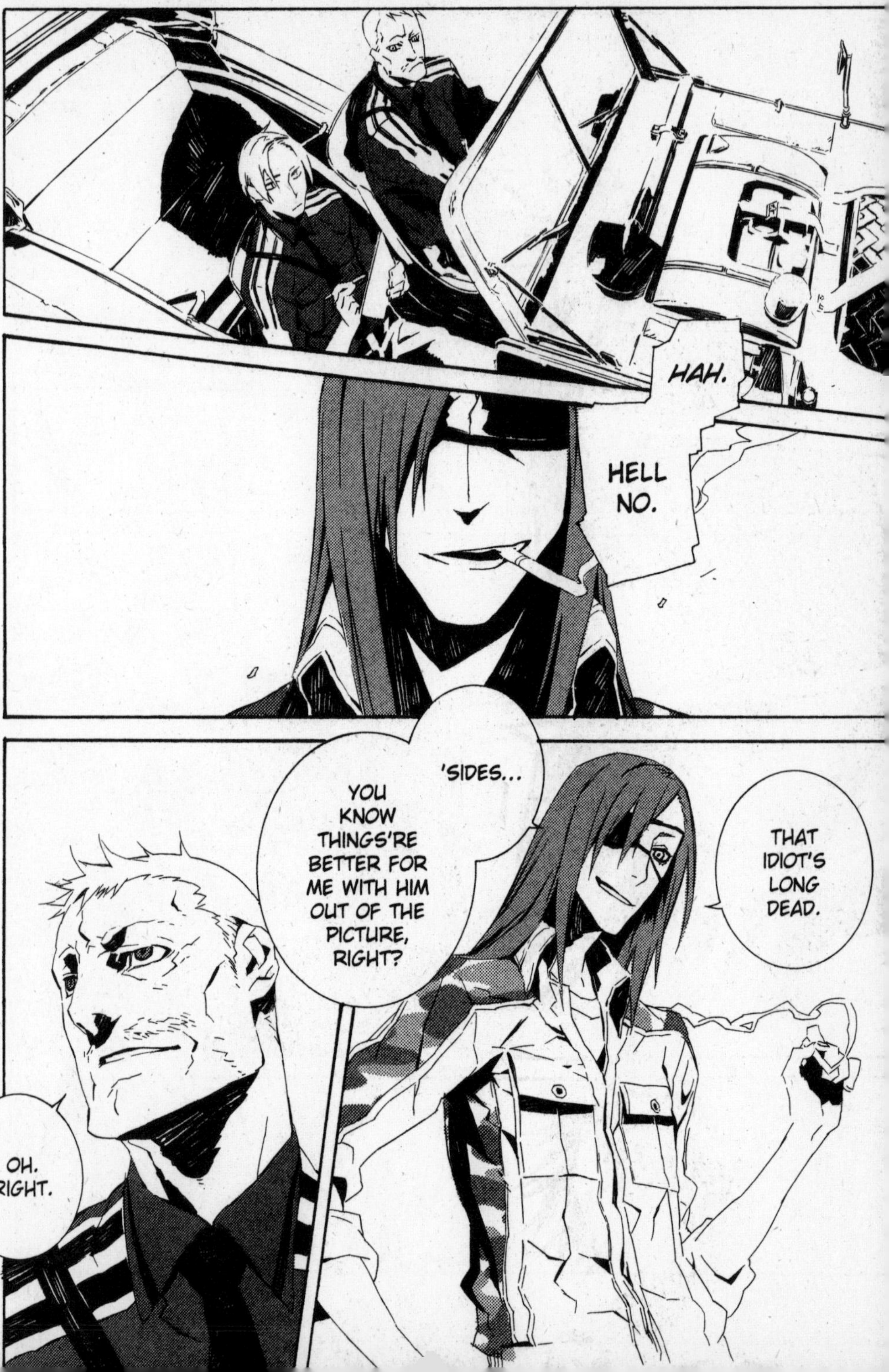

HAH.
HELL NO.
THAT IDIOT'S LONG DEAD.
'SIDES...
YOU KNOW THINGS'RE BETTER FOR ME WITH HIM OUT OF THE PICTURE, RIGHT?
OH. RIGHT.

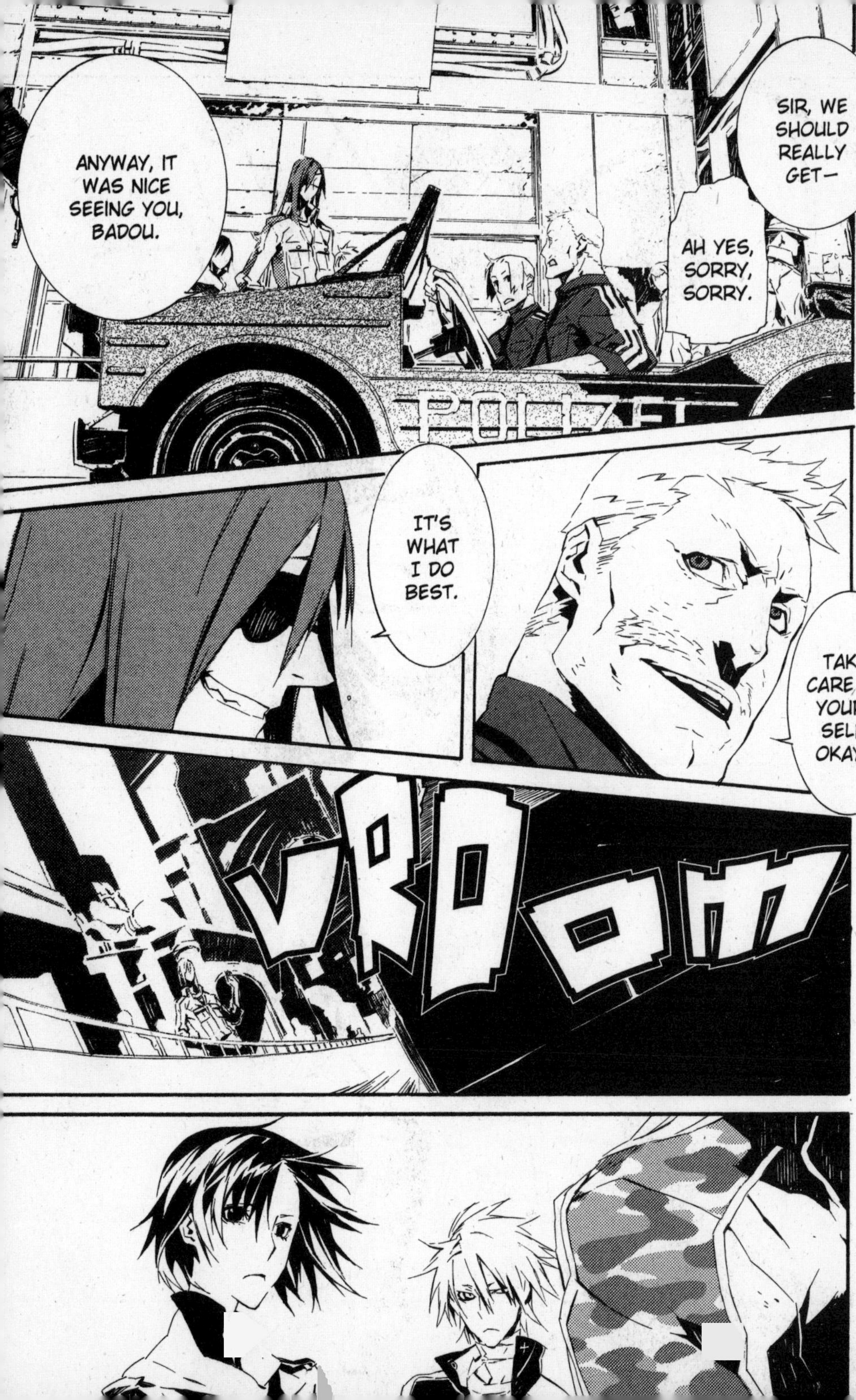
SIR, WE SHOULD REALLY GET—
AH YES, SORRY, SORRY.
ANYWAY, IT WAS NICE SEEING YOU, BADOU.
POLIZEI
TAKE CARE OF YOUR-SELF, OKAY?
IT'S WHAT I DO BEST.
VROOM

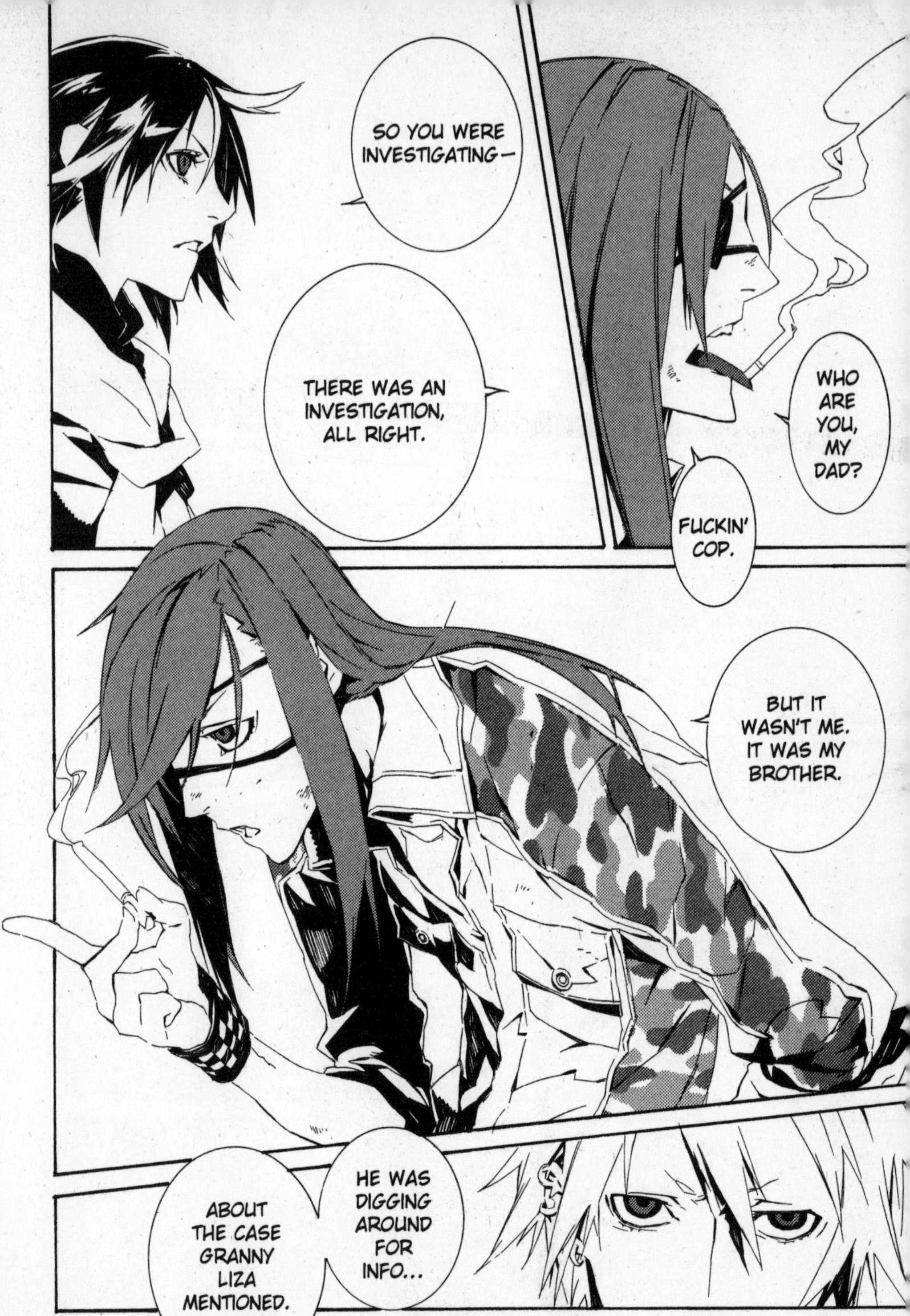
SO YOU WERE INVESTIGATING—
WHO ARE YOU, MY DAD?
FUCKIN' COP.
THERE WAS AN INVESTIGATION, ALL RIGHT.
BUT IT WASN'T ME. IT WAS MY BROTHER.
HE WAS DIGGING AROUND FOR INFO...
ABOUT THE CASE GRANNY LIZA MENTIONED.

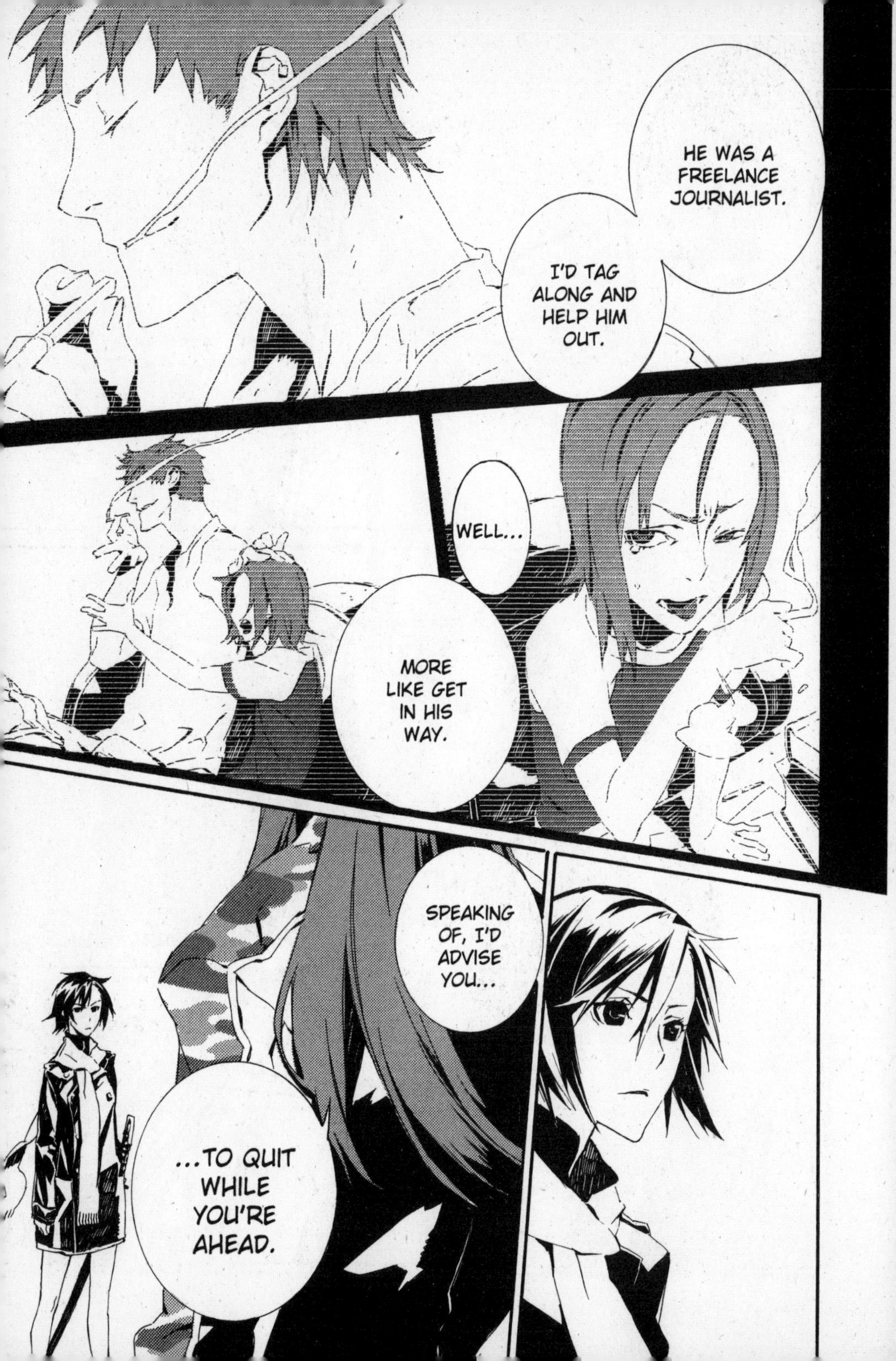
HE WAS A FREELANCE JOURNALIST.
I'D TAG ALONG AND HELP HIM OUT.
WELL...
MORE LIKE GET IN HIS WAY.
SPEAKING OF, I'D ADVISE YOU...
...TO QUIT WHILE YOU'RE AHEAD.

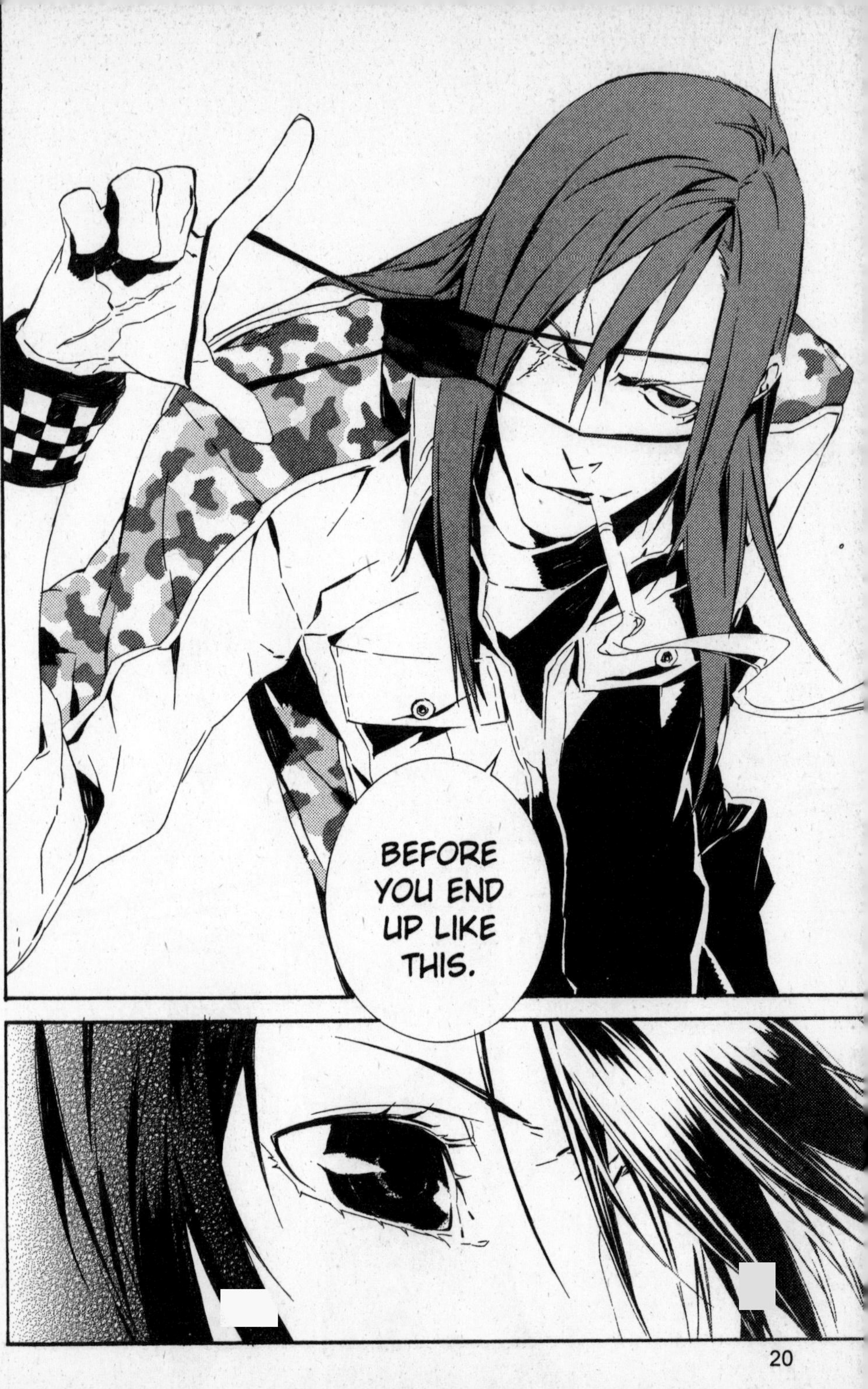
BEFORE YOU END UP LIKE THIS.

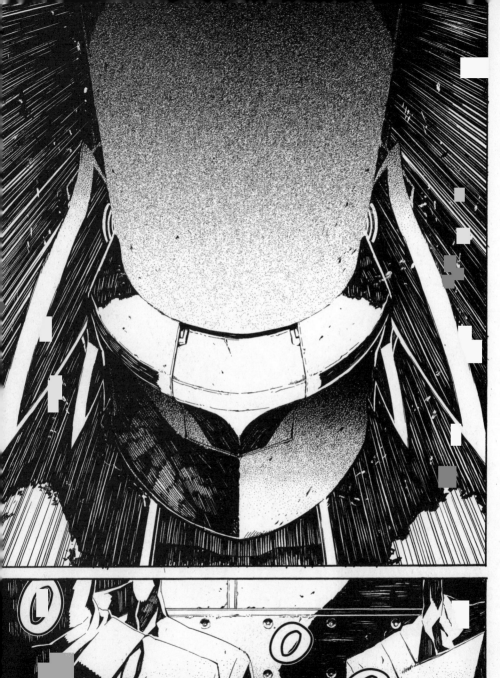

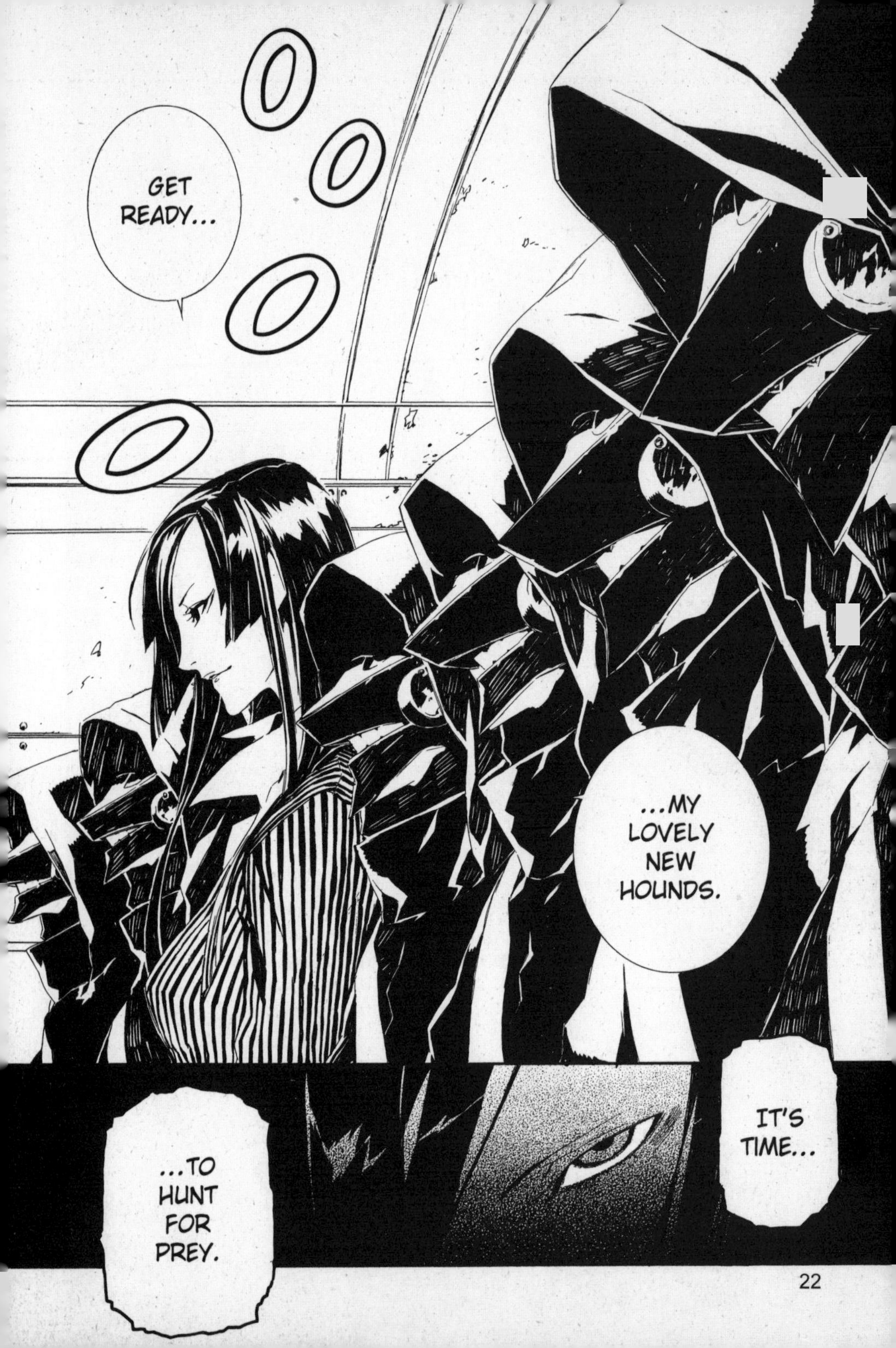
GET READY...
...MY LOVELY NEW HOUNDS.
IT'S TIME...
...TO HUNT FOR PREY.

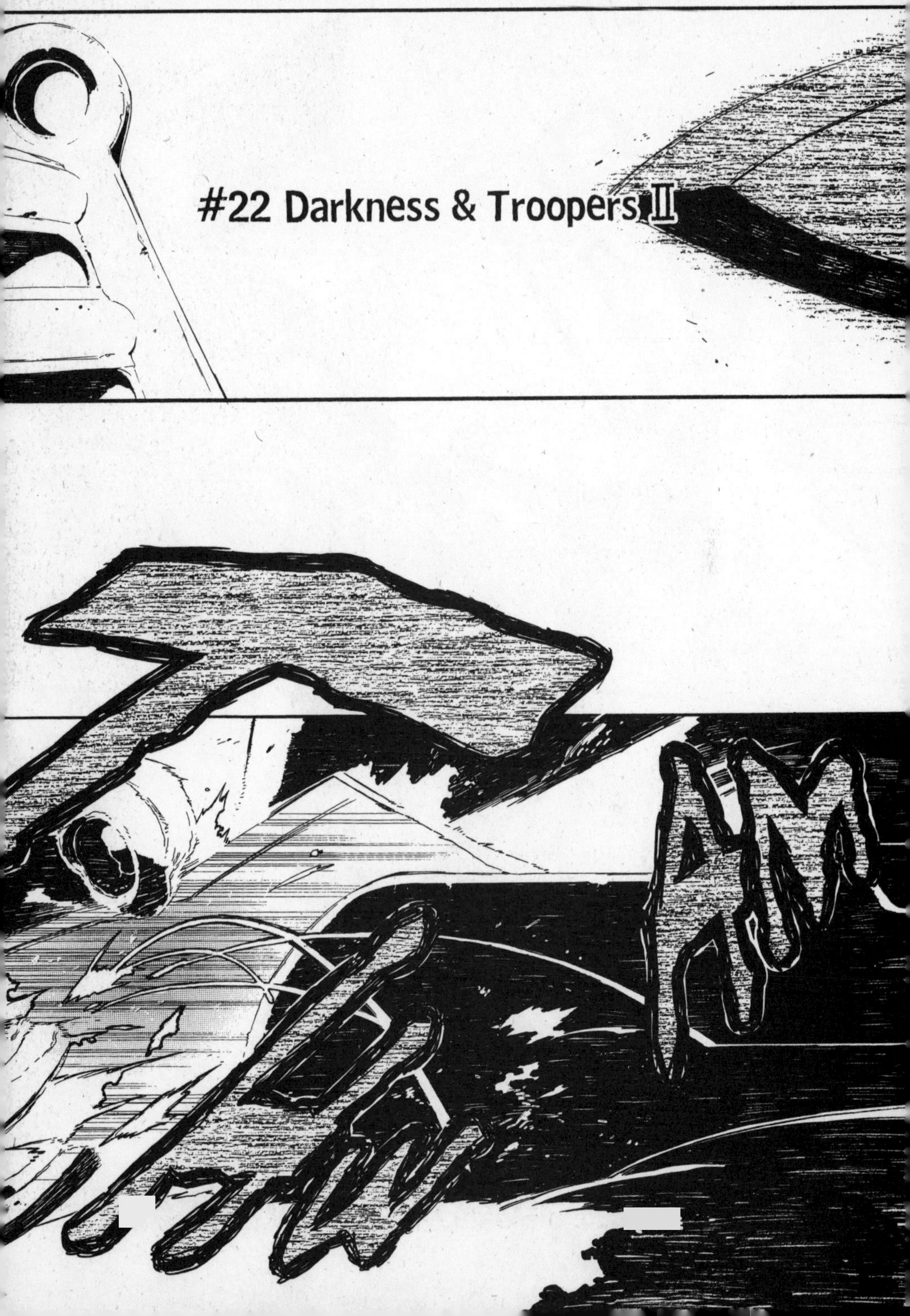
#22 Darkness & Troopers Ⅱ

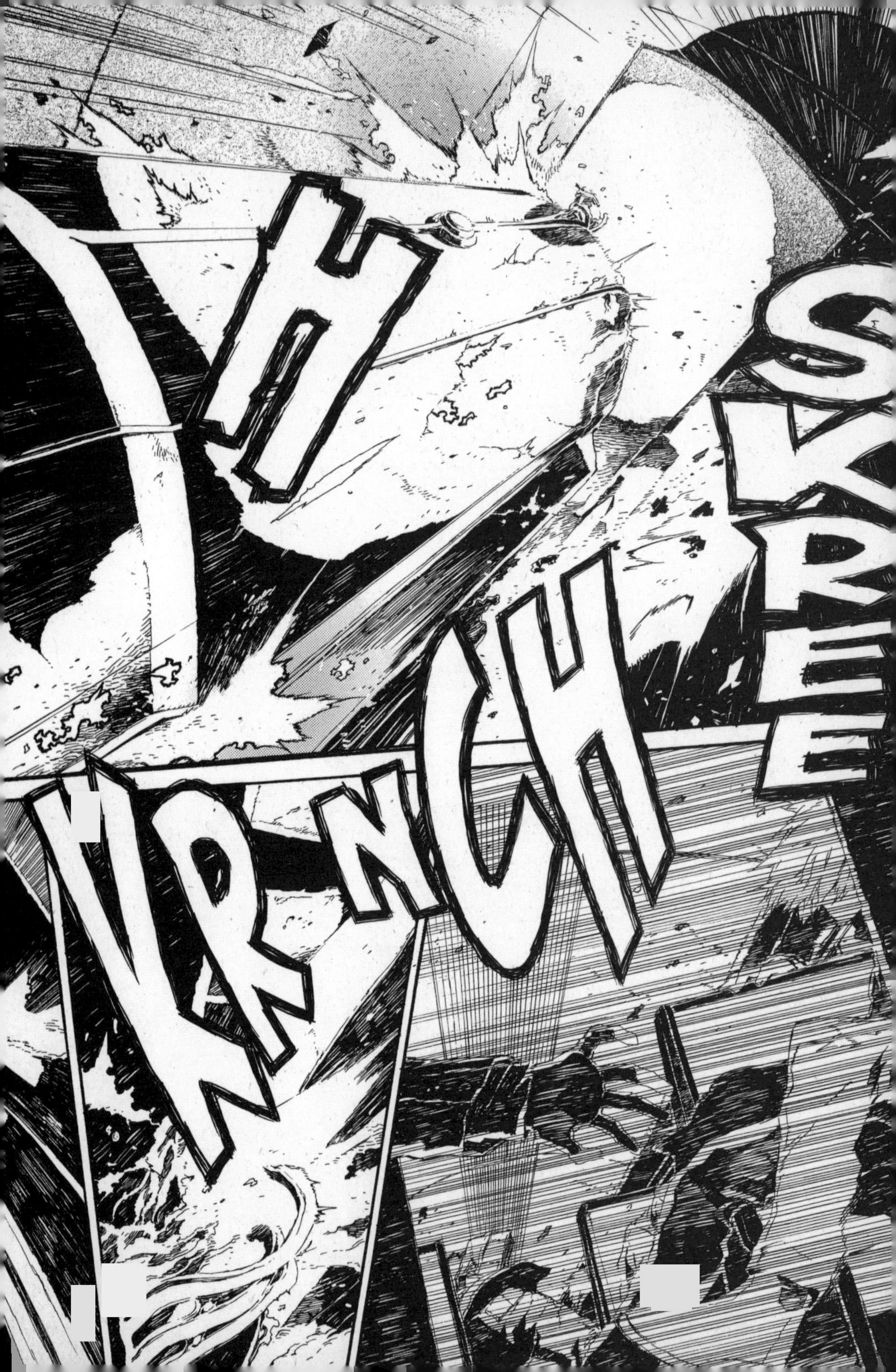

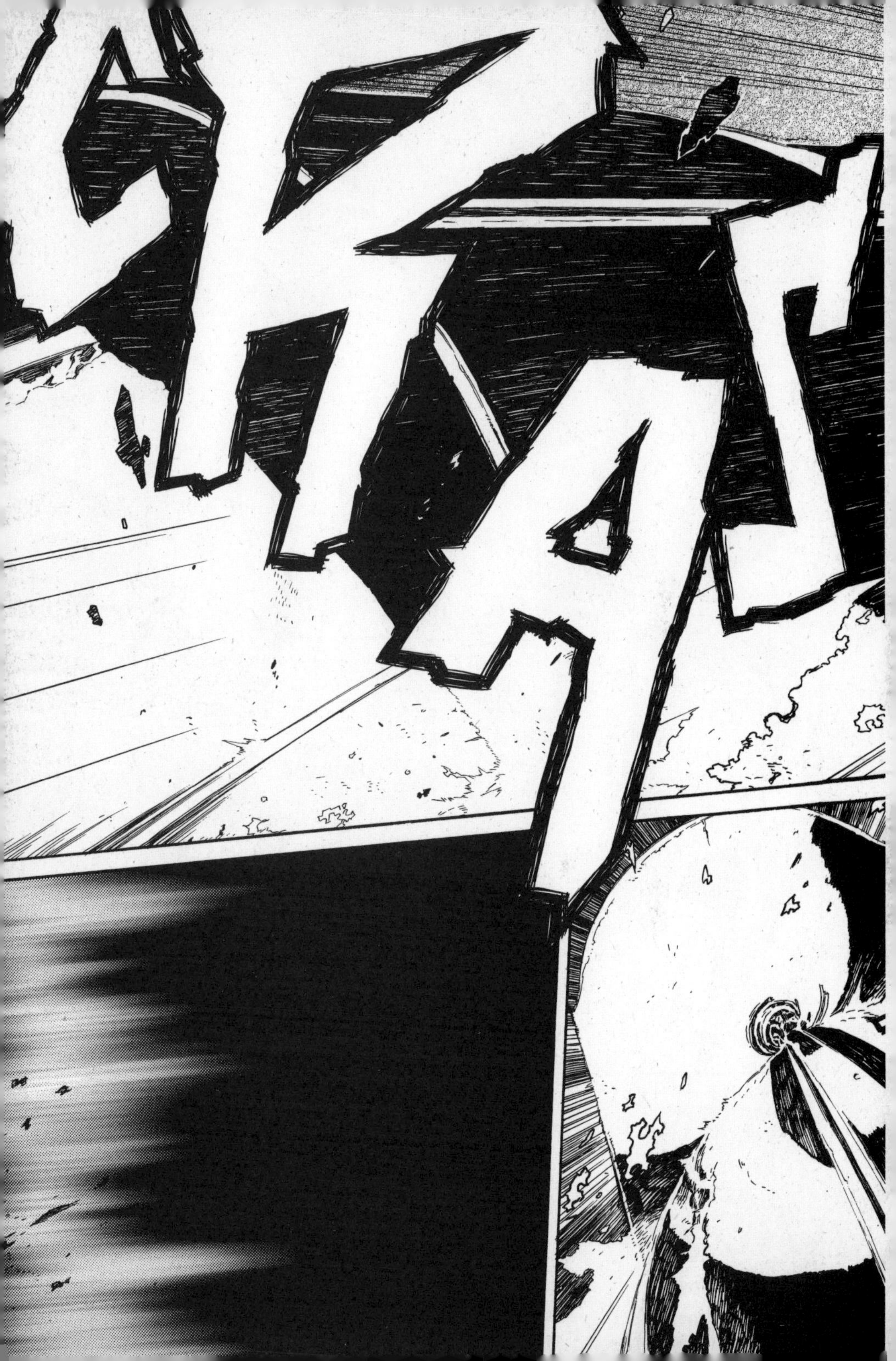

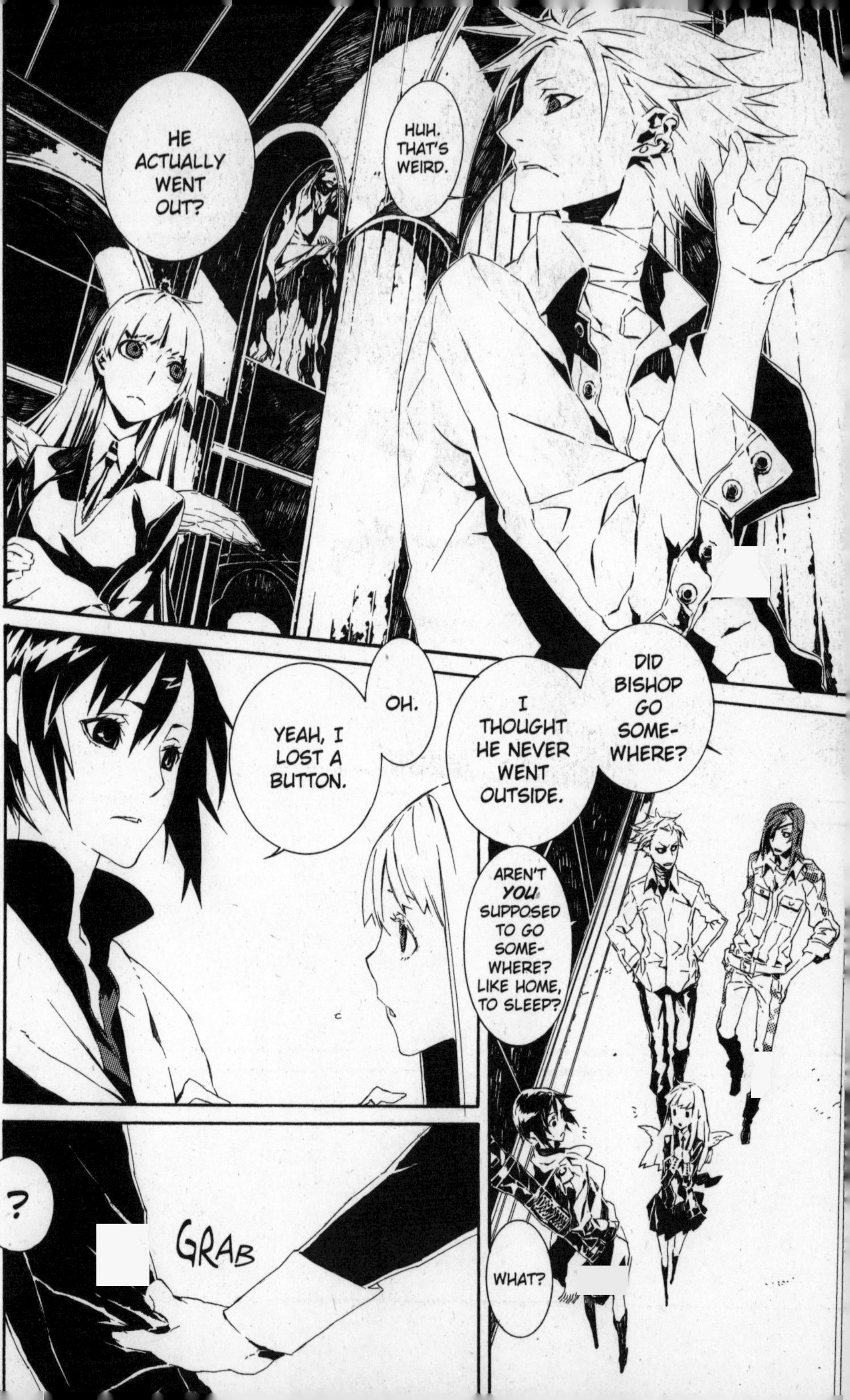
HUH. THAT'S WEIRD.
HE ACTUALLY WENT OUT?
DID BISHOP GO SOME-WHERE?
I THOUGHT HE NEVER WENT OUTSIDE.
AREN'T *YOU* SUPPOSED TO GO SOME-WHERE? LIKE HOME, TO SLEEP?
WHAT?
OH.
YEAH, I LOST A BUTTON.
?
GRAB

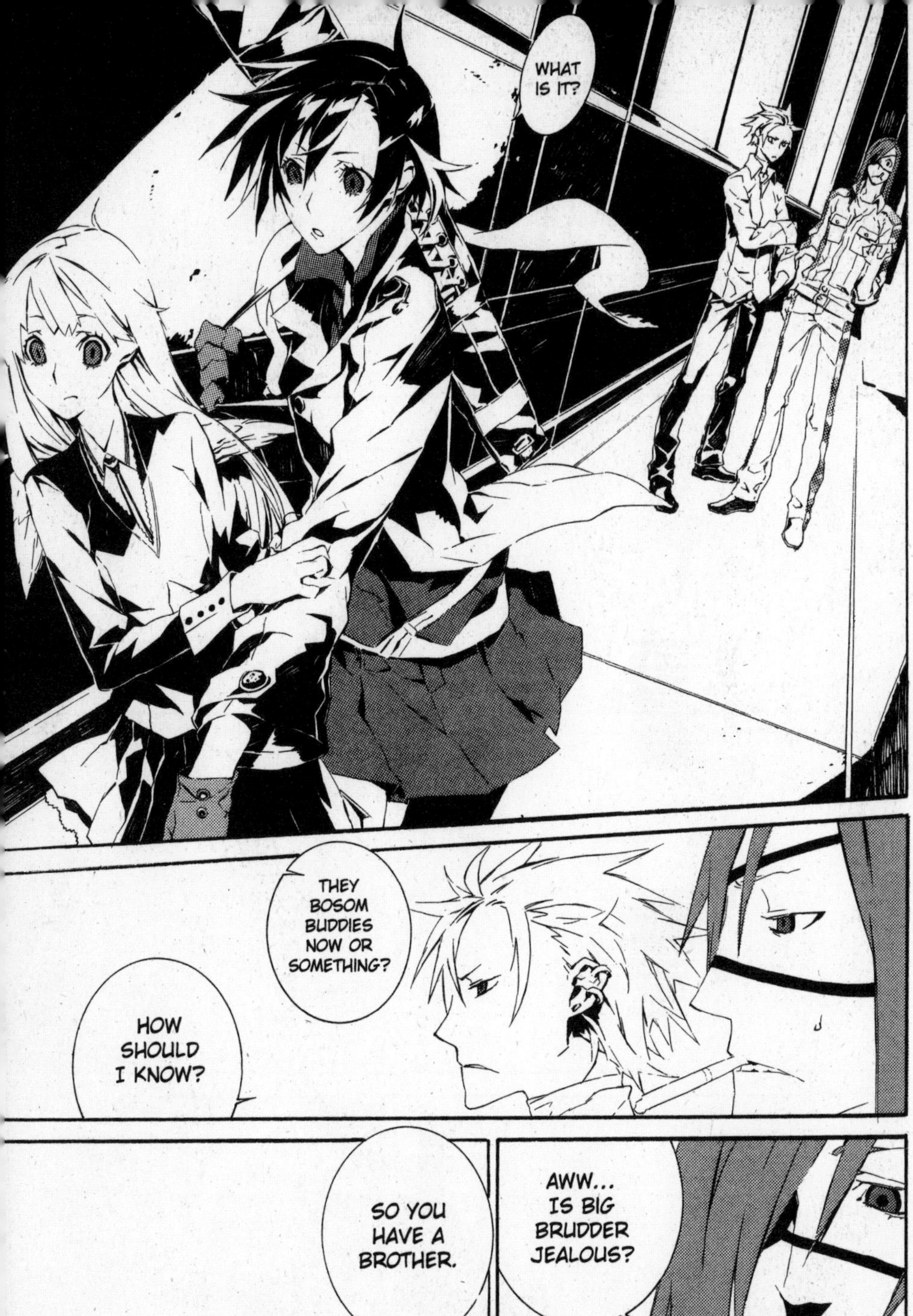
WHAT IS IT?
THEY BOSOM BUDDIES NOW OR SOMETHING?
HOW SHOULD I KNOW?
AWW... IS BIG BRUDDER JEALOUS?
SO YOU HAVE A BROTHER.

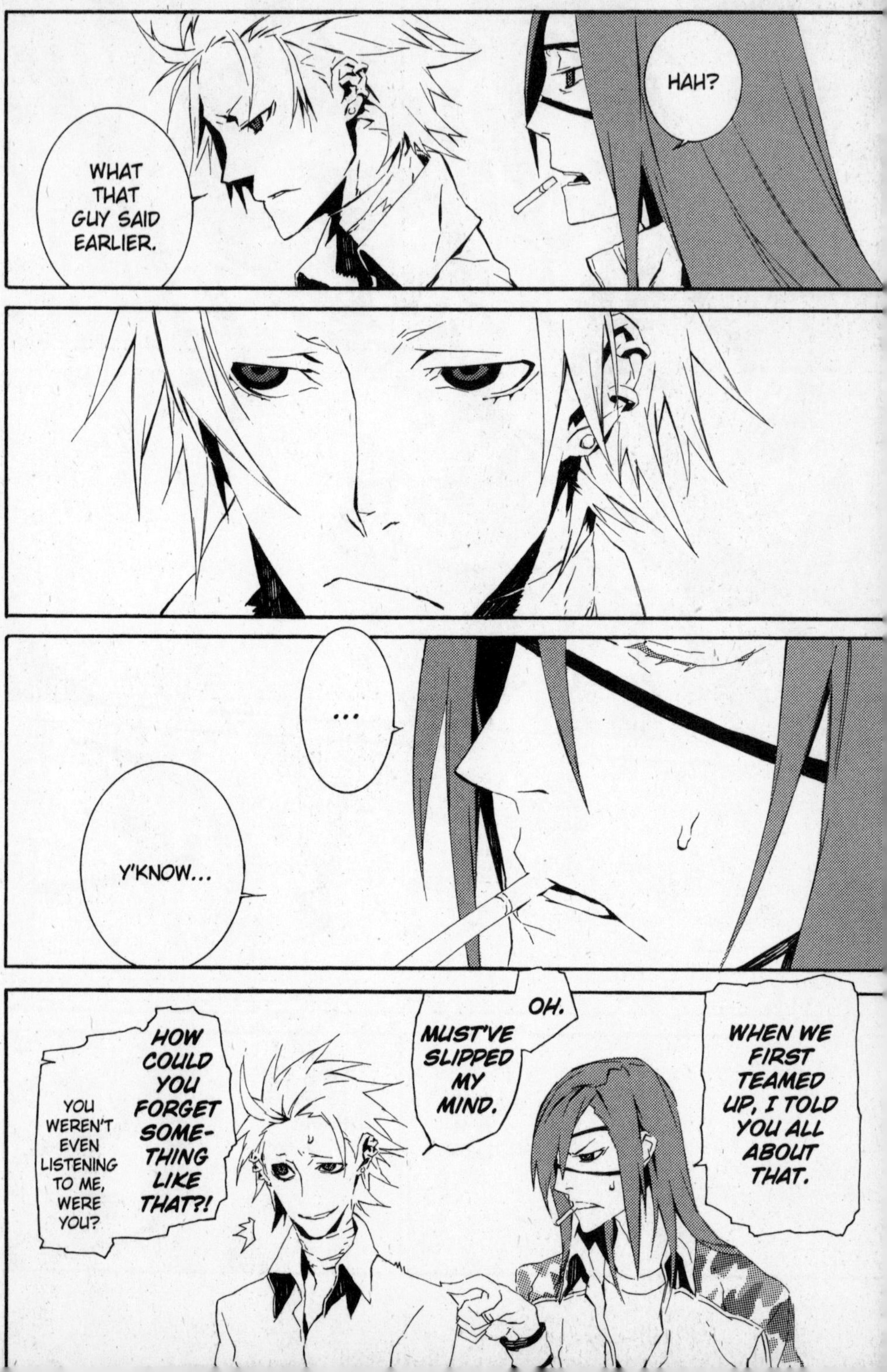
HAH?
WHAT THAT GUY SAID EARLIER.
...
Y'KNOW...
WHEN WE FIRST TEAMED UP, I TOLD YOU ALL ABOUT THAT.
OH.
MUST'VE SLIPPED MY MIND.
HOW COULD YOU FORGET SOME-THING LIKE THAT?!
YOU WEREN'T EVEN LISTENING TO ME, WERE YOU?

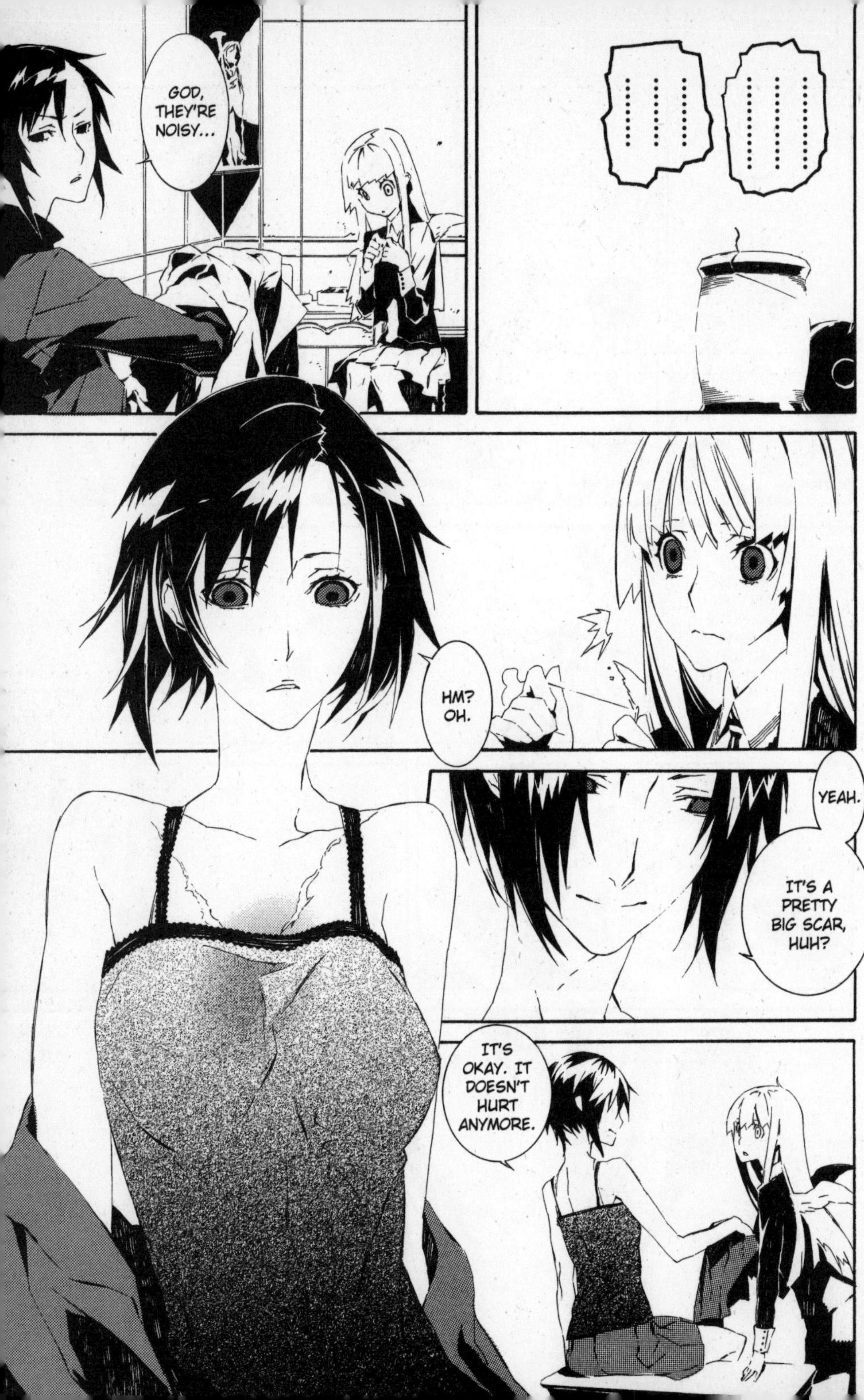
......
......
GOD, THEY'RE NOISY...
HM? OH.
YEAH.
IT'S A PRETTY BIG SCAR, HUH?
IT'S OKAY. IT DOESN'T HURT ANYMORE.

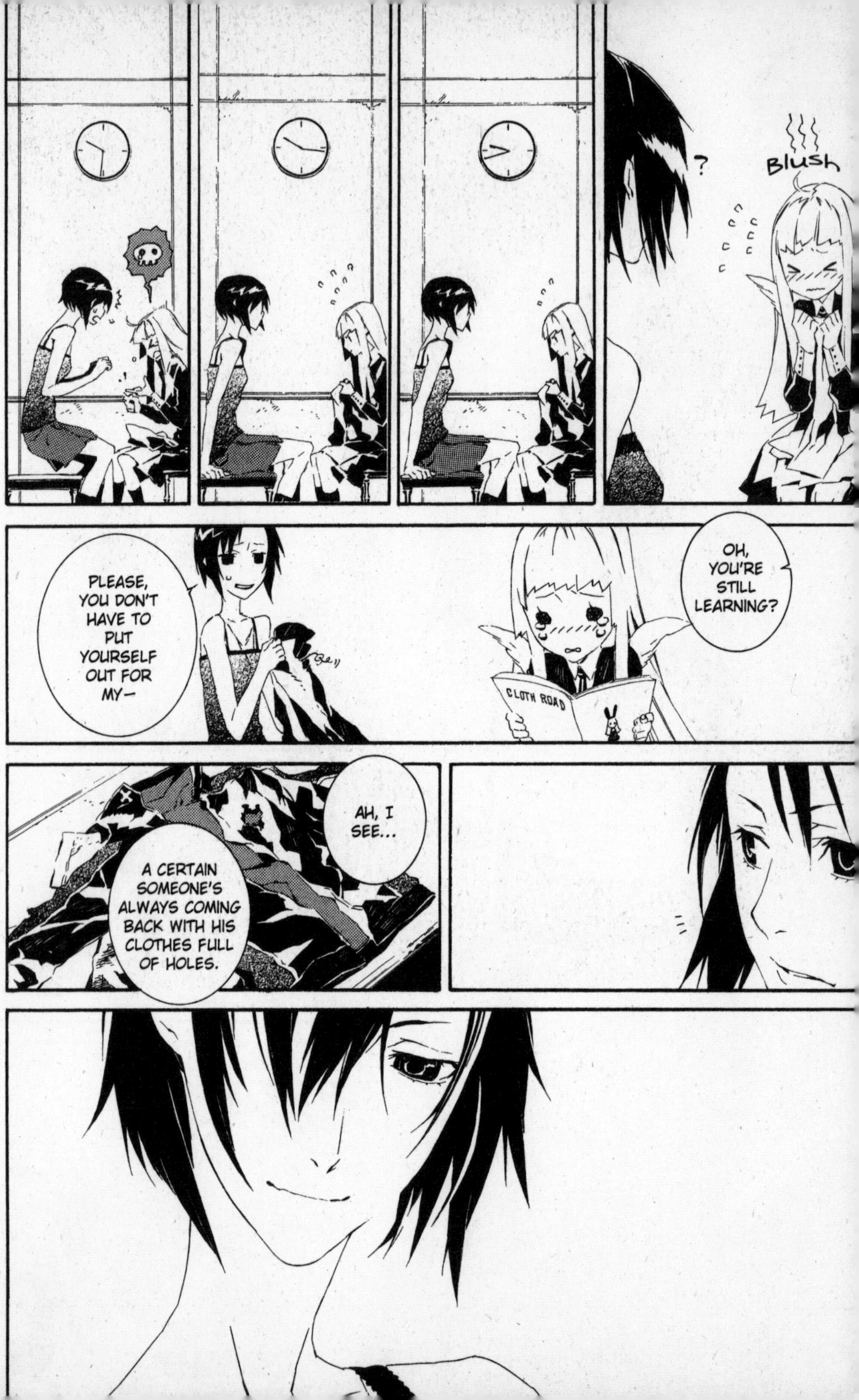
Blush
?
OH, YOU'RE STILL LEARNING?
CLOTH ROAD
PLEASE, YOU DON'T HAVE TO PUT YOURSELF OUT FOR MY–
AH, I SEE...
A CERTAIN SOMEONE'S ALWAYS COMING BACK WITH HIS CLOTHES FULL OF HOLES.

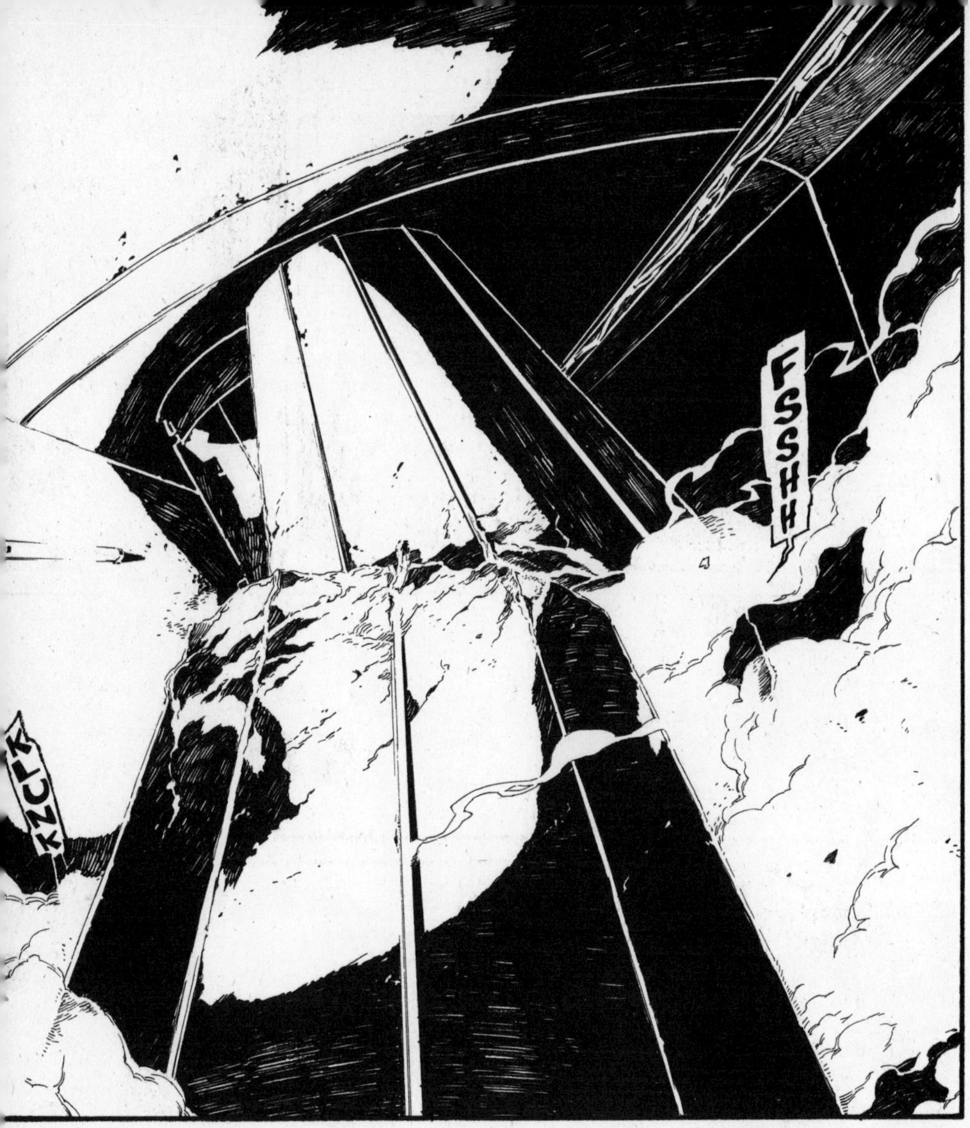
FSSHH
KZCPK

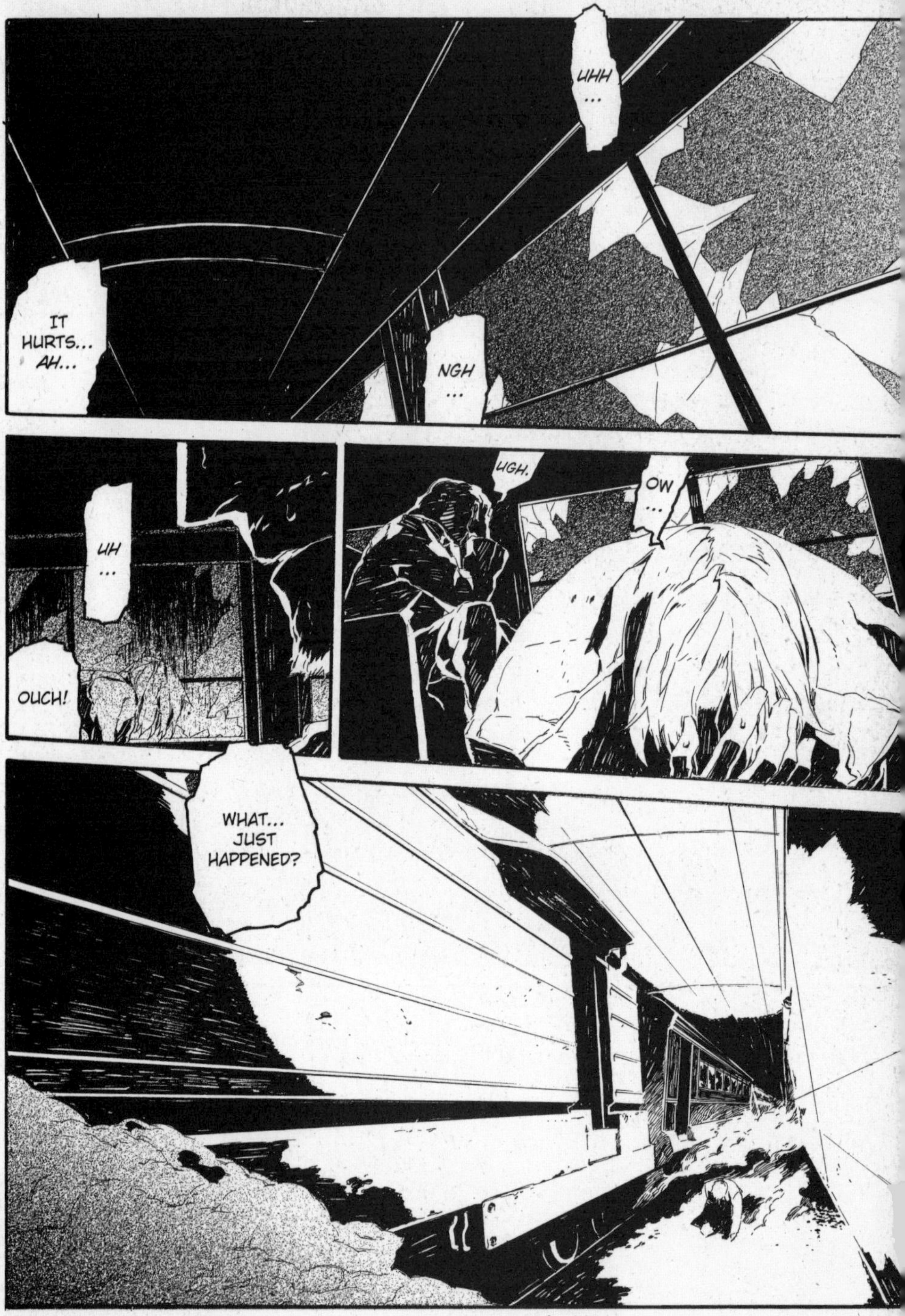
UHH...
NGH...
IT HURTS... AH...
OW...
UGH.
UH...
OUCH!
WHAT... JUST HAPPENED?

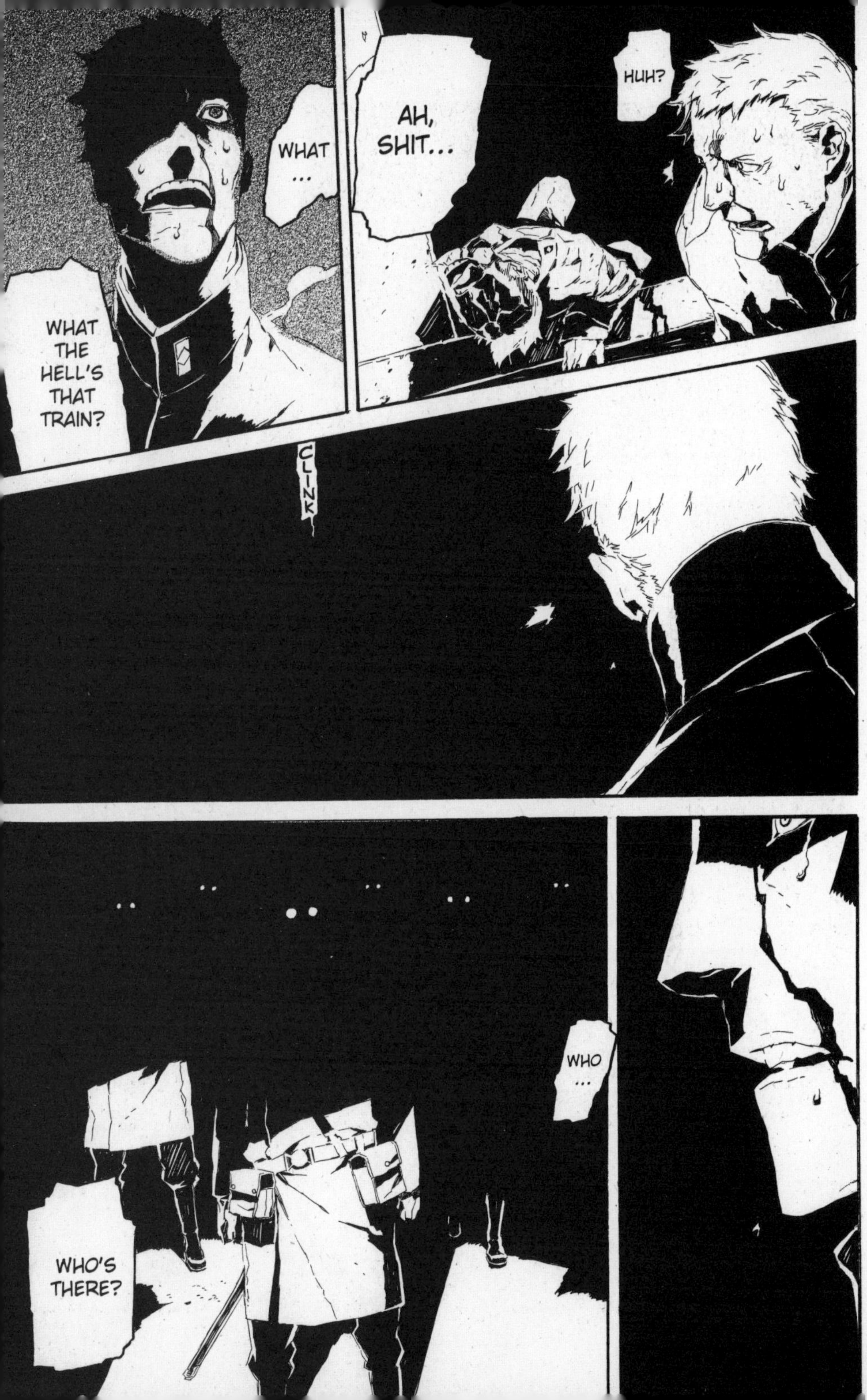
HUH?
AH, SHIT...
WHAT ...
WHAT THE HELL'S THAT TRAIN?
CLINK
WHO ...
WHO'S THERE?

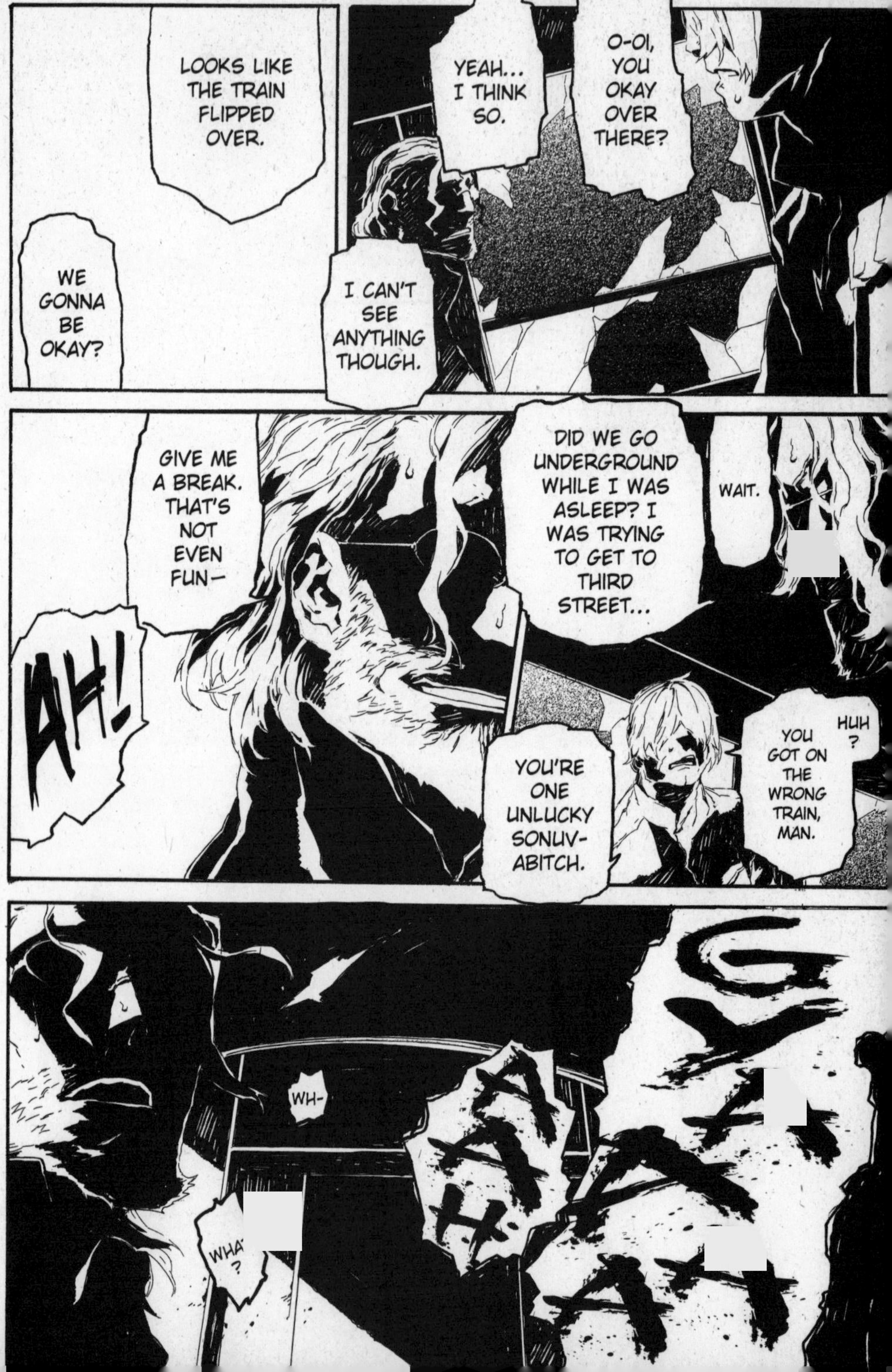
O-OI, YOU OKAY OVER THERE?
YEAH... I THINK SO.
I CAN'T SEE ANYTHING THOUGH.
LOOKS LIKE THE TRAIN FLIPPED OVER.
WE GONNA BE OKAY?
WAIT.
DID WE GO UNDERGROUND WHILE I WAS ASLEEP? I WAS TRYING TO GET TO THIRD STREET...
HUH?
YOU GOT ON THE WRONG TRAIN, MAN.
YOU'RE ONE UNLUCKY SONUV-ABITCH.
GIVE ME A BREAK. THAT'S NOT EVEN FUN—
AH!
WH-
WHAT?

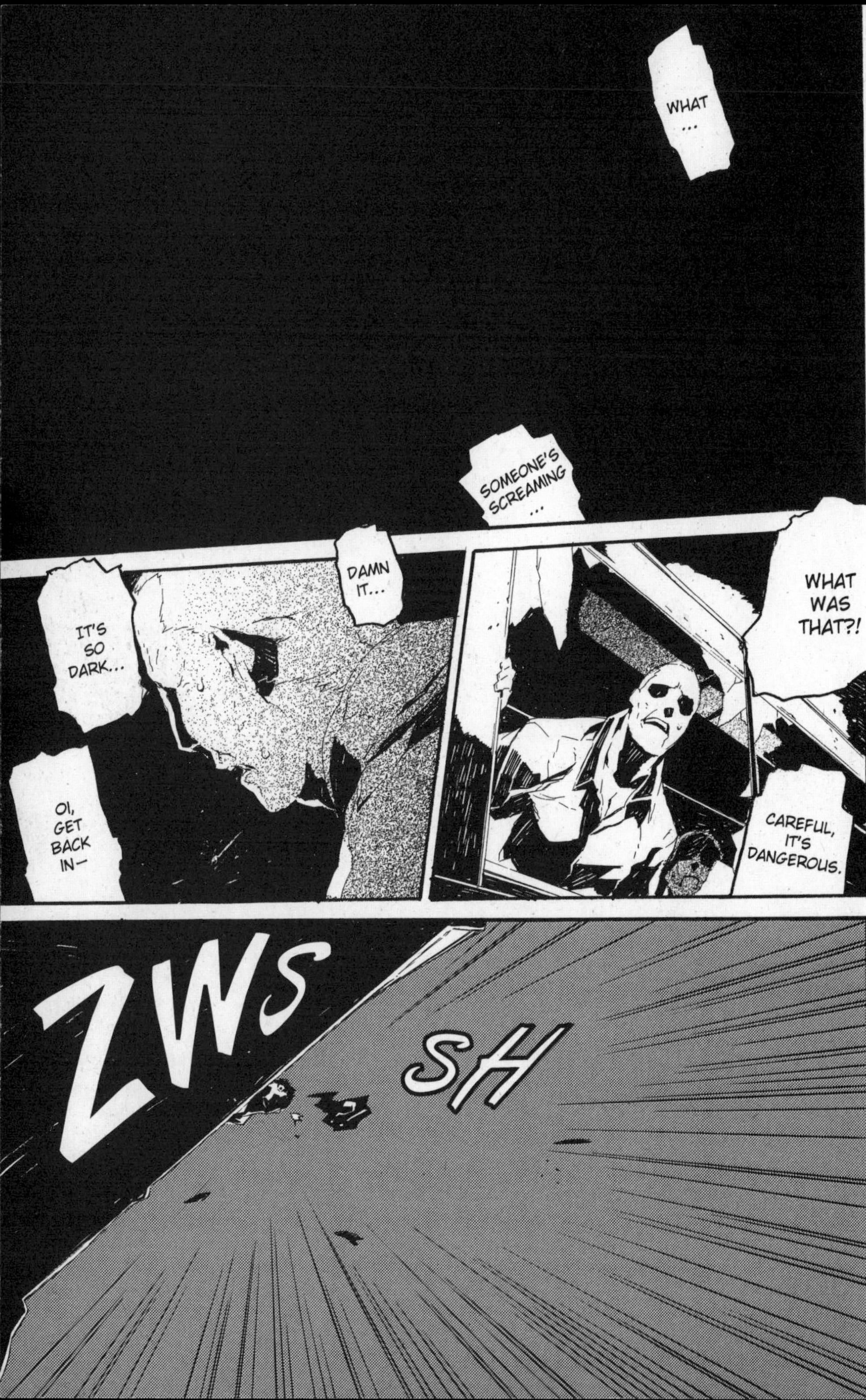
WHAT ...
SOMEONE'S SCREAMING ...
WHAT WAS THAT?!
CAREFUL, IT'S DANGEROUS.
DAMN IT...
IT'S SO DARK...
OI, GET BACK IN—
ZWS SH

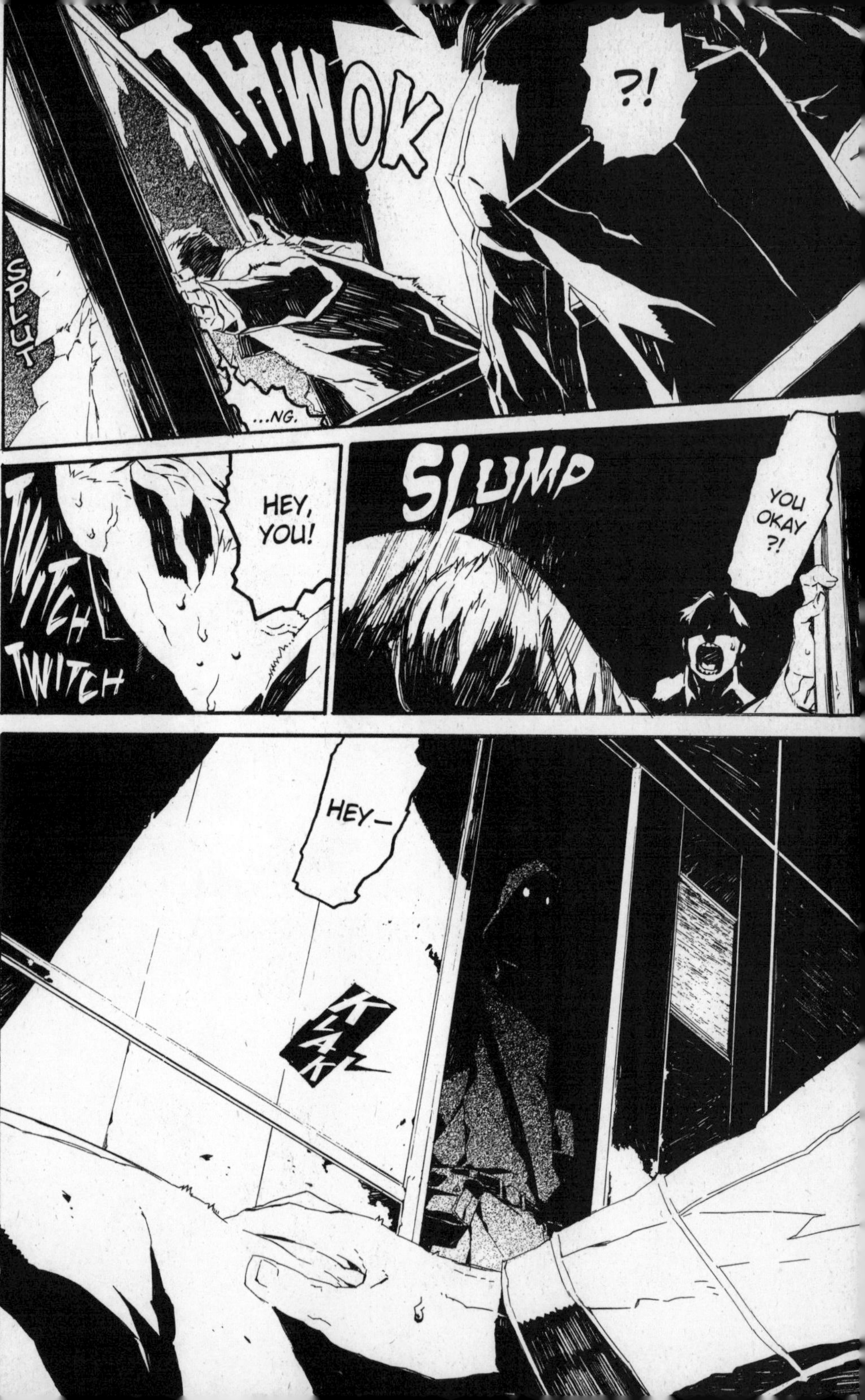
?!
THWOK
SPLUT
...NG.
YOU OKAY ?!
SLUMP
HEY, YOU!
TWITCH TWITCH
HEY—
KLAK

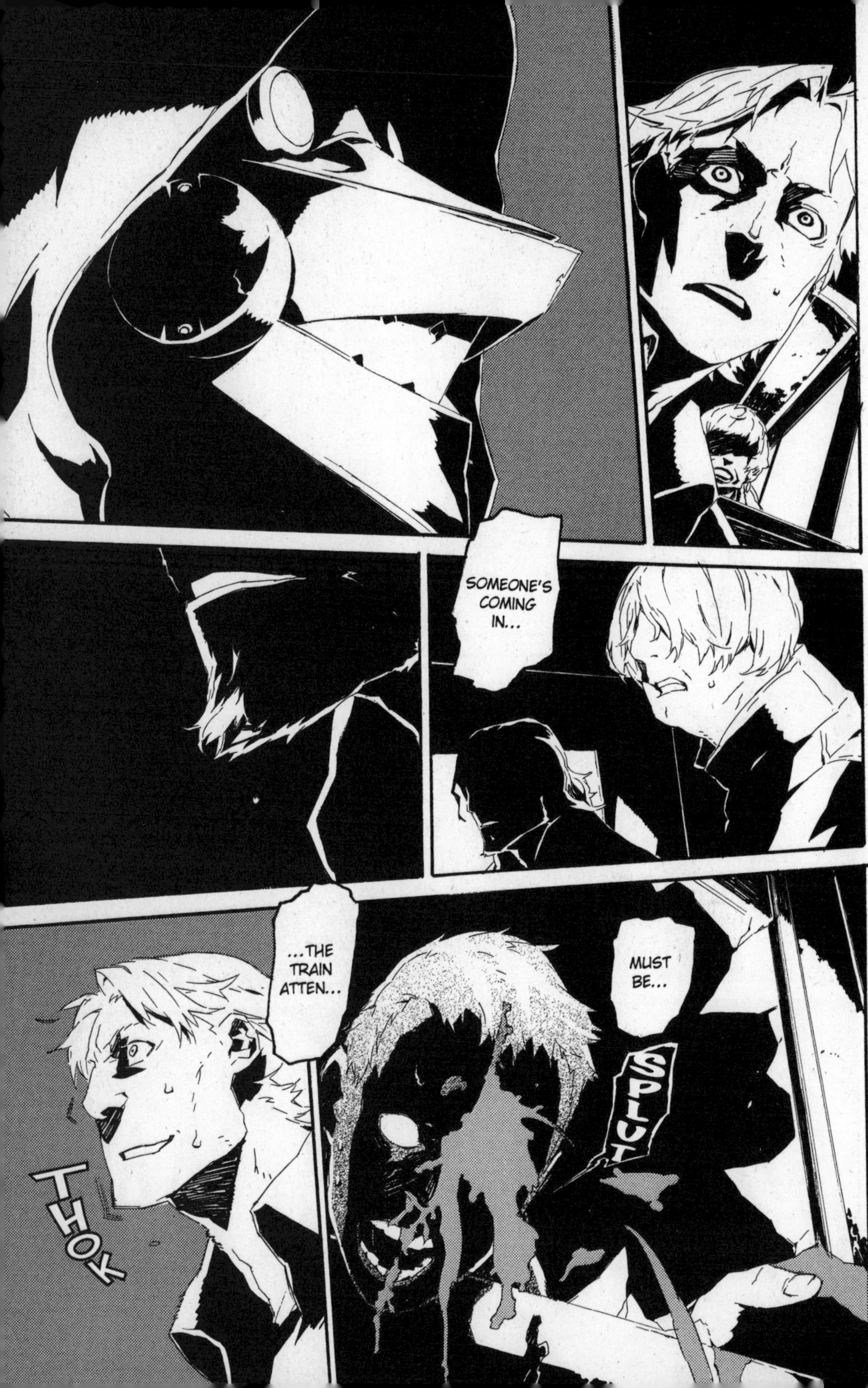
SOMEONE'S COMING IN...
MUST BE...
SPLUT
...THE TRAIN ATTEN...
THOK

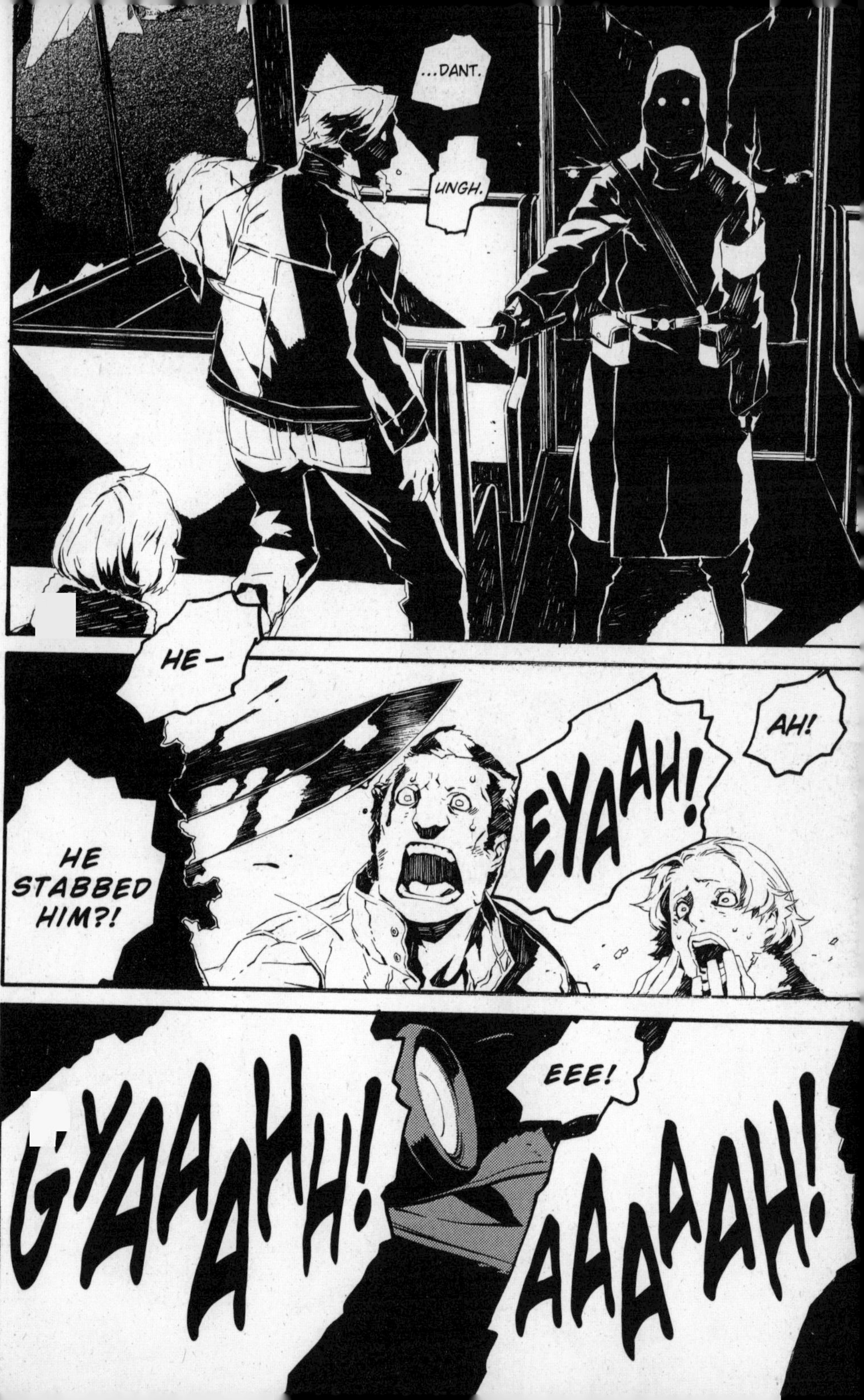
...DANT.
UNGH.
AH!
EYAAH!
HE—
HE STABBED HIM?!
AAAAAH!
EEE!
GYAAAHH!

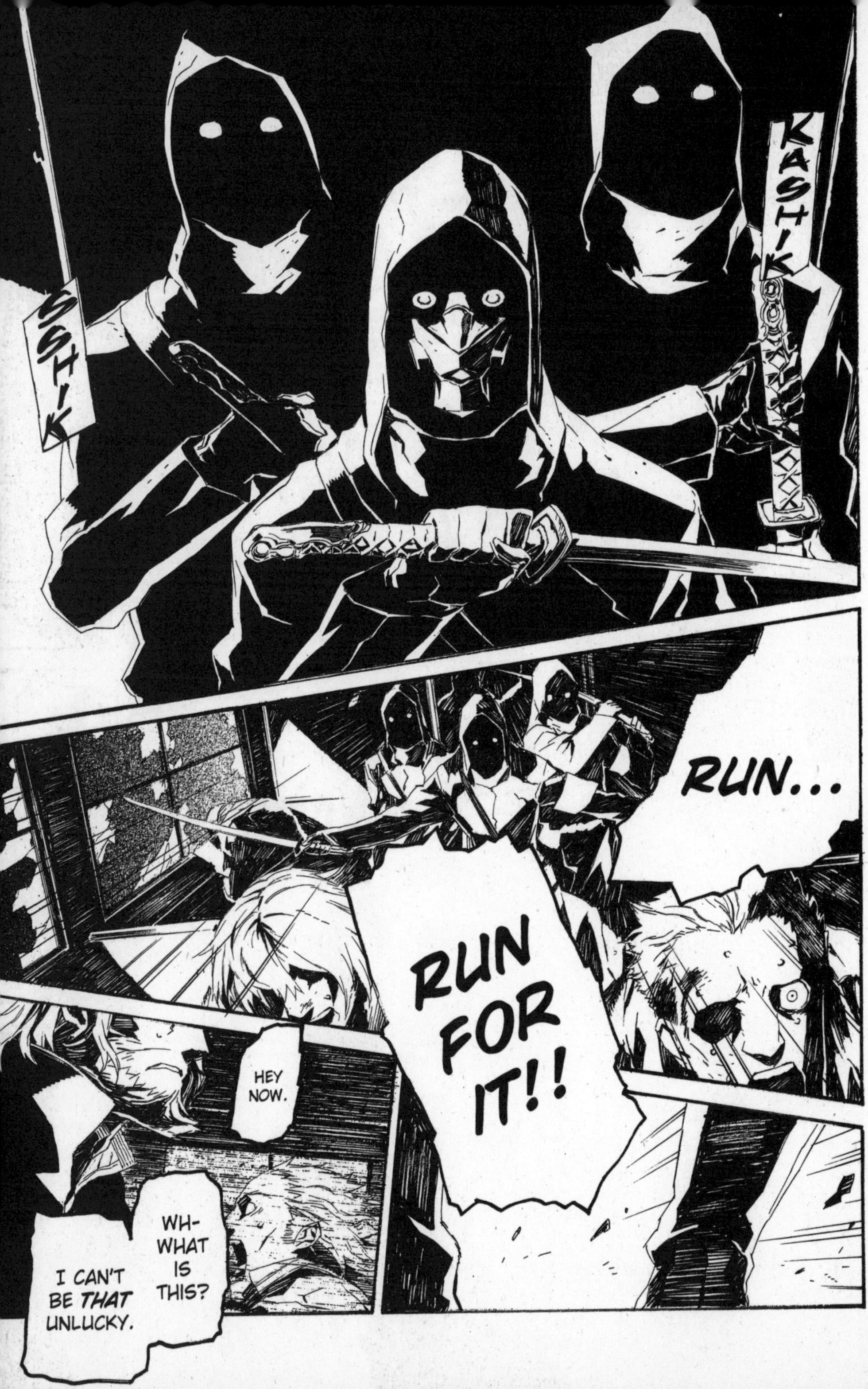
KASHIK
SSHIK
RUN...
RUN FOR IT!!
HEY NOW.
WH- WHAT IS THIS?
I CAN'T BE *THAT* UNLUCKY.

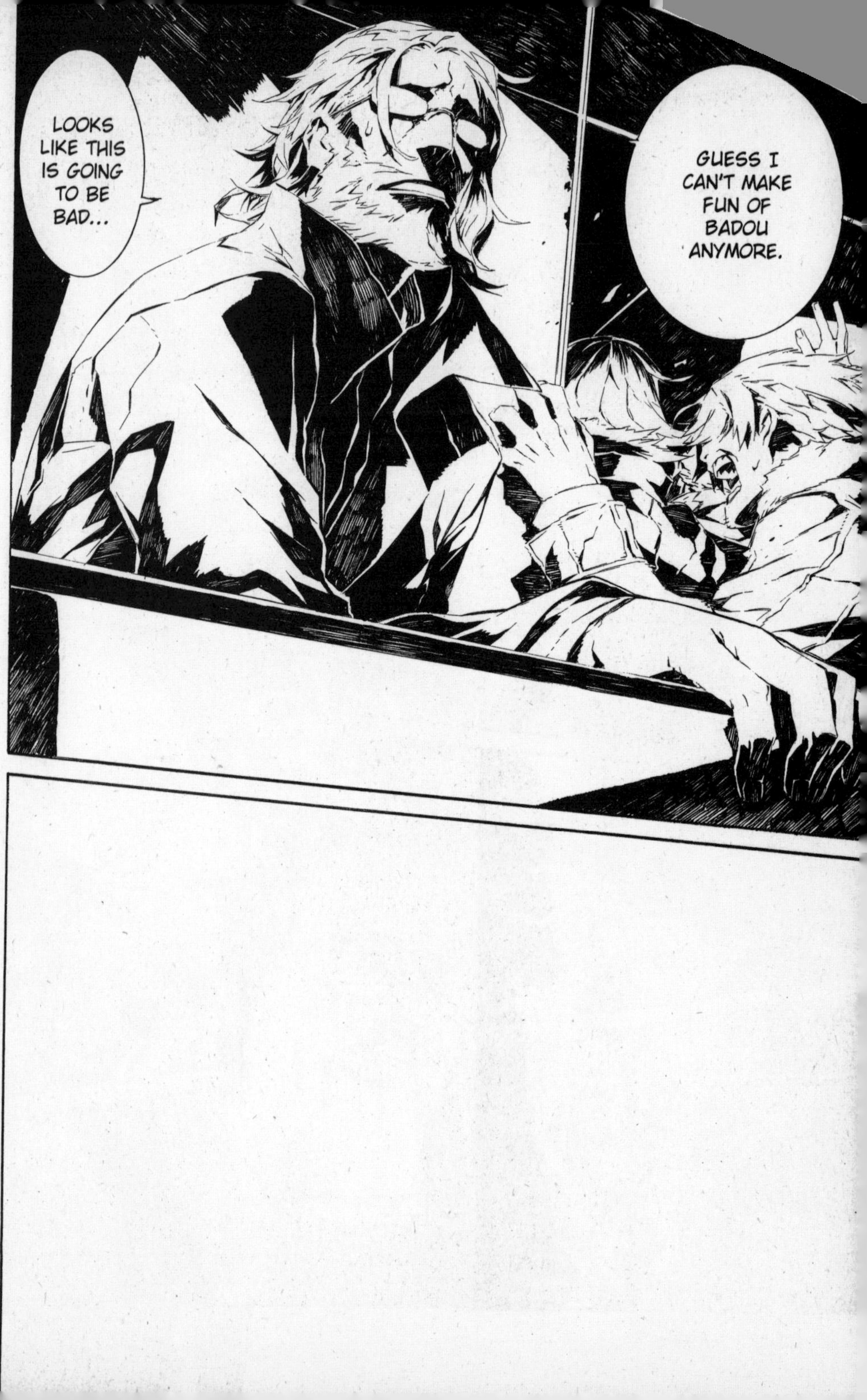
GUESS I CAN'T MAKE FUN OF BADOU ANYMORE.
LOOKS LIKE THIS IS GOING TO BE BAD...

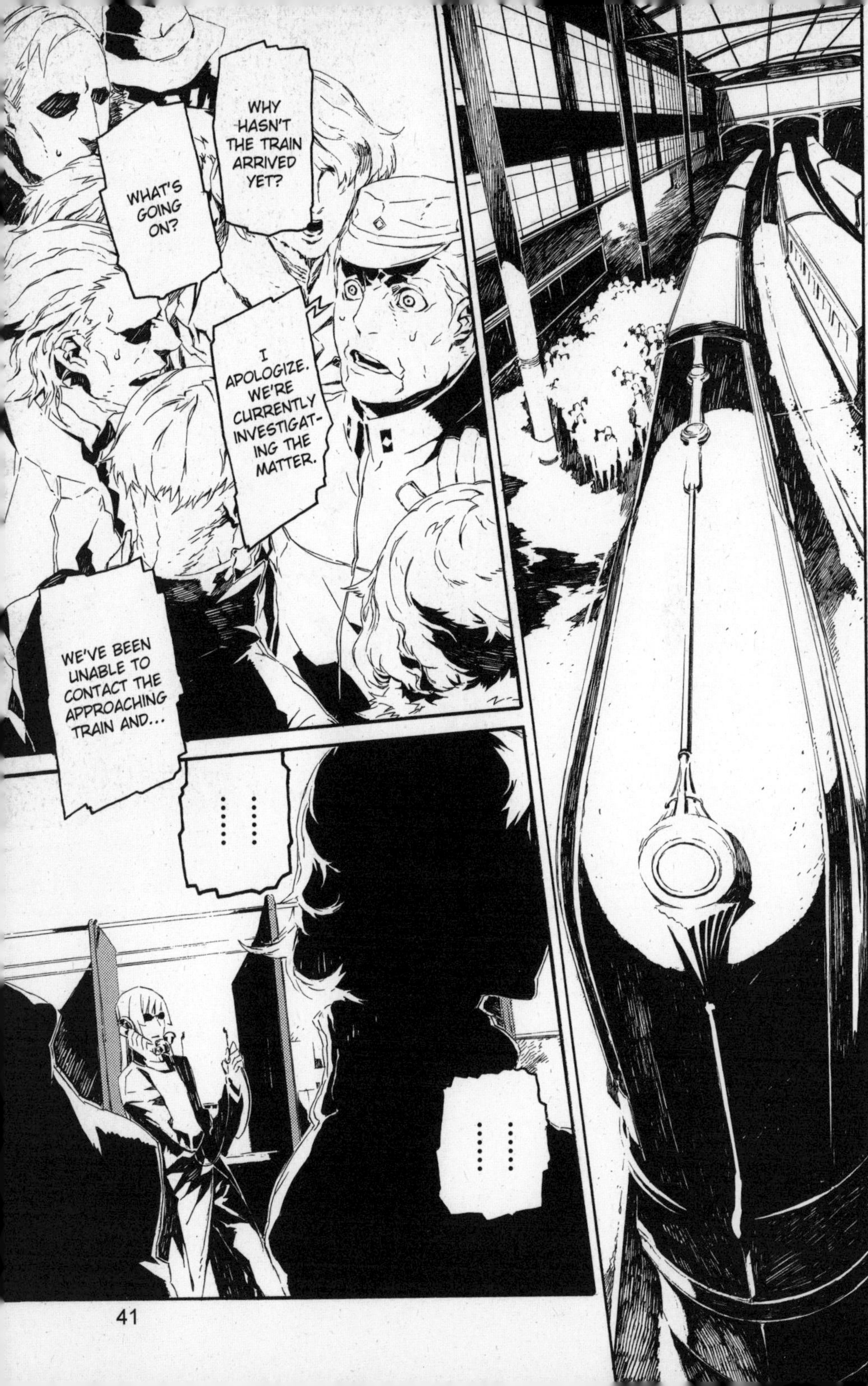

WHY HASN'T THE TRAIN ARRIVED YET?
WHAT'S GOING ON?
I APOLOGIZE. WE'RE CURRENTLY INVESTIGATING THE MATTER.
WE'VE BEEN UNABLE TO CONTACT THE APPROACHING TRAIN AND...
......
......

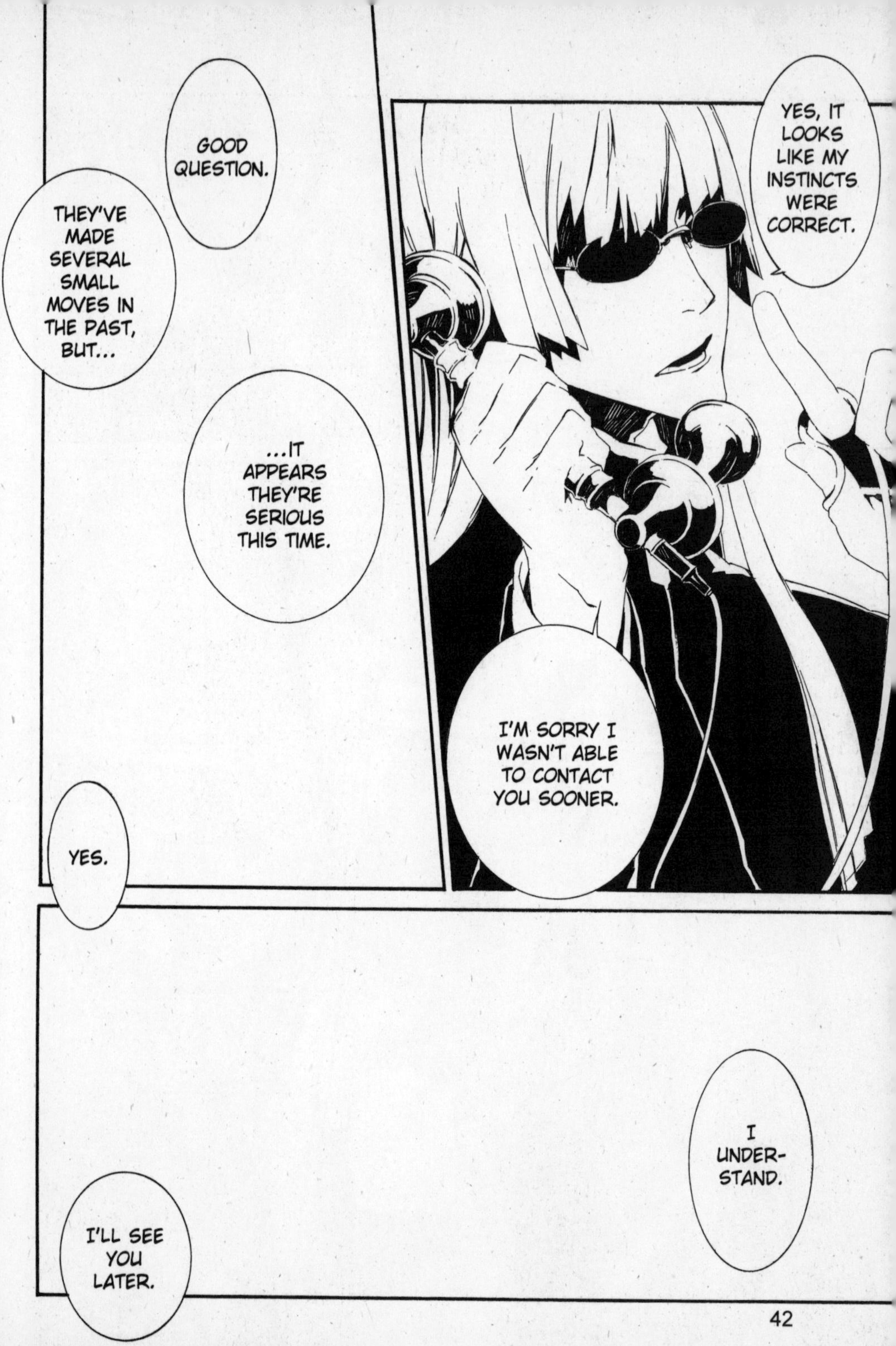
YES, IT LOOKS LIKE MY INSTINCTS WERE CORRECT.
I'M SORRY I WASN'T ABLE TO CONTACT YOU SOONER.
GOOD QUESTION.
THEY'VE MADE SEVERAL SMALL MOVES IN THE PAST, BUT...
...IT APPEARS THEY'RE SERIOUS THIS TIME.
YES.
I UNDER-STAND.
I'LL SEE YOU LATER.

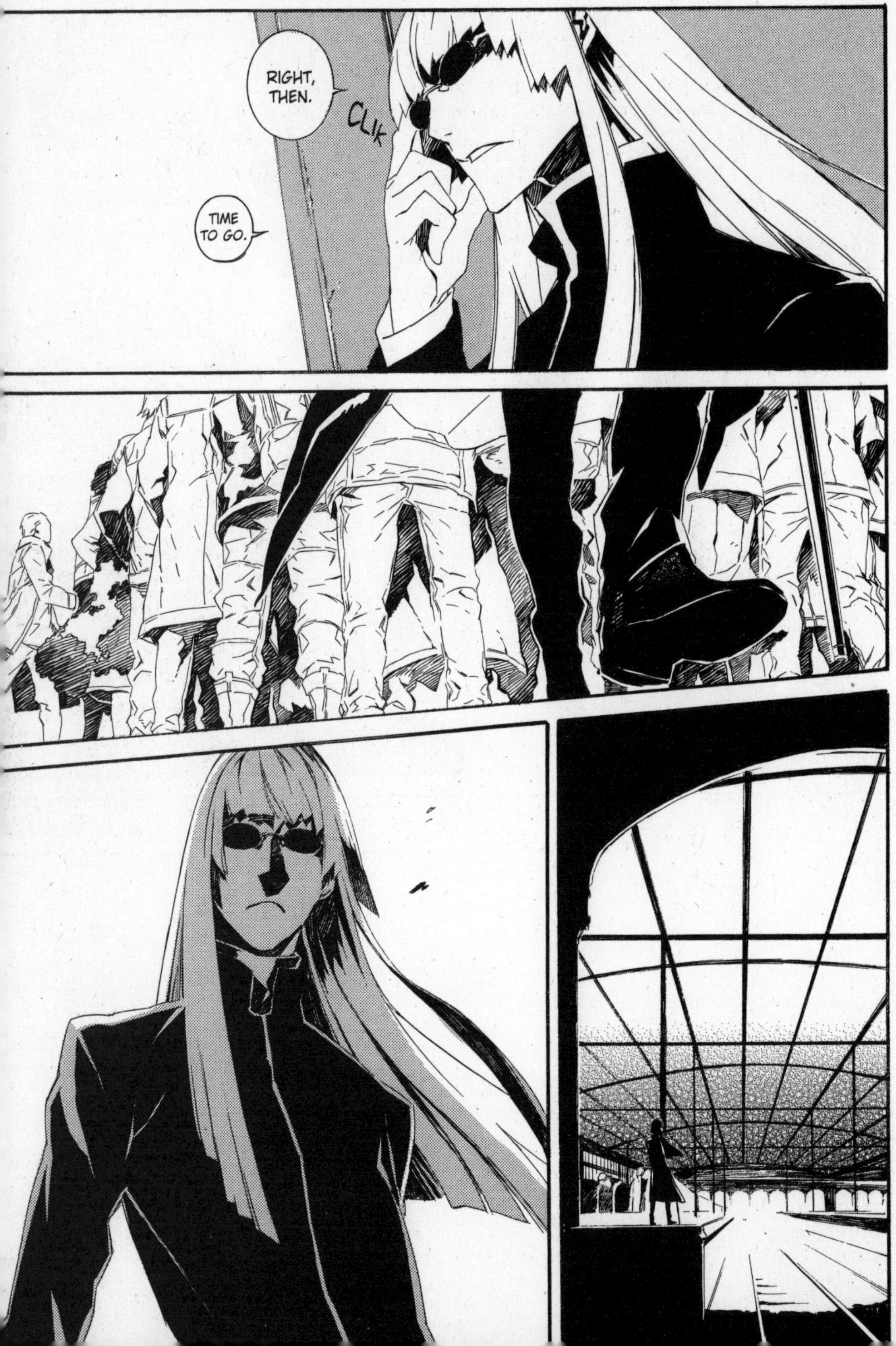
RIGHT, THEN.
CLIK
TIME TO GO.

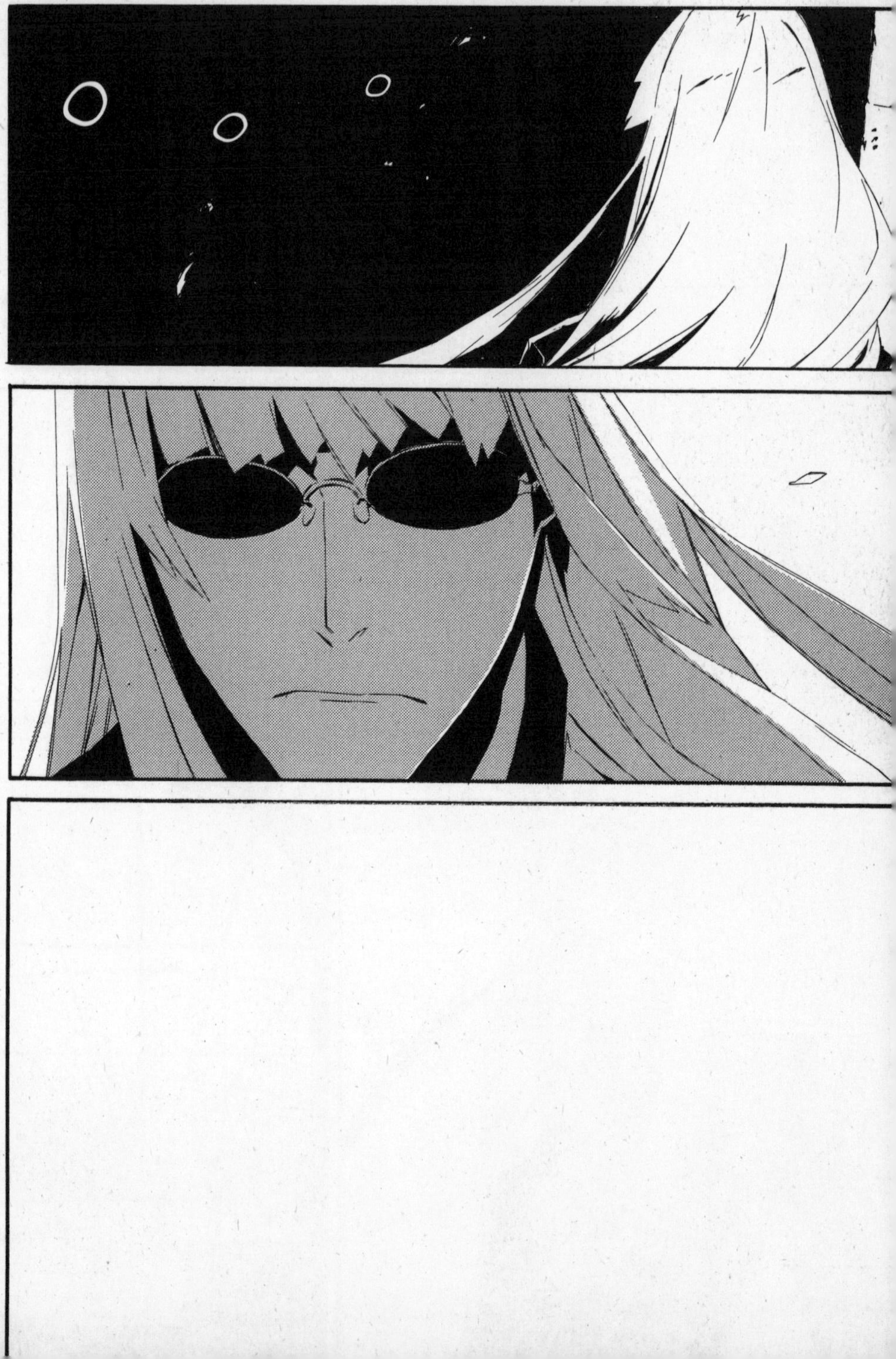

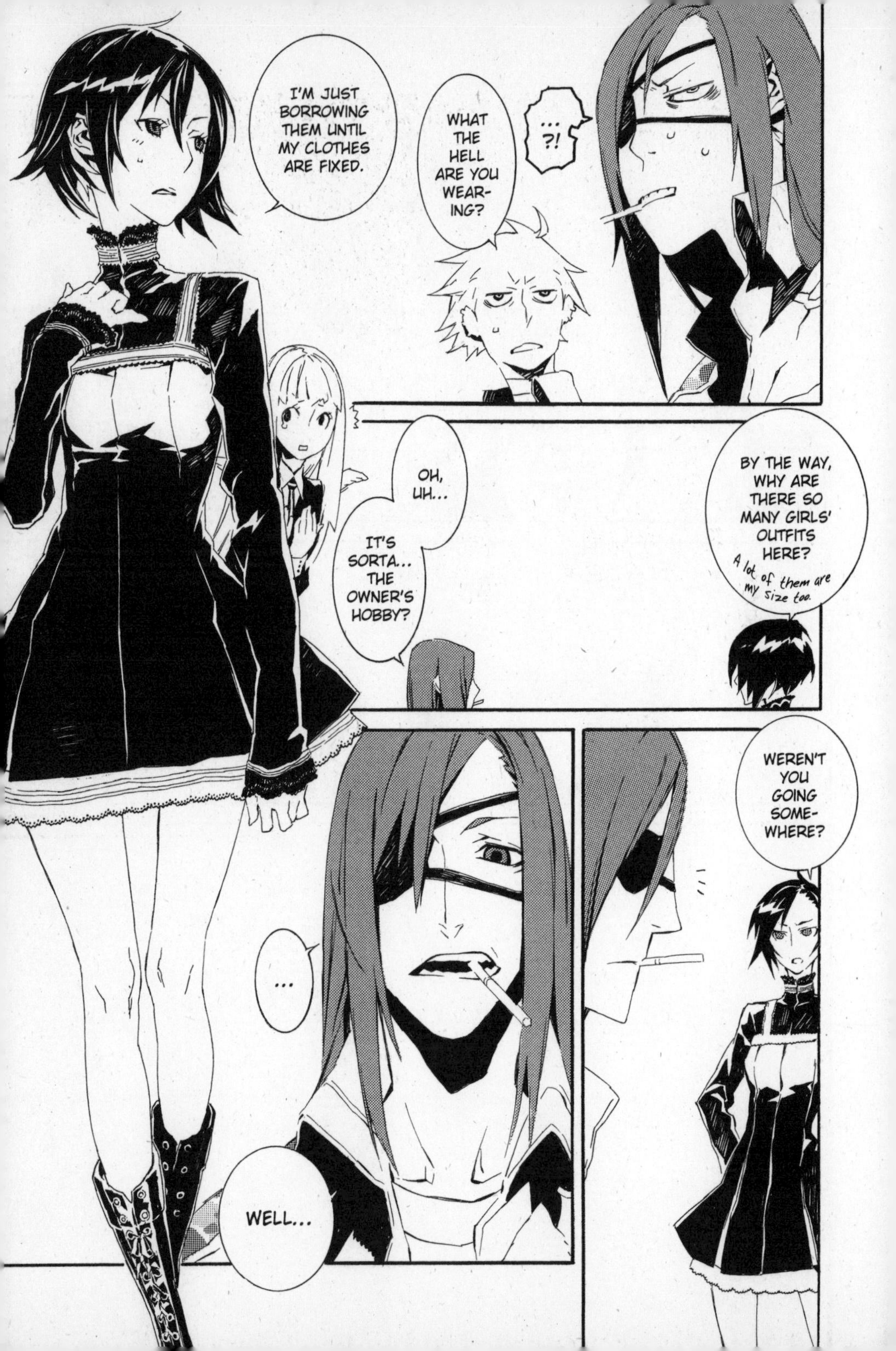

...?!
WHAT THE HELL ARE YOU WEARING?
I'M JUST BORROWING THEM UNTIL MY CLOTHES ARE FIXED.
BY THE WAY, WHY ARE THERE SO MANY GIRLS' OUTFITS HERE?
A lot of them are my size too.
OH, UH...
IT'S SORTA... THE OWNER'S HOBBY?
WEREN'T YOU GOING SOMEWHERE?
...
WELL...

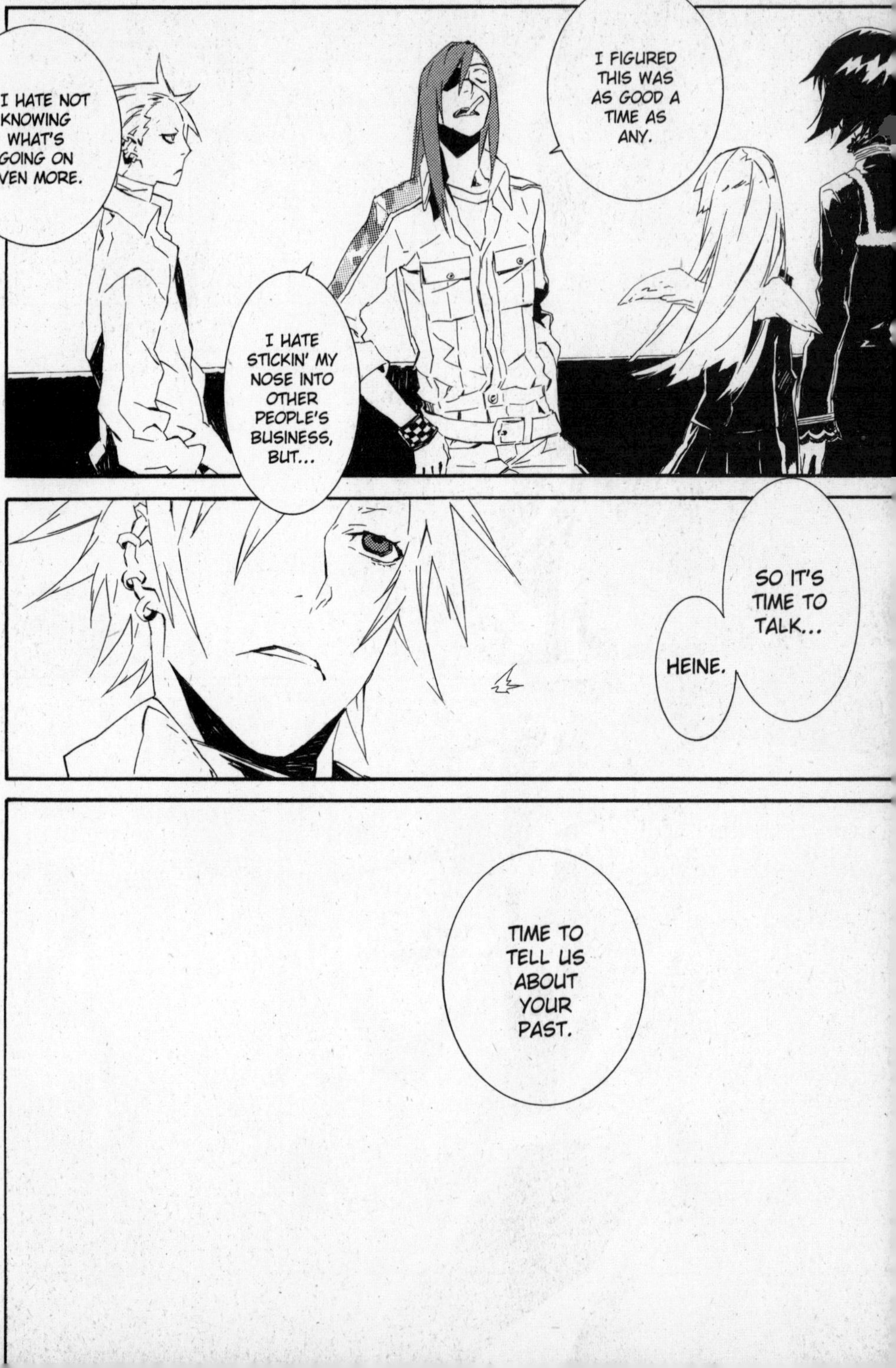
I FIGURED THIS WAS AS GOOD A TIME AS ANY.
I HATE STICKIN' MY NOSE INTO OTHER PEOPLE'S BUSINESS, BUT...
...I HATE NOT KNOWING WHAT'S GOING ON EVEN MORE.
SO IT'S TIME TO TALK...
HEINE.
TIME TO TELL US ABOUT YOUR PAST.

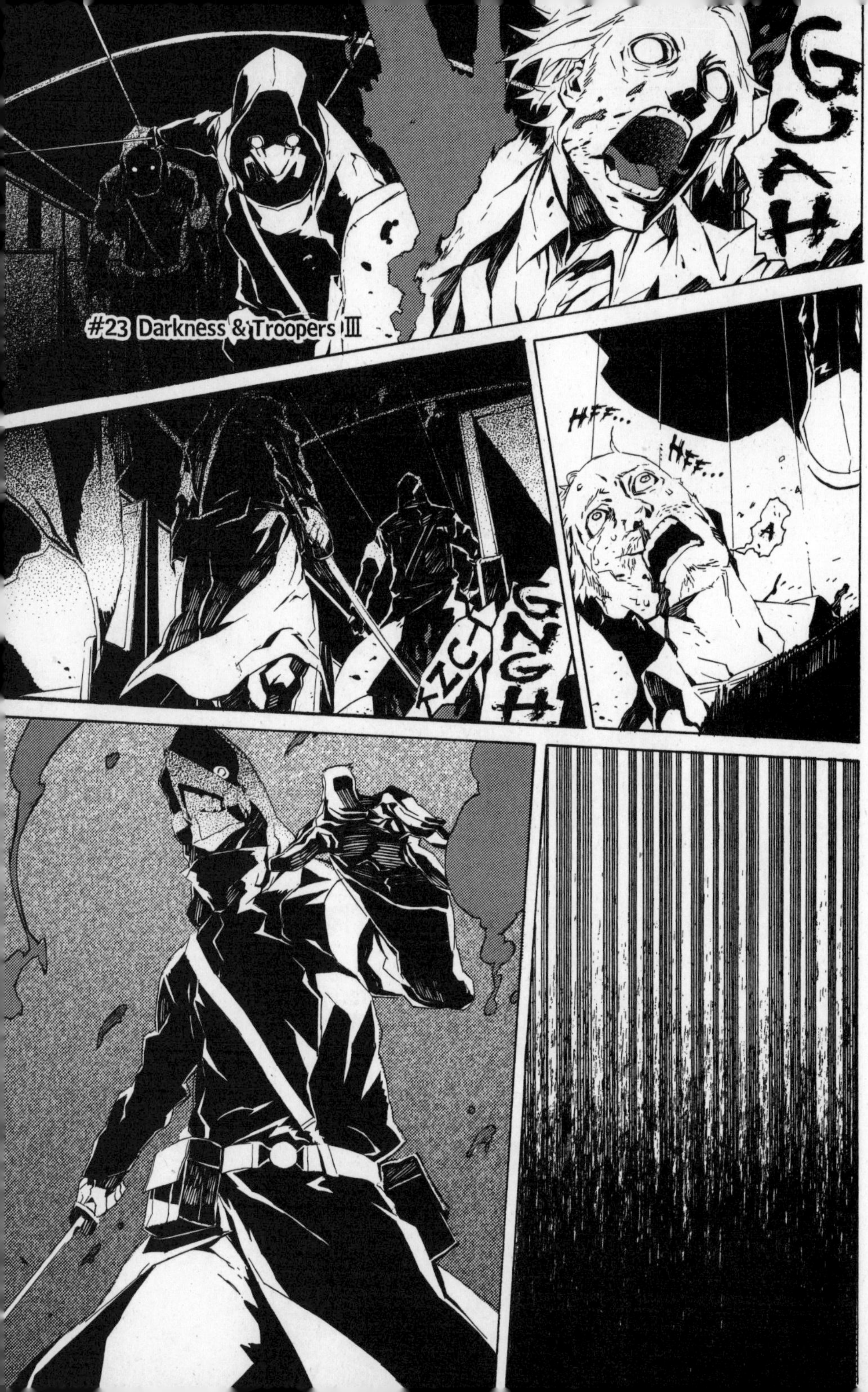
GUAH
#23 Darkness & Troopers III
HFF...
HFF...
A
GNGH
KZCH

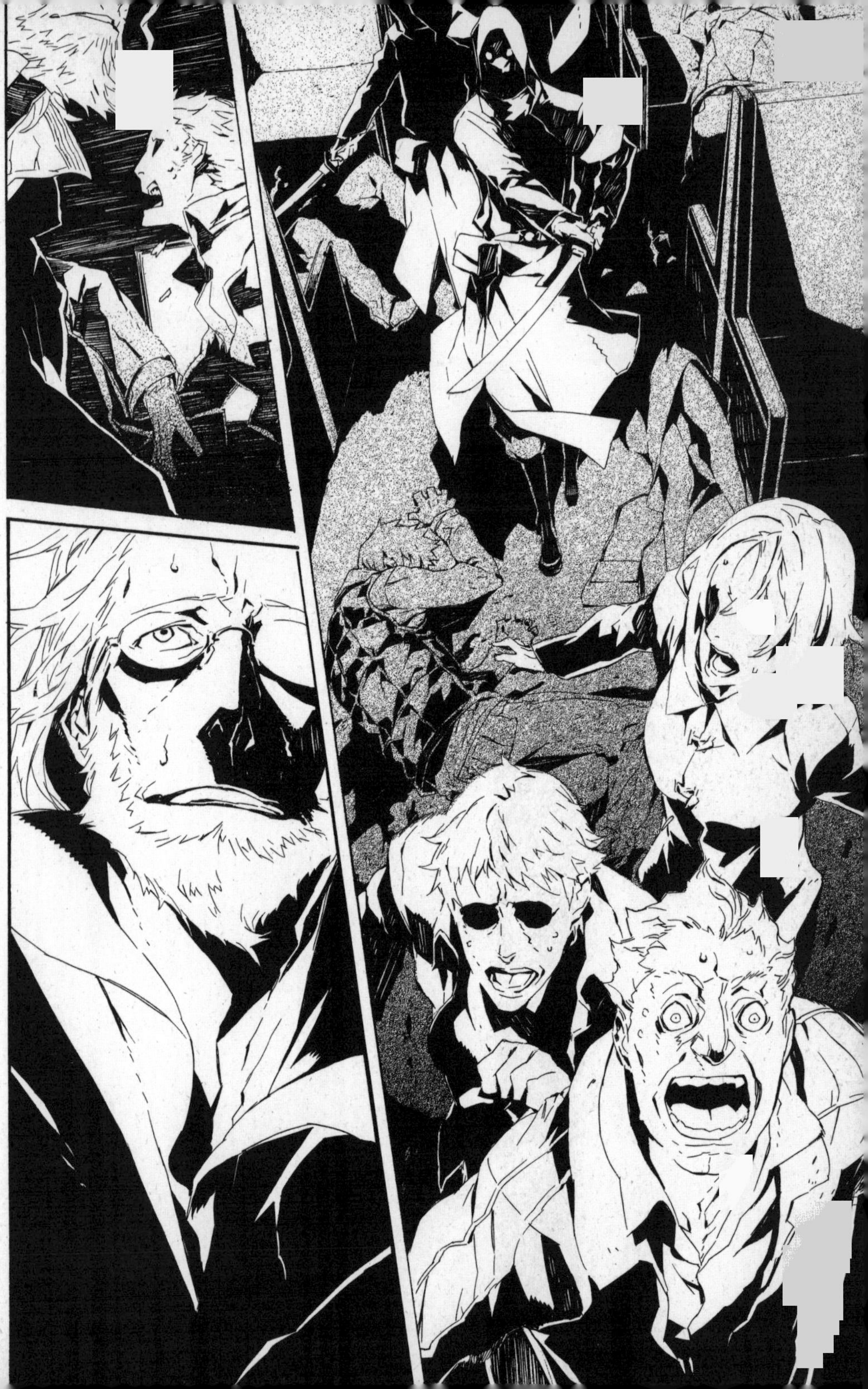

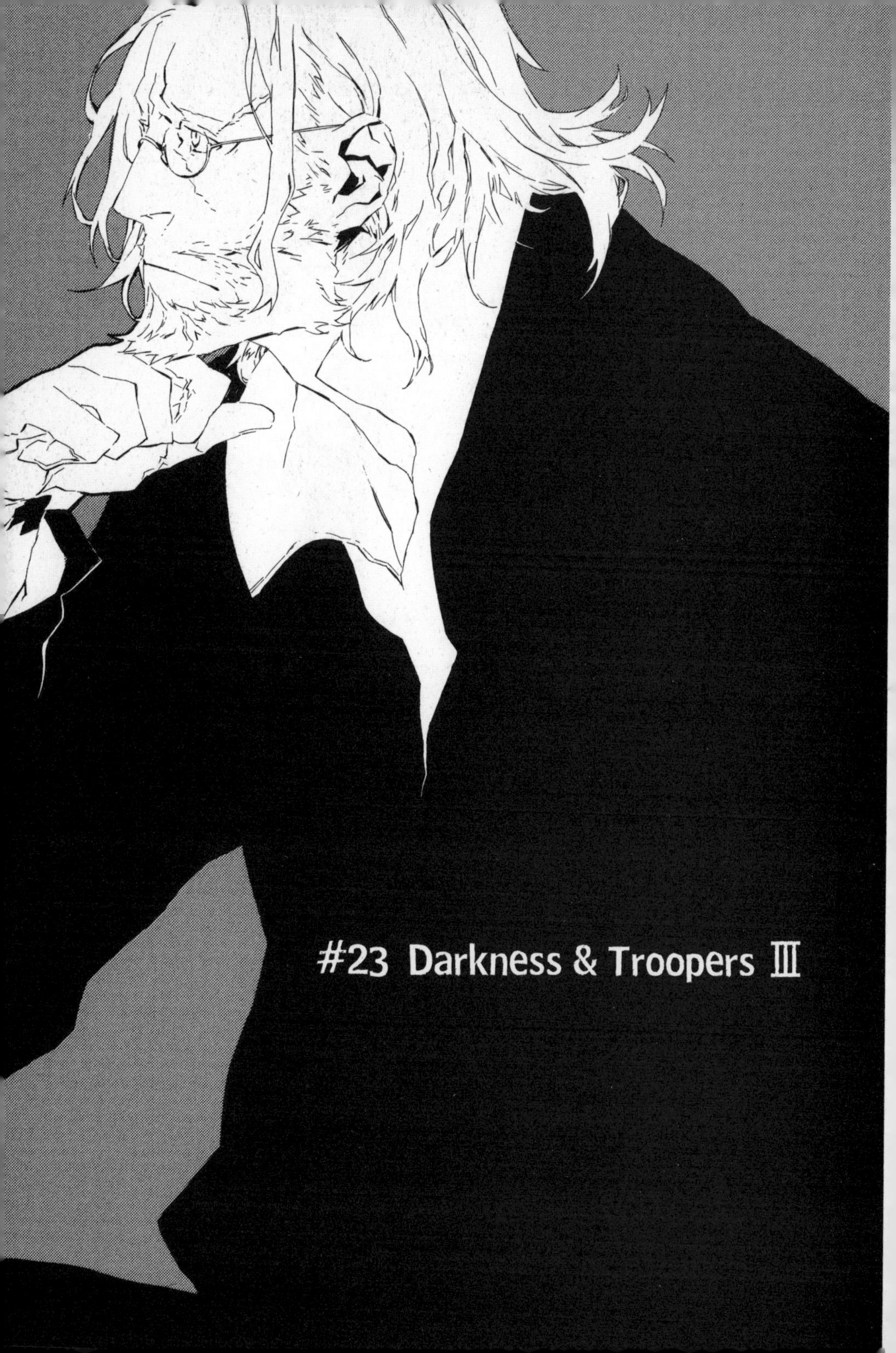
#23 Darkness & Troopers III

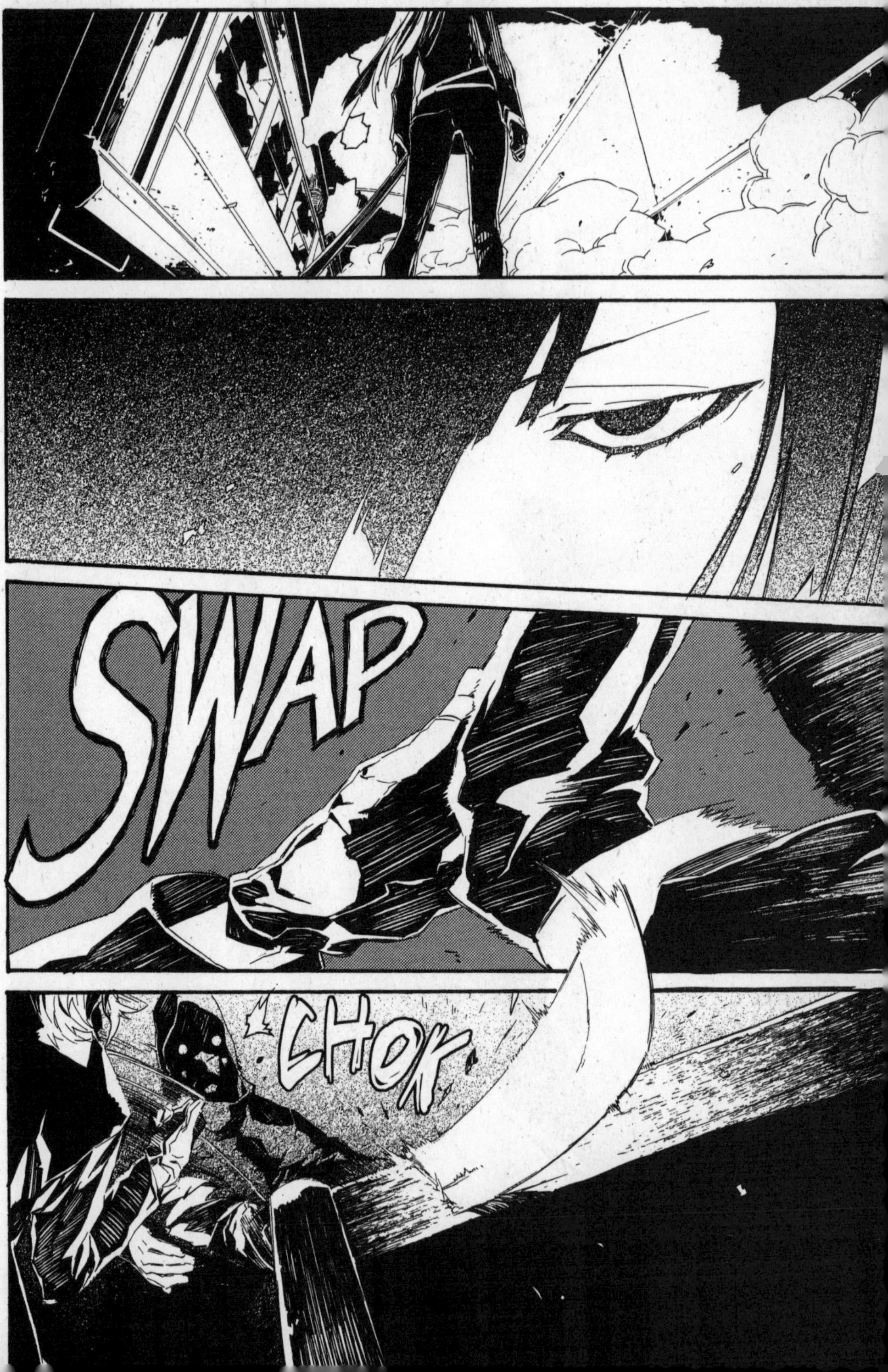
SWAP
CHOK

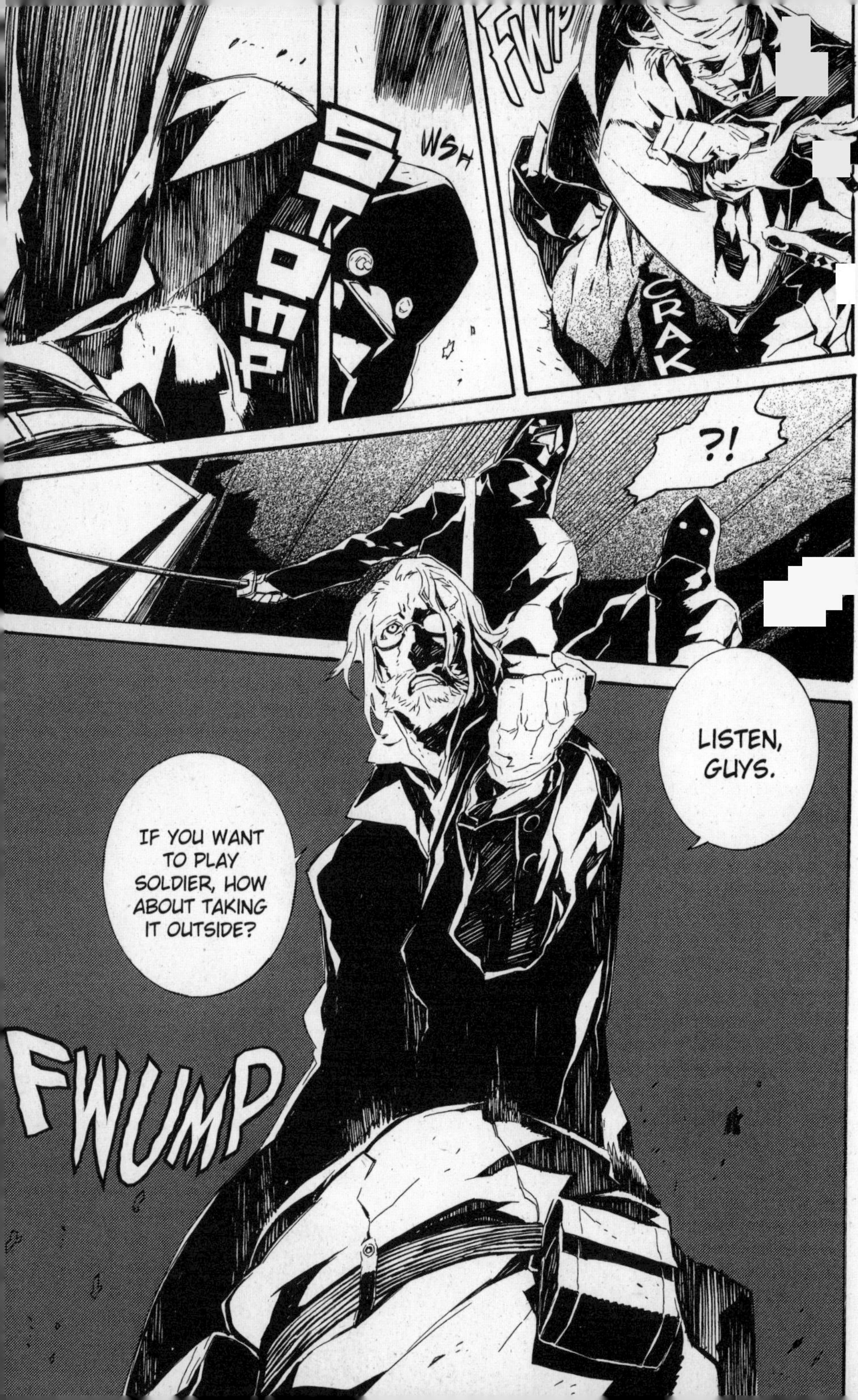
FWIP
CRAK
WSH
STOMP
?!
LISTEN, GUYS.
IF YOU WANT TO PLAY SOLDIER, HOW ABOUT TAKING IT OUTSIDE?
FWUMP

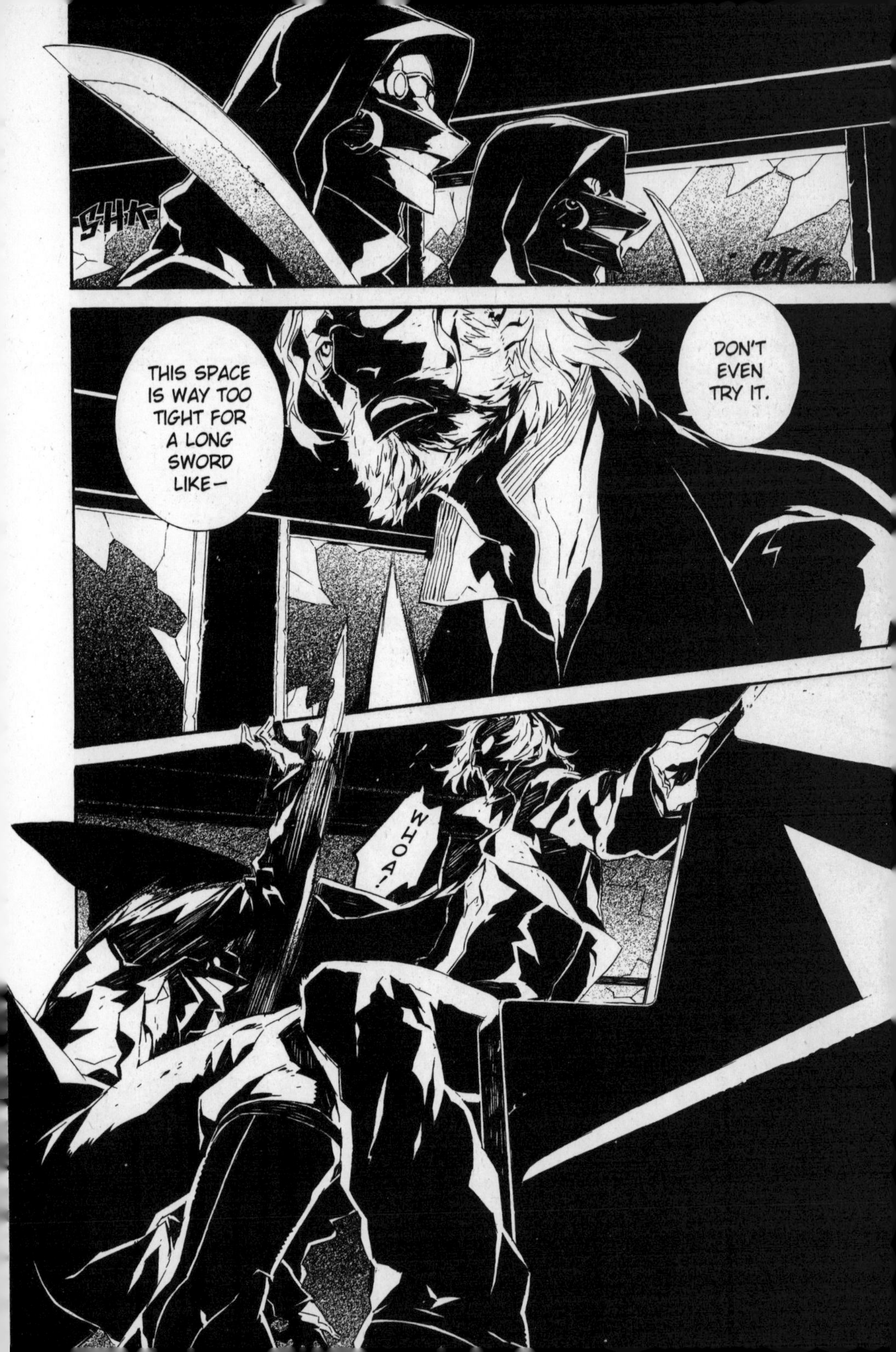
SHK-
DON'T EVEN TRY IT.
THIS SPACE IS WAY TOO TIGHT FOR A LONG SWORD LIKE—
WHOA!

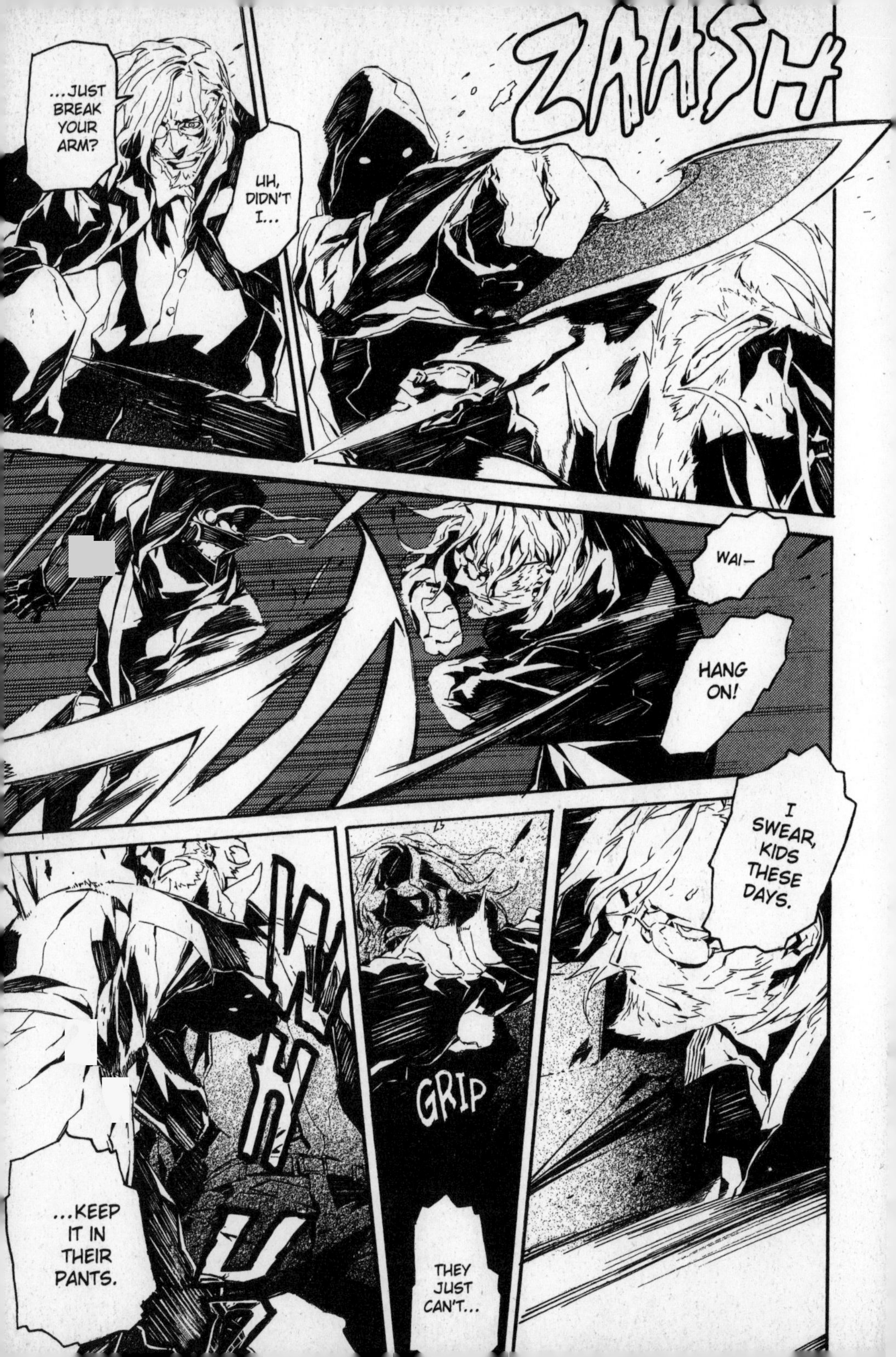
ZAASH
UH, DIDN'T I...
...JUST BREAK YOUR ARM?
WAI—
HANG ON!
I SWEAR, KIDS THESE DAYS.
GRIP
THEY JUST CAN'T...
...KEEP IT IN THEIR PANTS.

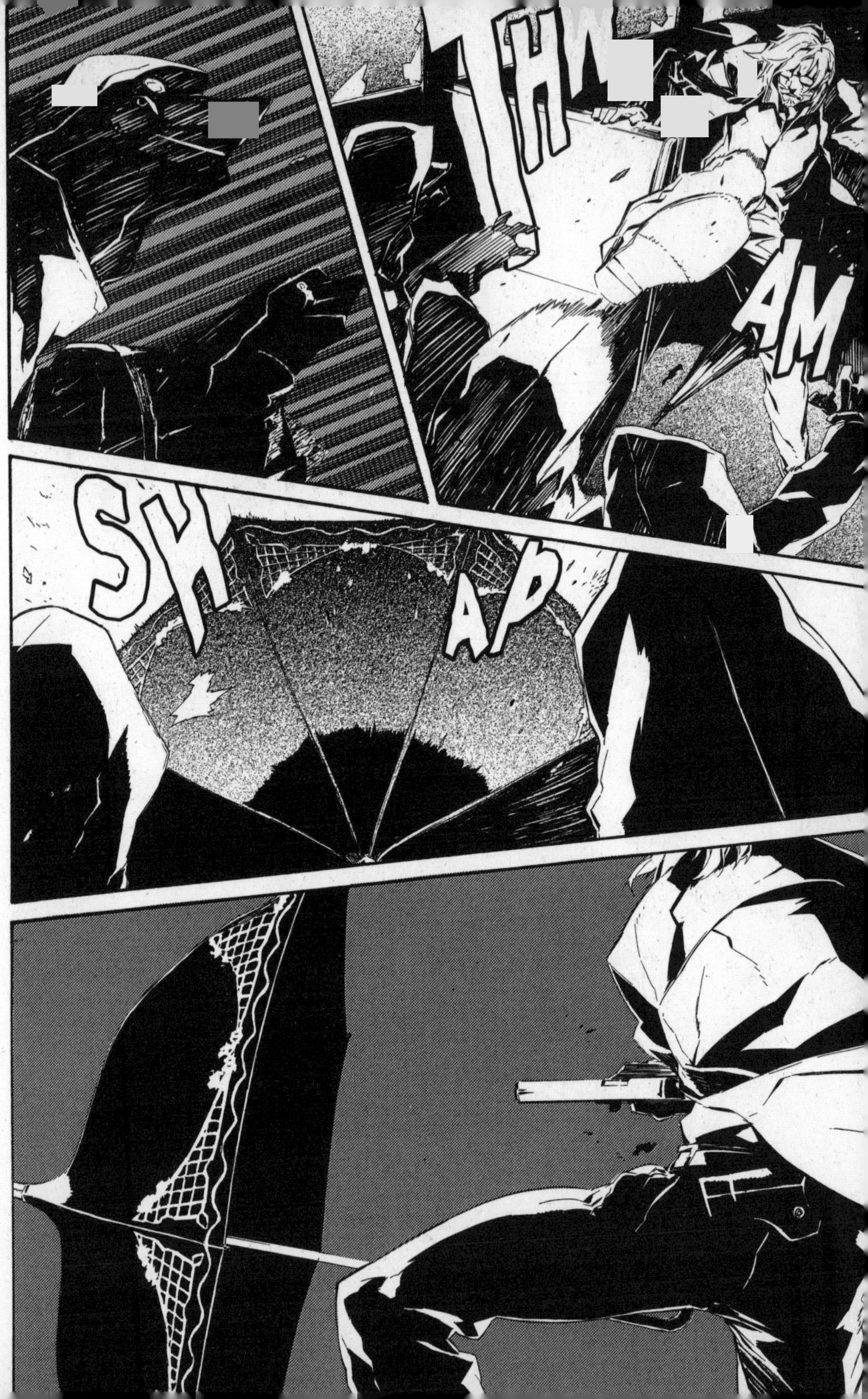
TH
AM
SHAP

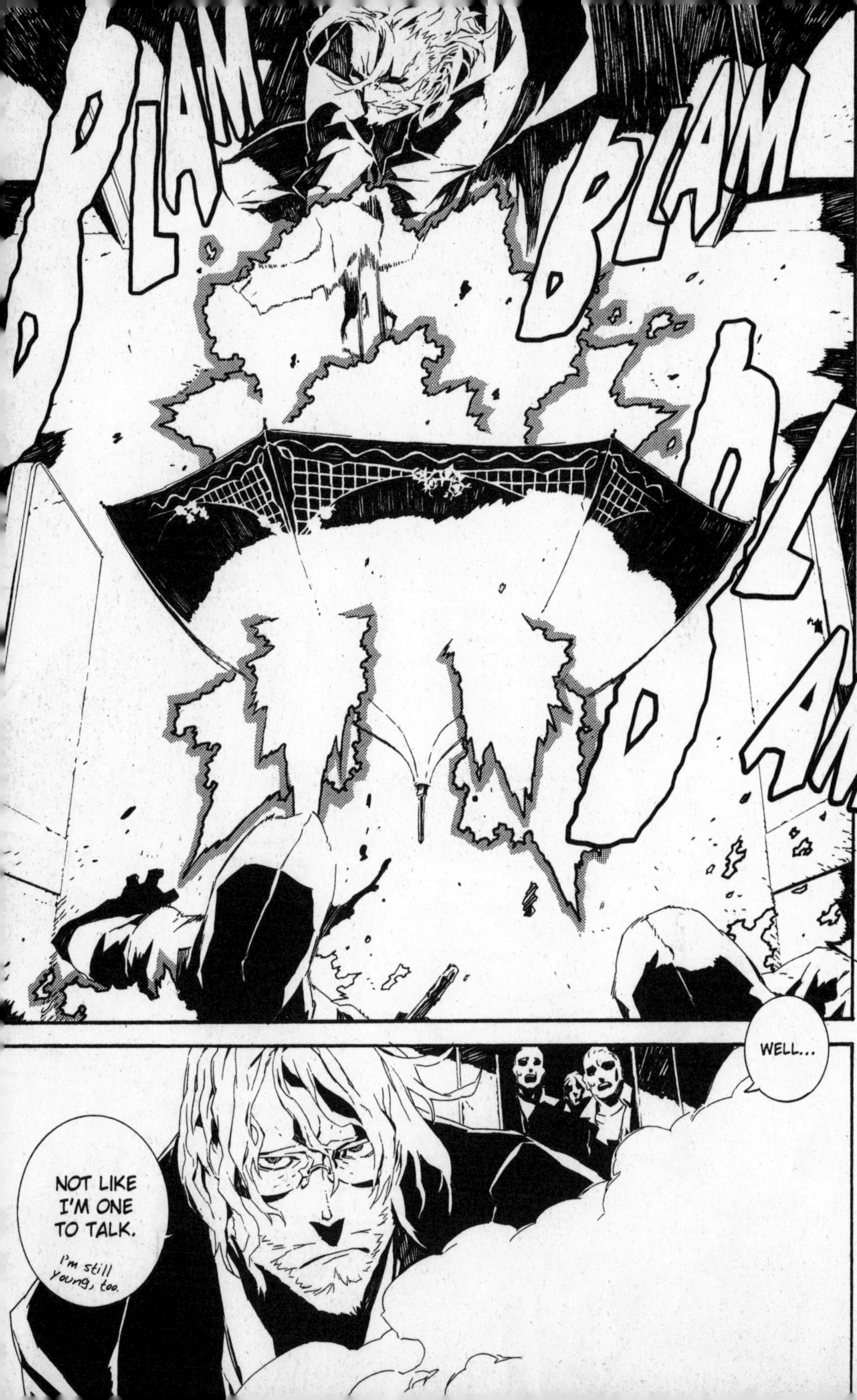
BLAM
BLAM
BLAM
WELL...
NOT LIKE I'M ONE TO TALK.
I'm still young, too.

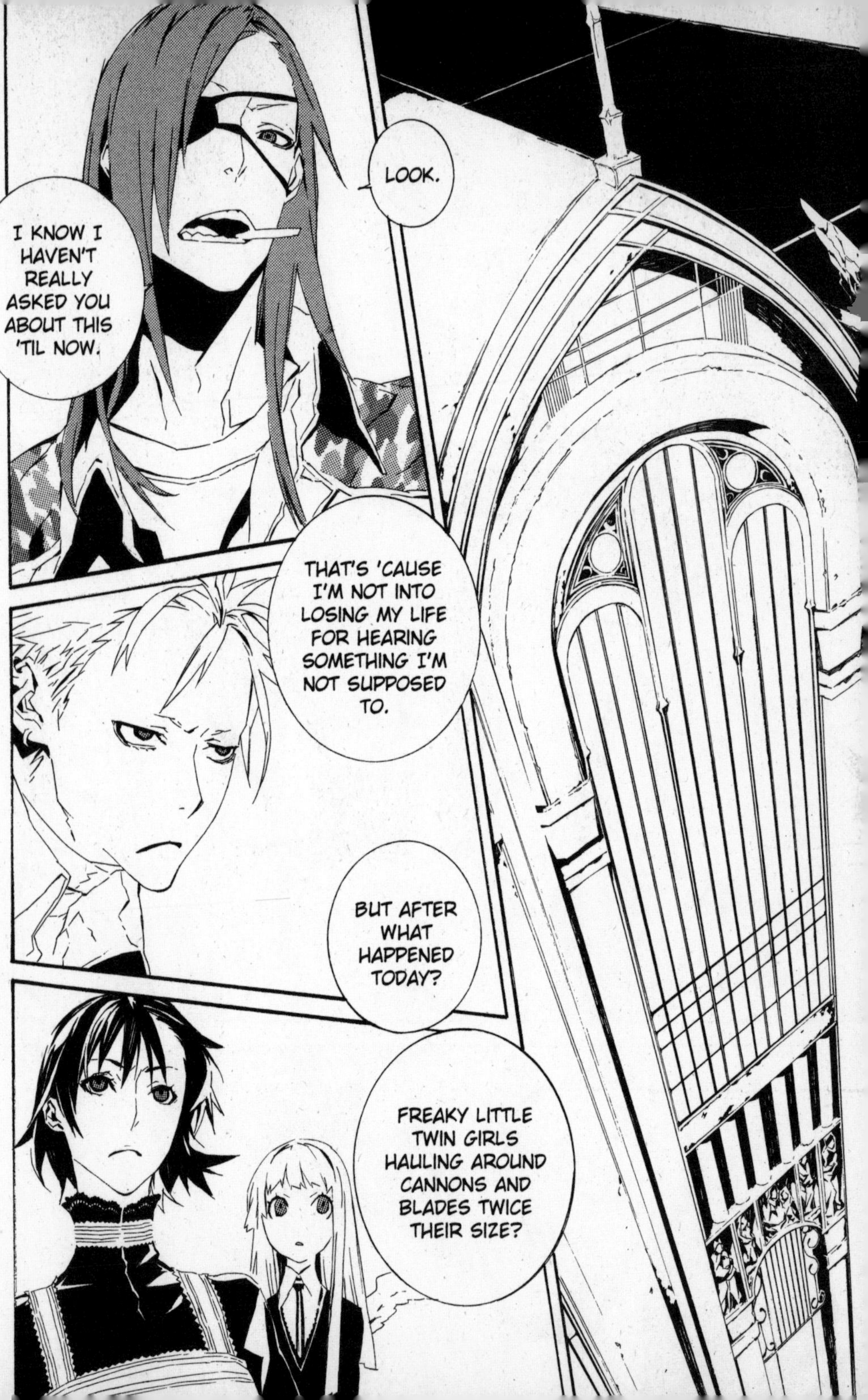
LOOK.
I KNOW I HAVEN'T REALLY ASKED YOU ABOUT THIS 'TIL NOW.
THAT'S 'CAUSE I'M NOT INTO LOSING MY LIFE FOR HEARING SOMETHING I'M NOT SUPPOSED TO.
BUT AFTER WHAT HAPPENED TODAY?
FREAKY LITTLE TWIN GIRLS HAULING AROUND CANNONS AND BLADES TWICE THEIR SIZE?

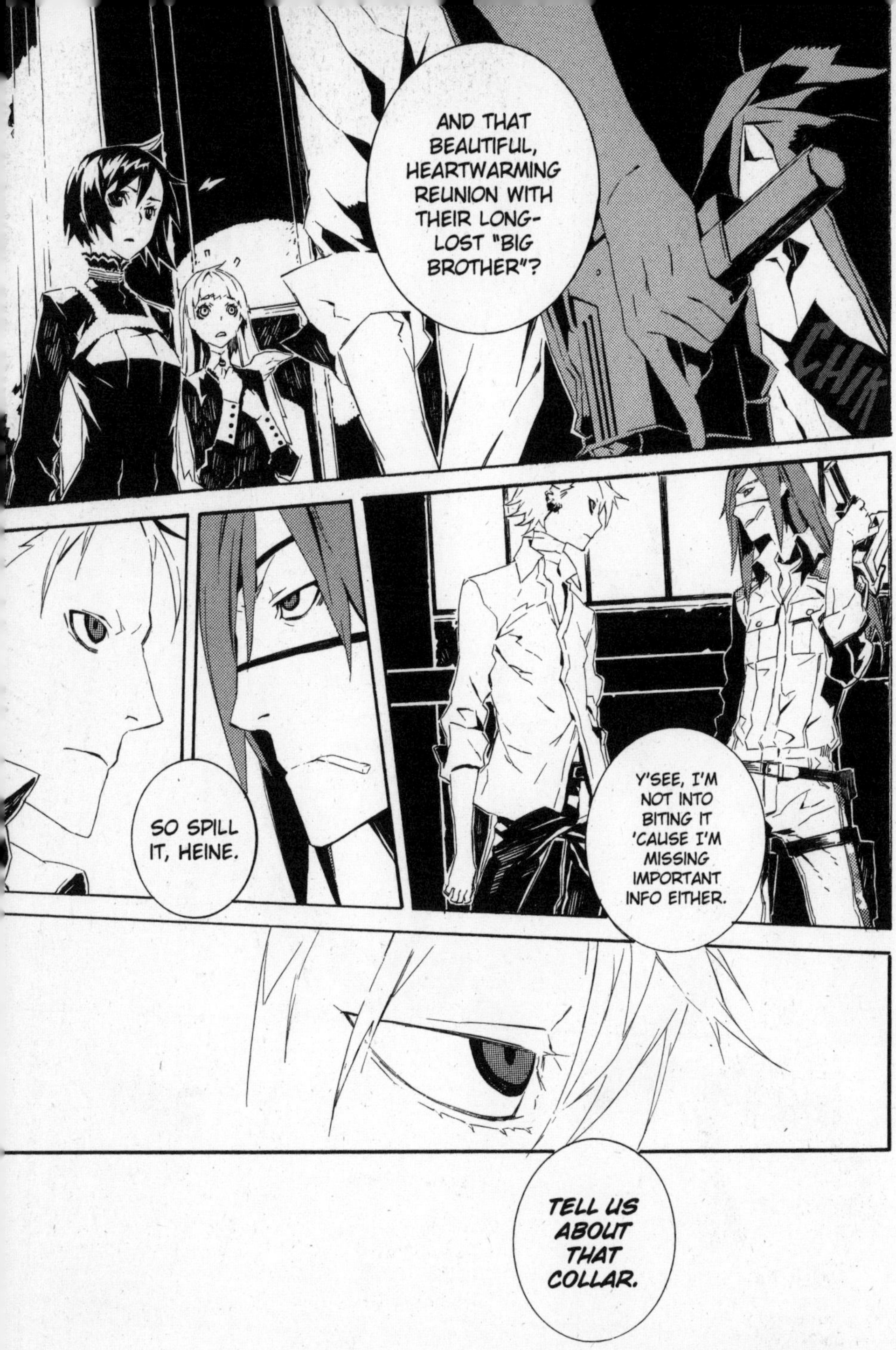
AND THAT BEAUTIFUL, HEARTWARMING REUNION WITH THEIR LONG-LOST "BIG BROTHER"?
CHIK
Y'SEE, I'M NOT INTO BITING IT 'CAUSE I'M MISSING IMPORTANT INFO EITHER.
SO SPILL IT, HEINE.
TELL US ABOUT THAT COLLAR.

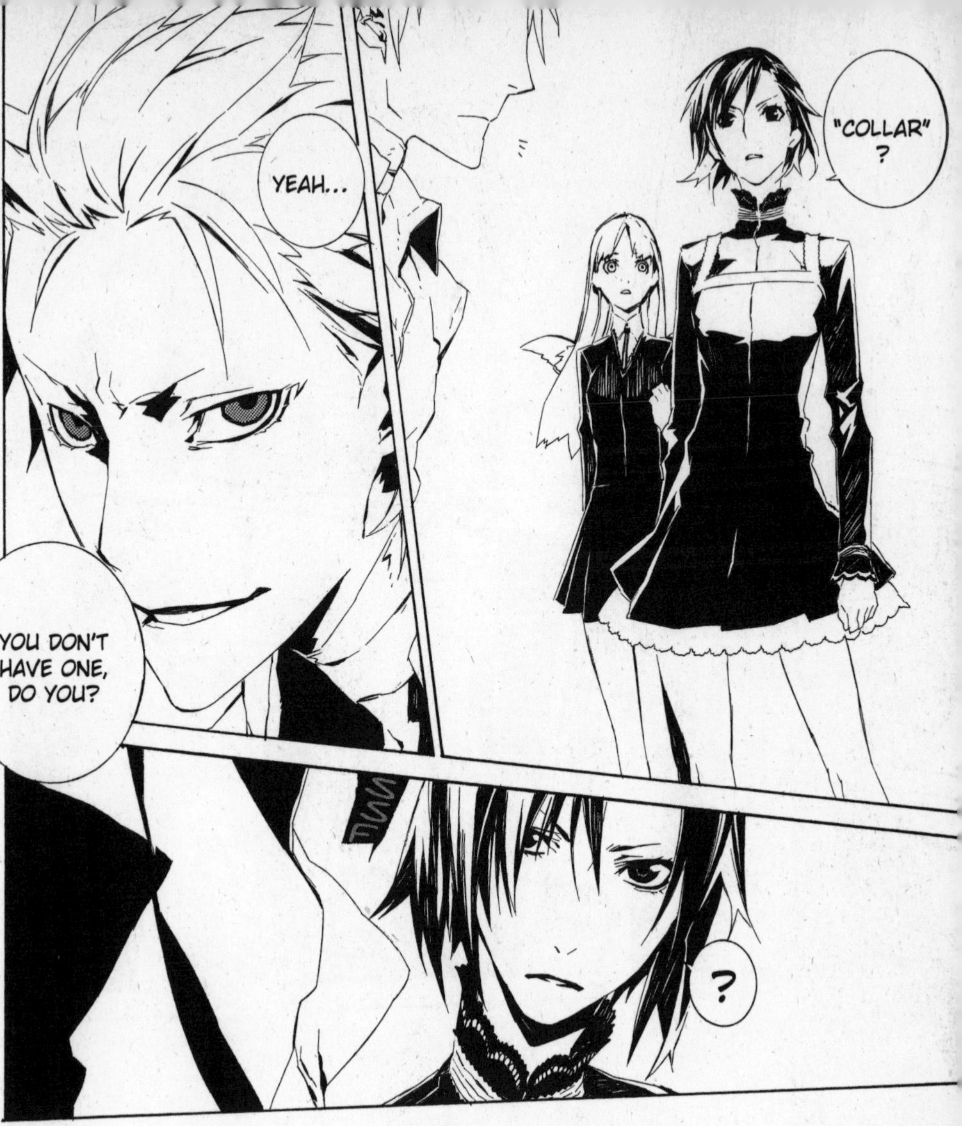
"COLLAR"
?
YEAH...
YOU DON'T
HAVE ONE,
DO YOU?
?

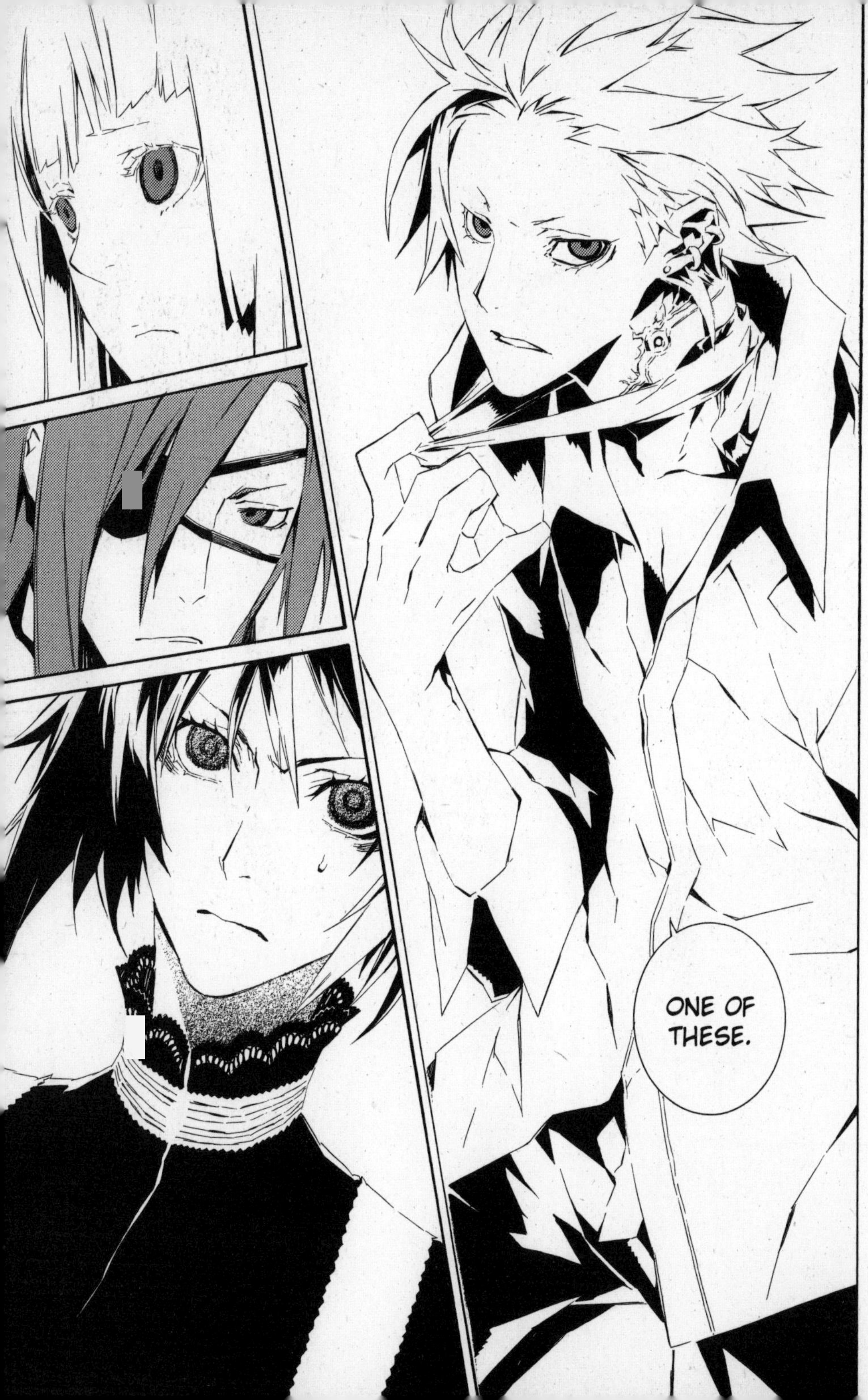
ONE OF THESE.

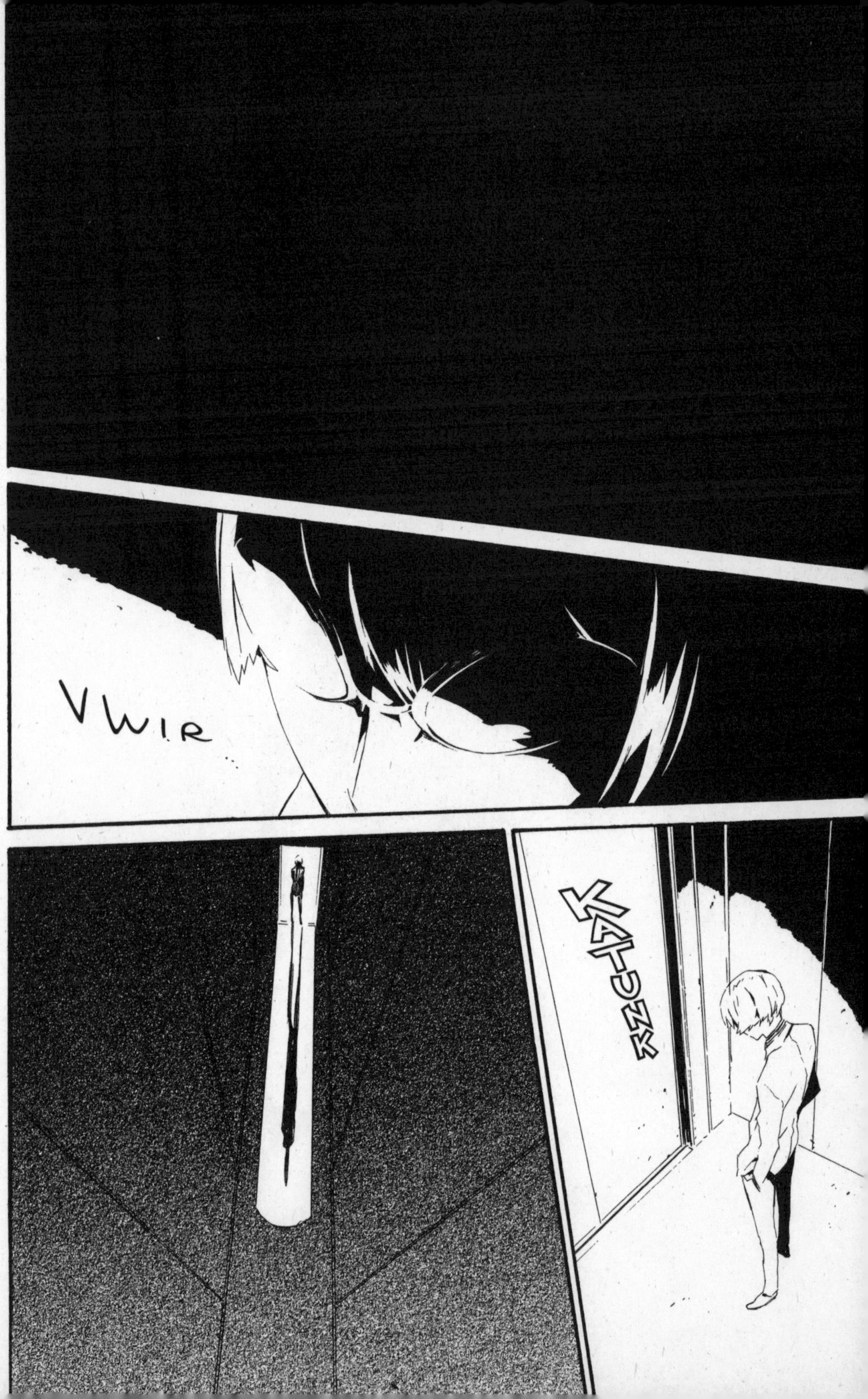
VWIR
KATUNK

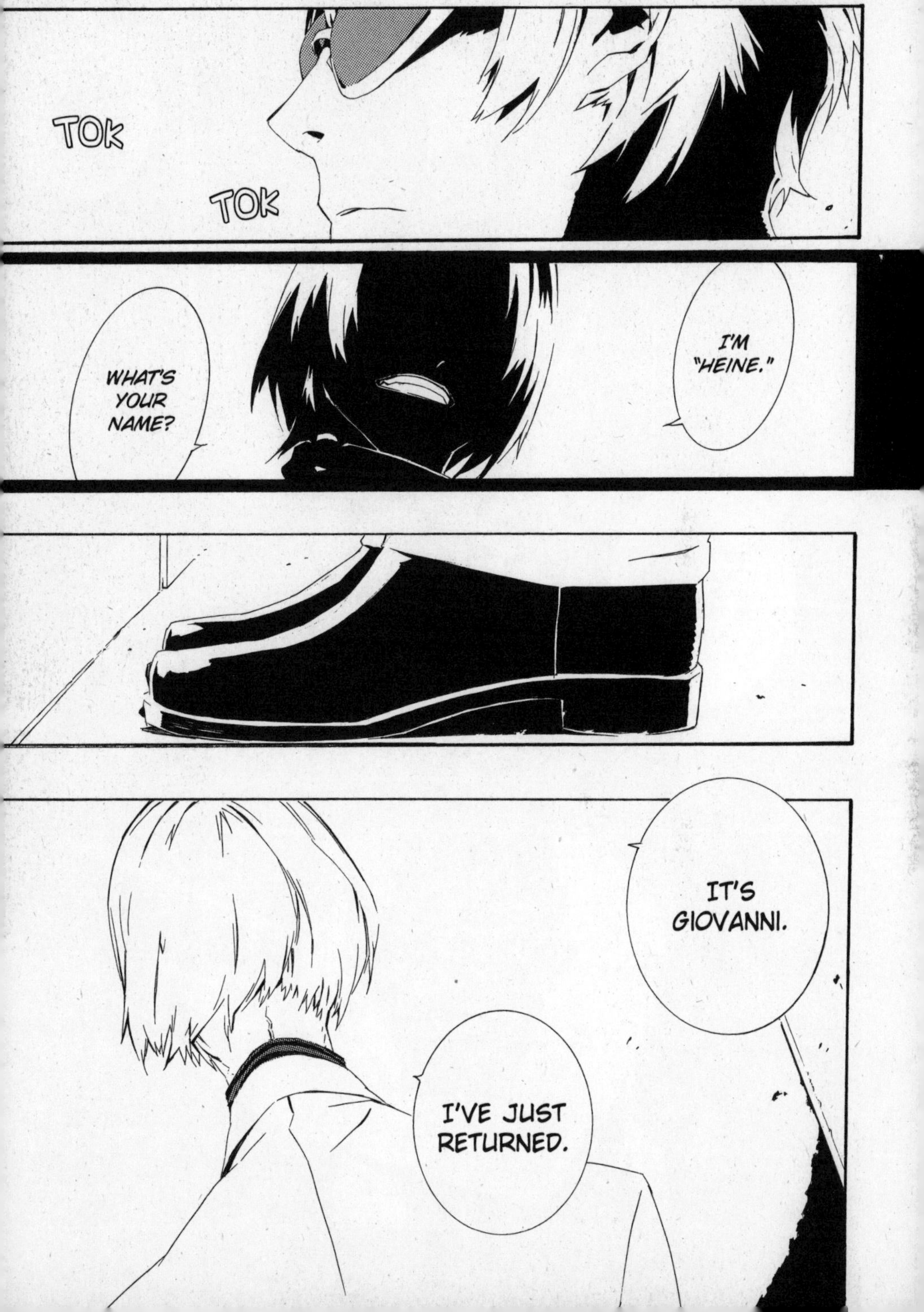
TOK
TOK
I'M "HEINE."
WHAT'S YOUR NAME?
IT'S GIOVANNI.
I'VE JUST RETURNED.

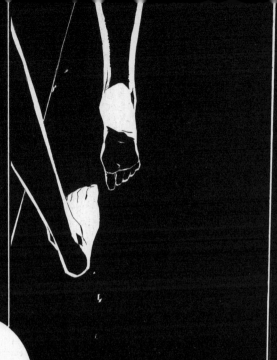

WHEN I WOKE UP, EVERYTHING WAS DARK.

AND I HAD NO MEMORIES LEFT OF ANYTHING BEFORE THAT MOMENT.

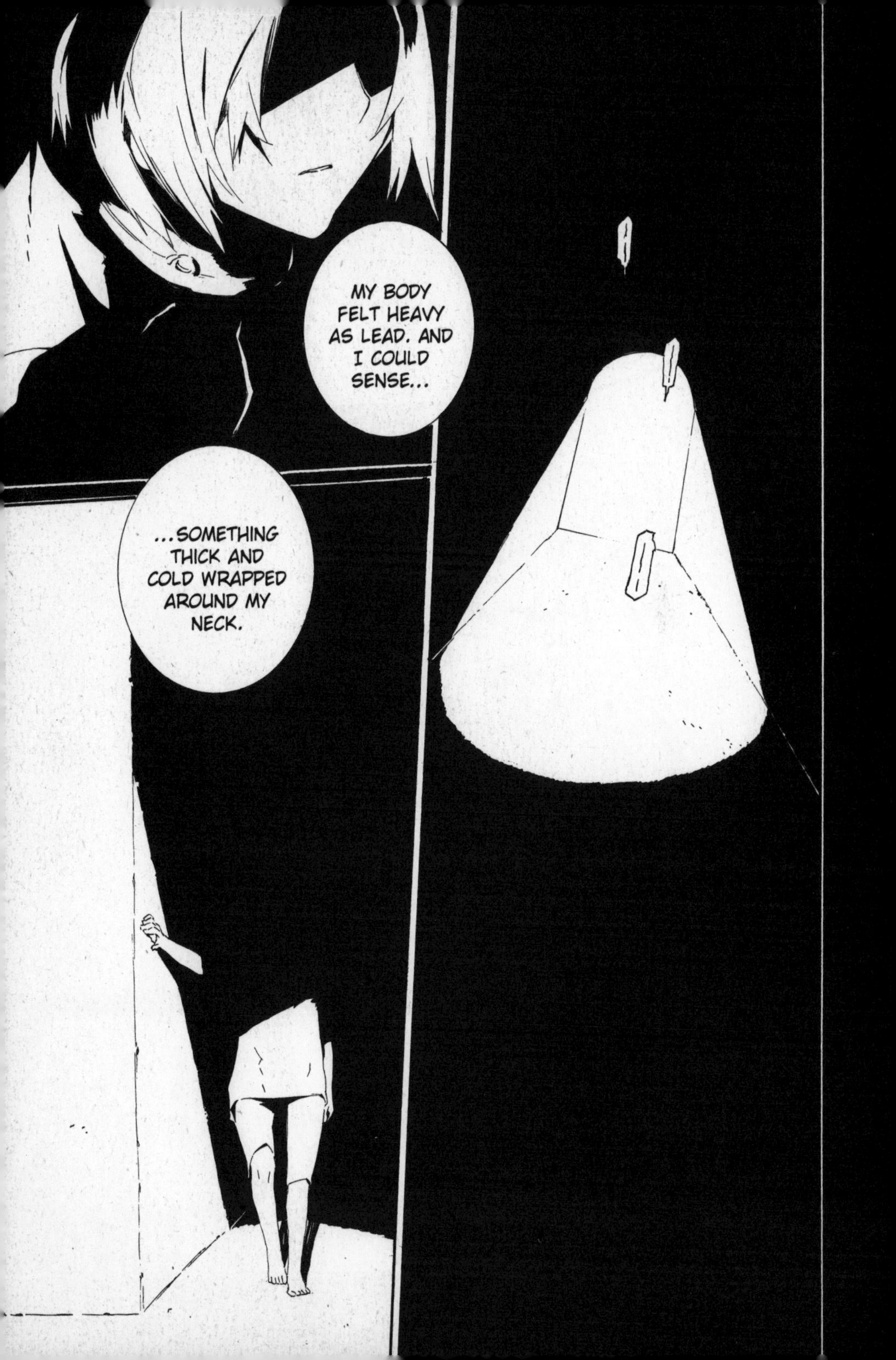
MY BODY FELT HEAVY AS LEAD. AND I COULD SENSE...
...SOMETHING THICK AND COLD WRAPPED AROUND MY NECK.

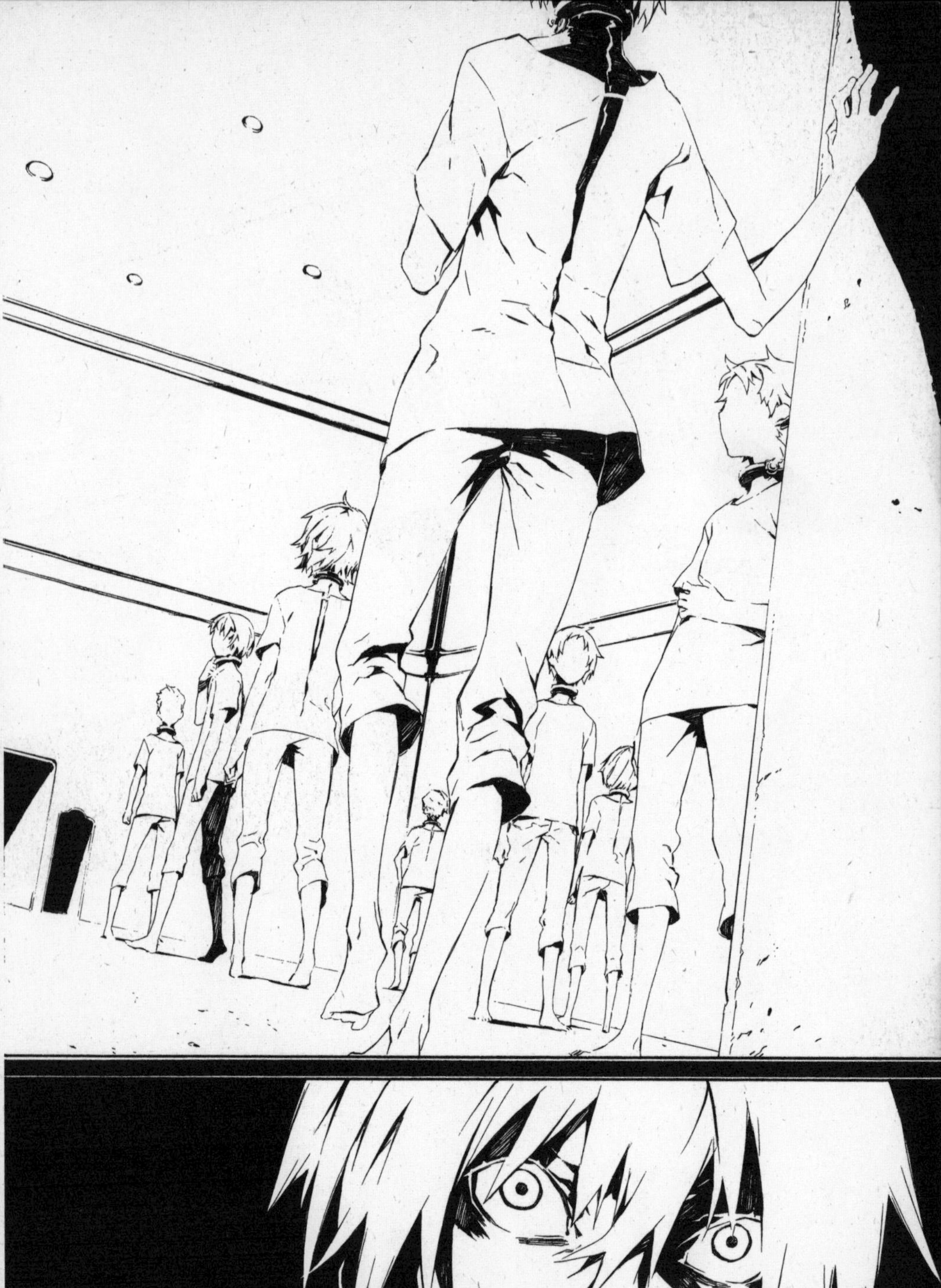

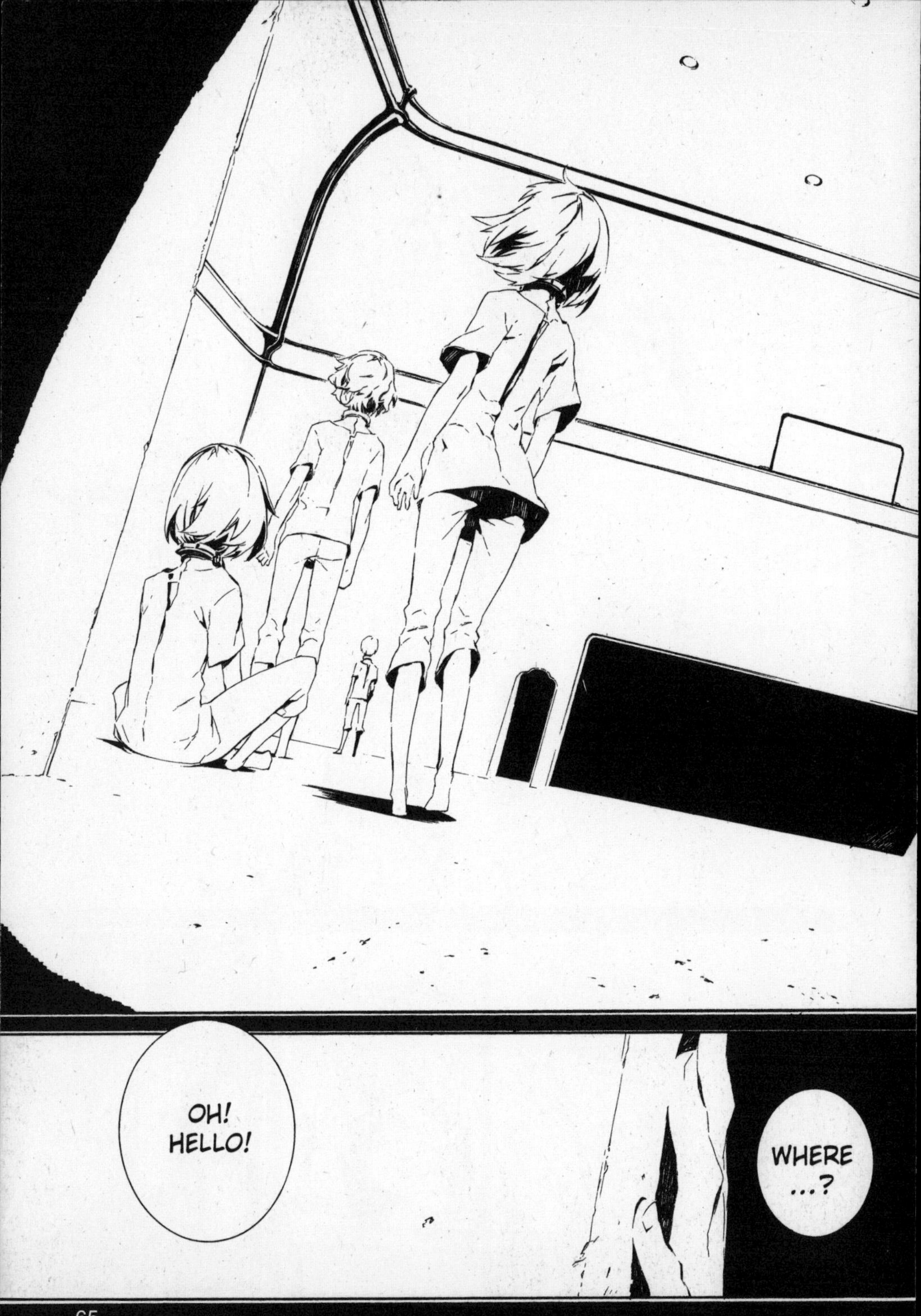
WHERE ...?
OH! HELLO!

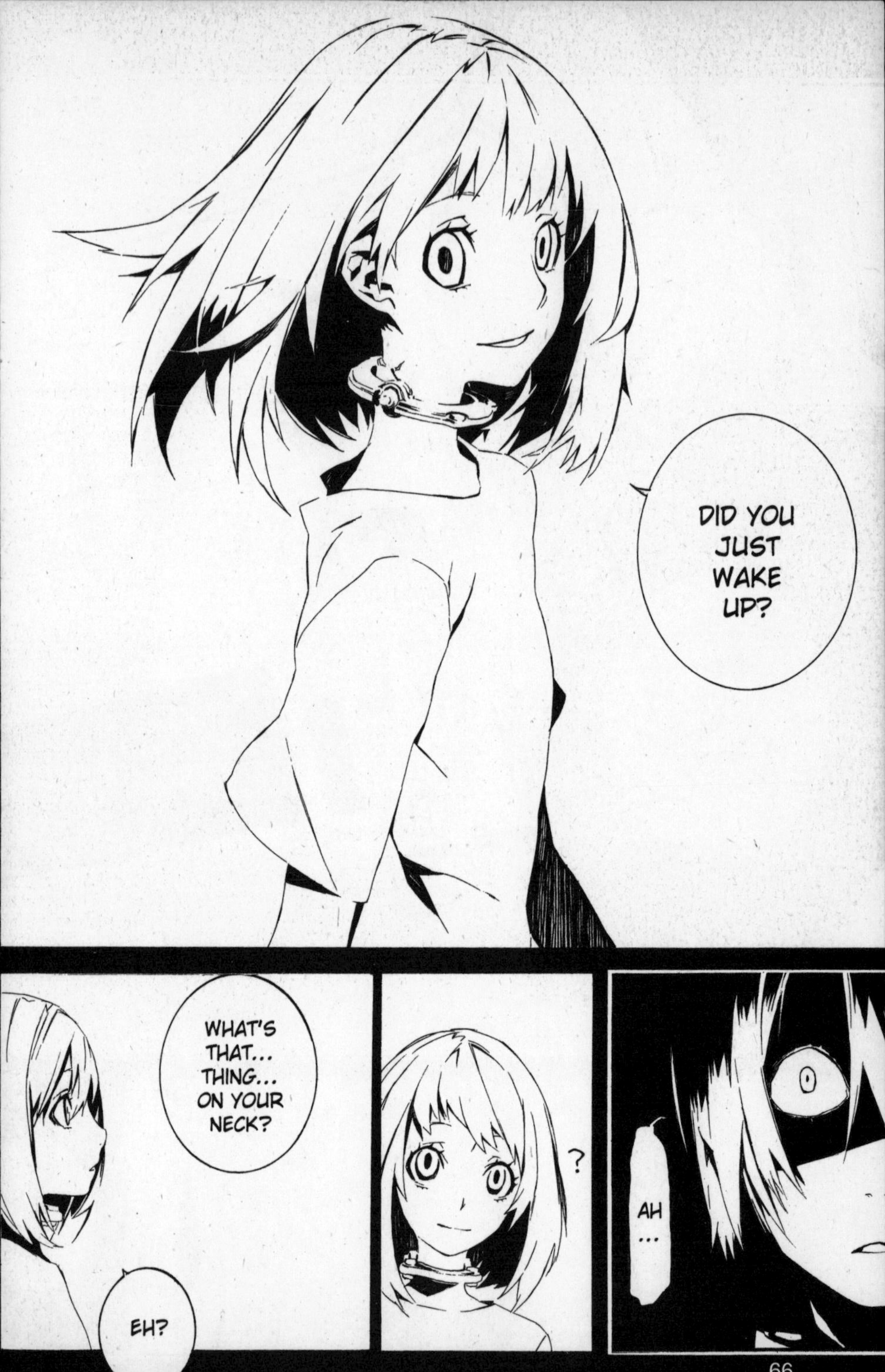
DID YOU JUST WAKE UP?
AH ...
?
WHAT'S THAT... THING... ON YOUR NECK?
EH?

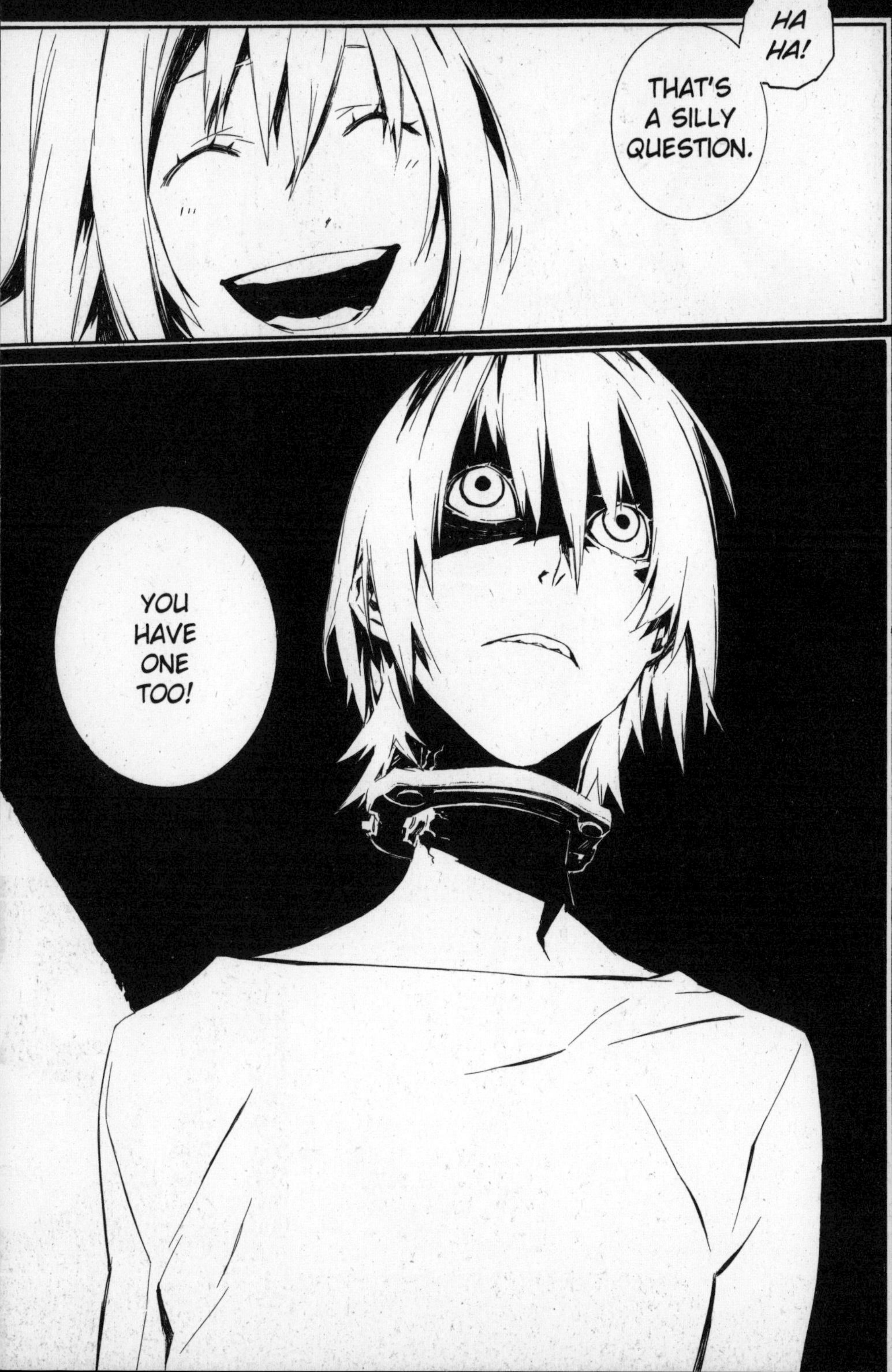
HA HA!
THAT'S A SILLY QUESTION.
YOU HAVE ONE TOO!

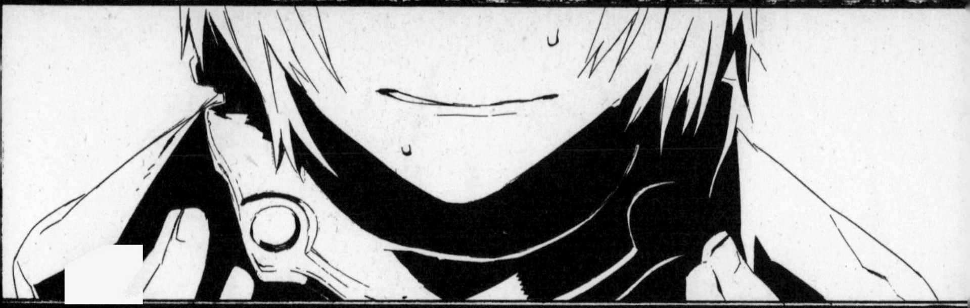

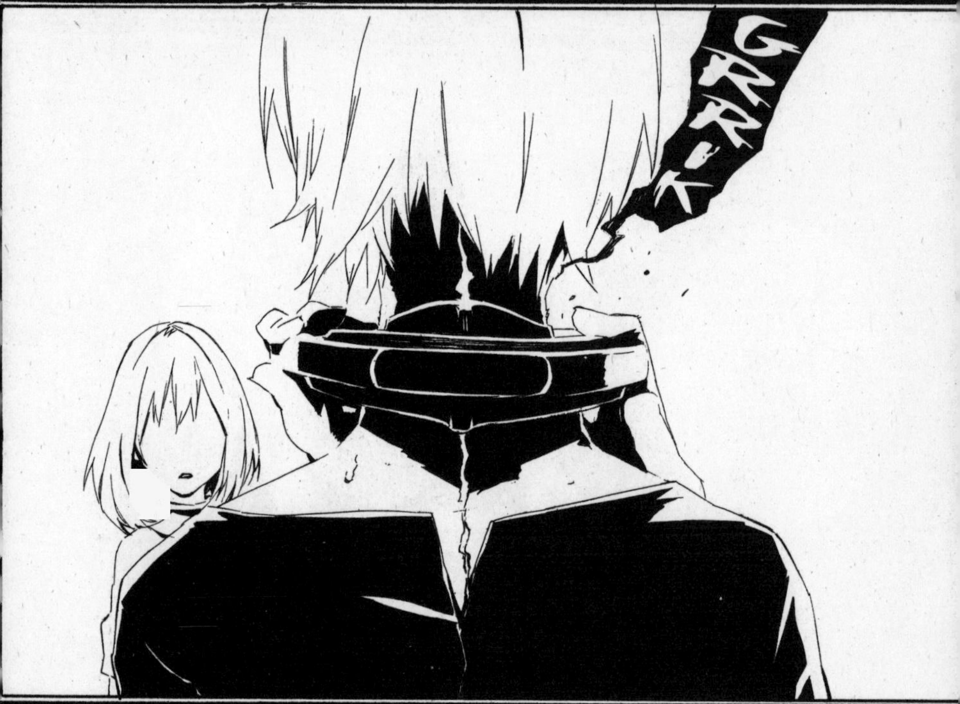
GRRIK

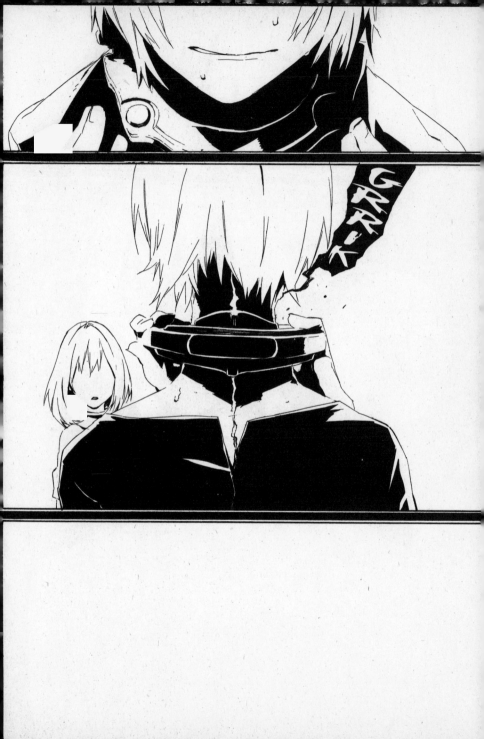

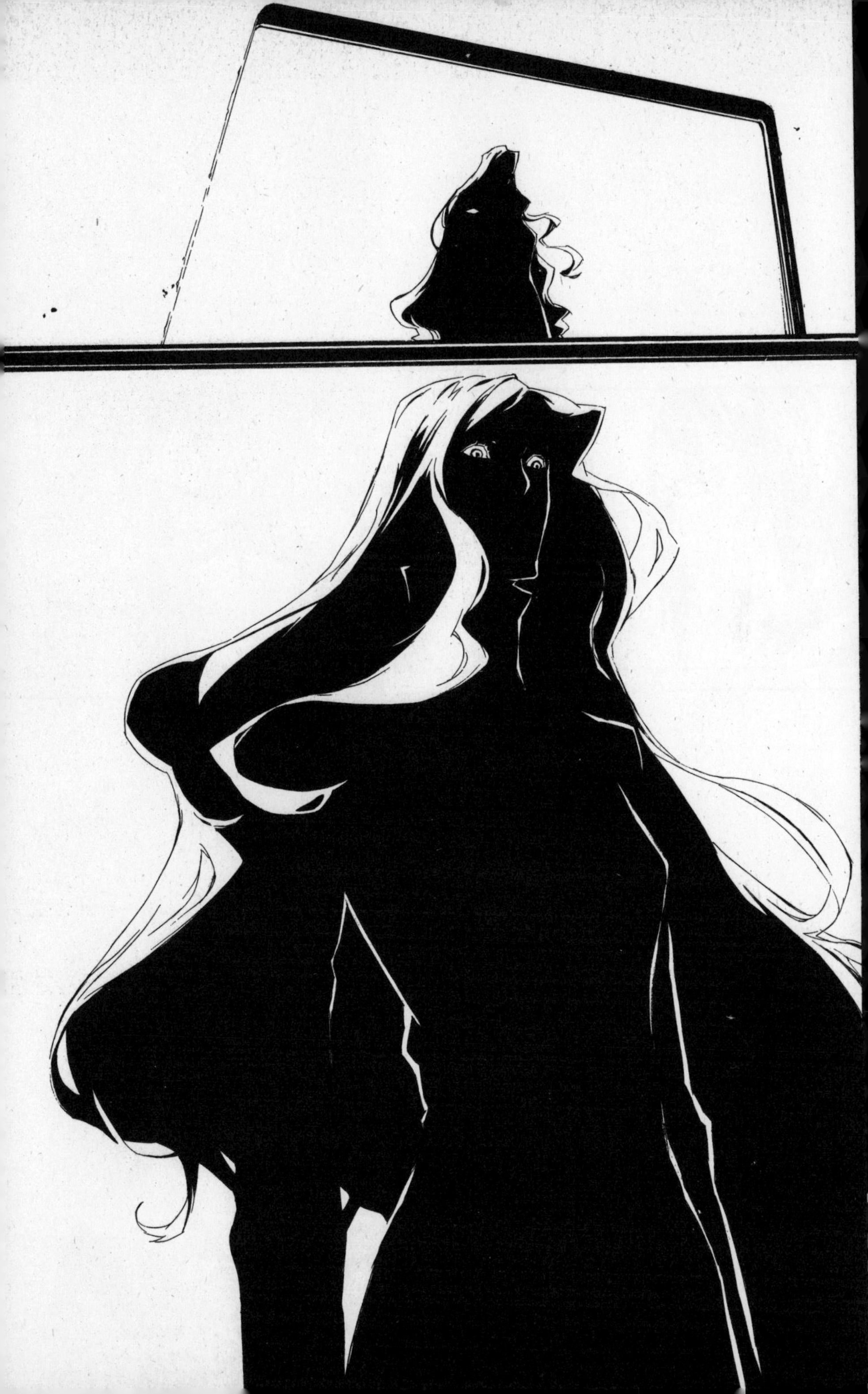

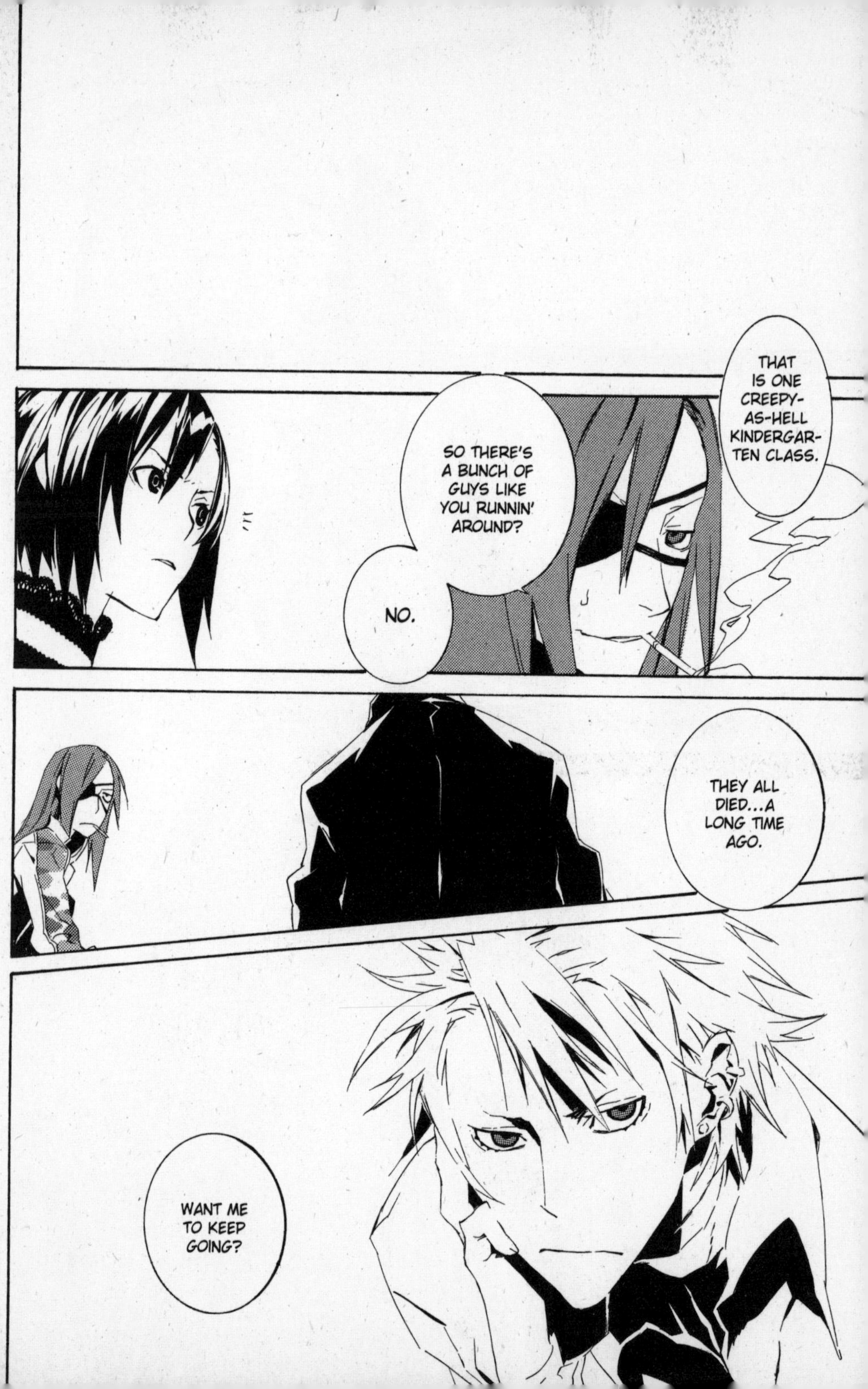
THAT IS ONE CREEPY-AS-HELL KINDERGARTEN CLASS.
SO THERE'S A BUNCH OF GUYS LIKE YOU RUNNIN' AROUND?
NO.
THEY ALL DIED...A LONG TIME AGO.
WANT ME TO KEEP GOING?

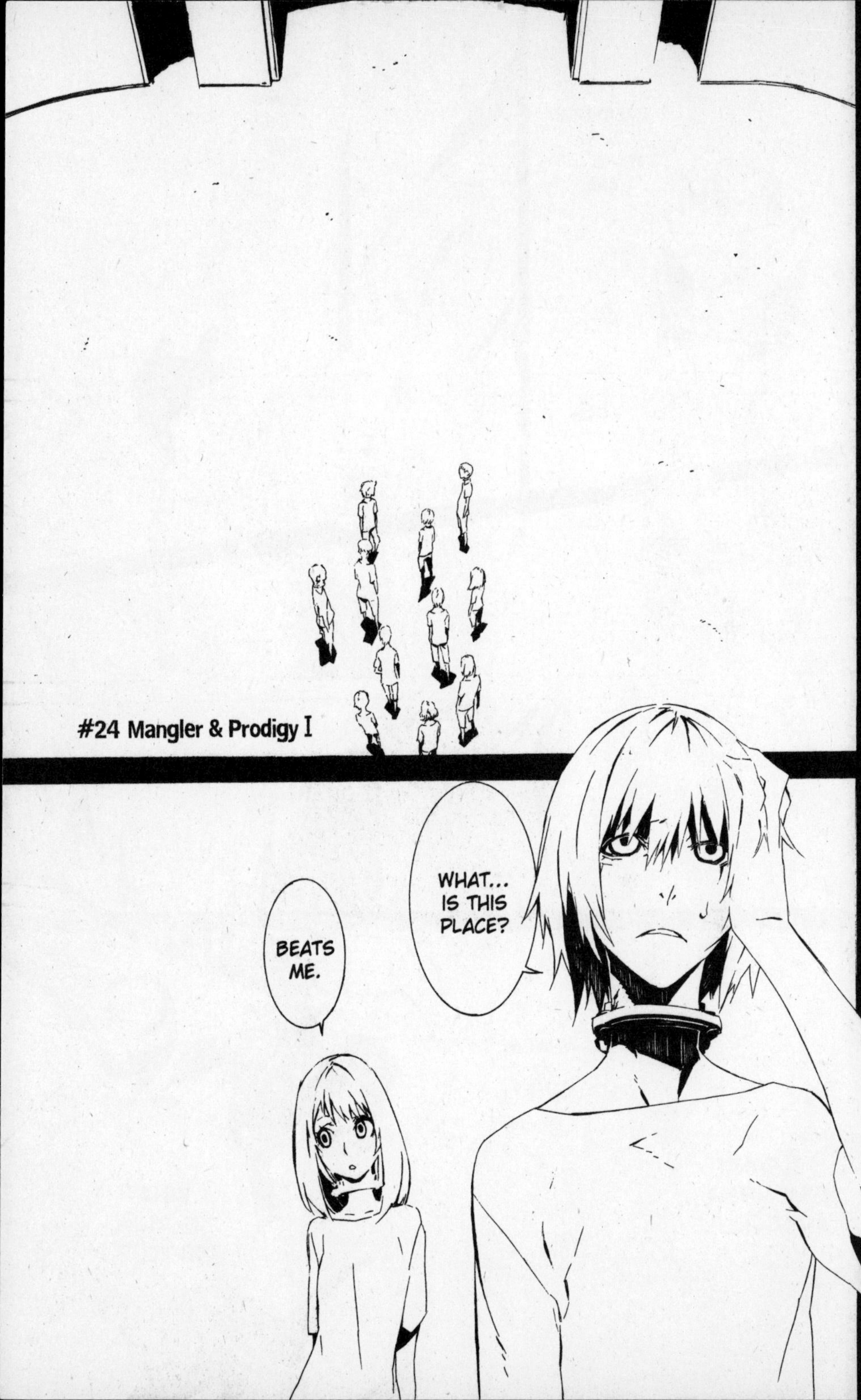
#24 Mangler & Prodigy I
WHAT... IS THIS PLACE?
BEATS ME.

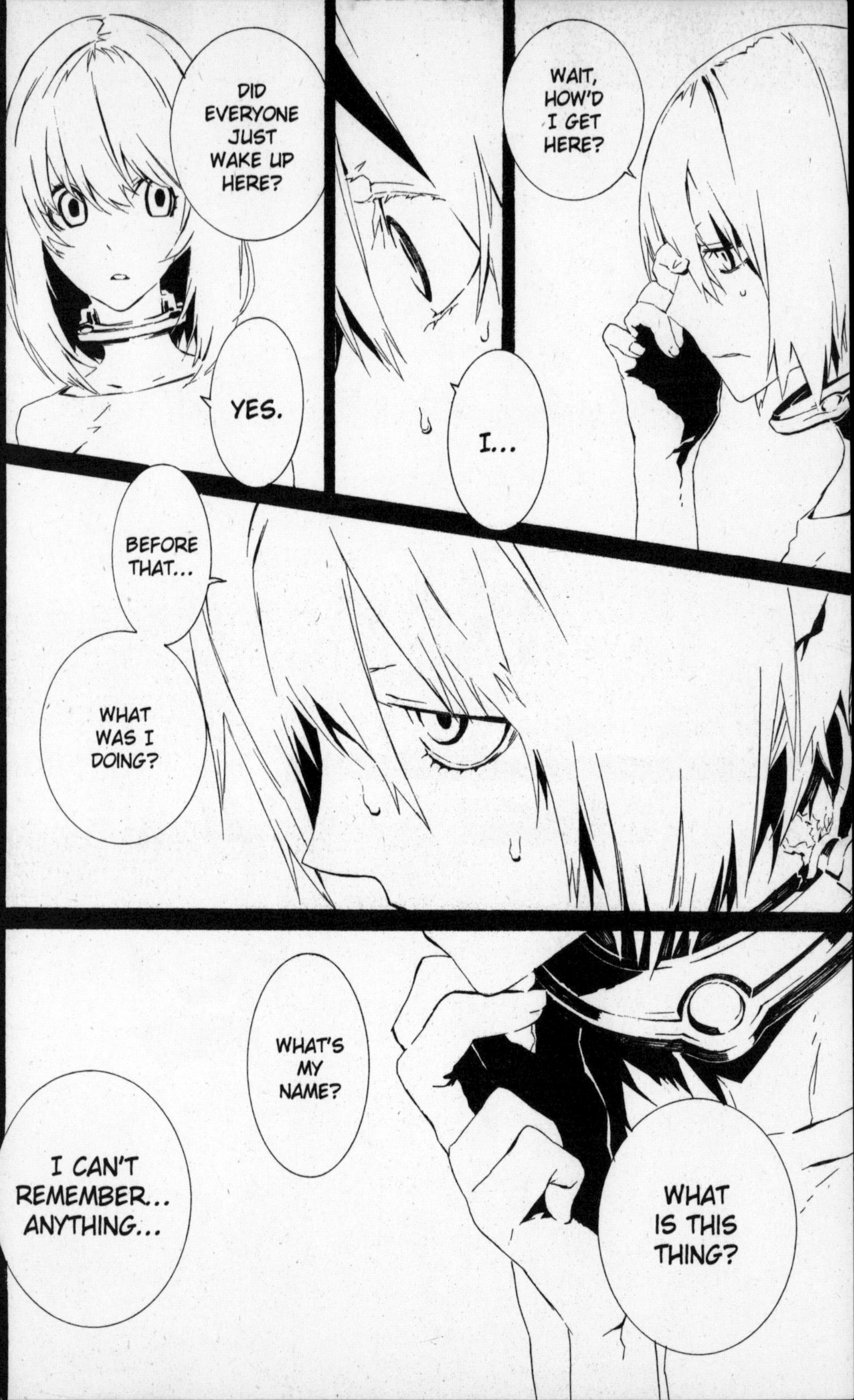

WAIT, HOW'D I GET HERE?
I...
DID EVERYONE JUST WAKE UP HERE?
YES.
BEFORE THAT...
WHAT WAS I DOING?
WHAT IS THIS THING?
WHAT'S MY NAME?
I CAN'T REMEMBER... ANYTHING...

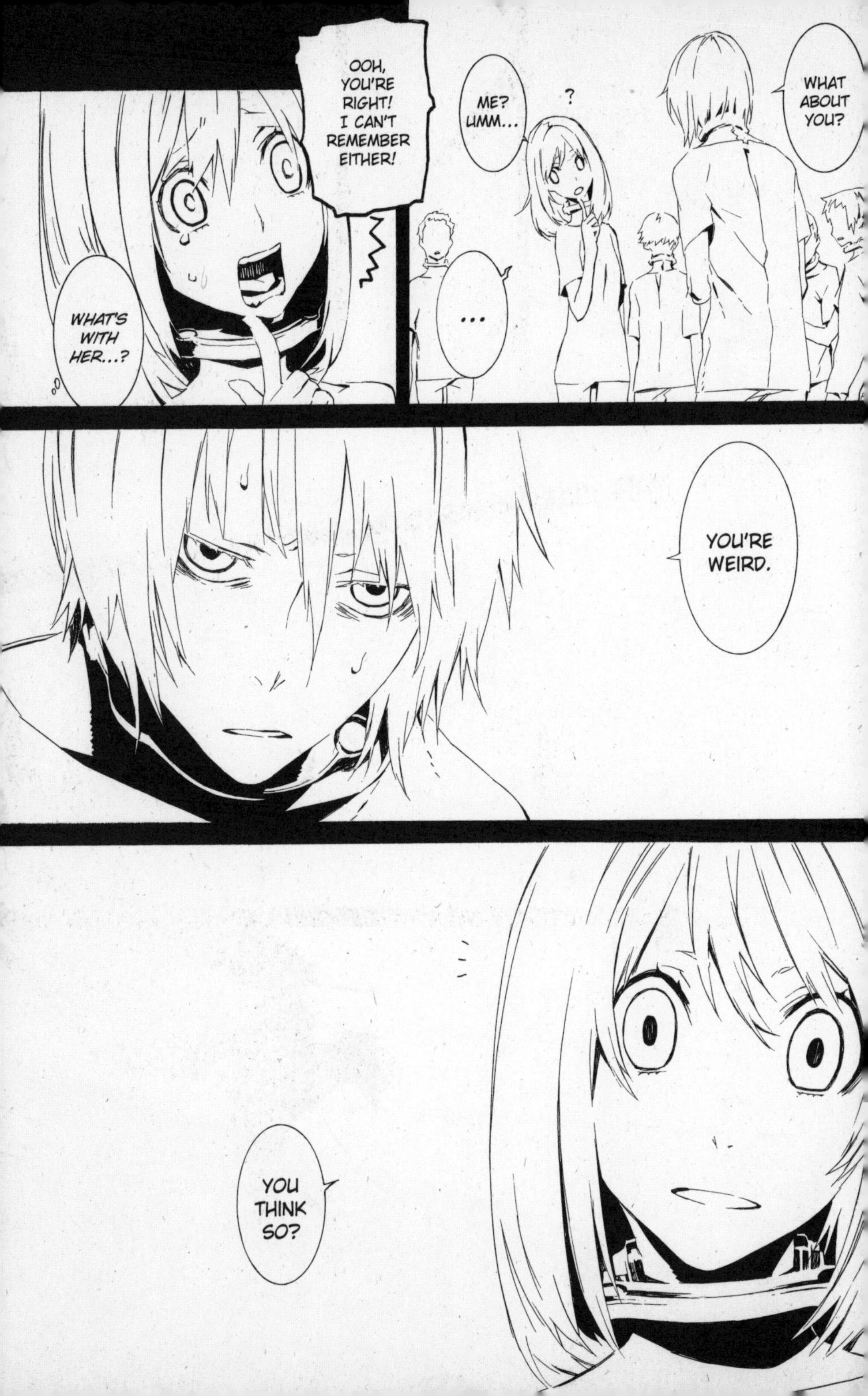

WHAT ABOUT YOU?
?
ME? UMM...
...
OOH, YOU'RE RIGHT! I CAN'T REMEMBER EITHER!
WHAT'S WITH HER...?
YOU'RE WEIRD.
YOU THINK SO?

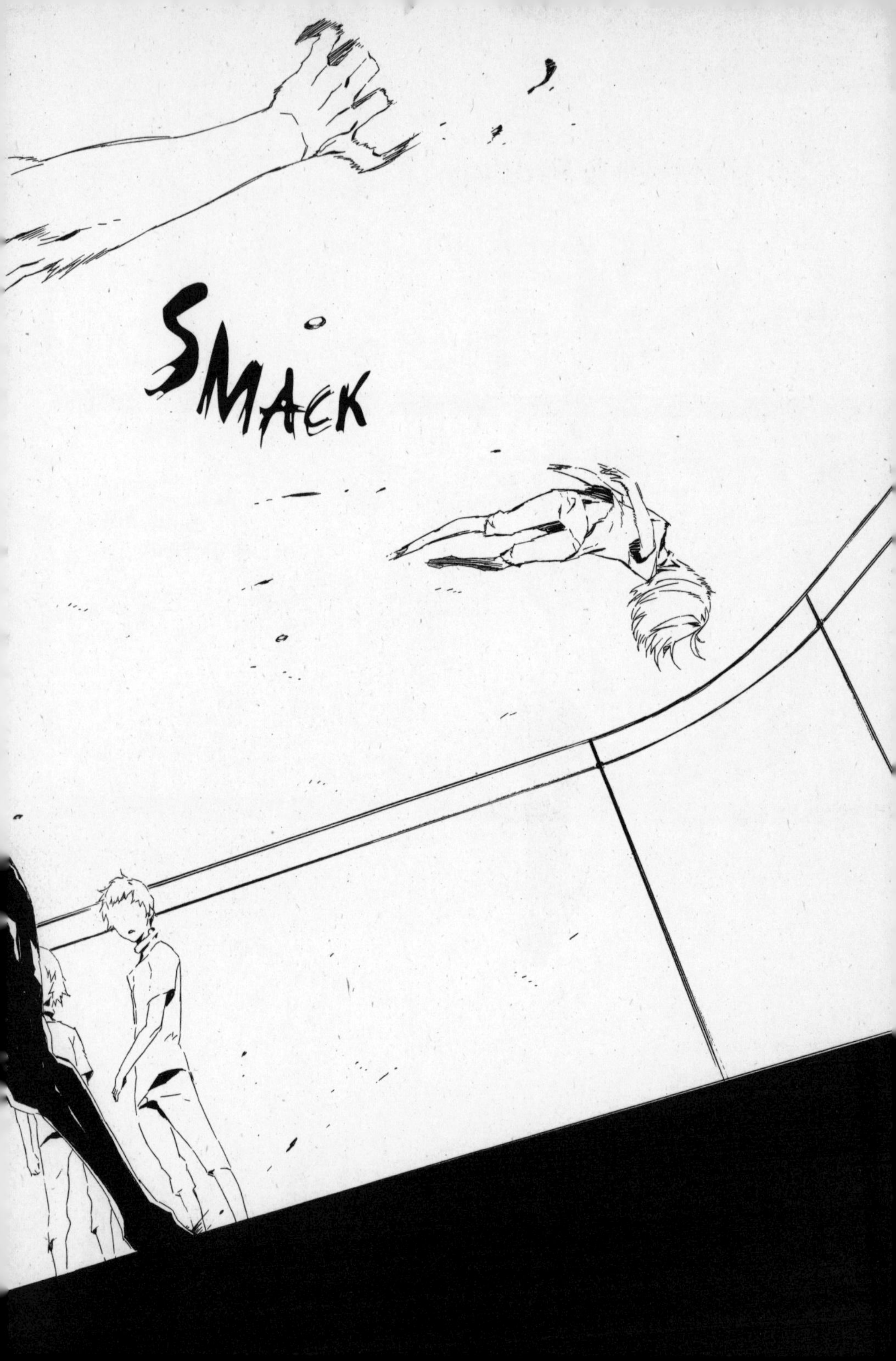
SMACK

#24 Mangler & Prodigy I

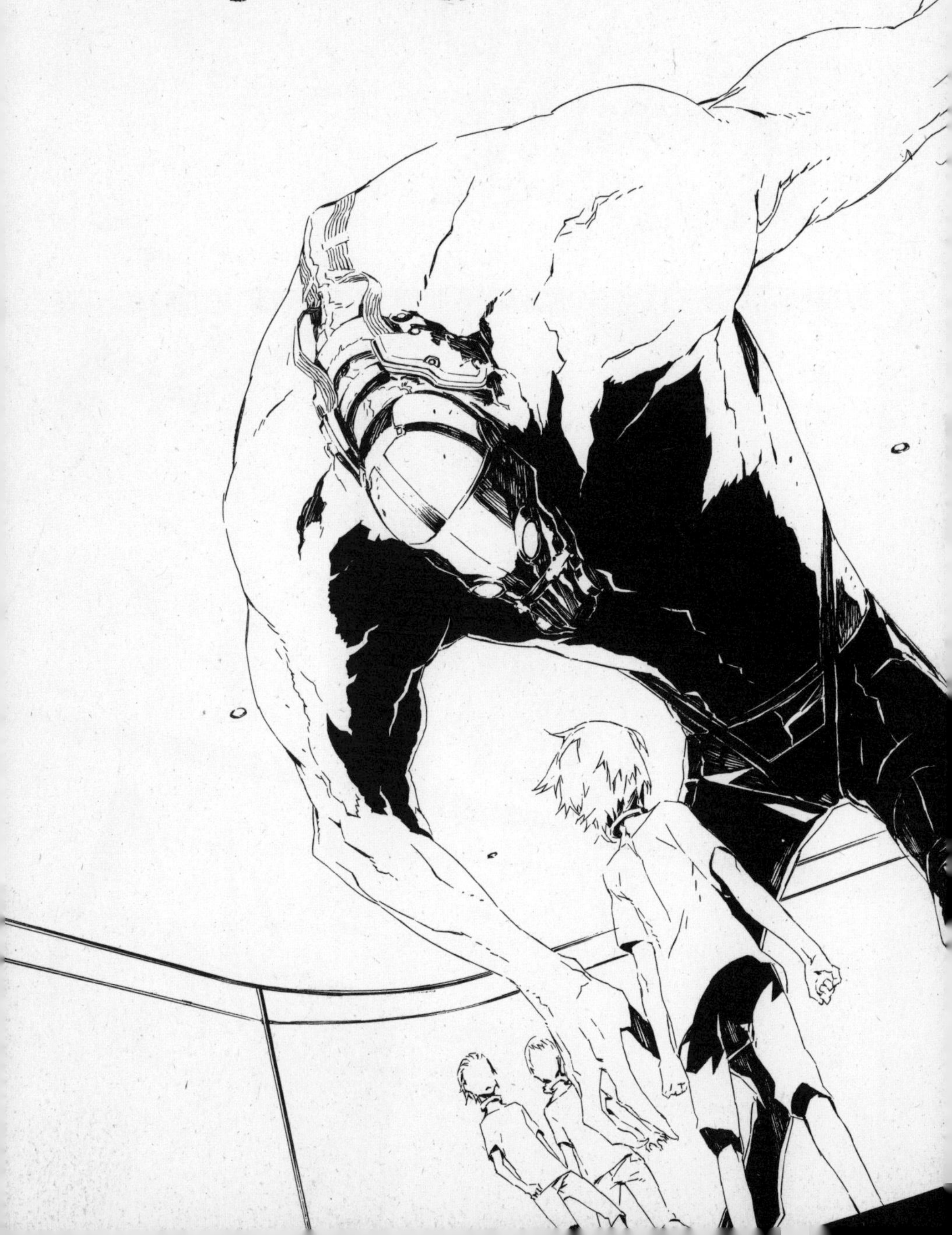

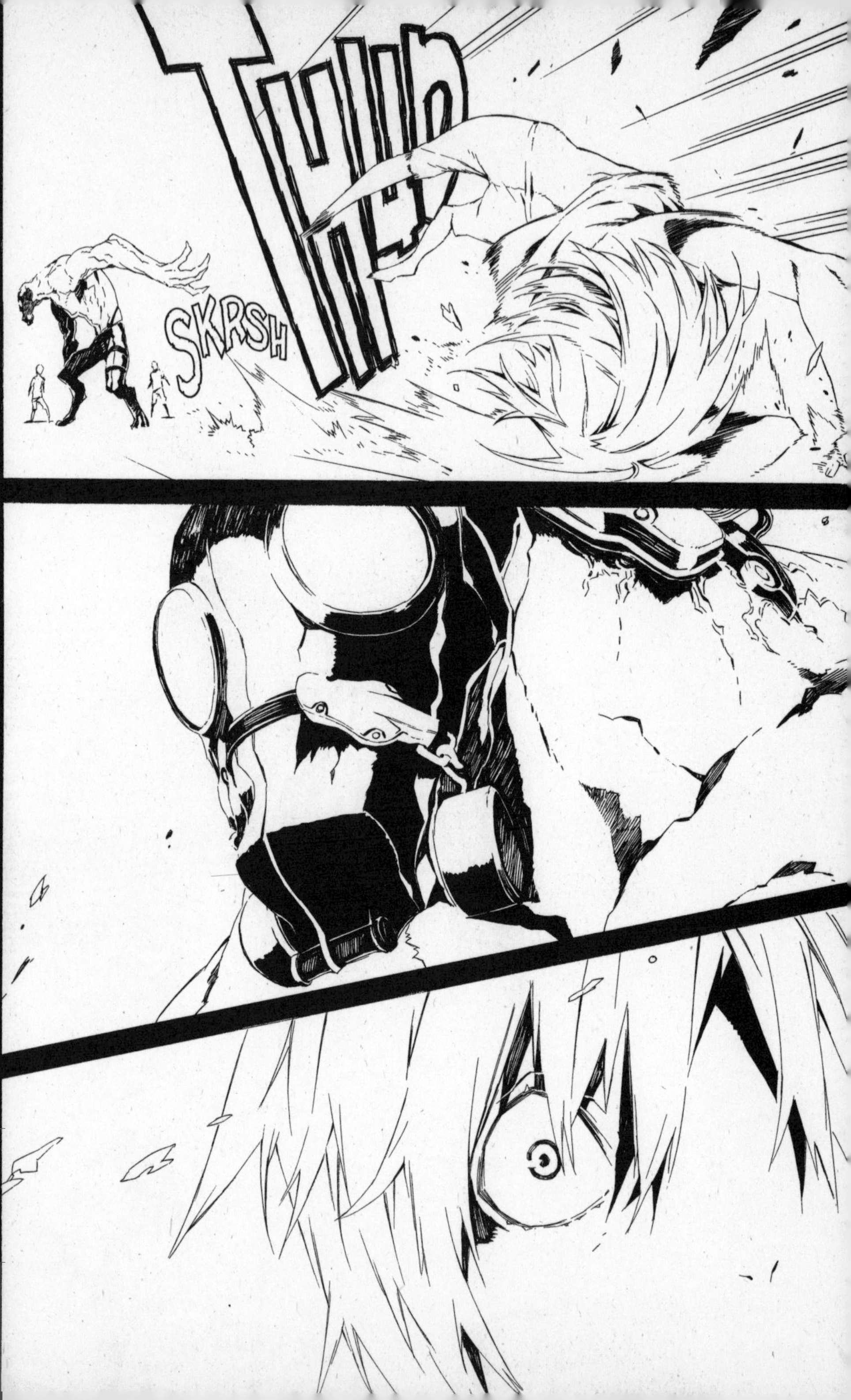
SKRSH

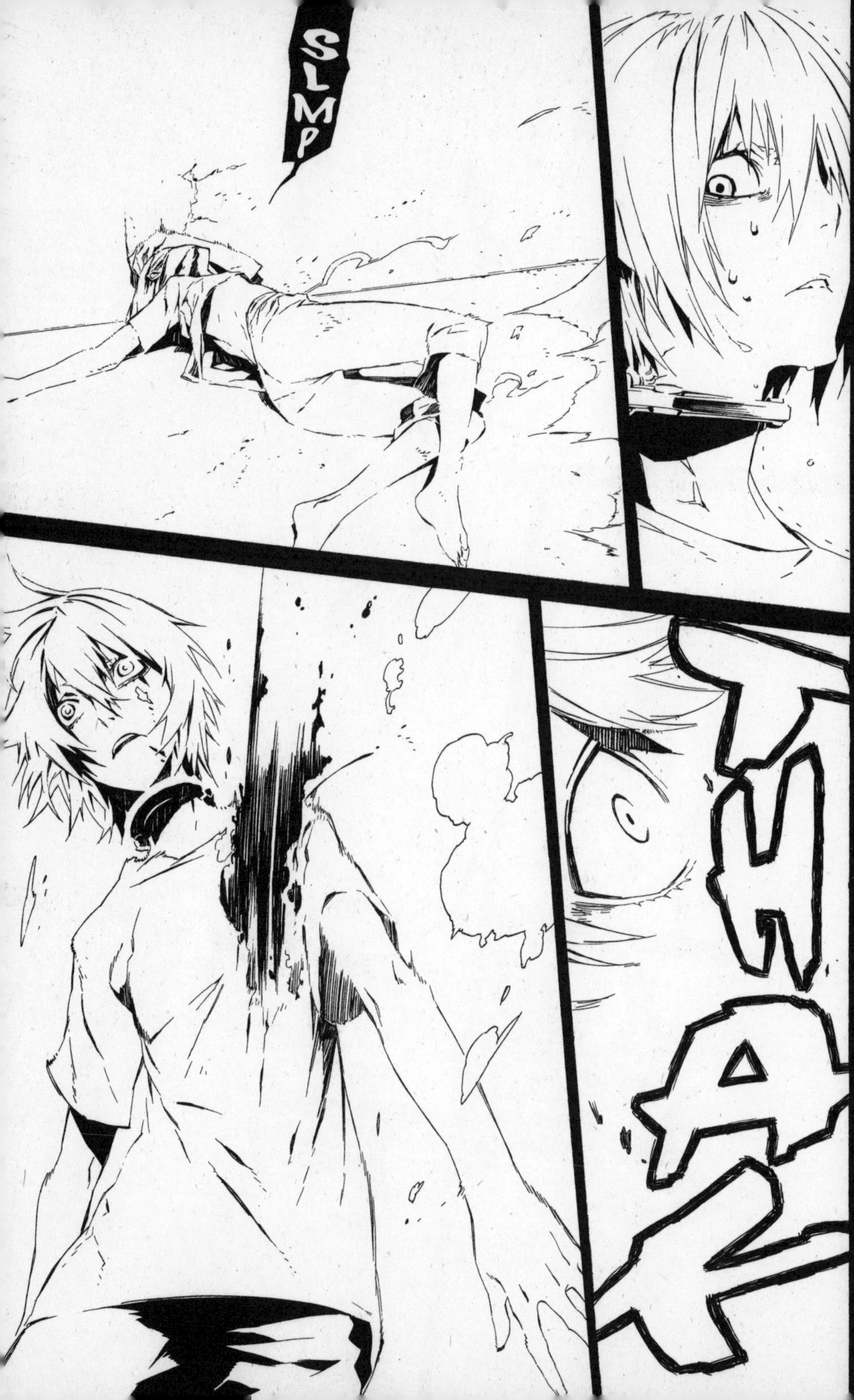
SLMP

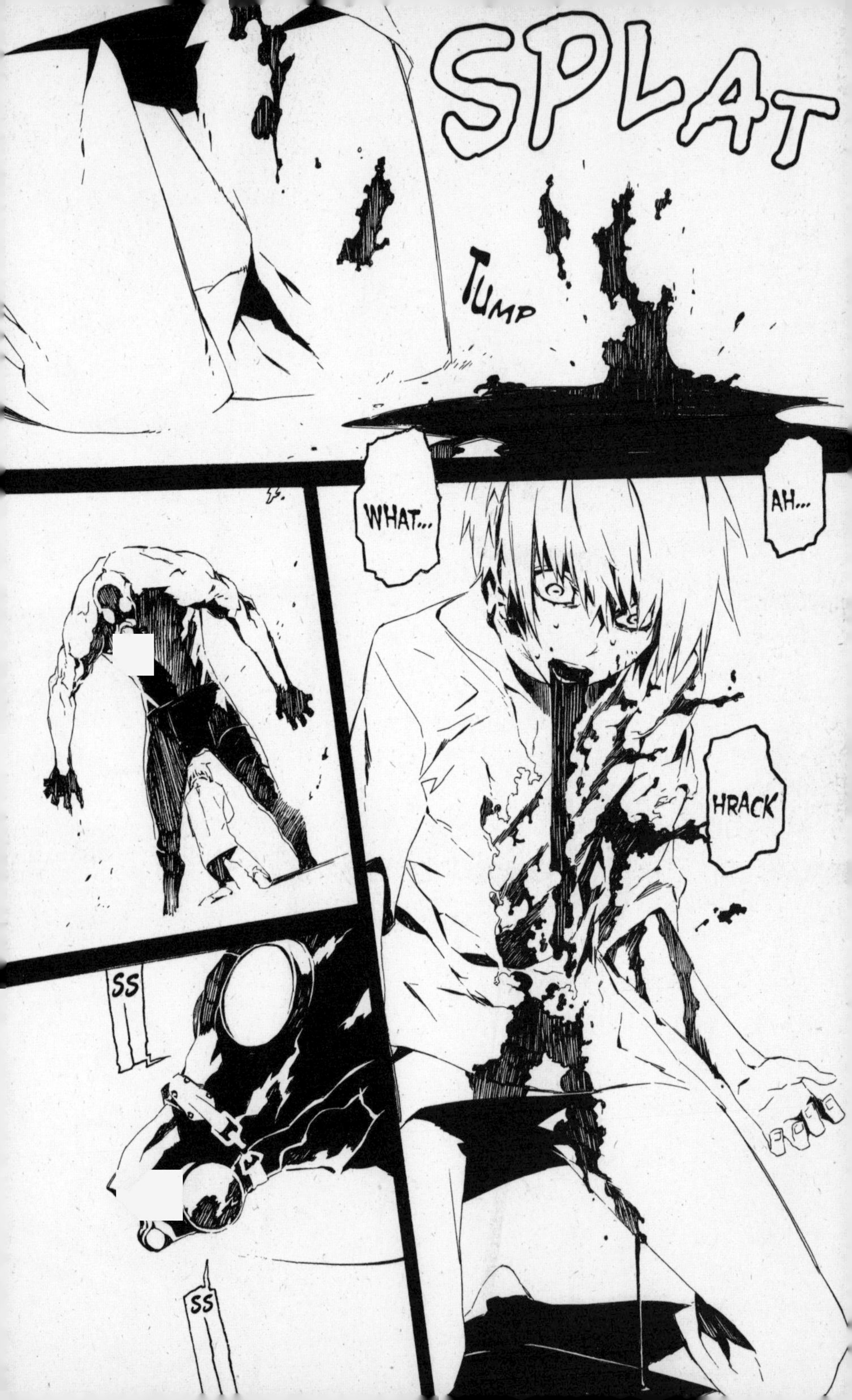
SPLAT
TUMP
AH...
WHAT...
HRACK
SS
SS

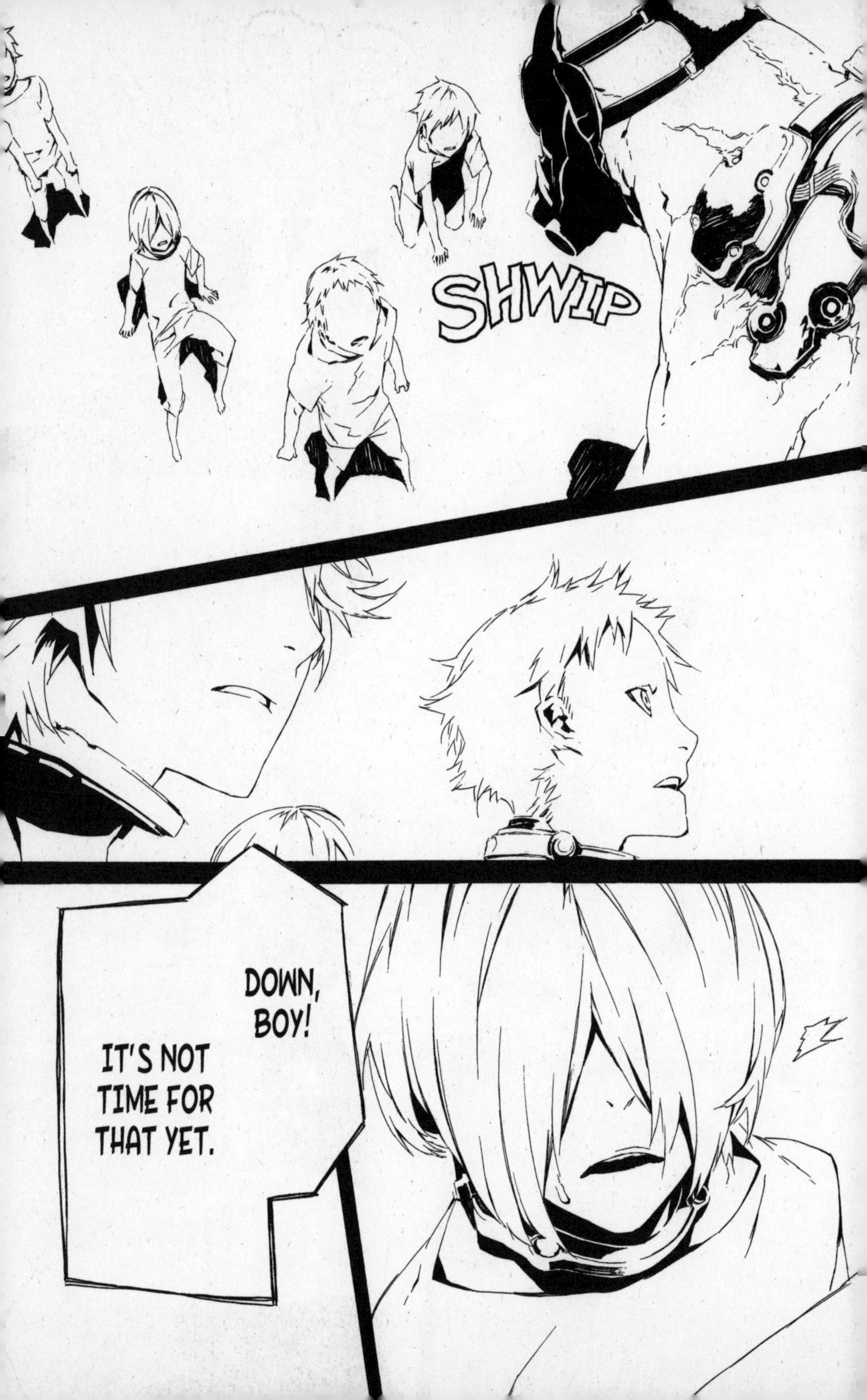
SHWIP
DOWN, BOY!
IT'S NOT TIME FOR THAT YET.

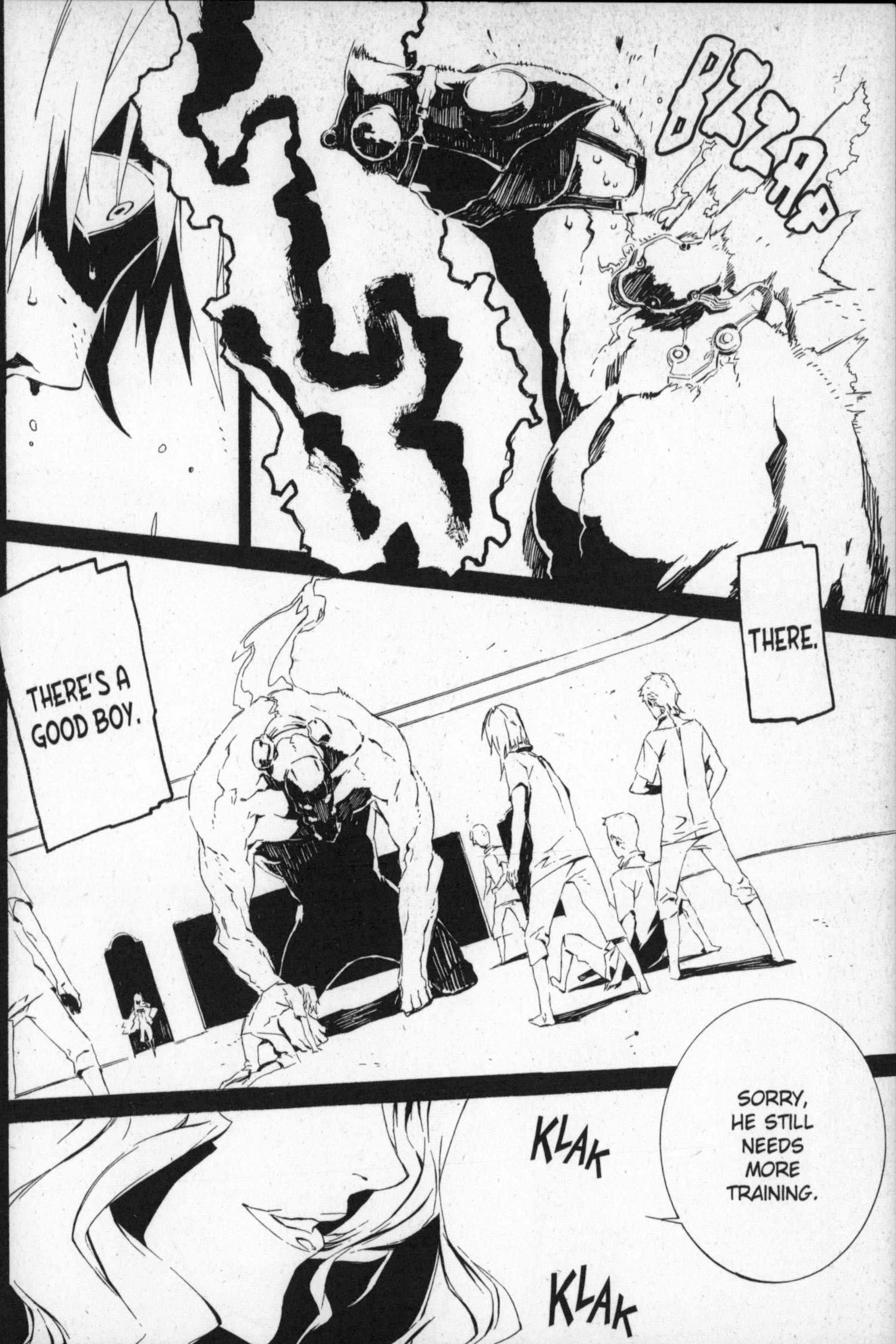
BZZAP
THERE.
THERE'S A GOOD BOY.
SORRY, HE STILL NEEDS MORE TRAINING.
KLAK
KLAK

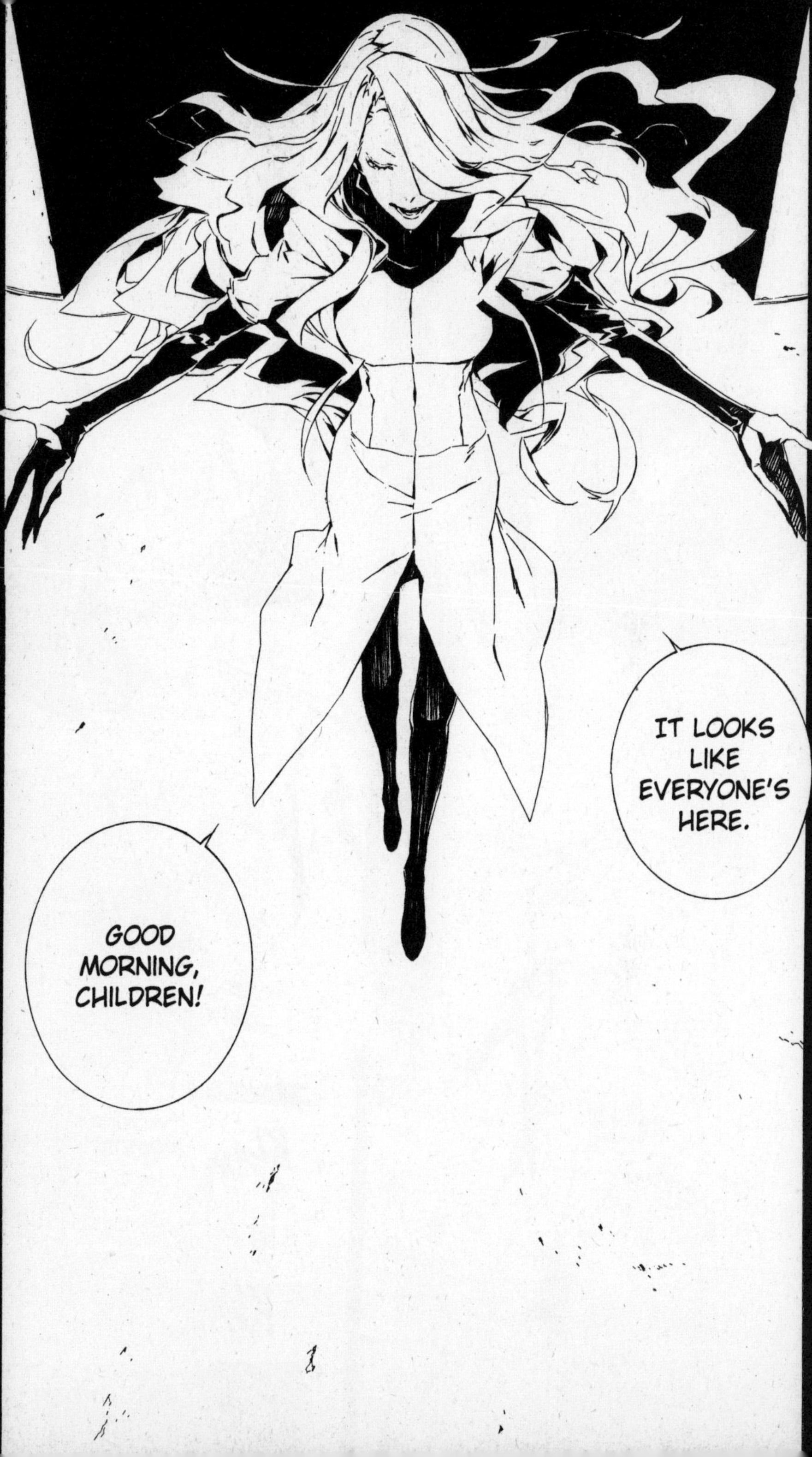
IT LOOKS LIKE EVERYONE'S HERE.
GOOD MORNING, CHILDREN!

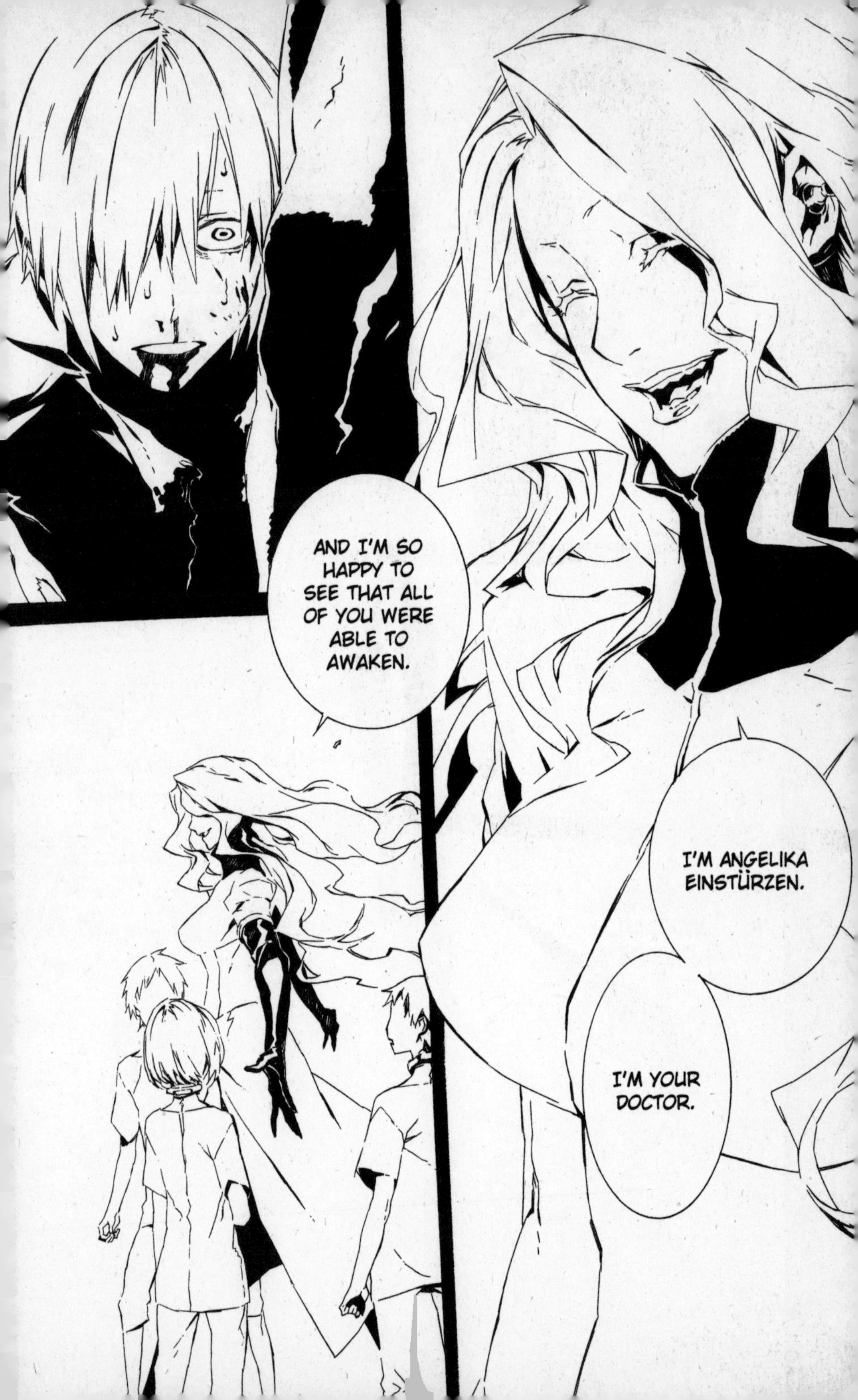
AND I'M SO HAPPY TO SEE THAT ALL OF YOU WERE ABLE TO AWAKEN.
I'M ANGELIKA EINSTÜRZEN.
I'M YOUR DOCTOR.

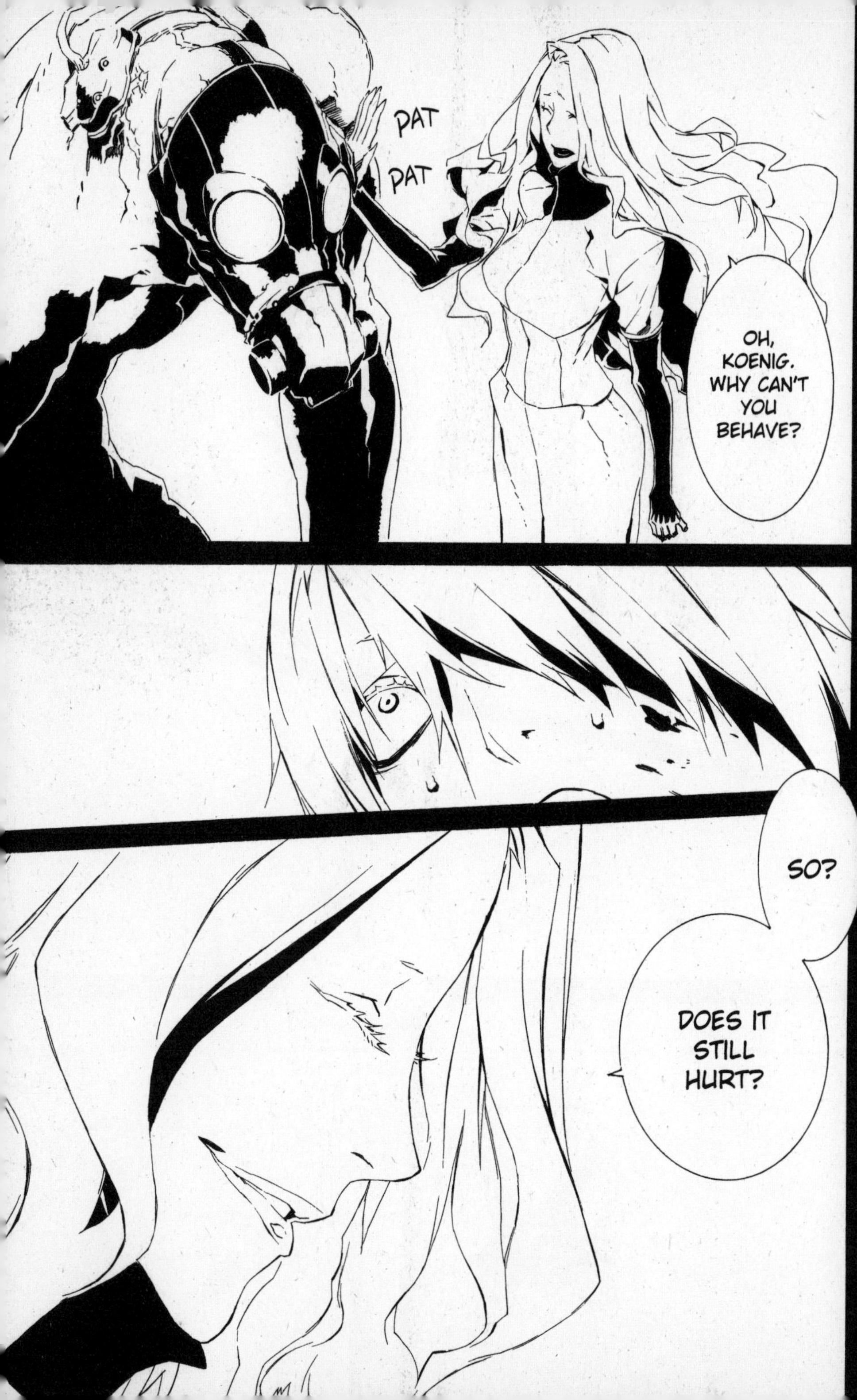
OH, KOENIG. WHY CAN'T YOU BEHAVE?
PAT
PAT
SO?
DOES IT STILL HURT?

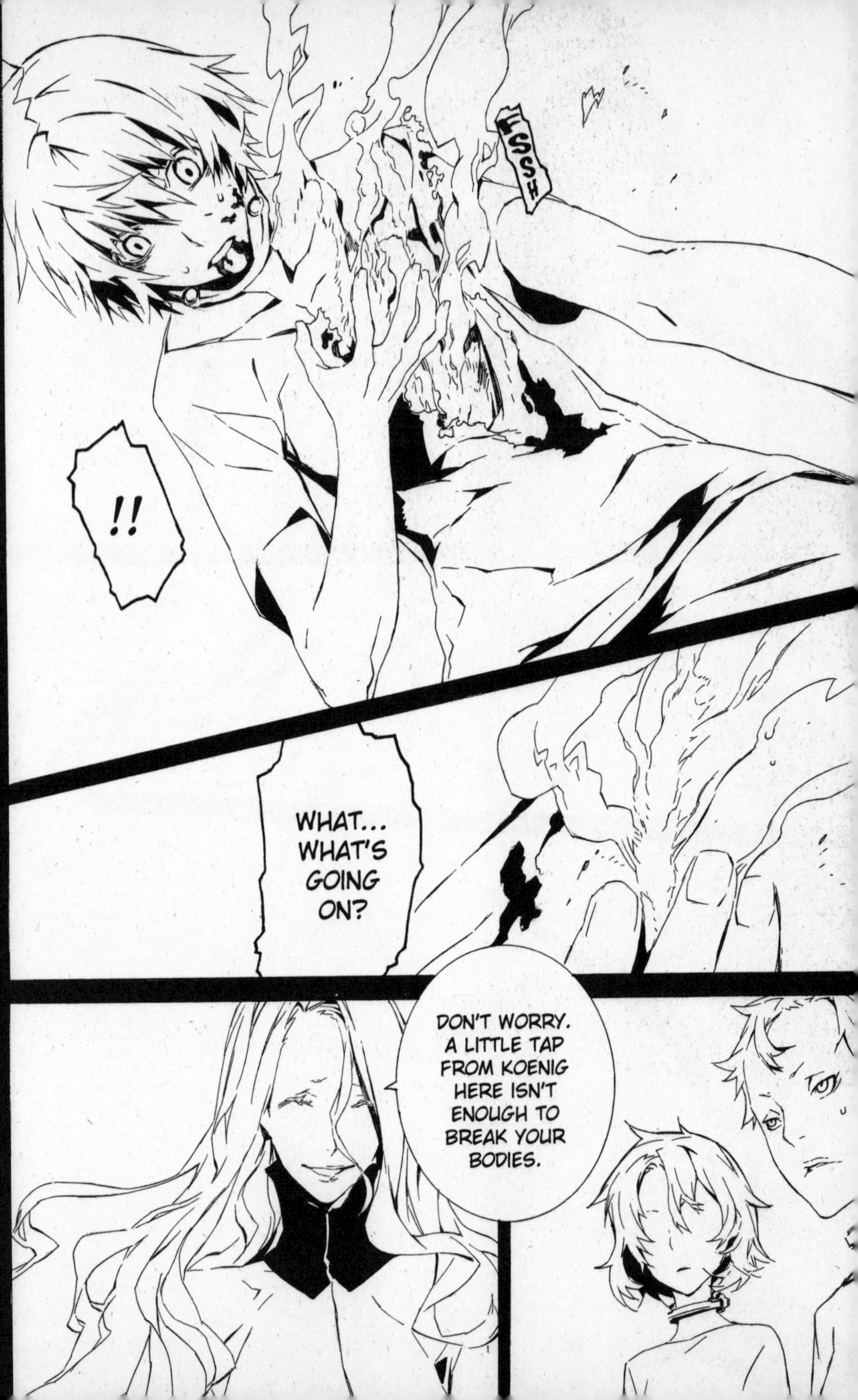
FSSH
!!
WHAT... WHAT'S GOING ON?
DON'T WORRY. A LITTLE TAP FROM KOENIG HERE ISN'T ENOUGH TO BREAK YOUR BODIES.

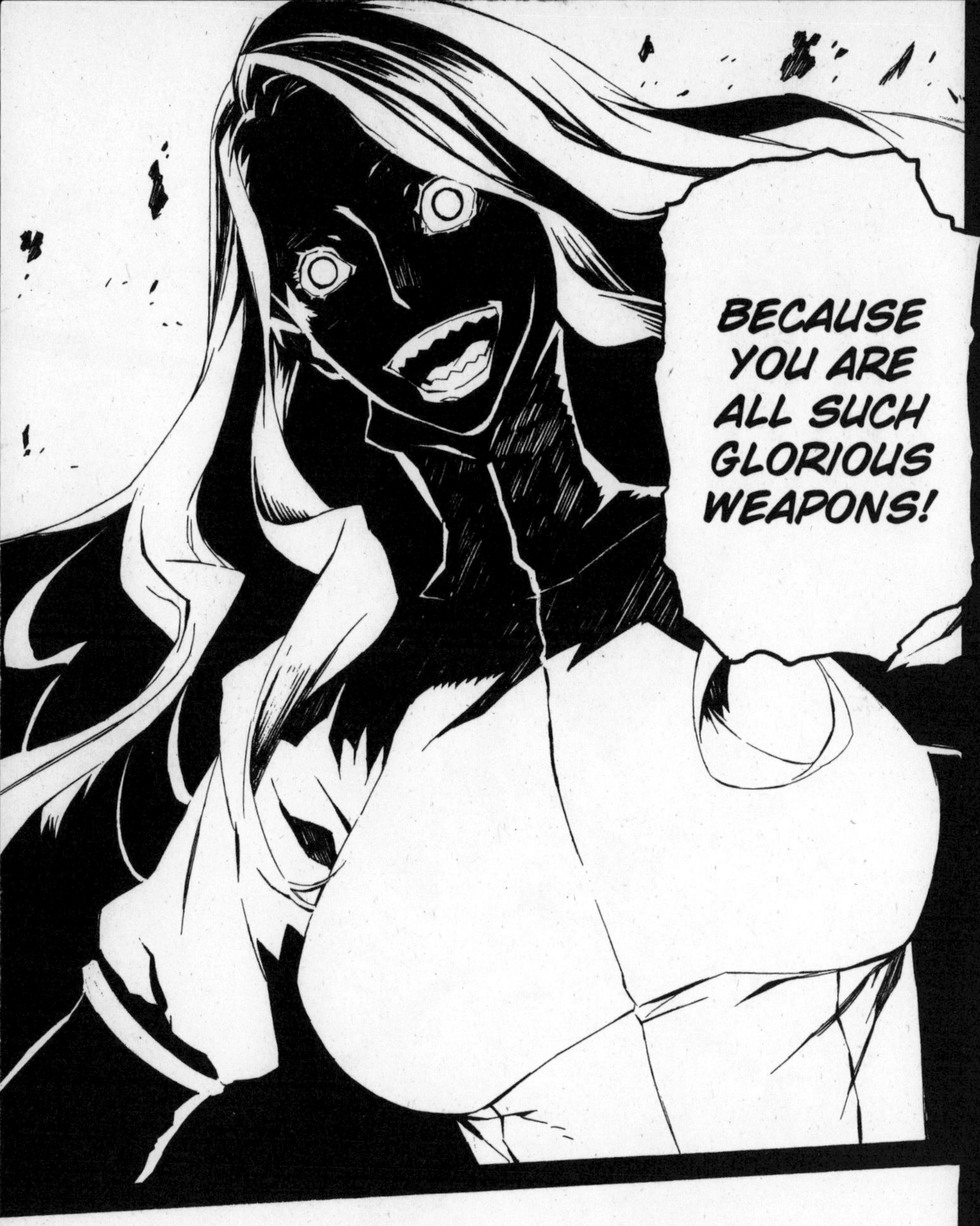
BECAUSE YOU ARE ALL SUCH GLORIOUS WEAPONS!

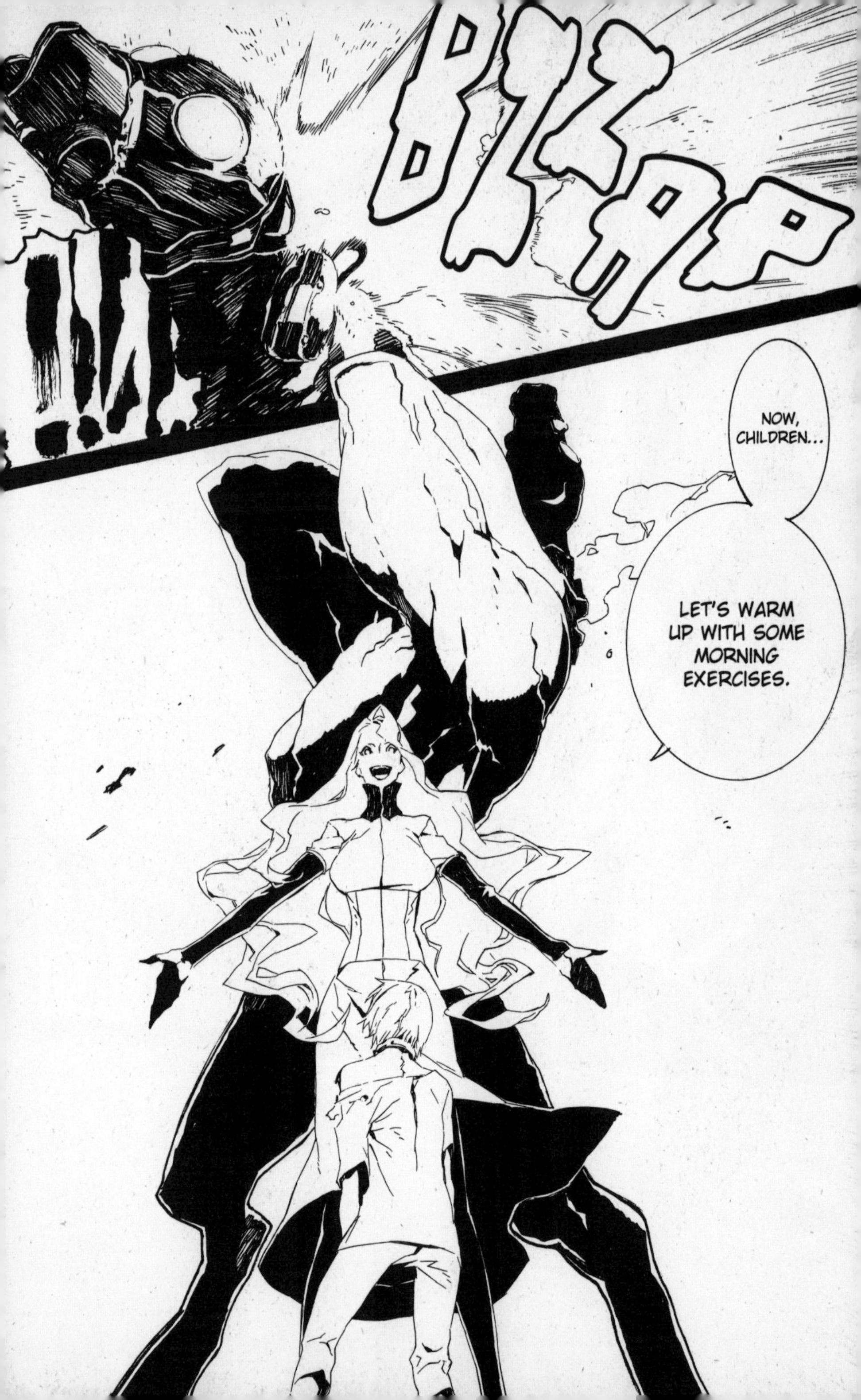
BLAP
NOW, CHILDREN...
LET'S WARM UP WITH SOME MORNING EXERCISES.

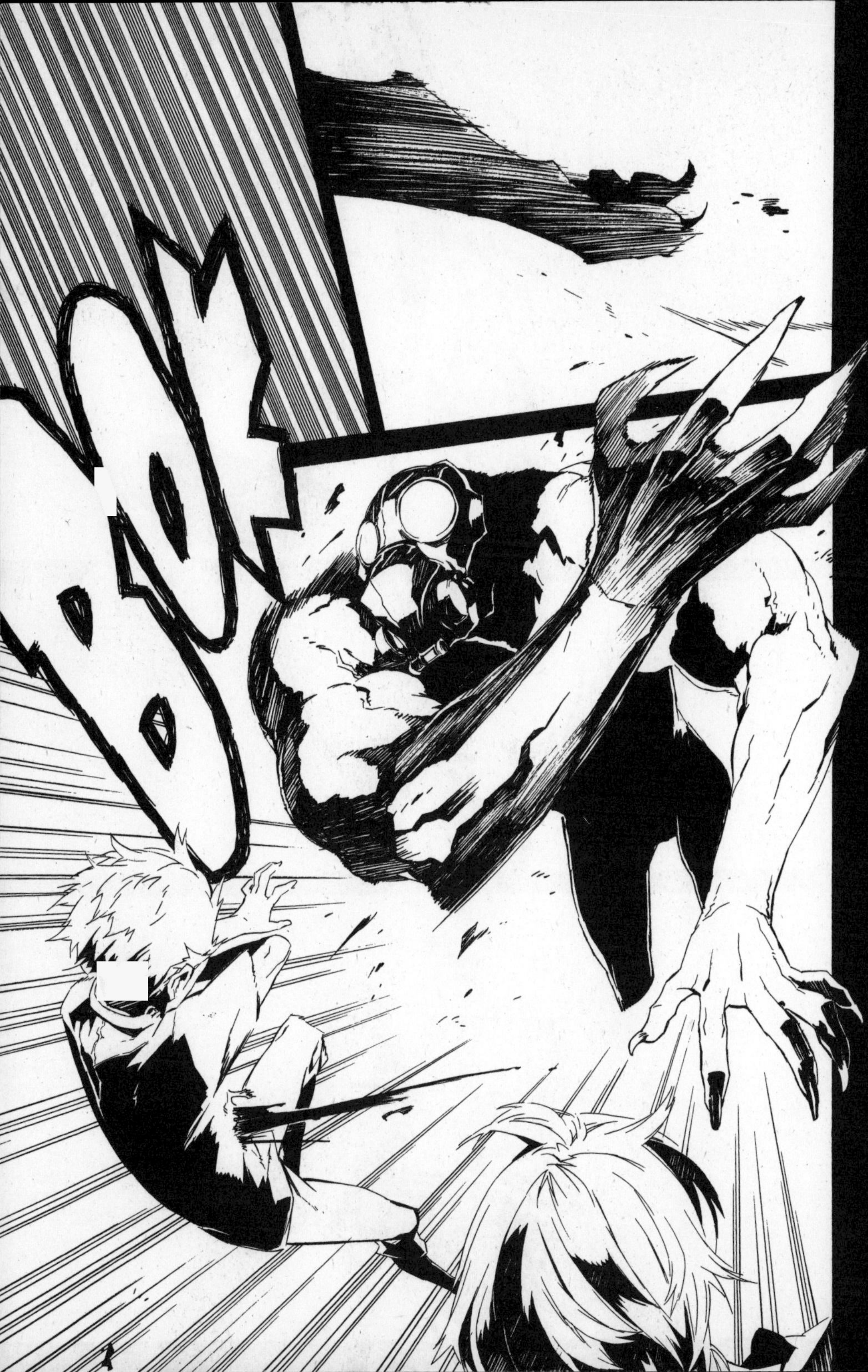

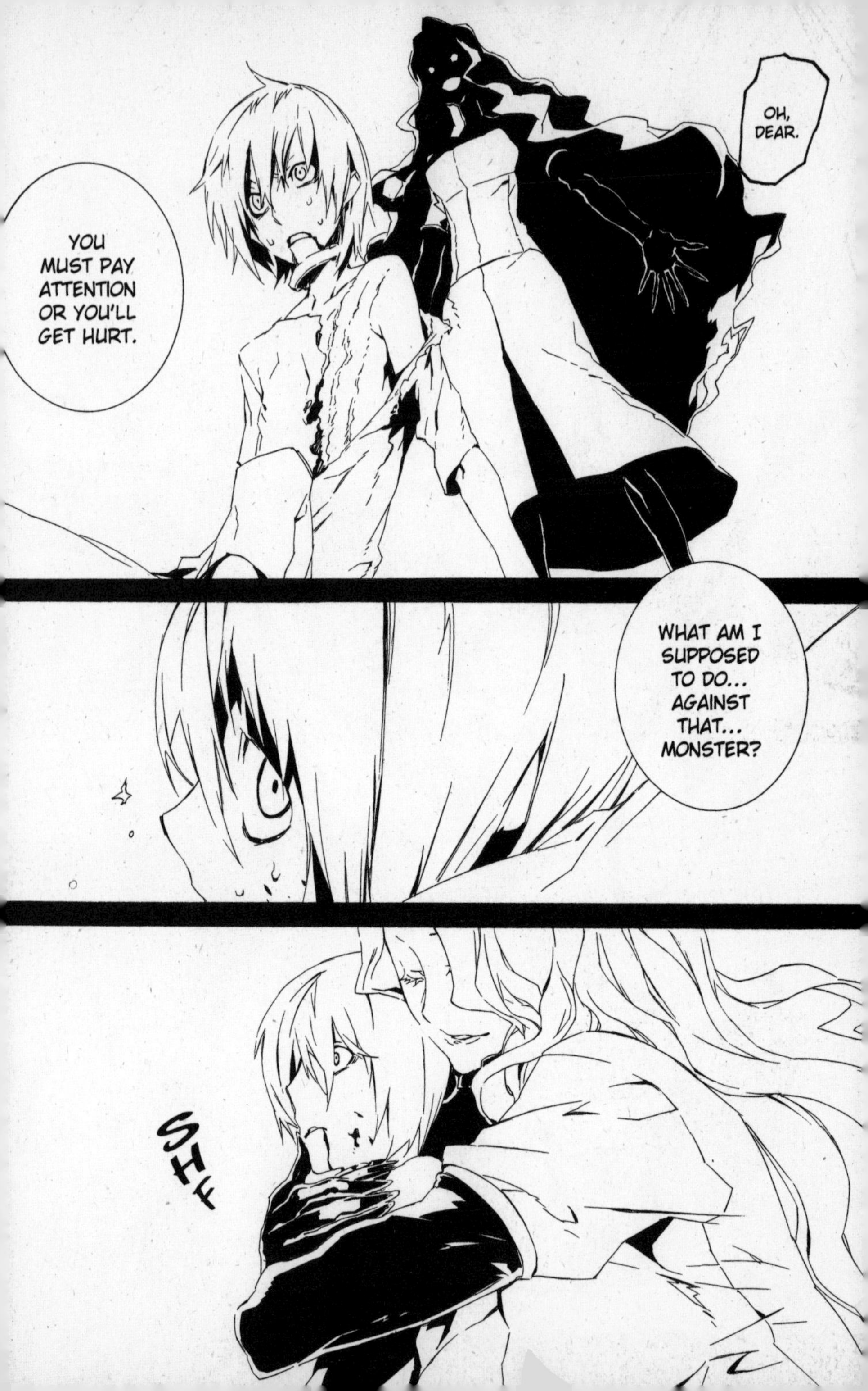
OH, DEAR.
YOU MUST PAY ATTENTION OR YOU'LL GET HURT.
WHAT AM I SUPPOSED TO DO... AGAINST THAT... MONSTER?
SHF

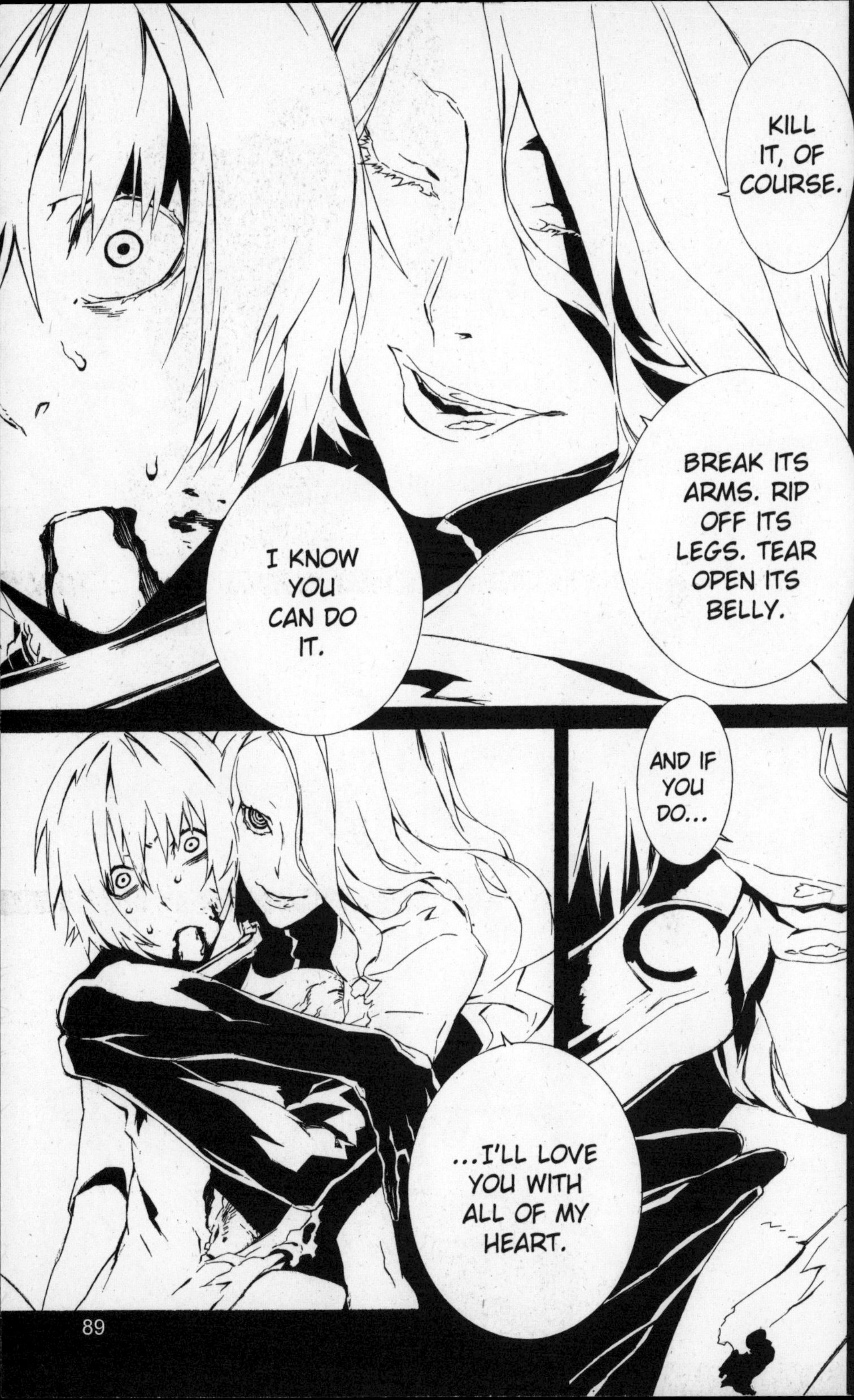
KILL IT, OF COURSE.
BREAK ITS ARMS. RIP OFF ITS LEGS. TEAR OPEN ITS BELLY.
I KNOW YOU CAN DO IT.
AND IF YOU DO...
...I'LL LOVE YOU WITH ALL OF MY HEART.

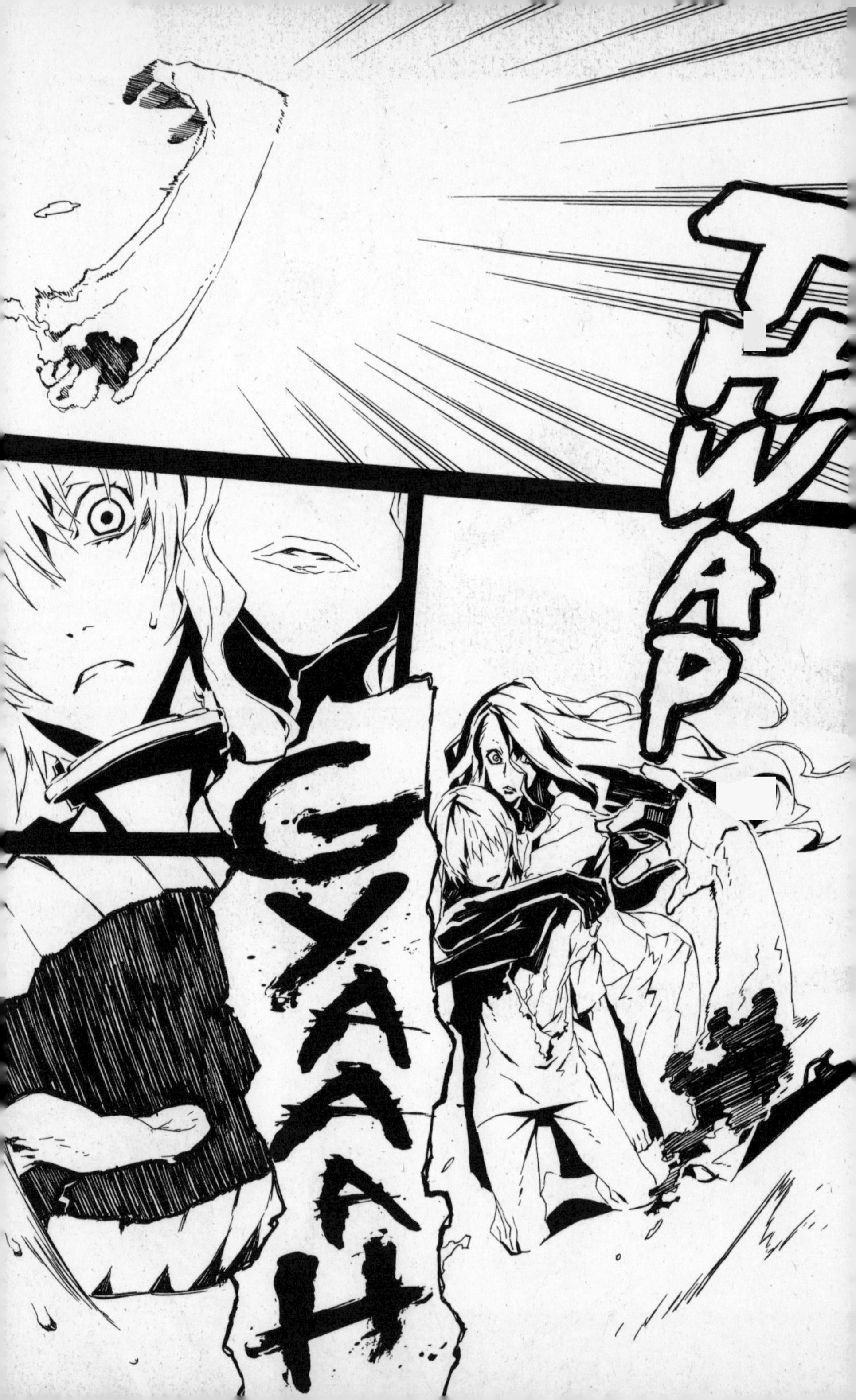
THWAP
GYAAAH

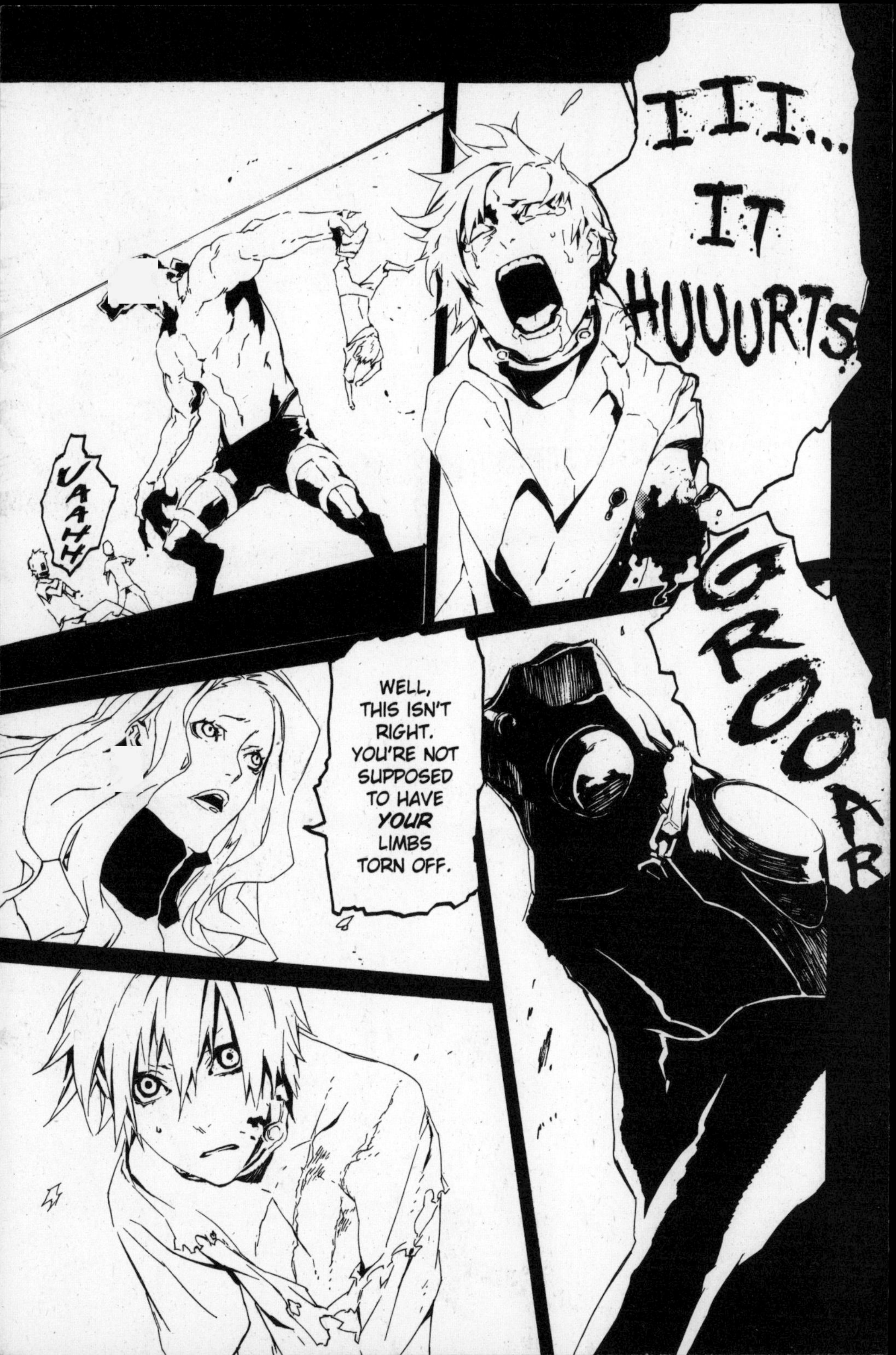
III... IT HUUURTS
UAAHH
GROOOAR
WELL, THIS ISN'T RIGHT. YOU'RE NOT SUPPOSED TO HAVE *YOUR* LIMBS TORN OFF.

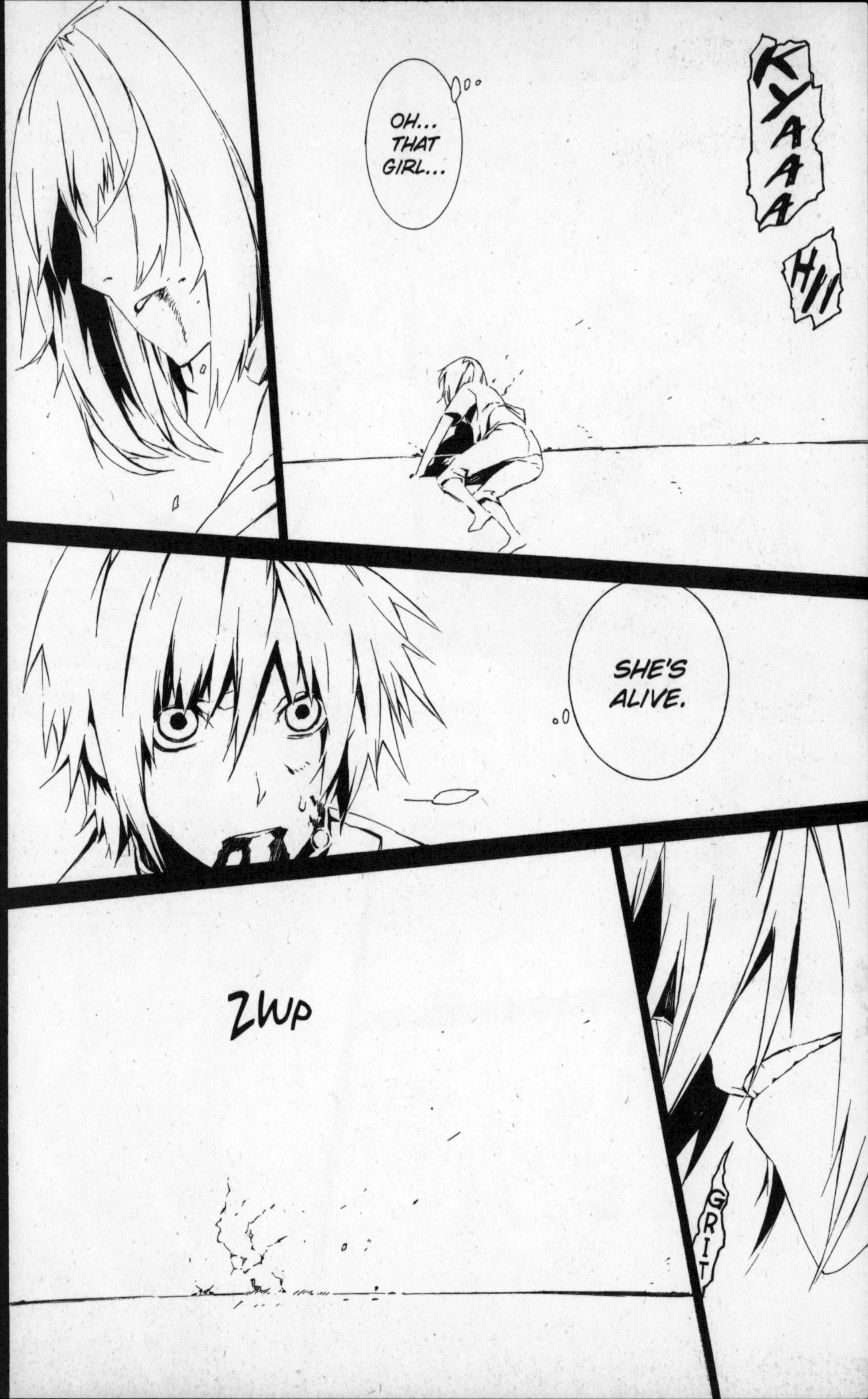
KYAAAHII
OH... THAT GIRL...
SHE'S ALIVE.
GRIT
ZWP

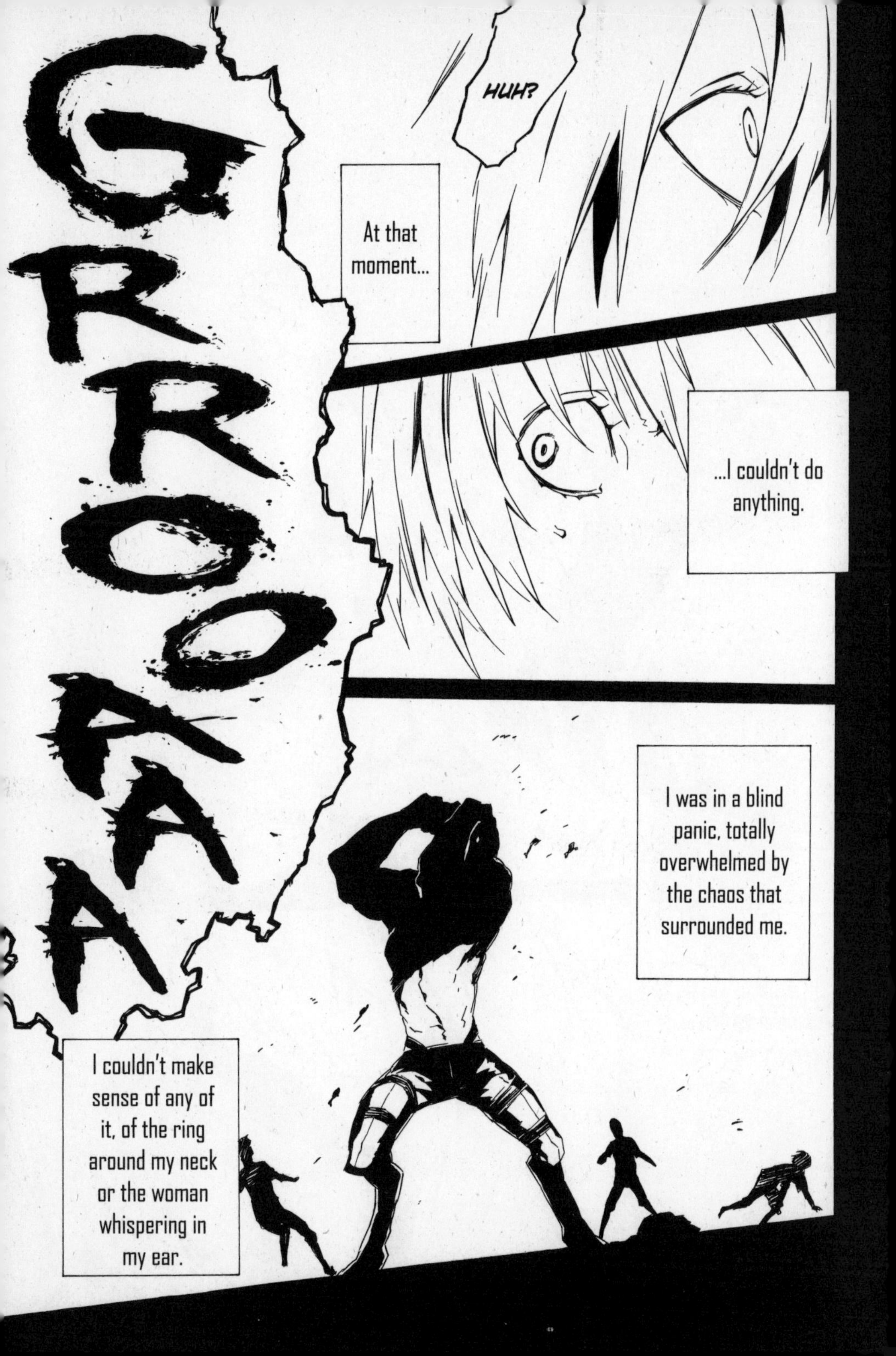
HUH?
At that moment...
...I couldn't do anything.
I was in a blind panic, totally overwhelmed by the chaos that surrounded me.
GRROOAAA
I couldn't make sense of any of it, of the ring around my neck or the woman whispering in my ear.

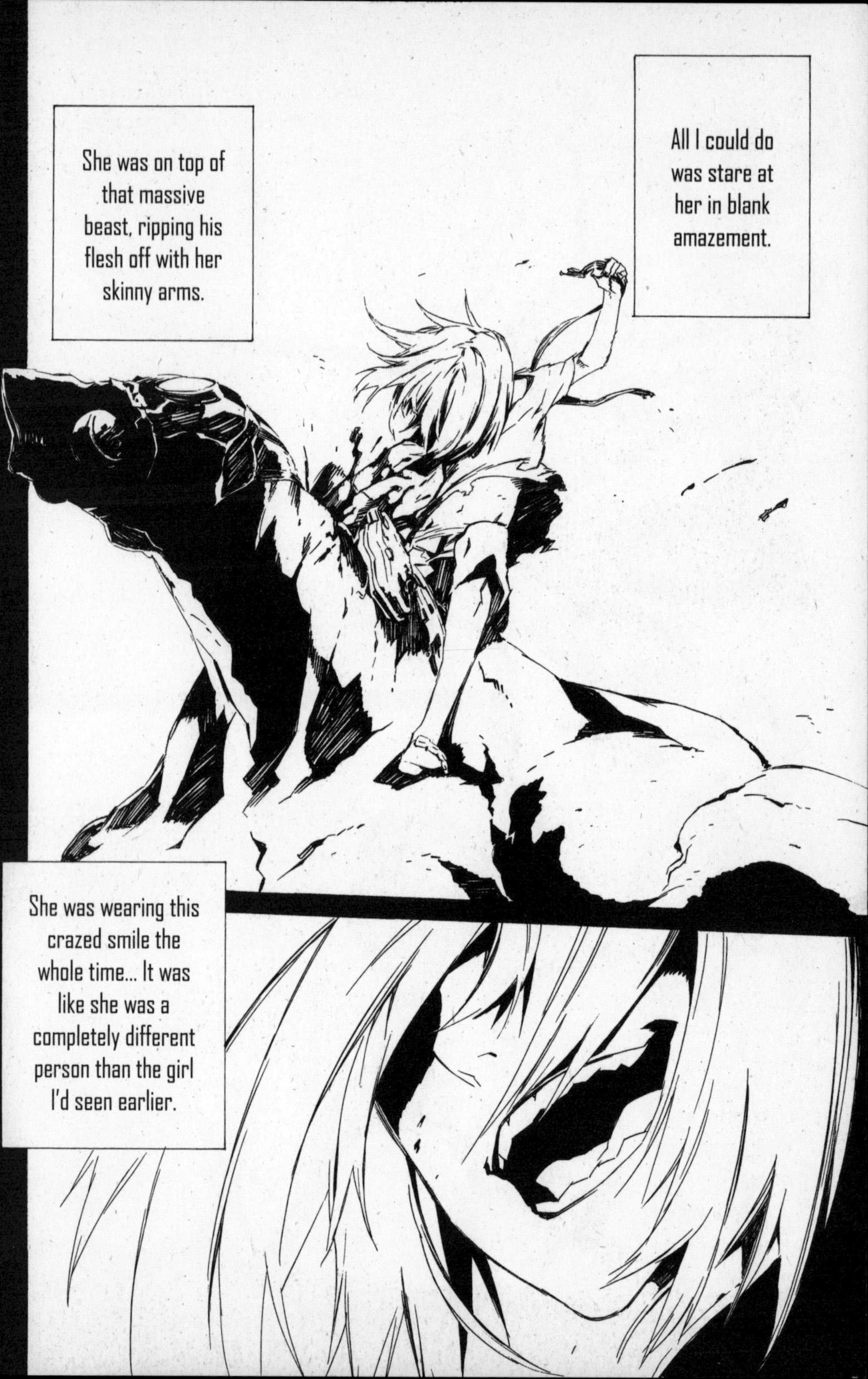
All I could do was stare at her in blank amazement.
She was on top of that massive beast, ripping his flesh off with her skinny arms.
She was wearing this crazed smile the whole time... It was like she was a completely different person than the girl I'd seen earlier.

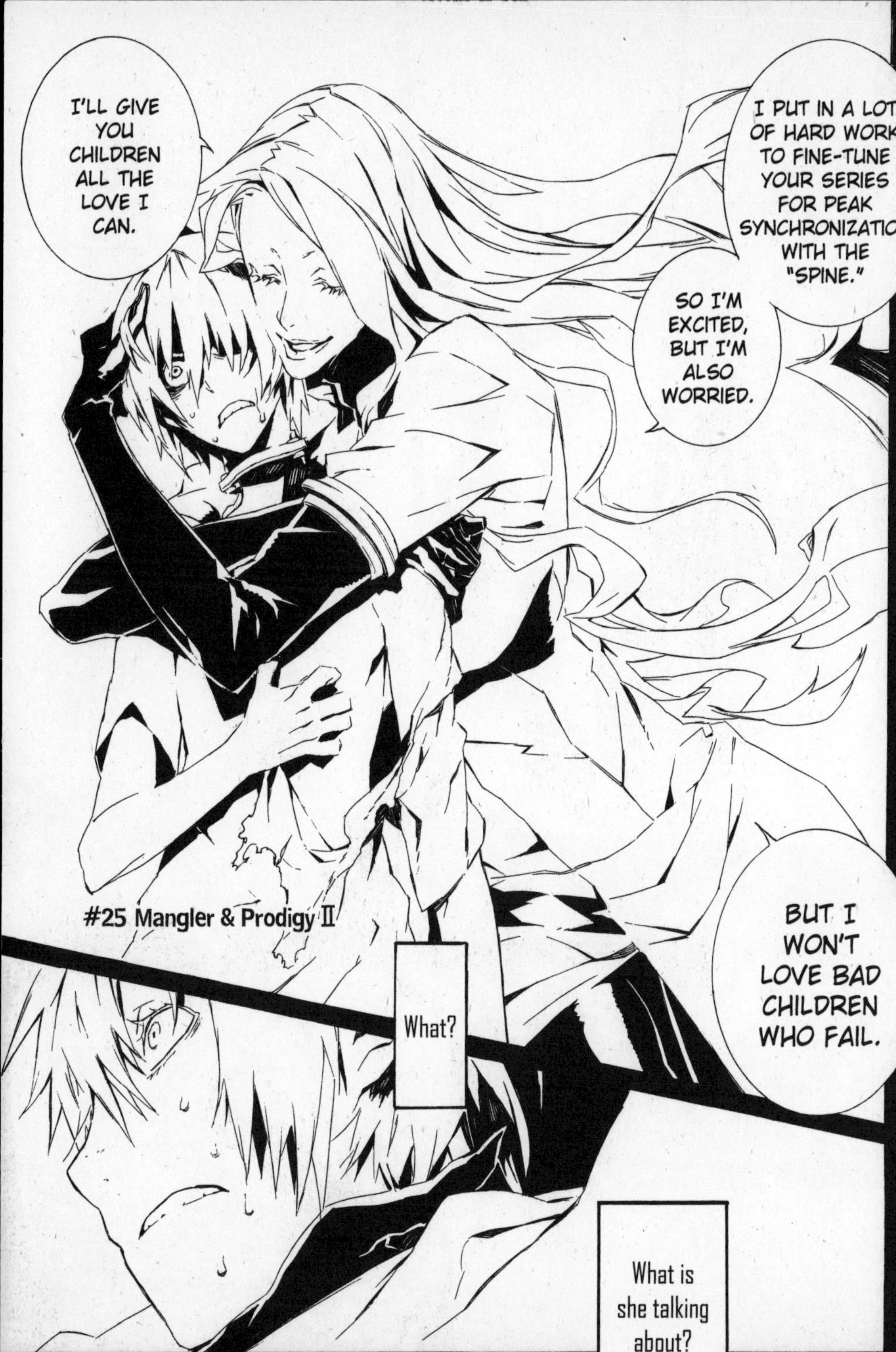
I PUT IN A LOT OF HARD WORK TO FINE-TUNE YOUR SERIES FOR PEAK SYNCHRONIZATION WITH THE "SPINE."
SO I'M EXCITED, BUT I'M ALSO WORRIED.
I'LL GIVE YOU CHILDREN ALL THE LOVE I CAN.
BUT I WON'T LOVE BAD CHILDREN WHO FAIL.
#25 Mangler & Prodigy II
What?
What is she talking about?

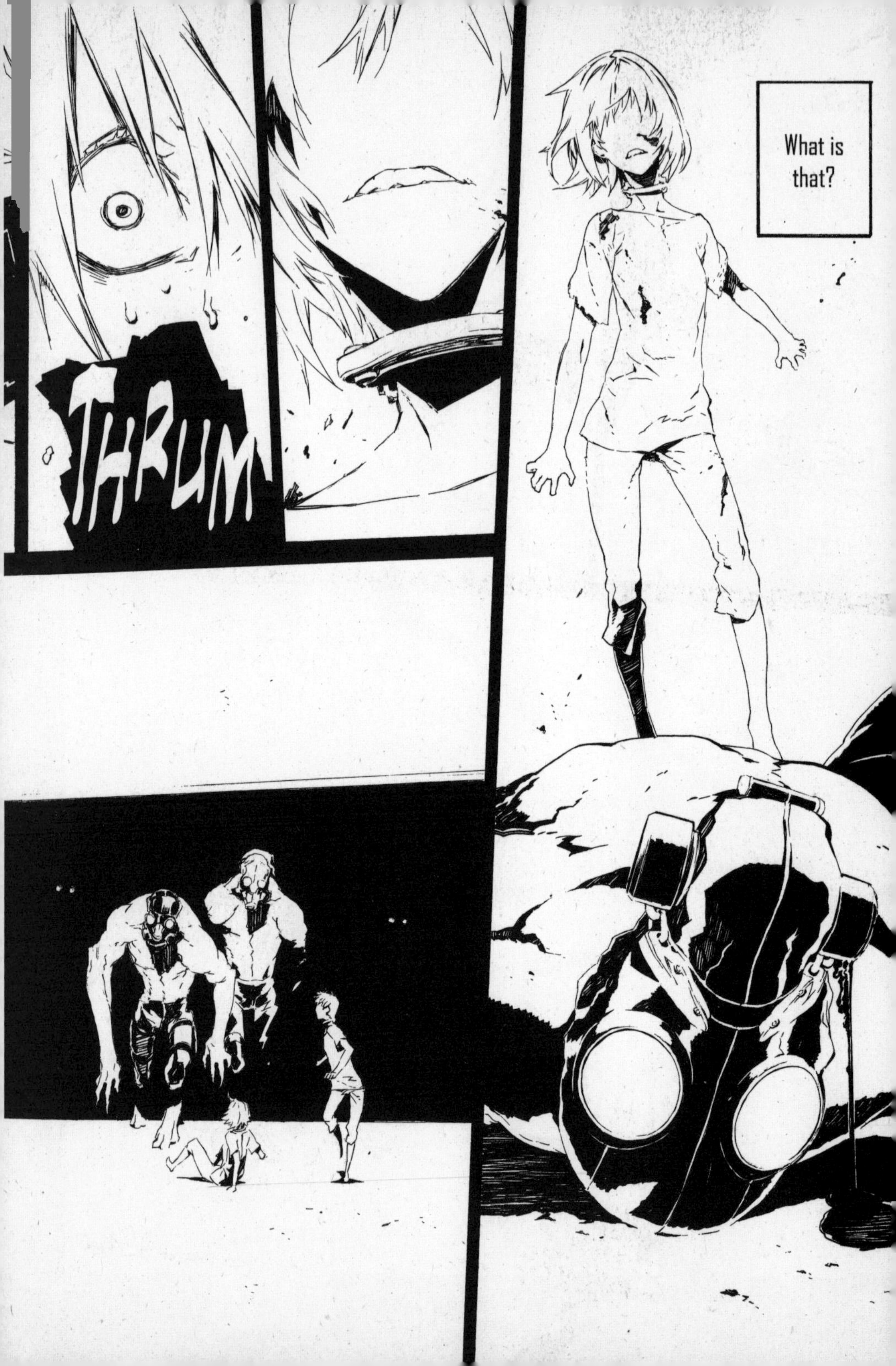
What is that?
THRUM

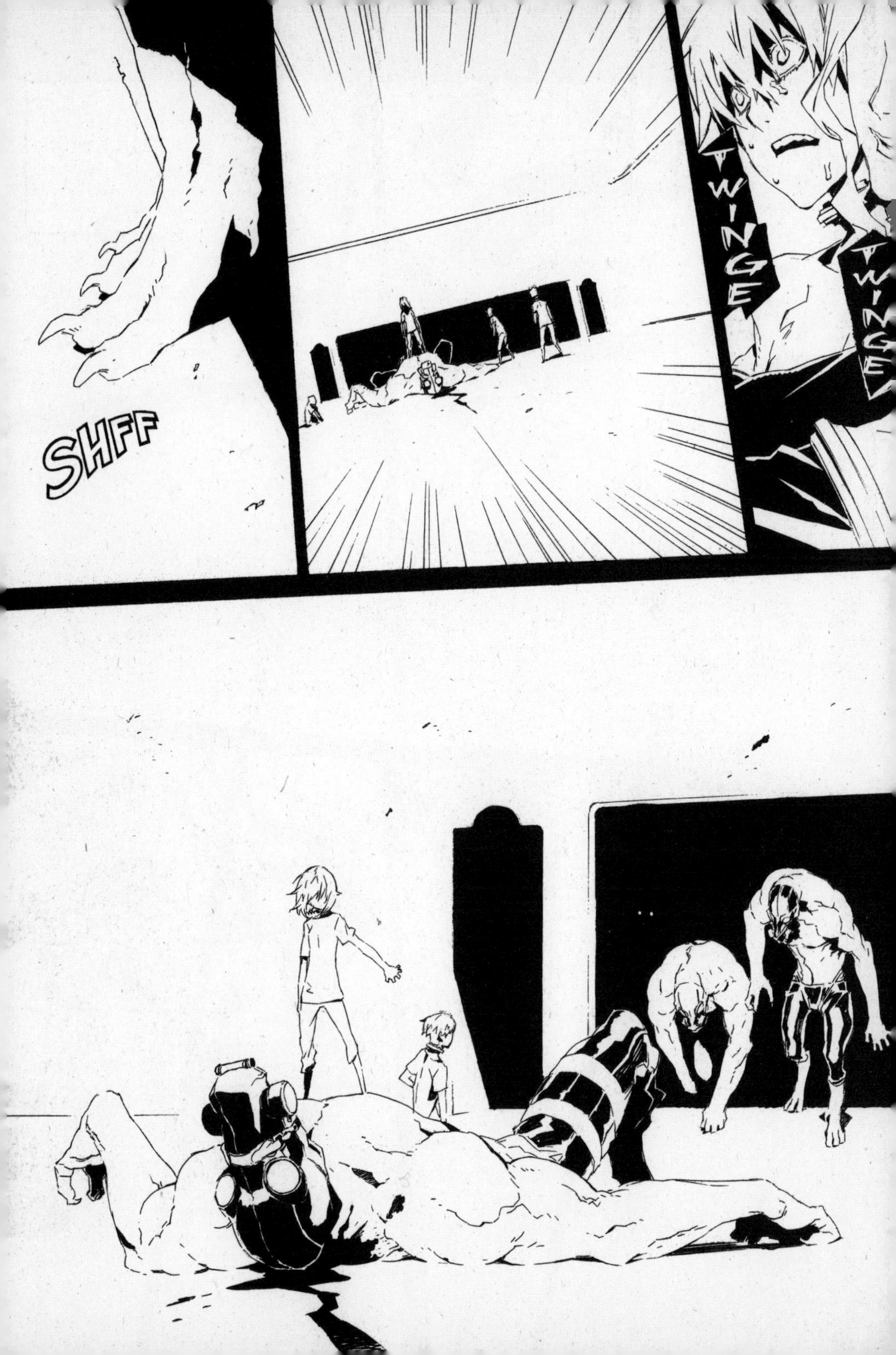
TWINGE
TWINGE
SHFF

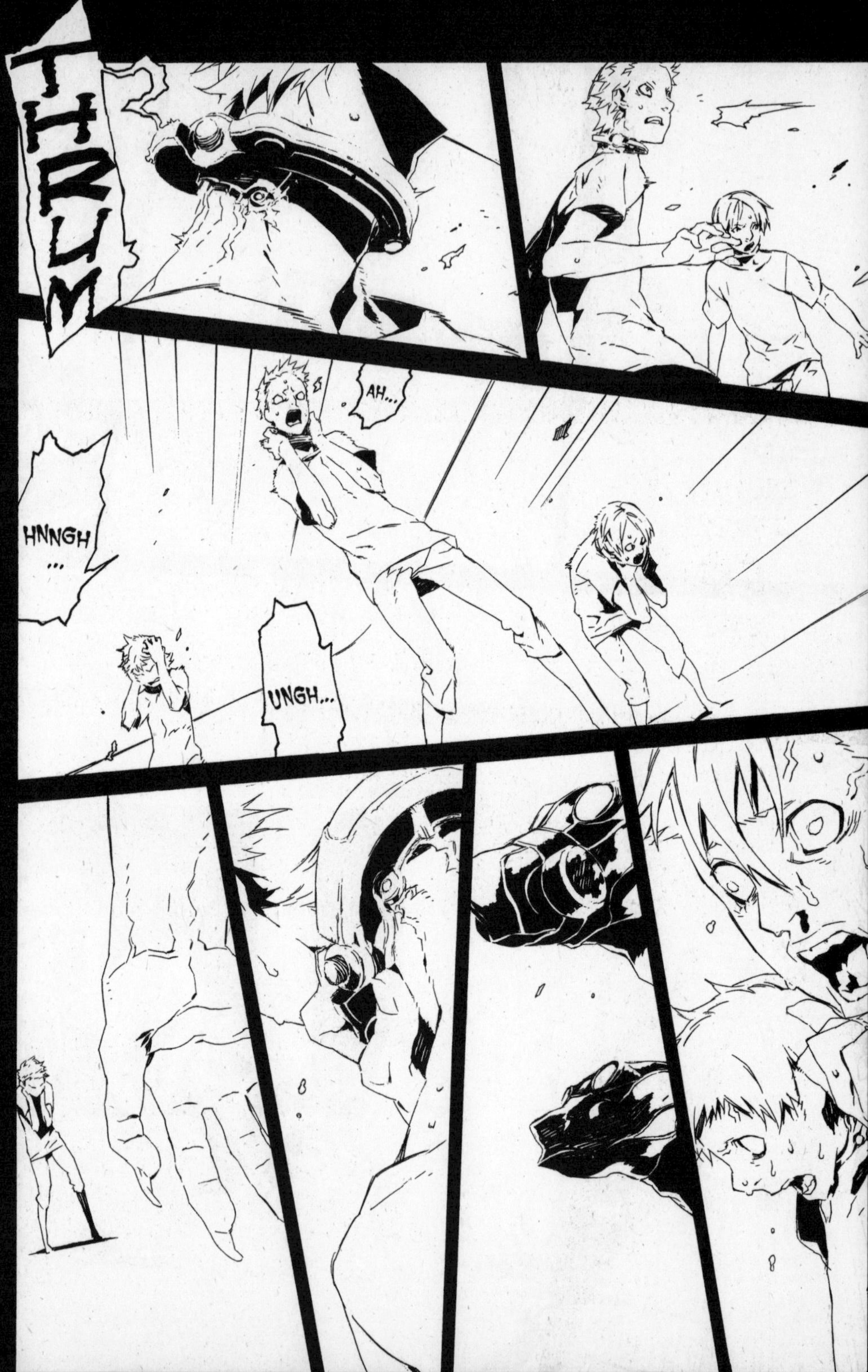
THRUM
AH...
HNNGH...
UNGH...

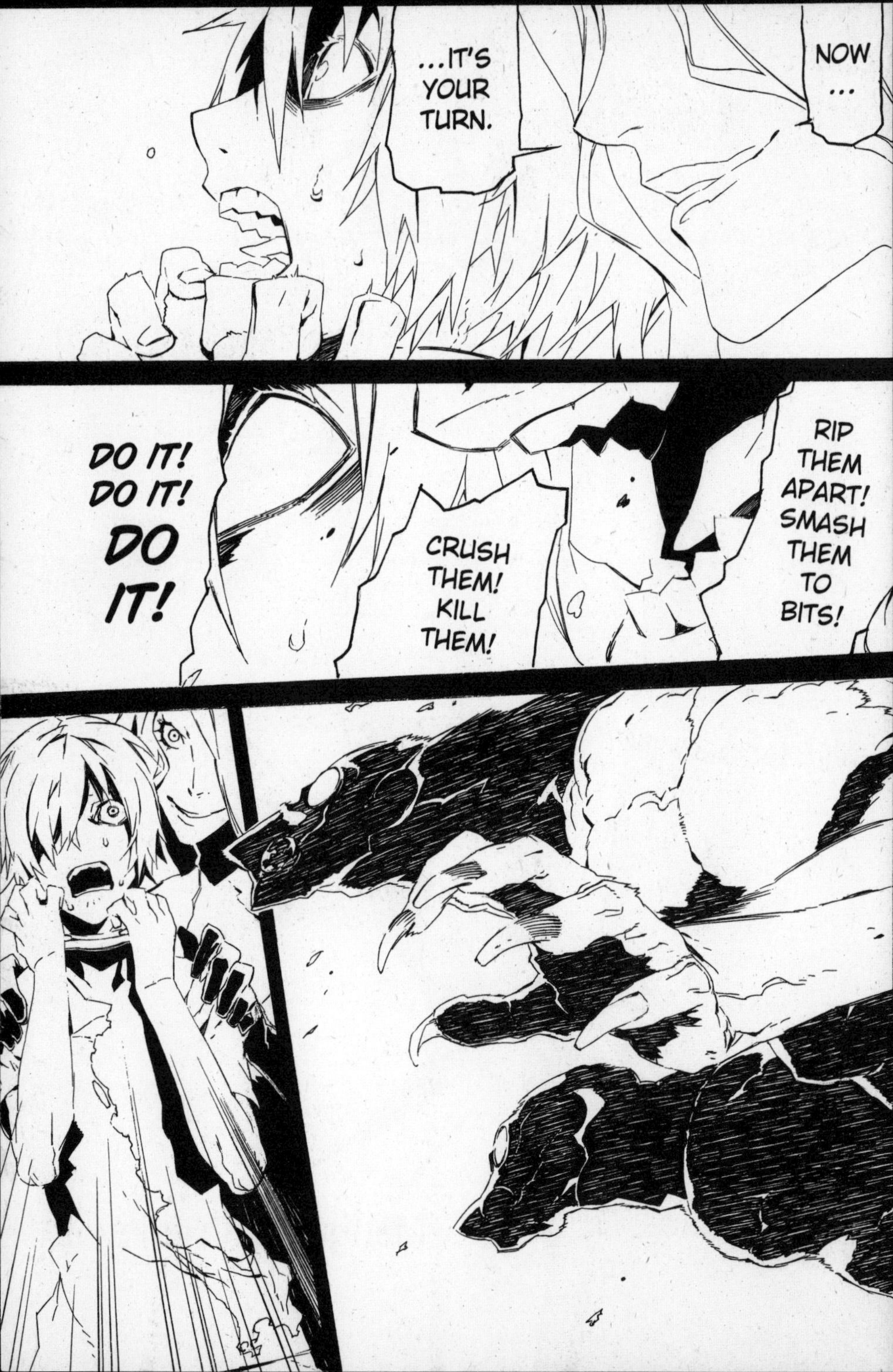
NOW ...
...IT'S YOUR TURN.
RIP THEM APART! SMASH THEM TO BITS!
CRUSH THEM! KILL THEM!
DO IT! DO IT! DO IT!

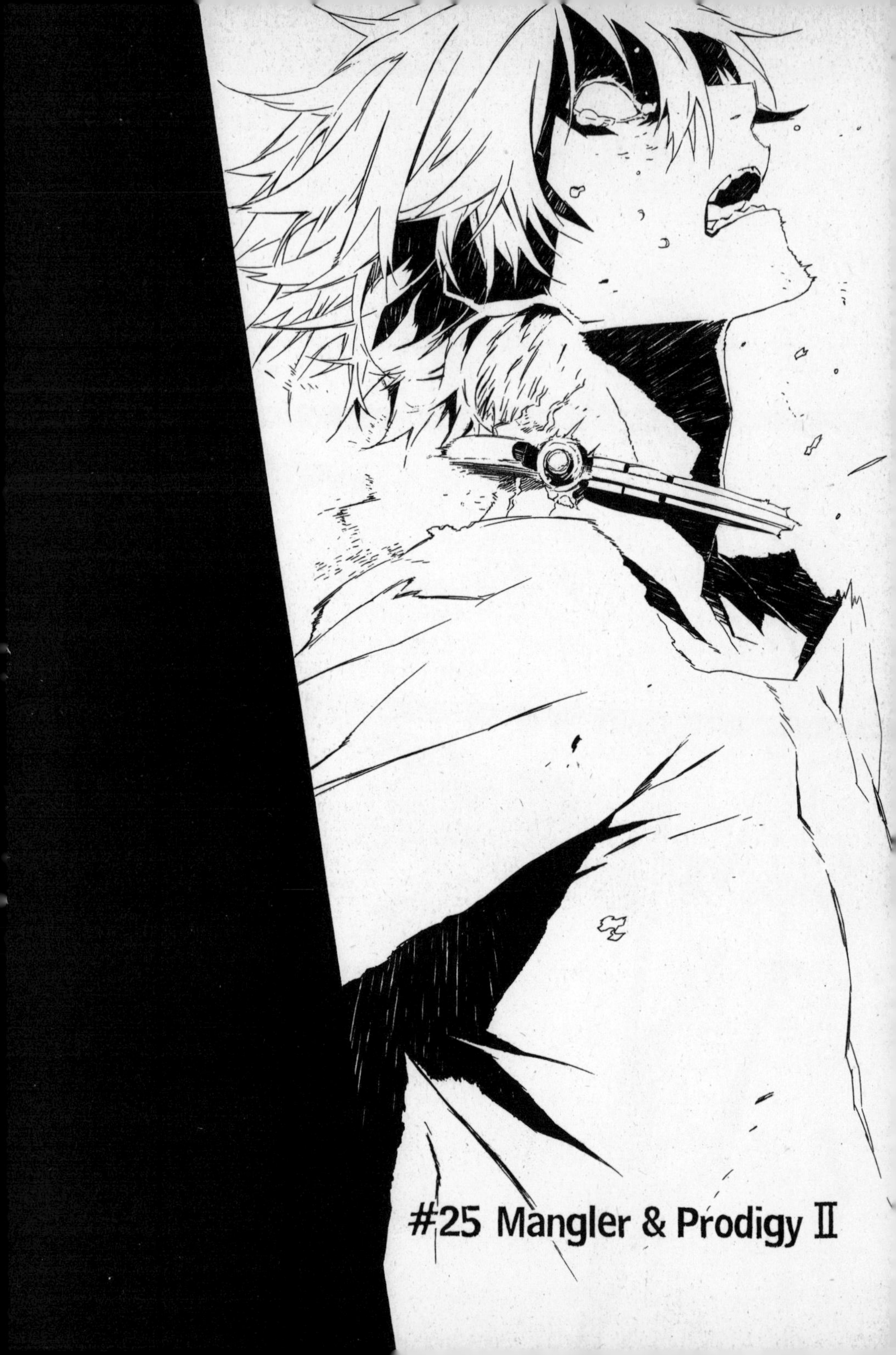

#25 Mangler & Prodigy Ⅱ

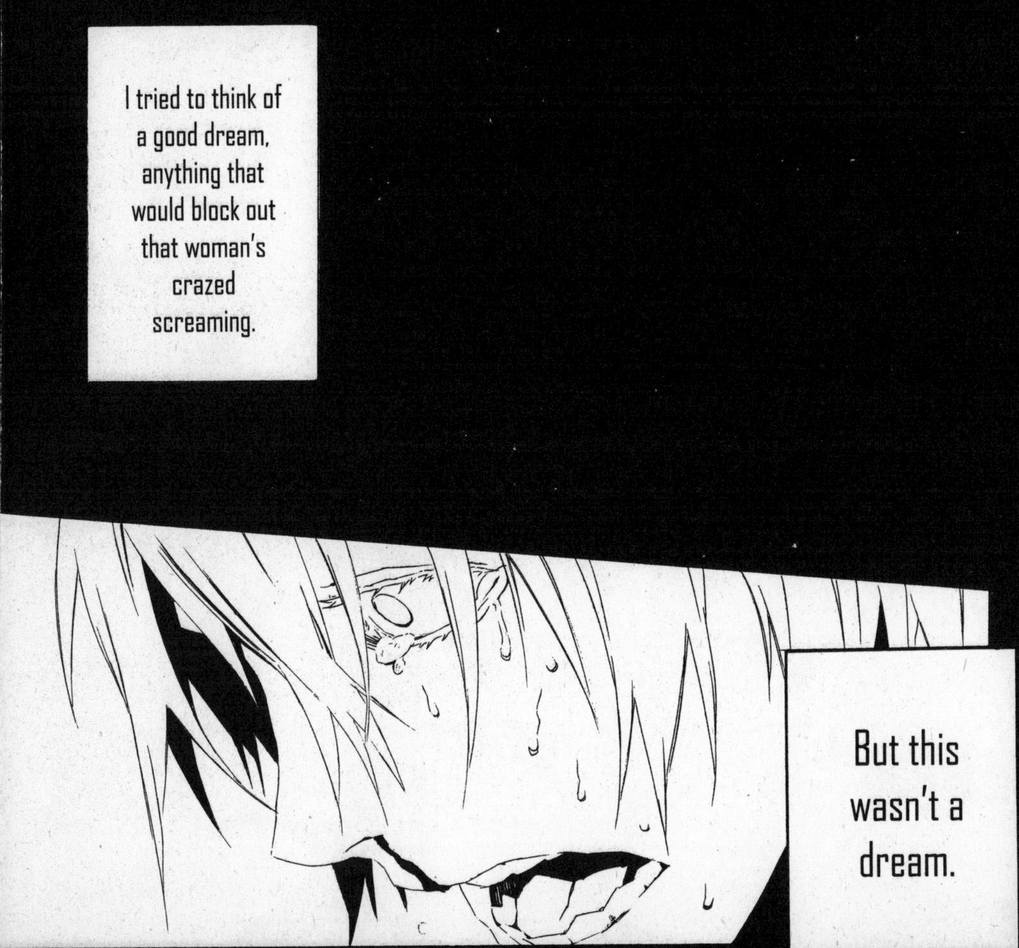
I tried to think of a good dream, anything that would block out that woman's crazed screaming.
But this wasn't a dream.

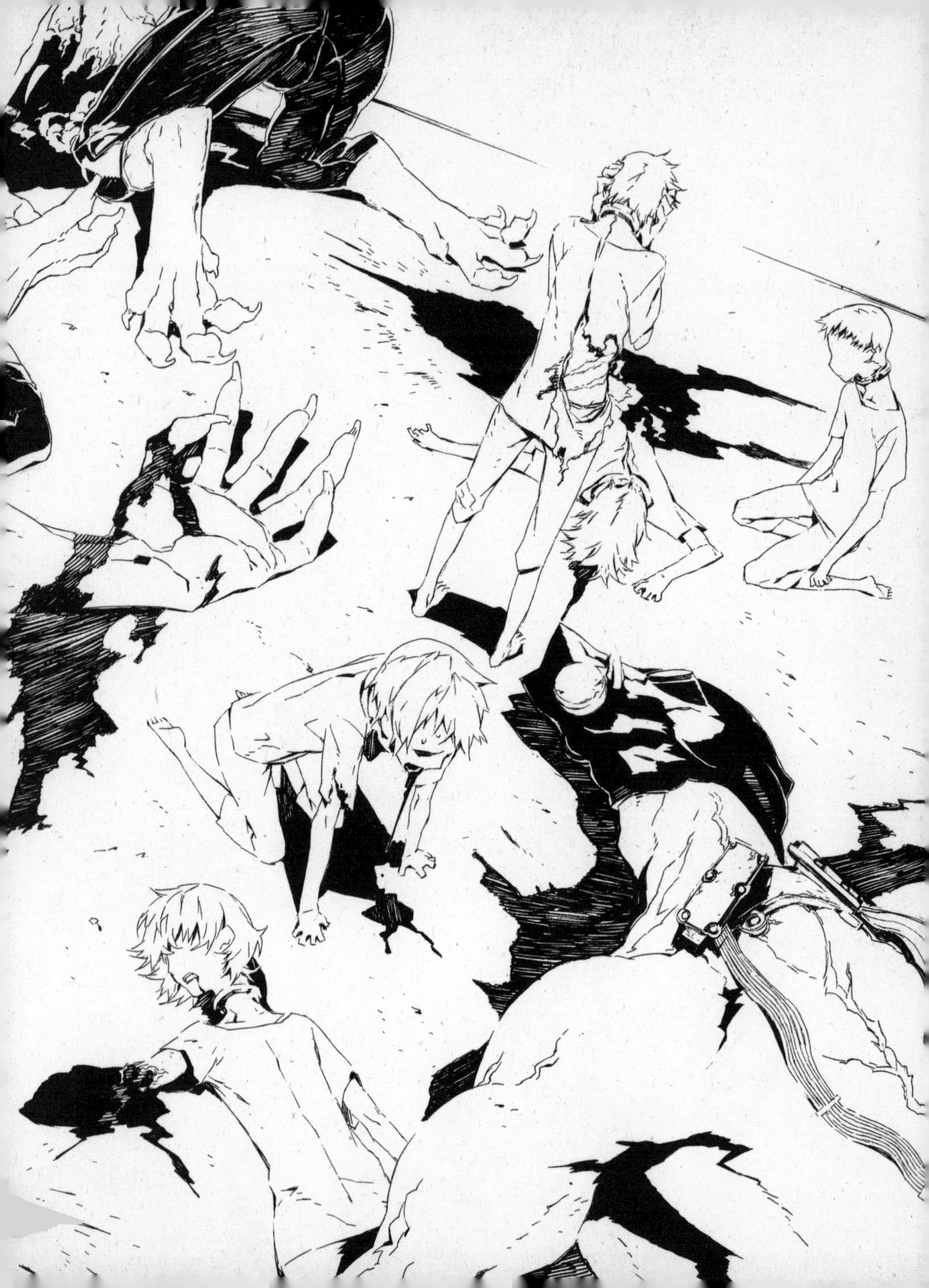

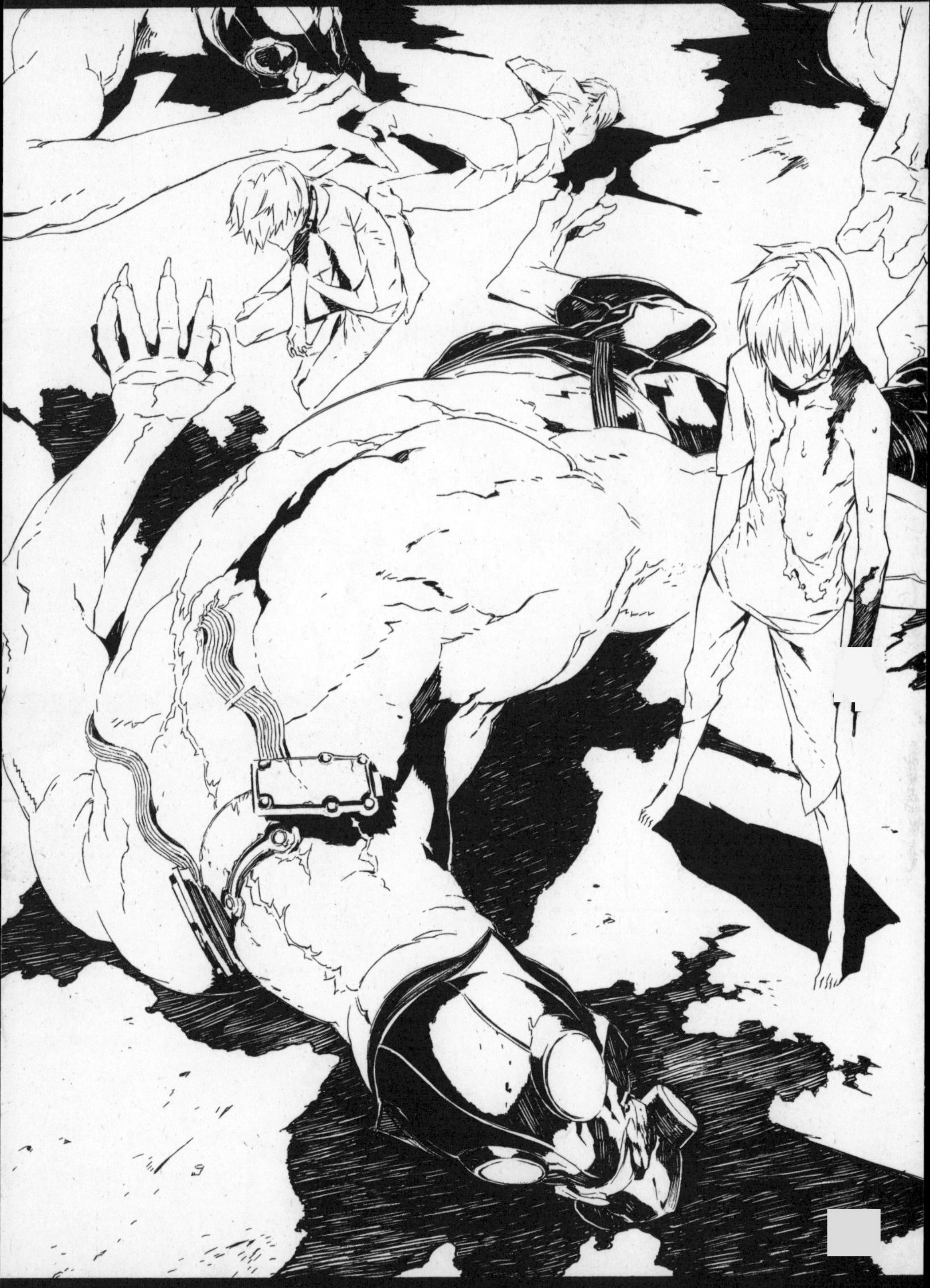

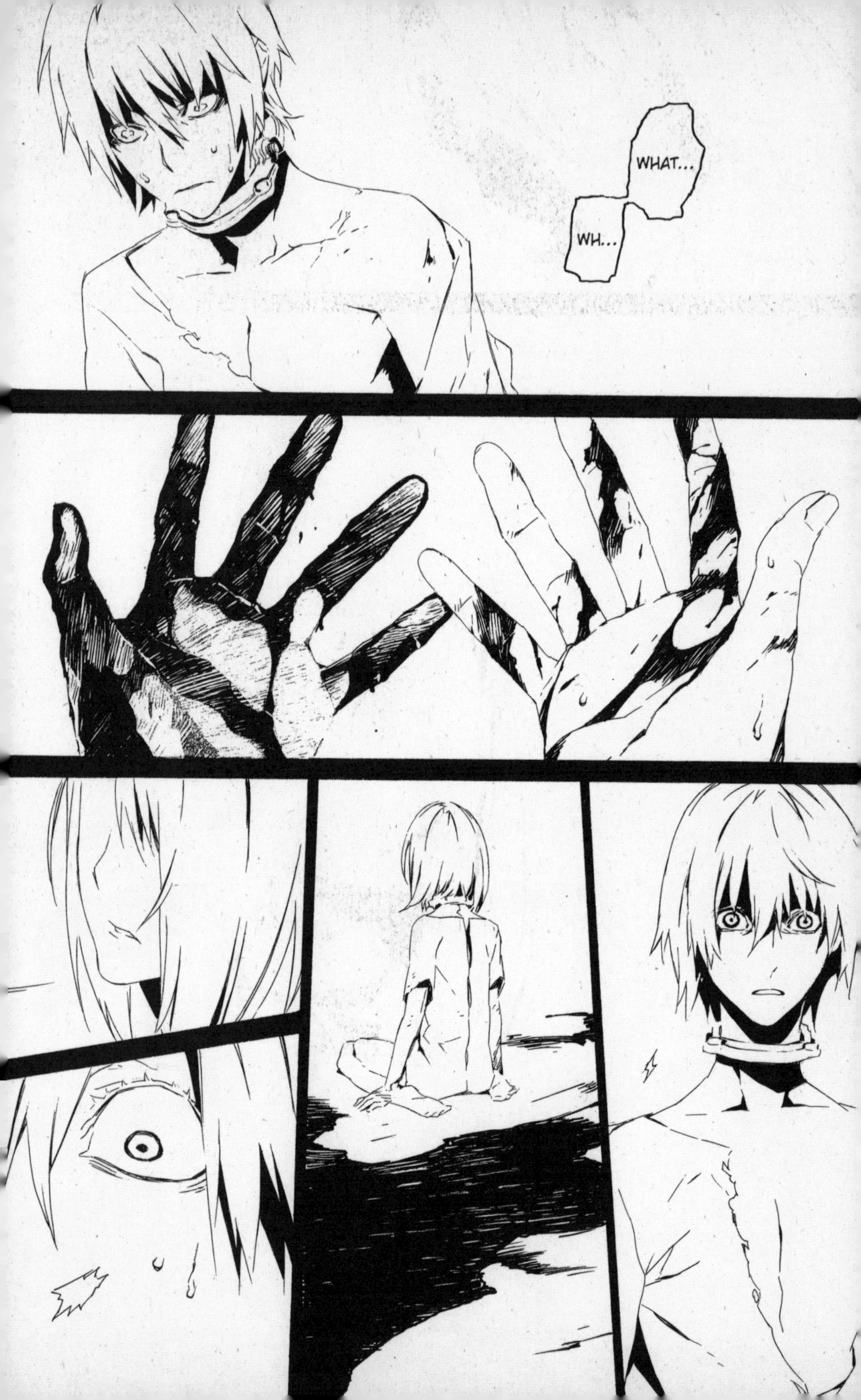
WHAT...
WH...

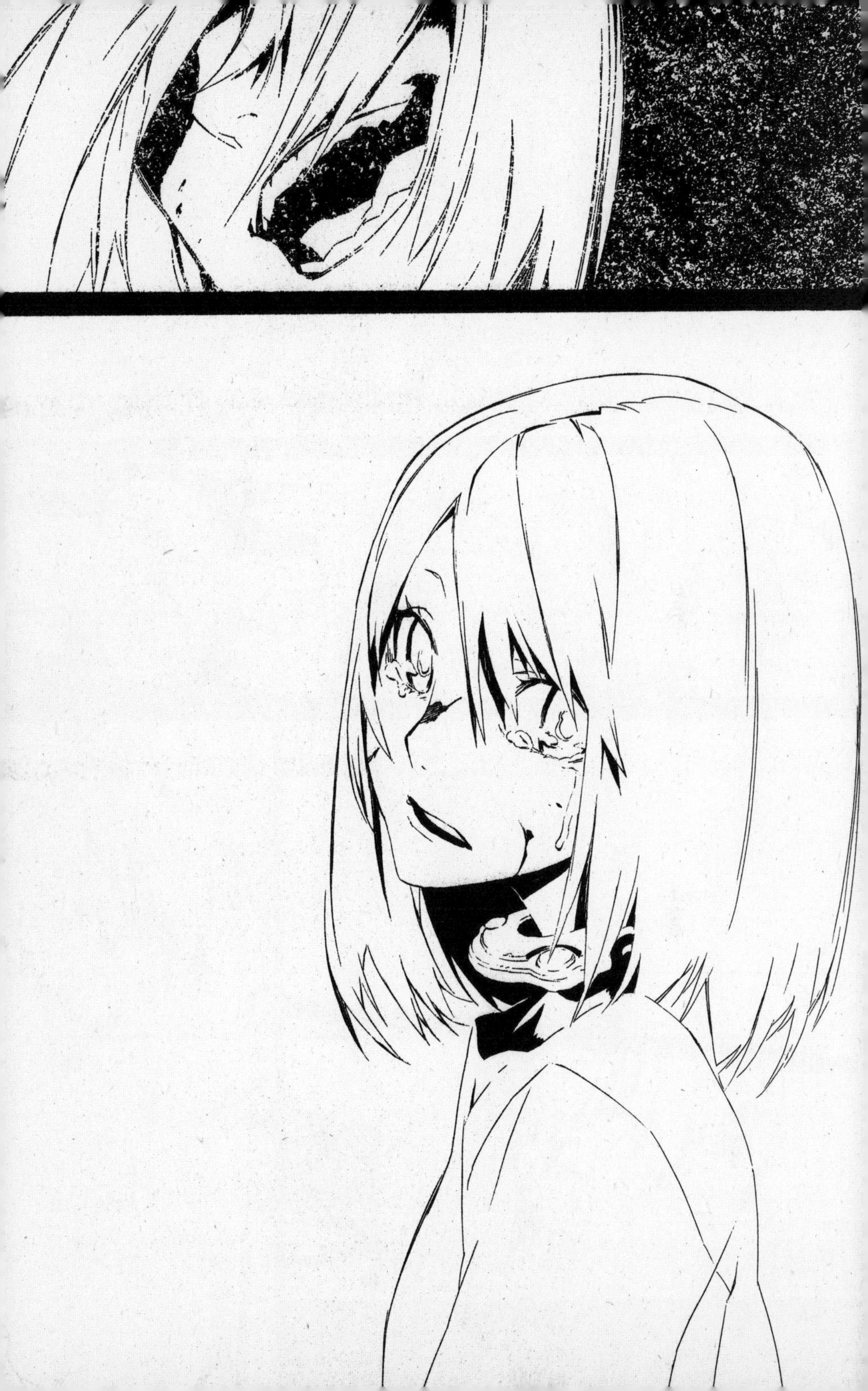

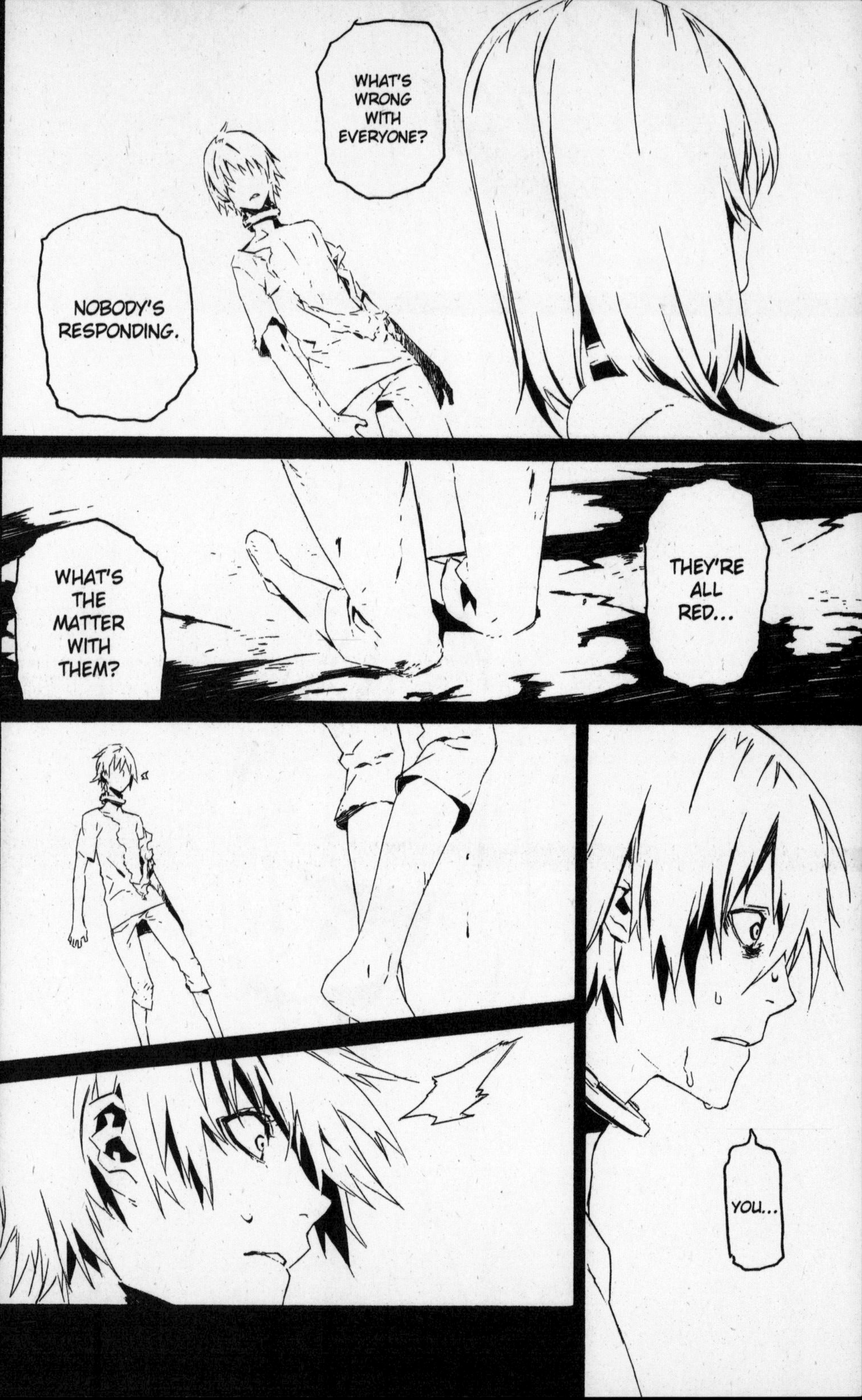
WHAT'S WRONG WITH EVERYONE?
NOBODY'S RESPONDING.
THEY'RE ALL RED...
WHAT'S THE MATTER WITH THEM?
YOU...

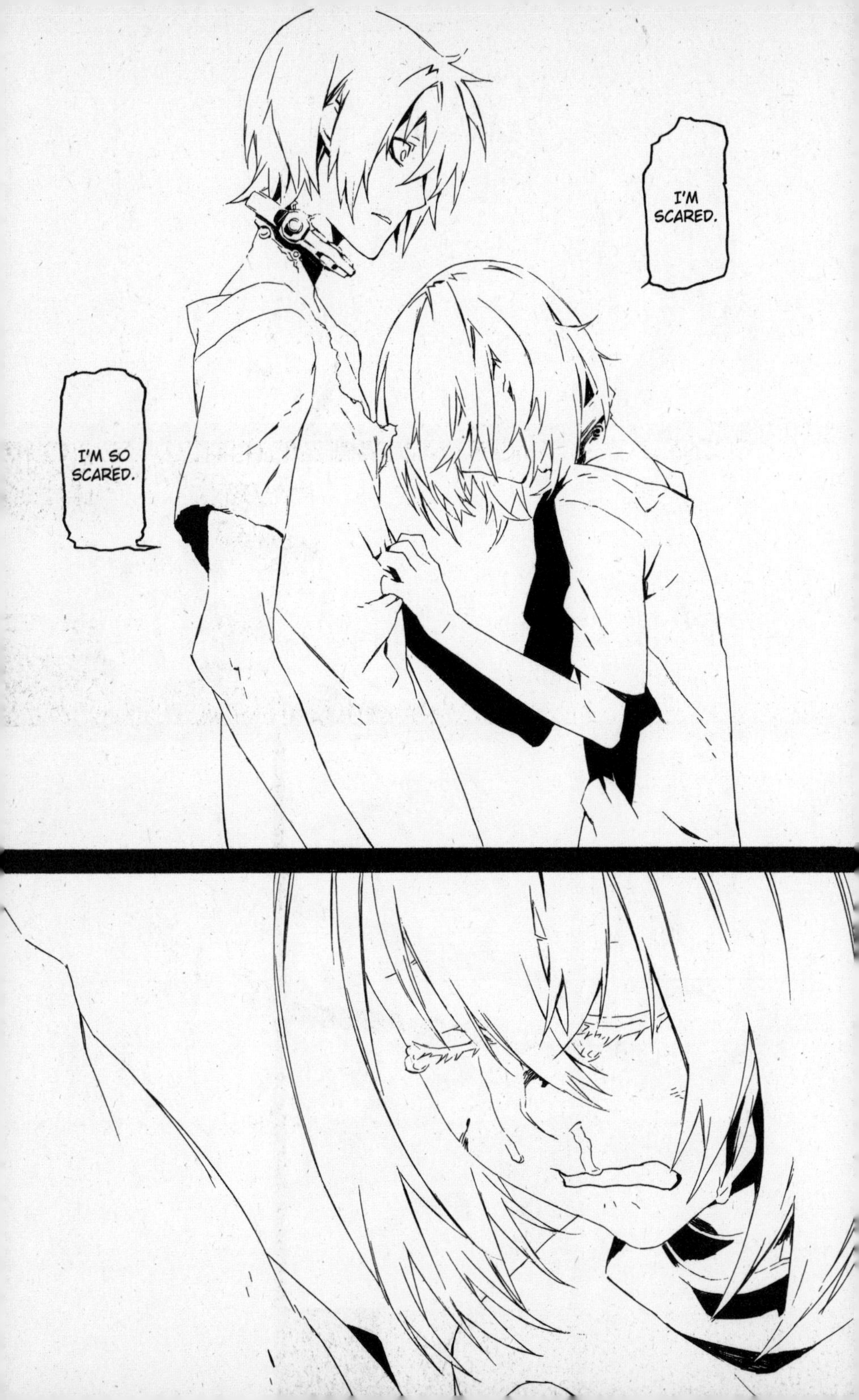
I'M SCARED.
I'M SO SCARED.

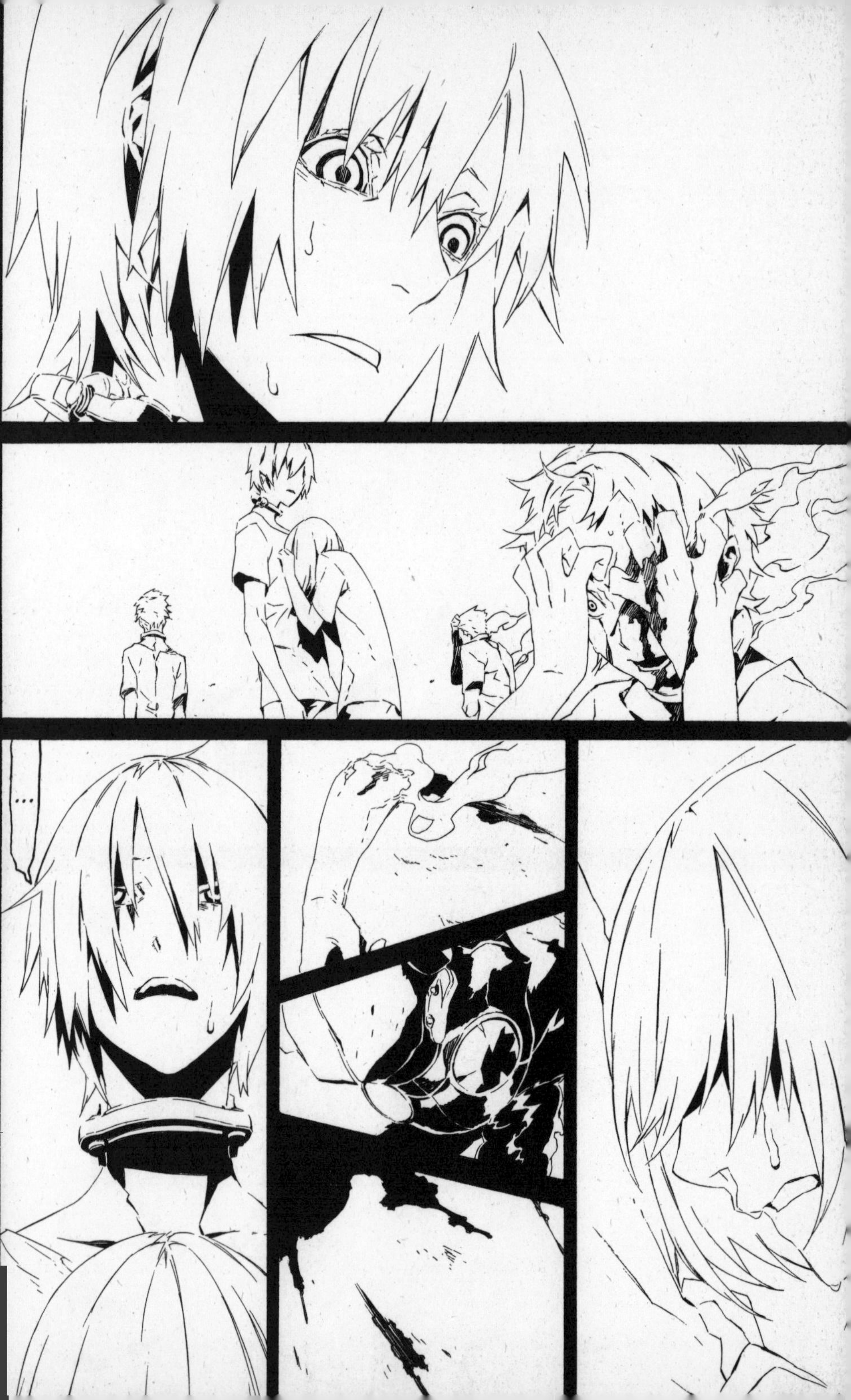
...

I DON'T... UNDERSTAND...

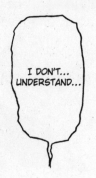

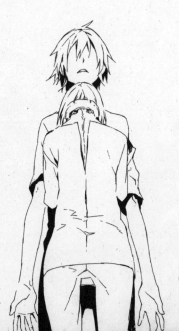

I DON'T GET IT.

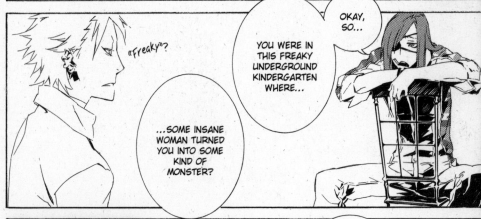

OKAY, SO...

YOU WERE IN THIS FREAKY UNDERGROUND KINDERGARTEN WHERE...

"Freaky"?

...SOME INSANE WOMAN TURNED YOU INTO SOME KIND OF MONSTER?

KLATTA

PUH-LEEZE... SOUNDS LIKE SOMETHING OUT OF A MANGA.

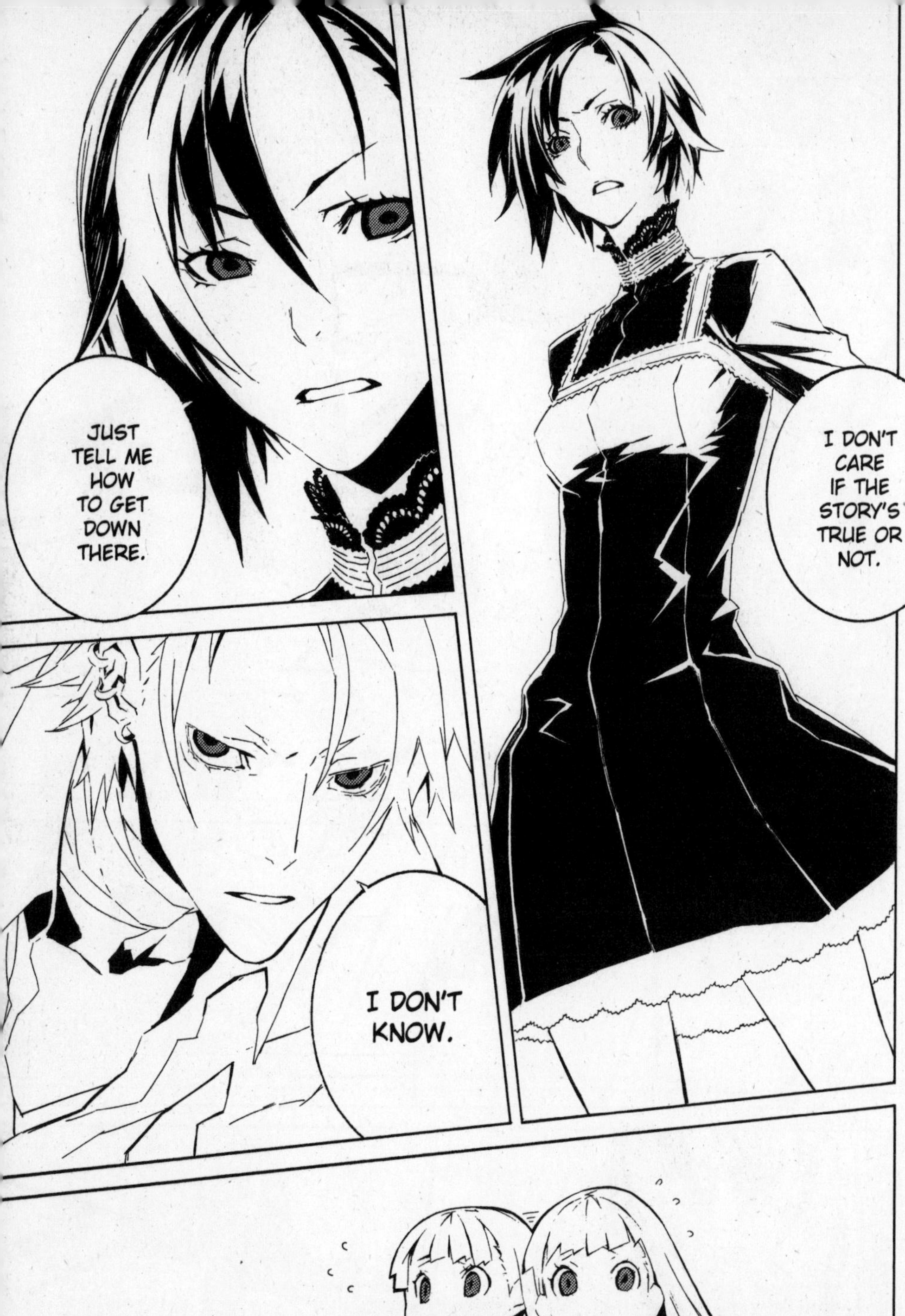
I DON'T CARE IF THE STORY'S TRUE OR NOT.
JUST TELL ME HOW TO GET DOWN THERE.
I DON'T KNOW.

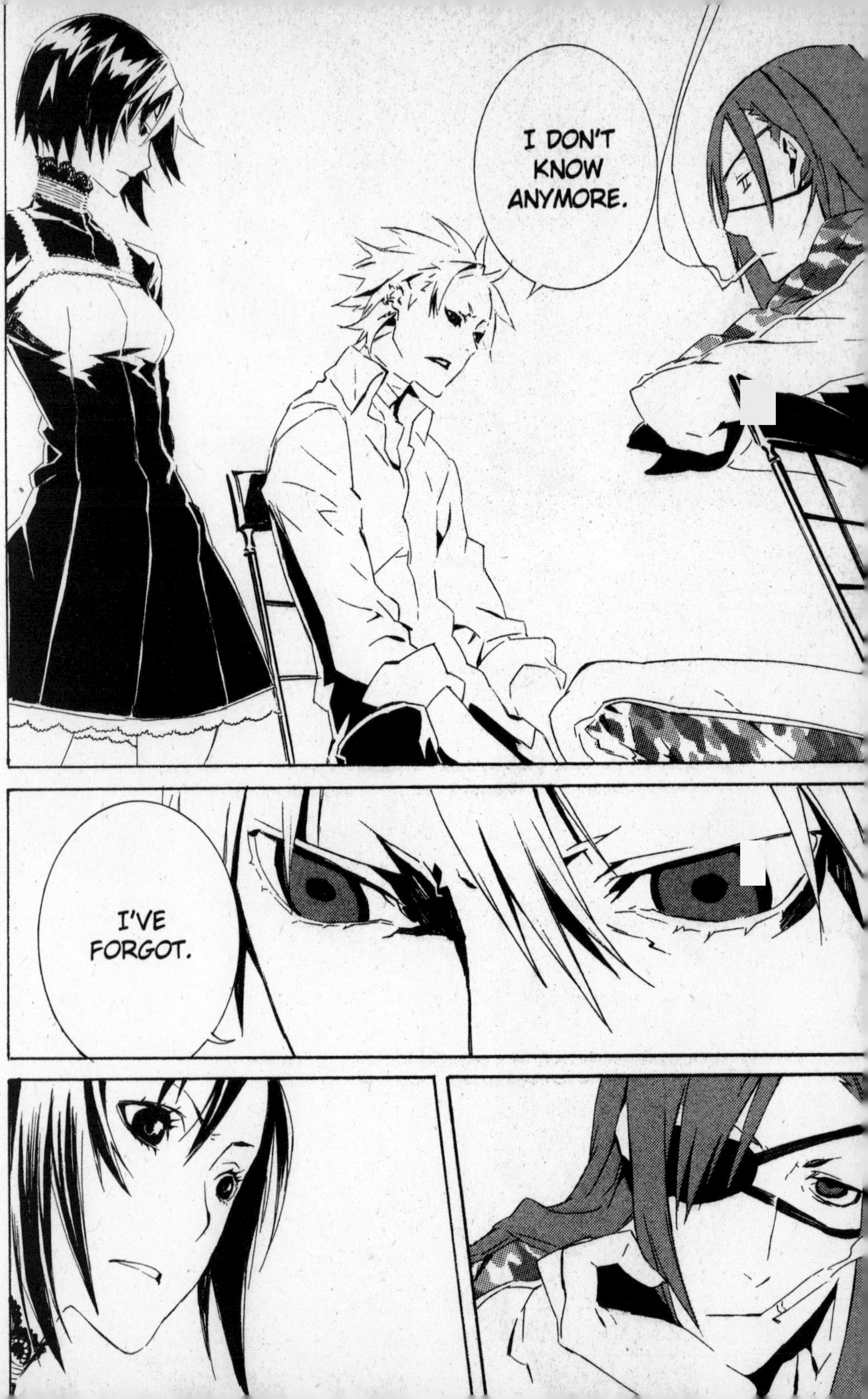
I DON'T KNOW ANYMORE.
I'VE FORGOT.

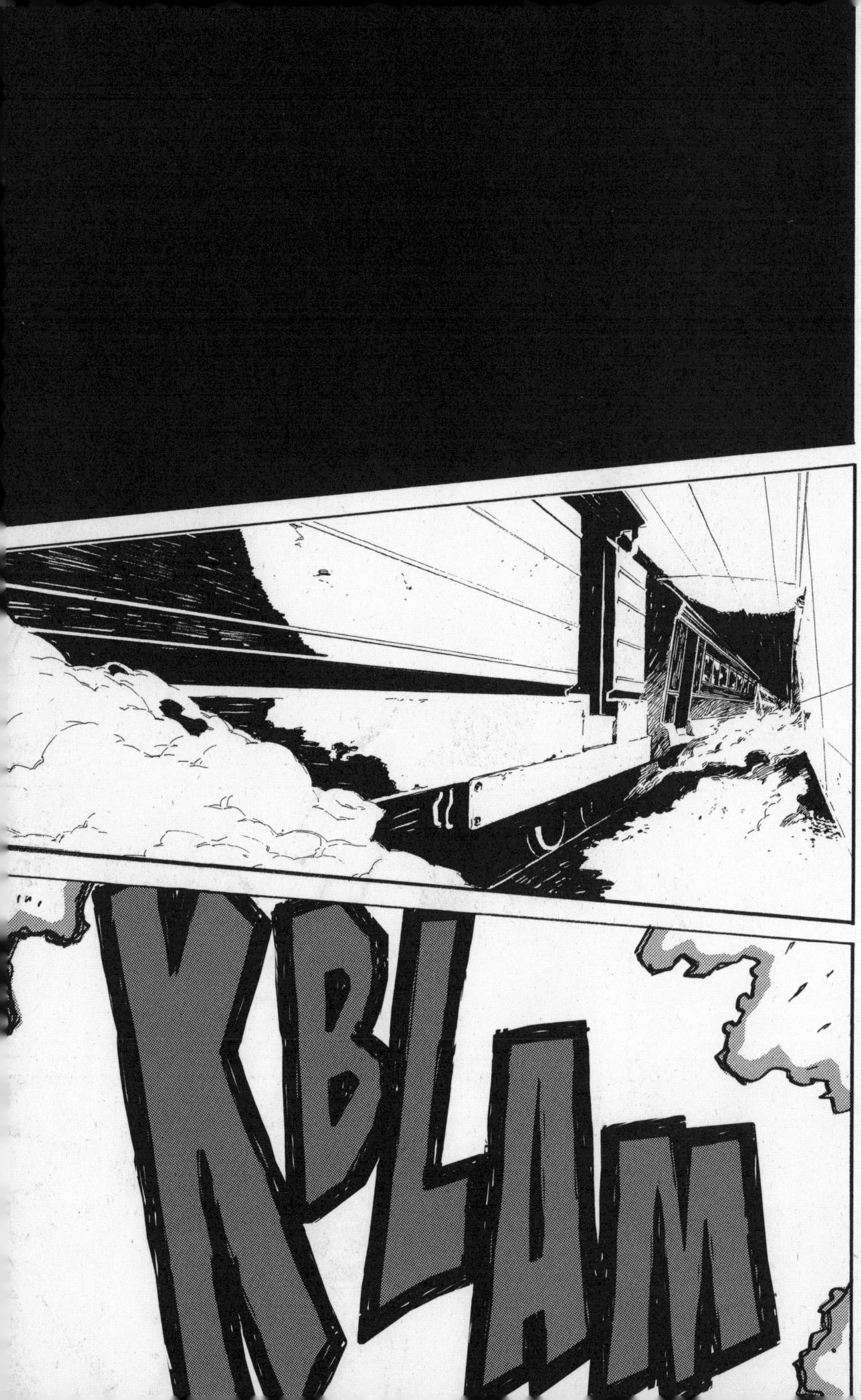
KBLAM

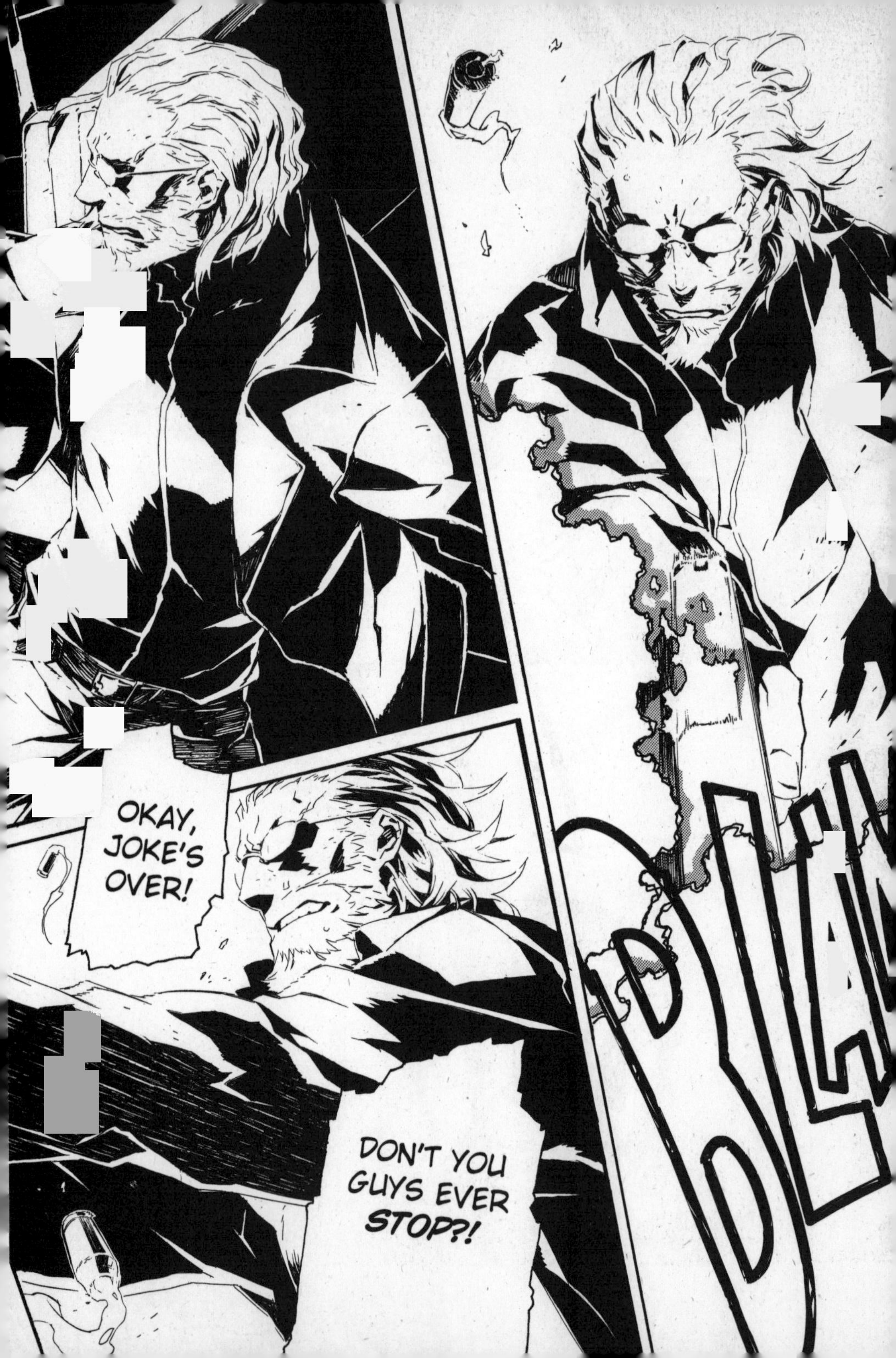
OKAY, JOKE'S OVER!
DON'T YOU GUYS EVER STOP?!

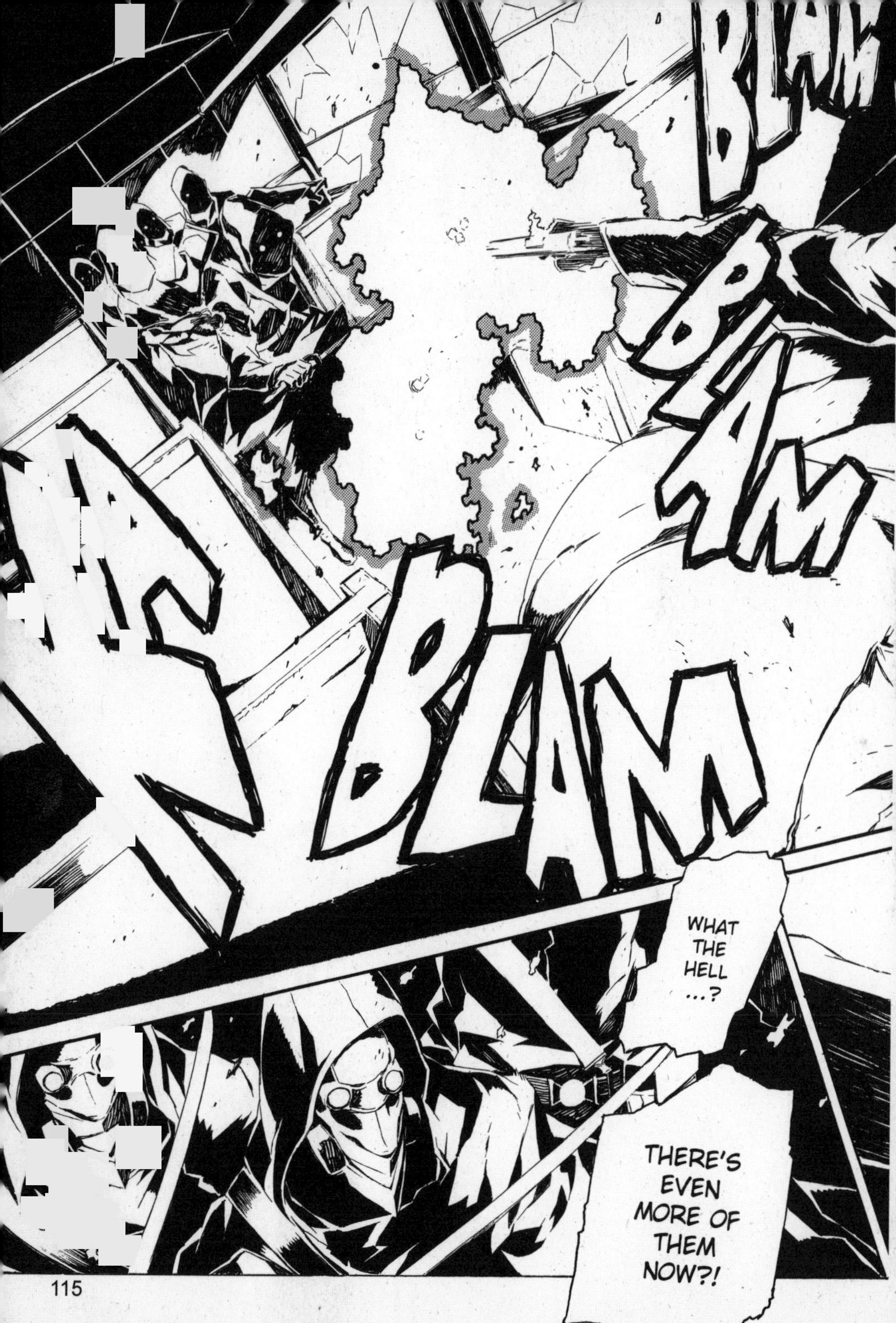
BLAM
BLAM
BLAM
WHAT THE HELL ...?
THERE'S EVEN MORE OF THEM NOW?!

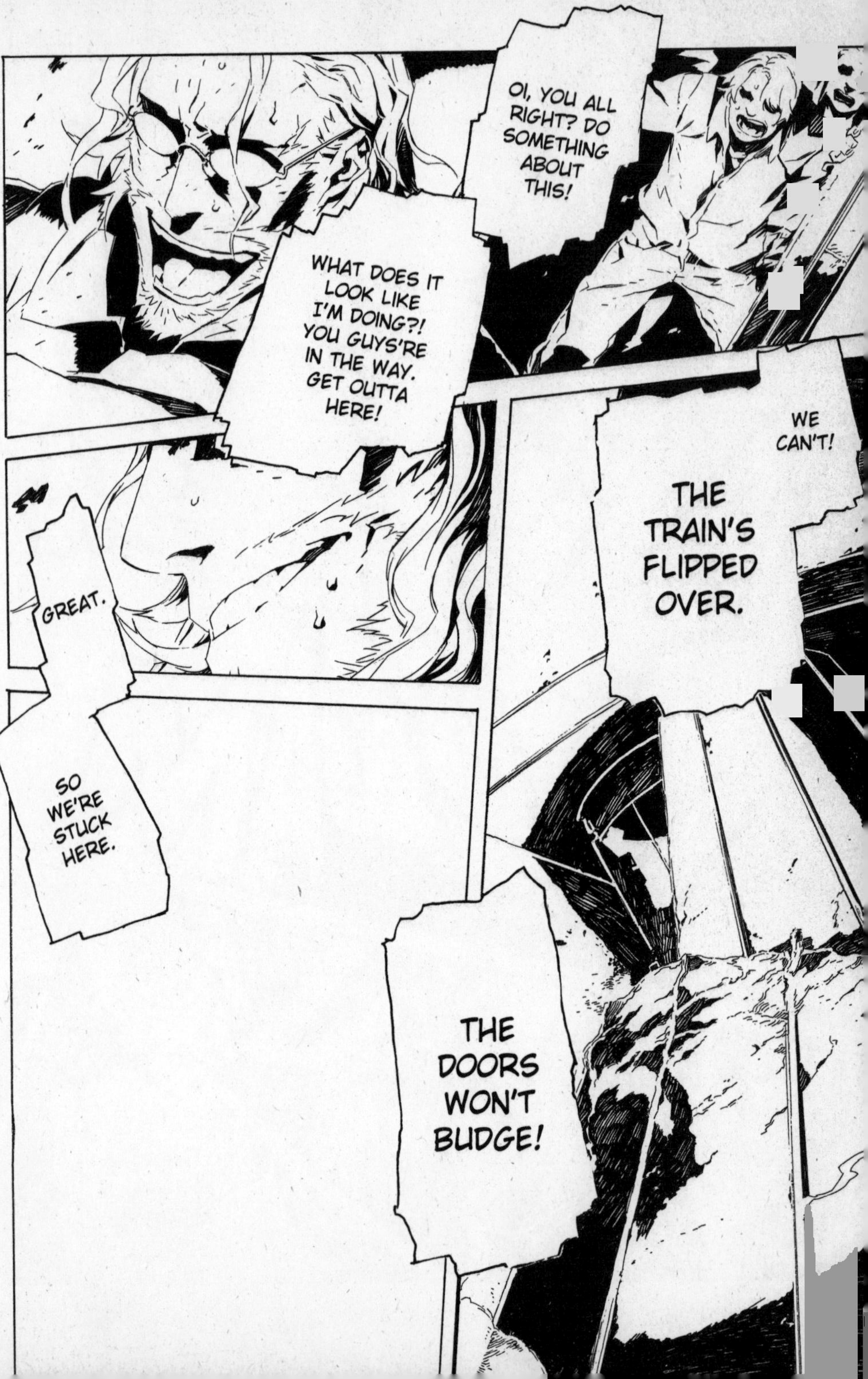
OI, YOU ALL RIGHT? DO SOMETHING ABOUT THIS!
WHAT DOES IT LOOK LIKE I'M DOING?! YOU GUYS'RE IN THE WAY. GET OUTTA HERE!
WE CAN'T!
THE TRAIN'S FLIPPED OVER.
THE DOORS WON'T BUDGE!
GREAT.
SO WE'RE STUCK HERE.

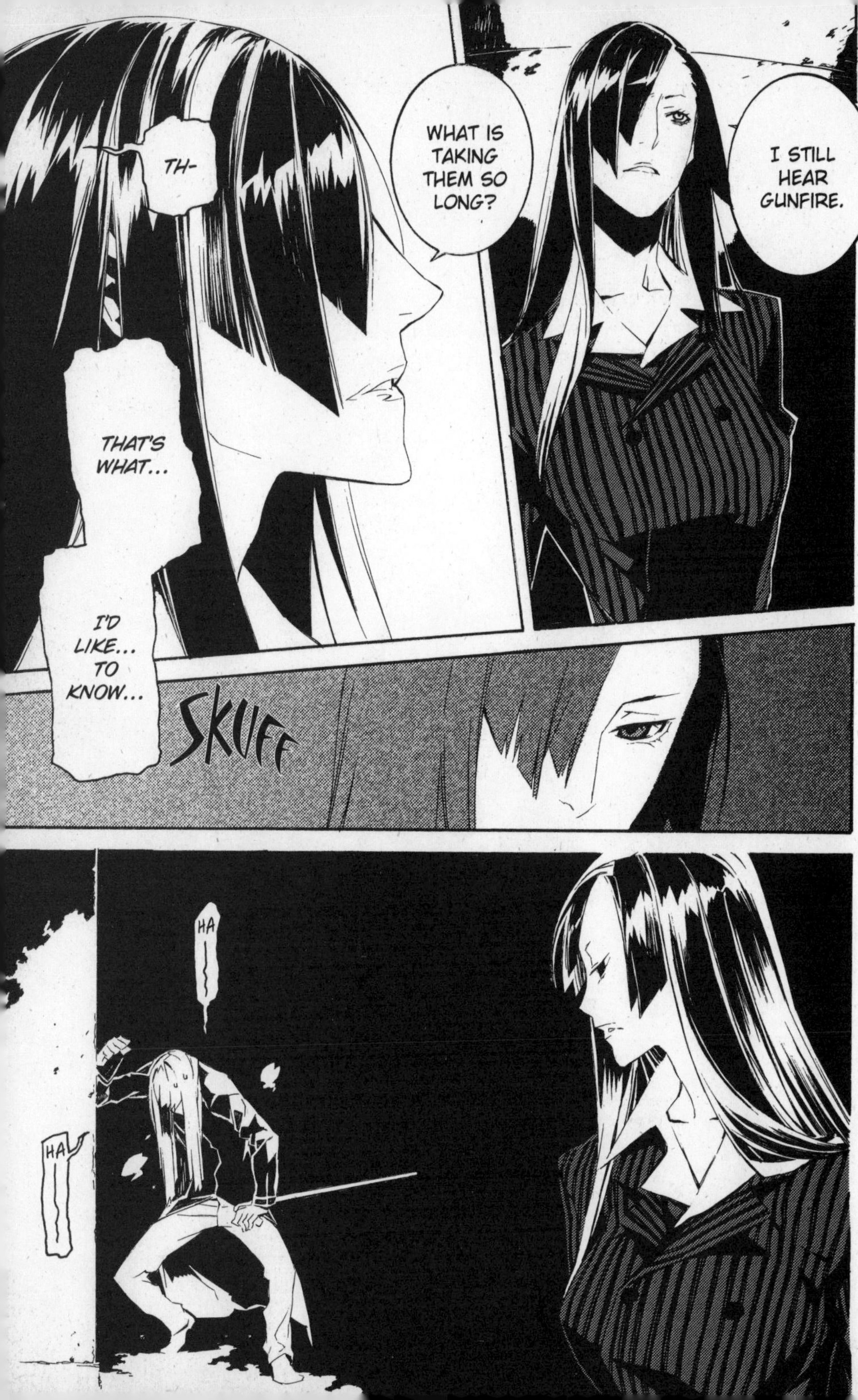
I STILL HEAR GUNFIRE.
WHAT IS TAKING THEM SO LONG?
TH-
THAT'S WHAT...
I'D LIKE... TO KNOW...
SKUFF
HA
HA

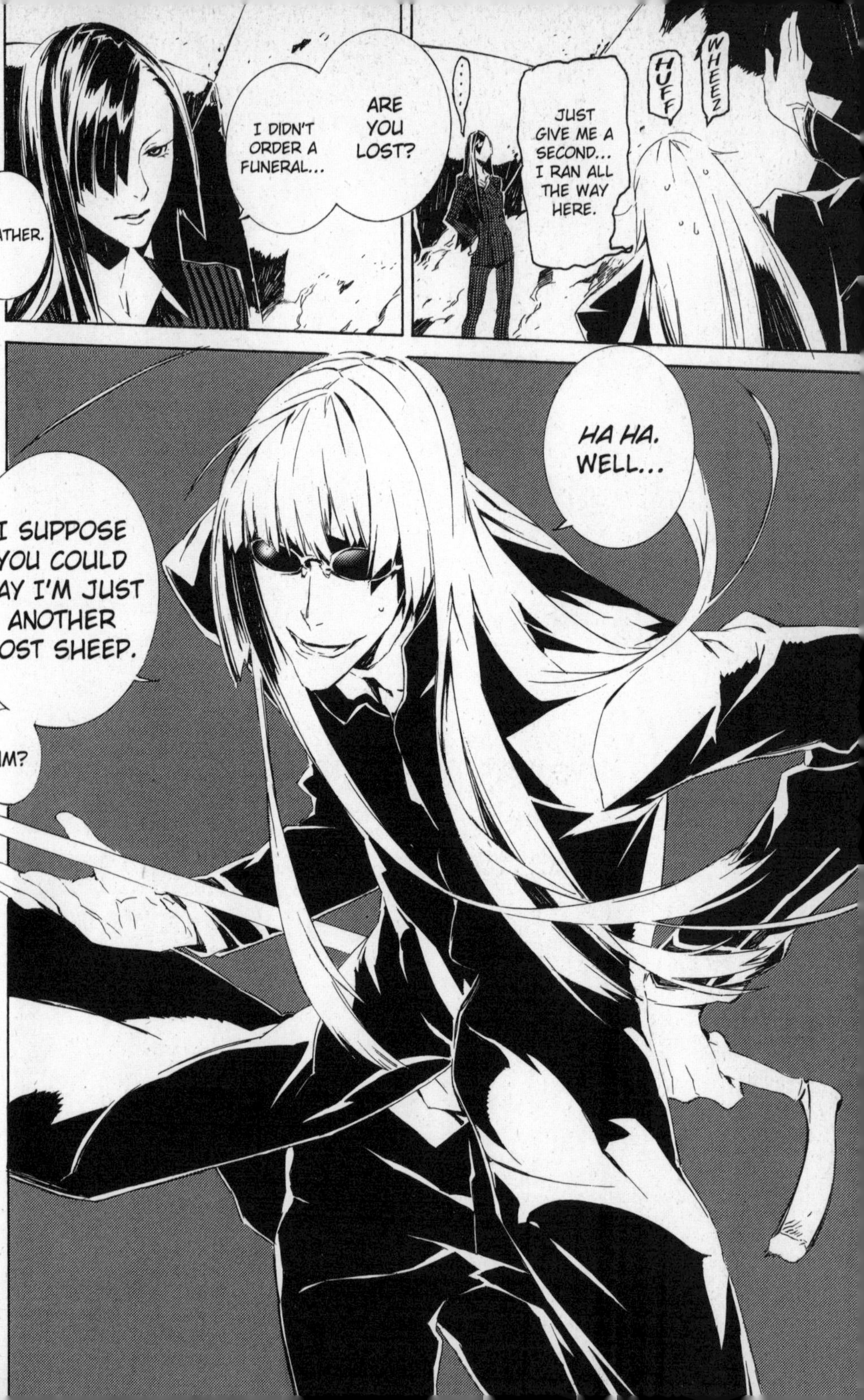
WHEEZ
HUFF
JUST GIVE ME A SECOND... I RAN ALL THE WAY HERE.
...
ARE YOU LOST?
I DIDN'T ORDER A FUNERAL...
...FATHER.
HA HA. WELL...
I SUPPOSE YOU COULD SAY I'M JUST ANOTHER LOST SHEEP.
HM?

#26 Blind Bishop & Strongest Elder

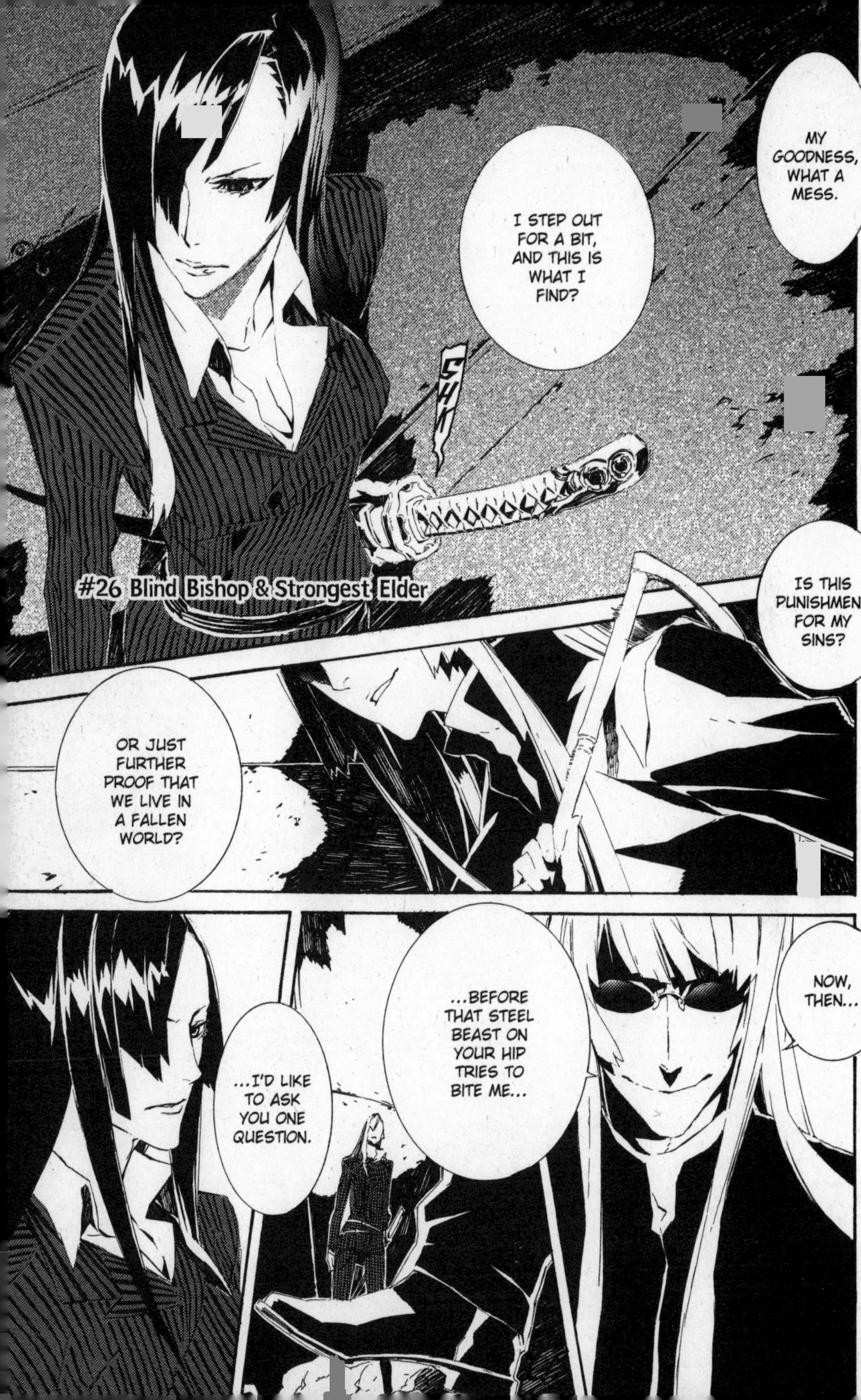
MY GOODNESS, WHAT A MESS.
I STEP OUT FOR A BIT, AND THIS IS WHAT I FIND?
SHK
IS THIS PUNISHMENT FOR MY SINS?
OR JUST FURTHER PROOF THAT WE LIVE IN A FALLEN WORLD?
NOW, THEN...
...BEFORE THAT STEEL BEAST ON YOUR HIP TRIES TO BITE ME...
...I'D LIKE TO ASK YOU ONE QUESTION.

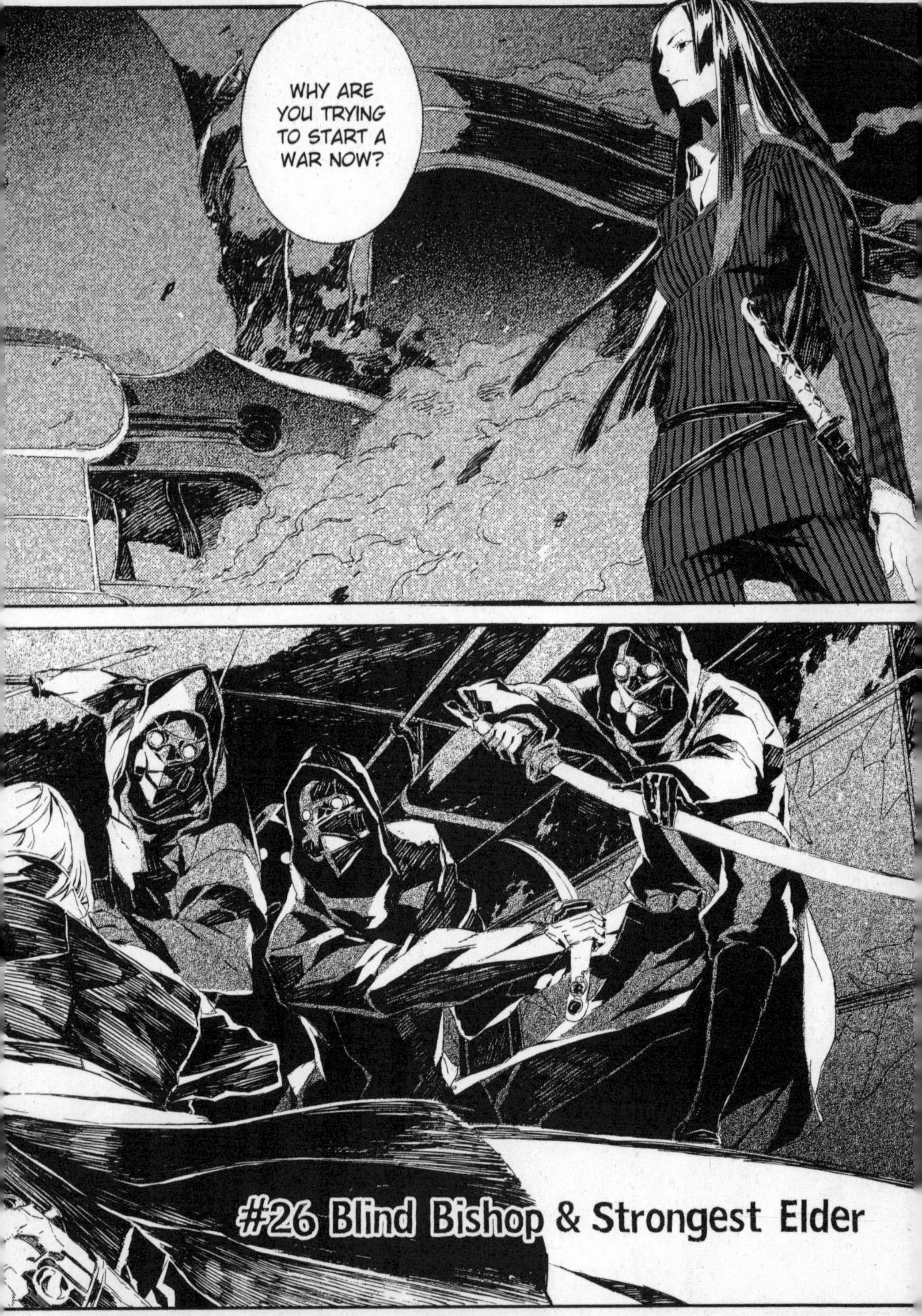
WHY ARE YOU TRYING TO START A WAR NOW?
#26 Blind Bishop & Strongest Elder

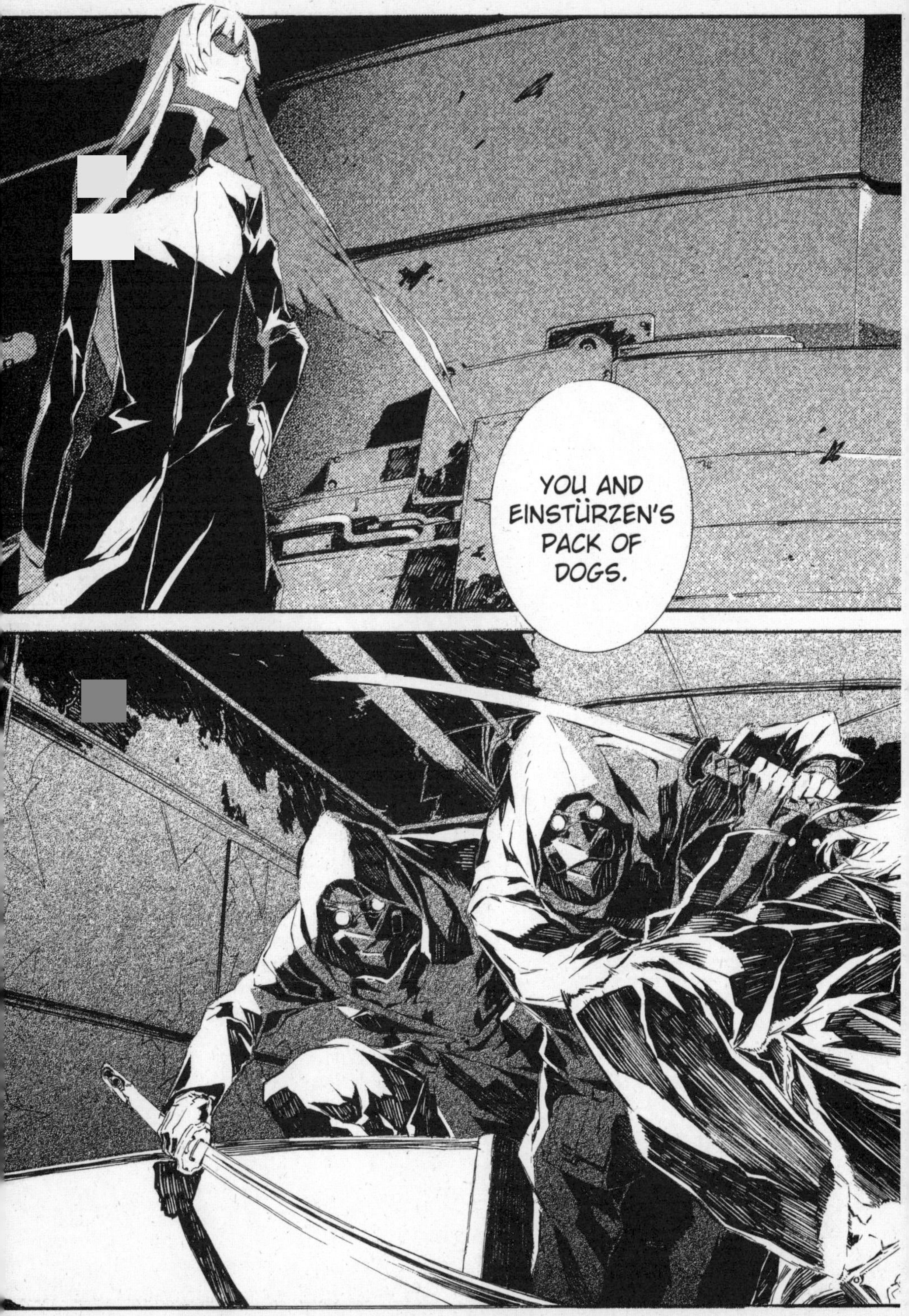
YOU AND EINSTÜRZEN'S PACK OF DOGS.

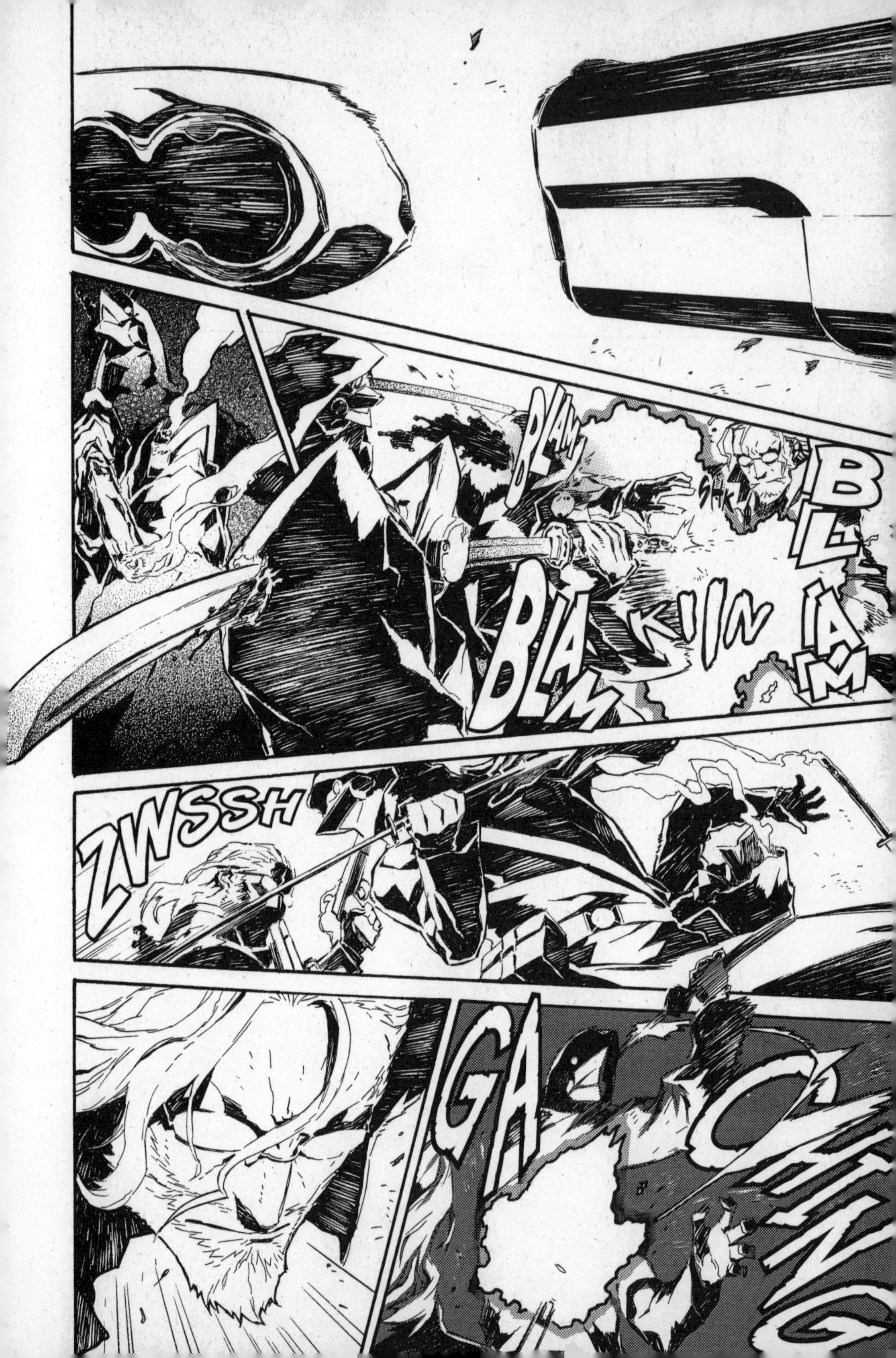
BLAM
BLAM
BLAM
KIIN
BLAM
ZWSSH
GA
CHING

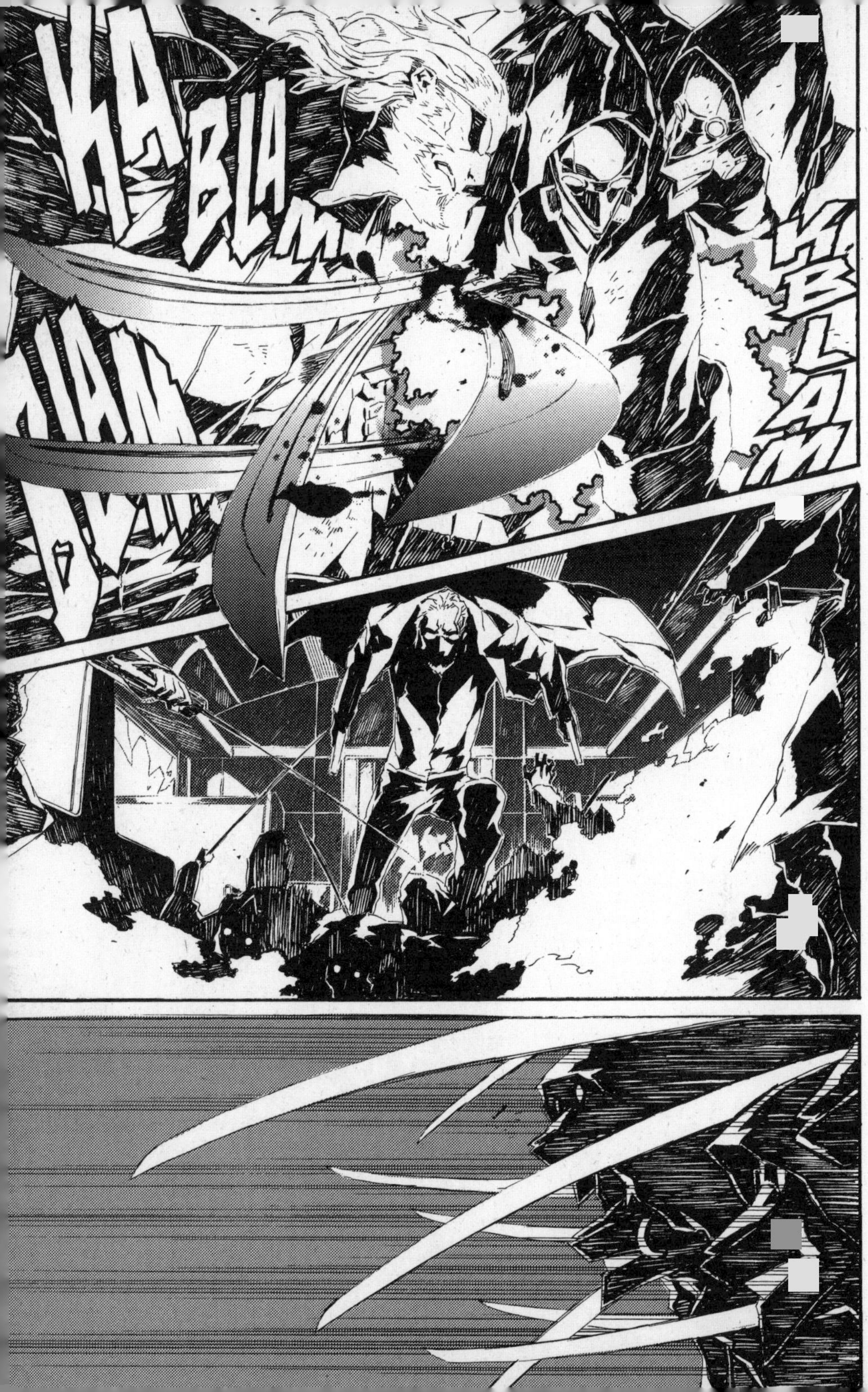
KBLAM
KA BLAM

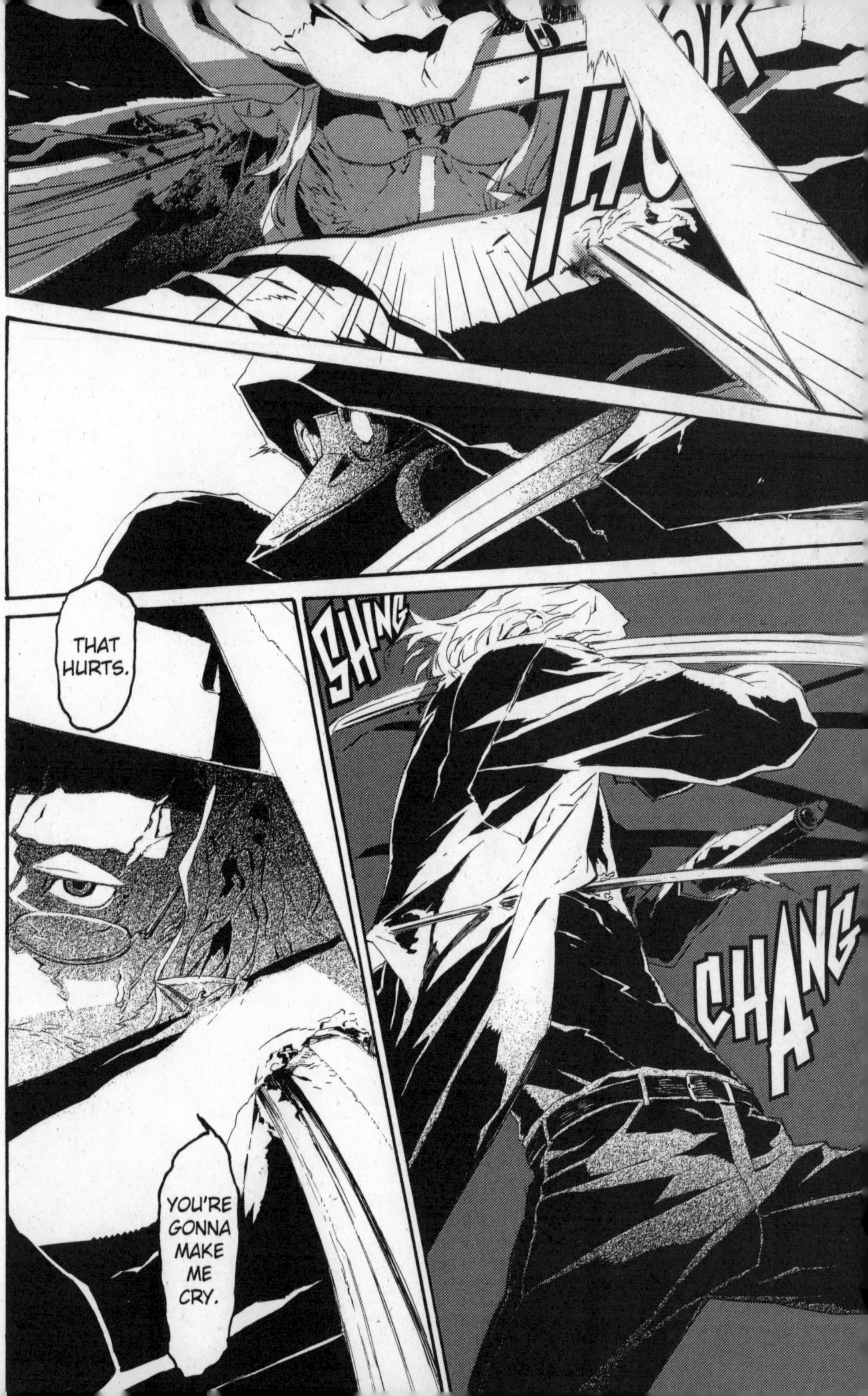
SHING
CHANG
THAT HURTS.
YOU'RE GONNA MAKE ME CRY.

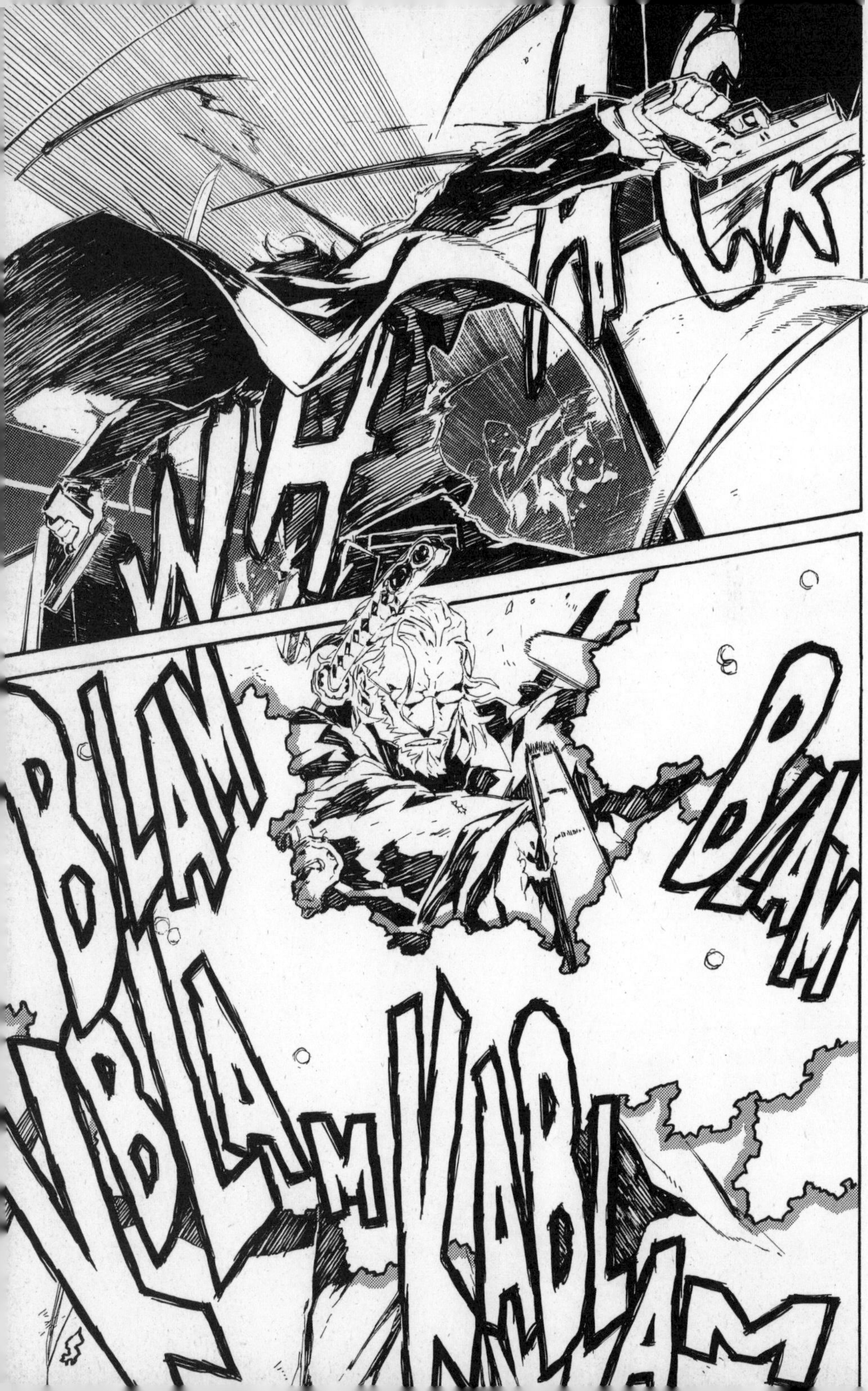
WHACK
BLAM
BLAM
KABLAM
KABLAM

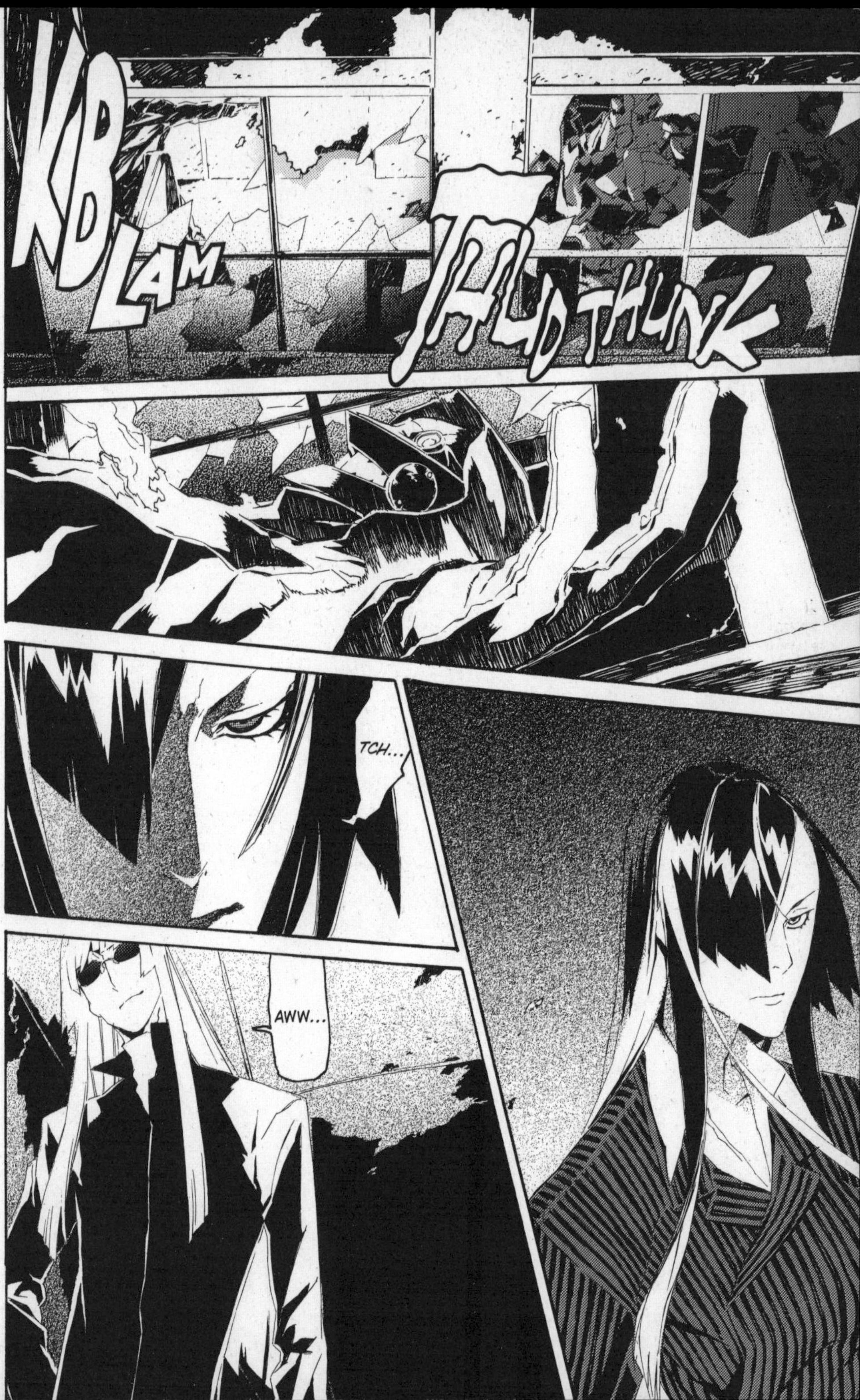
KBLAM
THUD THUNK
TCH...
AWW...

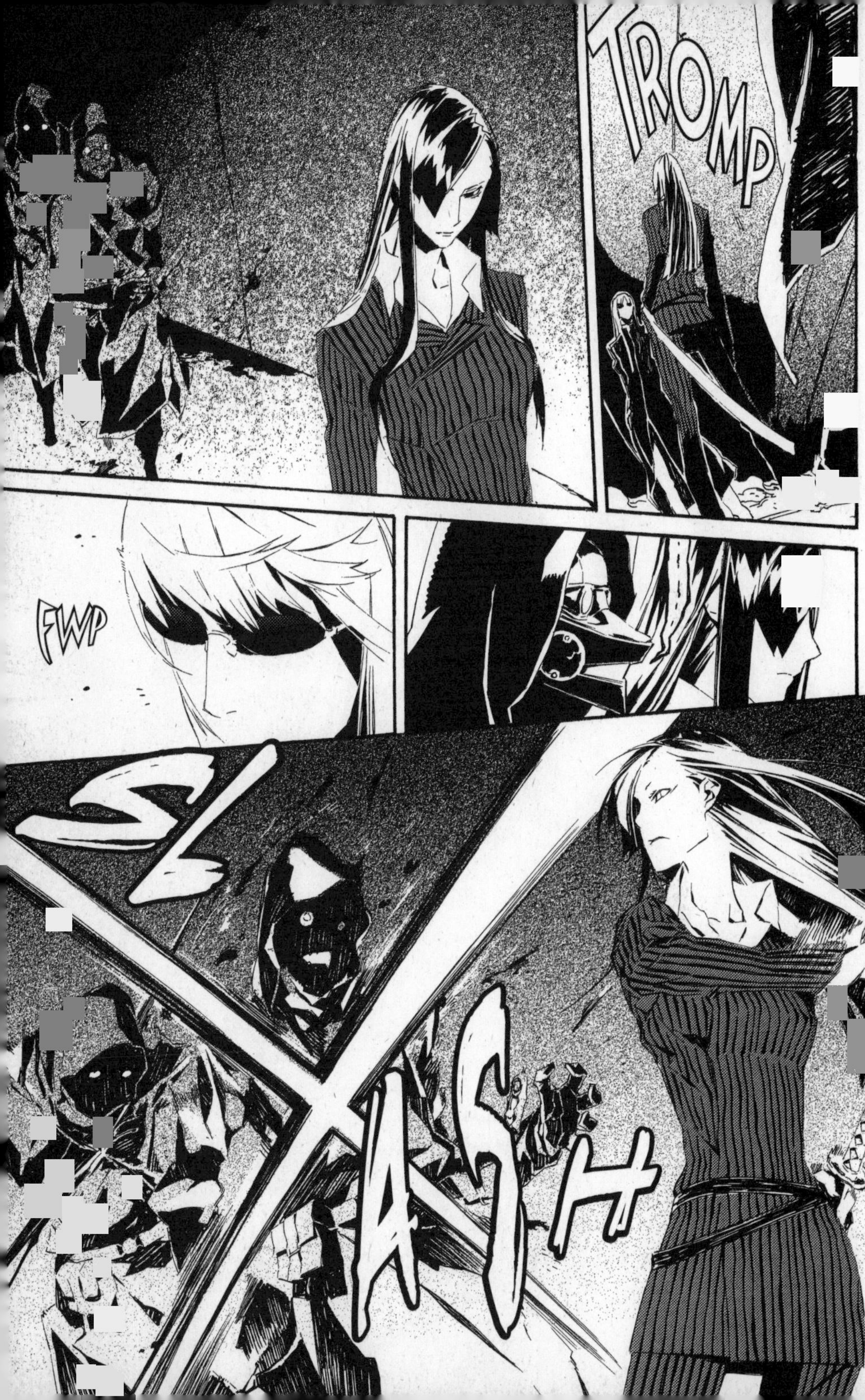
TROMP
FWP
SLASH

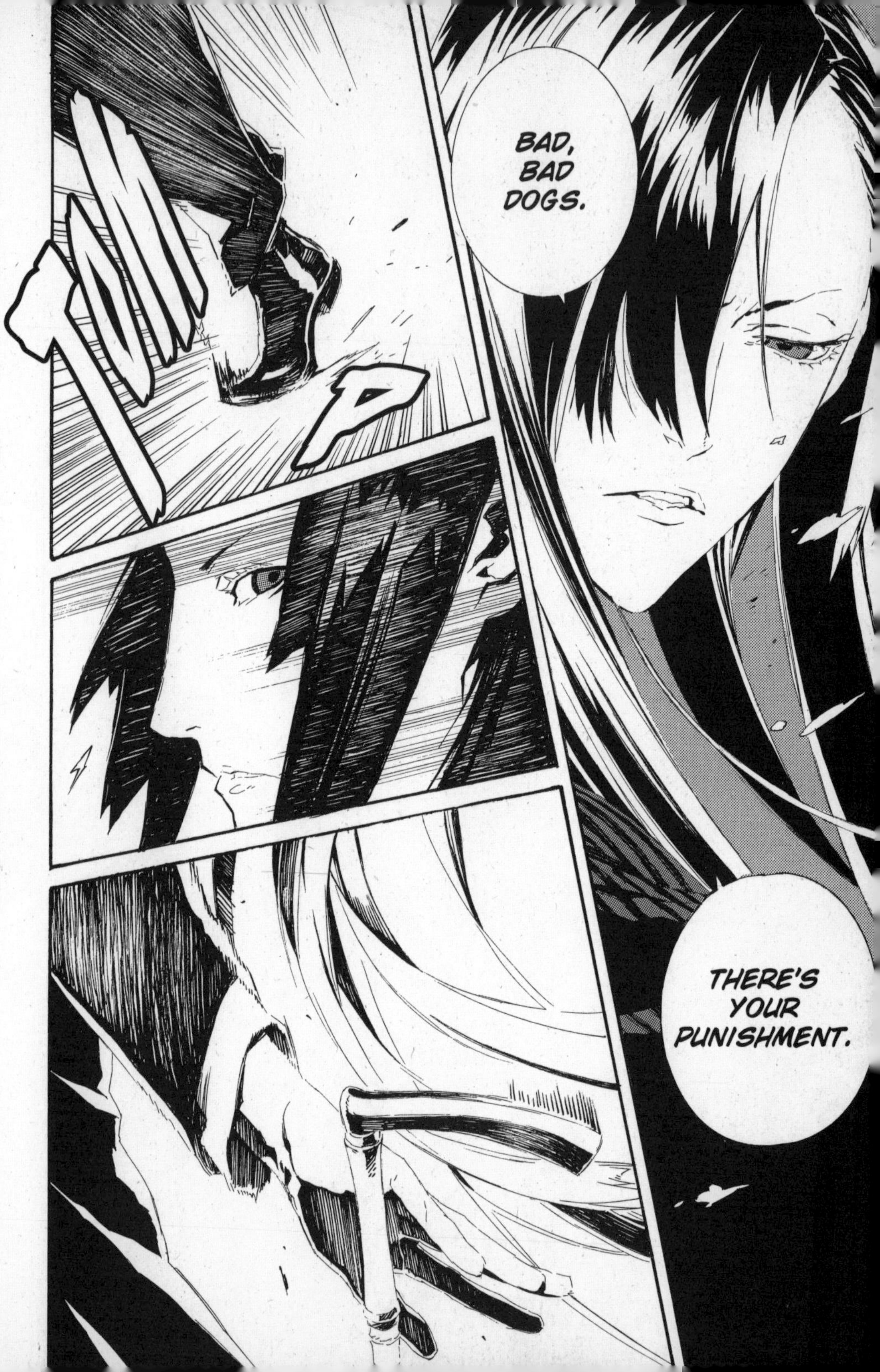
BAD, BAD DOGS.
THERE'S YOUR PUNISHMENT.

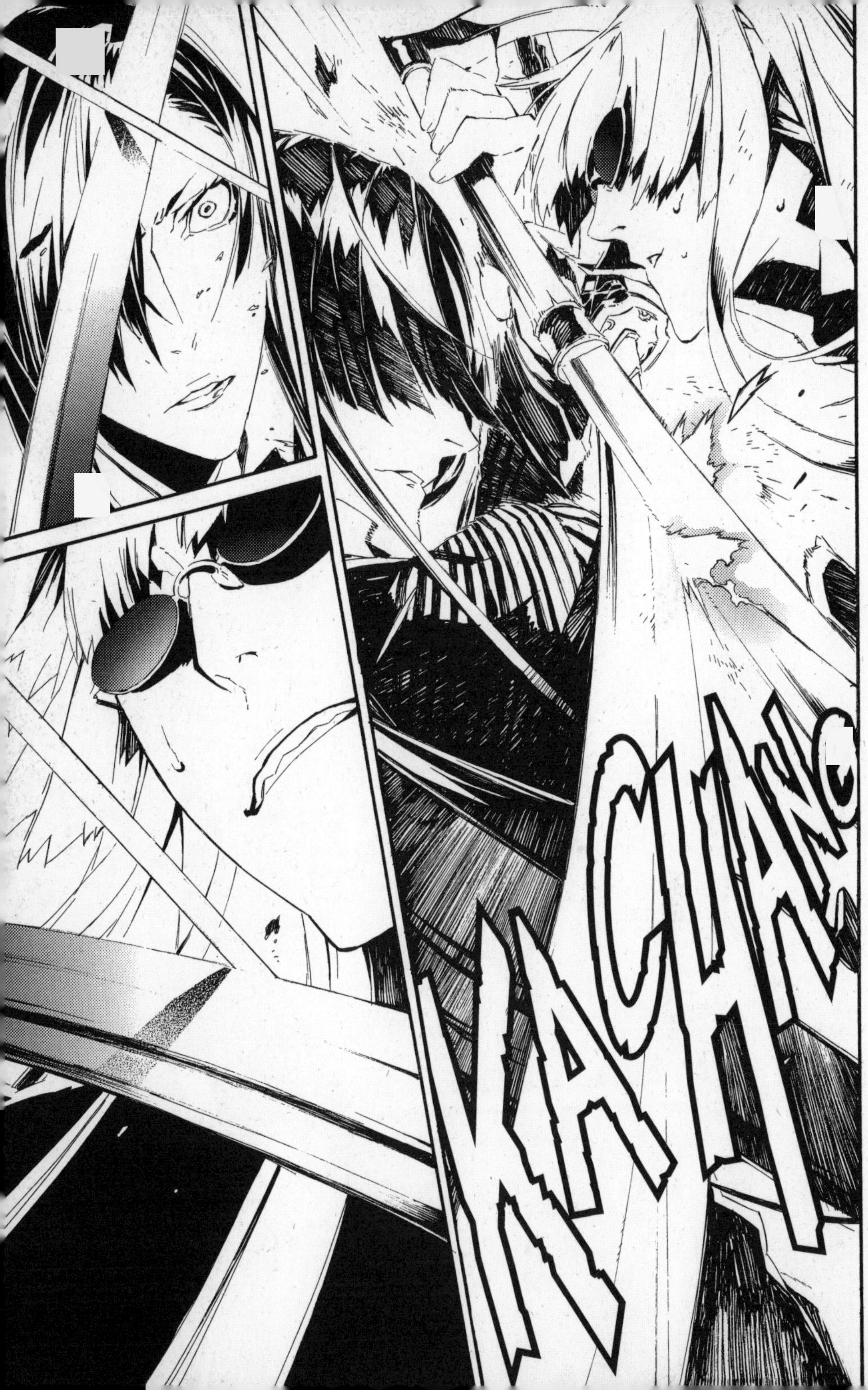
KACHANG

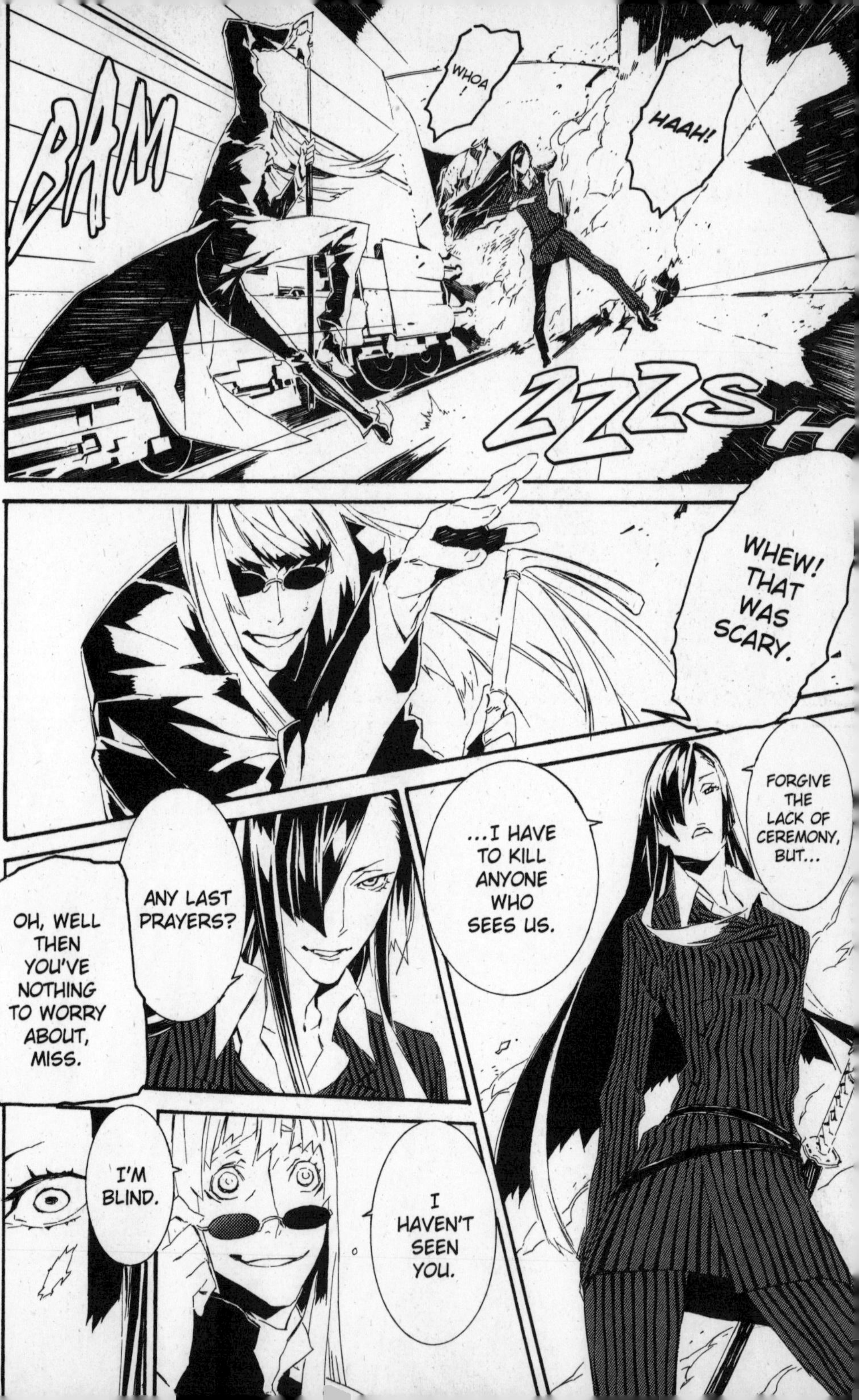
HAAH!
WHOA!
BAM
ZZZSH
WHEW! THAT WAS SCARY.
FORGIVE THE LACK OF CEREMONY, BUT...
...I HAVE TO KILL ANYONE WHO SEES US.
ANY LAST PRAYERS?
OH, WELL THEN YOU'VE NOTHING TO WORRY ABOUT, MISS.
I HAVEN'T SEEN YOU.
I'M BLIND.

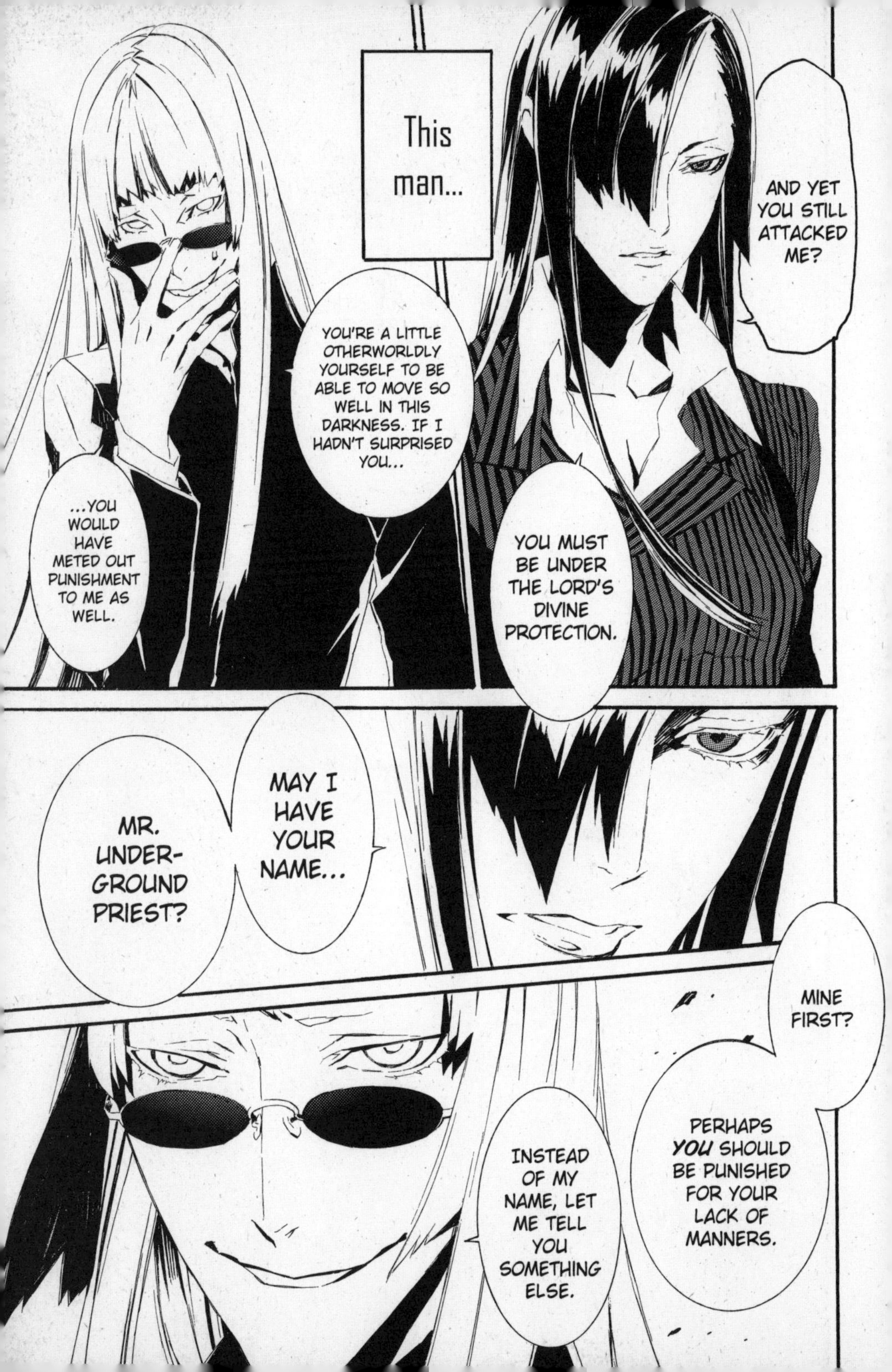
AND YET YOU STILL ATTACKED ME?
YOU MUST BE UNDER THE LORD'S DIVINE PROTECTION.
This man...
YOU'RE A LITTLE OTHERWORLDLY YOURSELF TO BE ABLE TO MOVE SO WELL IN THIS DARKNESS. IF I HADN'T SURPRISED YOU...
...YOU WOULD HAVE METED OUT PUNISHMENT TO ME AS WELL.
MAY I HAVE YOUR NAME...
MR. UNDER-GROUND PRIEST?
MINE FIRST?
PERHAPS *YOU* SHOULD BE PUNISHED FOR YOUR LACK OF MANNERS.
INSTEAD OF MY NAME, LET ME TELL YOU SOMETHING ELSE.

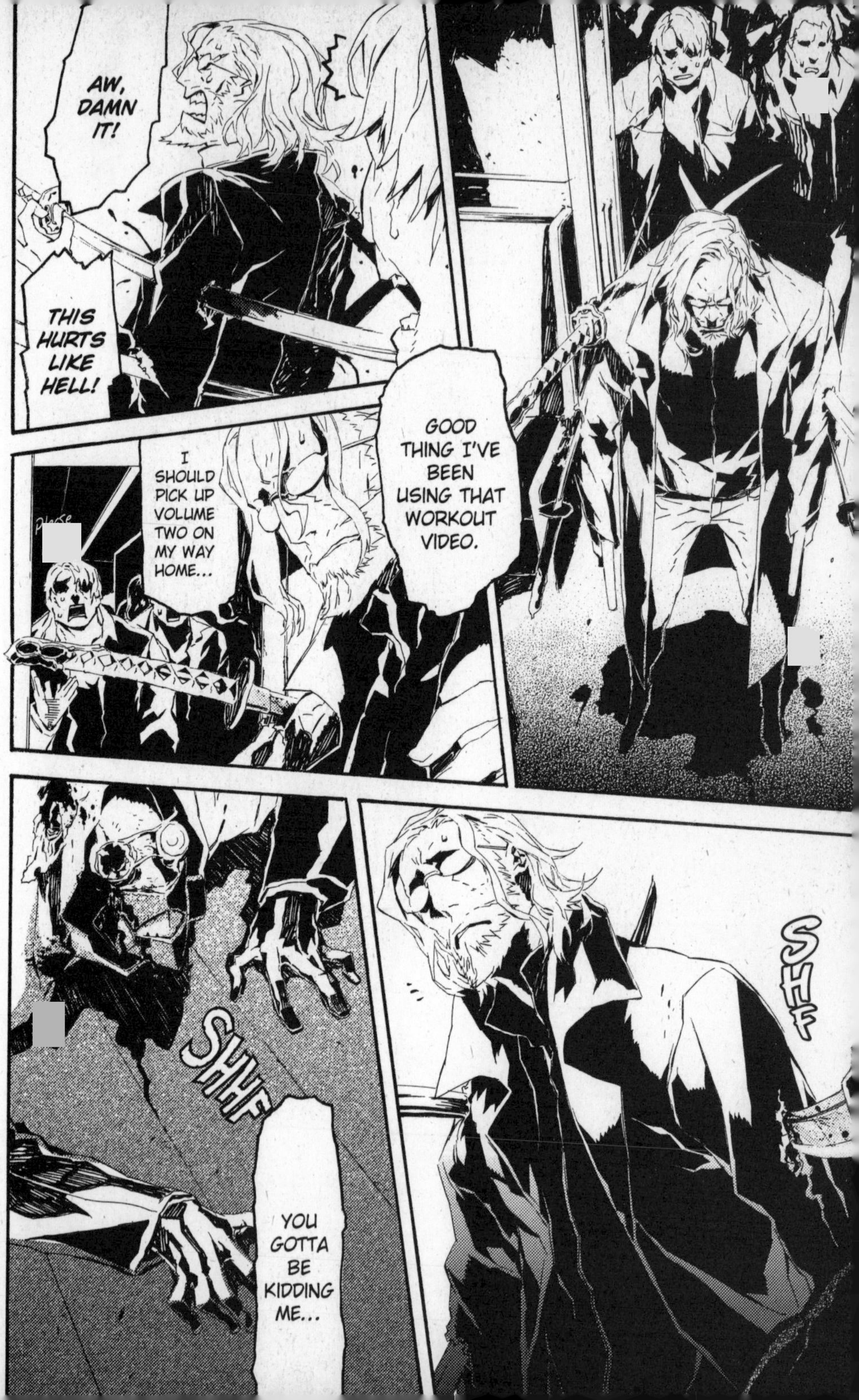
AW, DAMN IT!
THIS HURTS LIKE HELL!
GOOD THING I'VE BEEN USING THAT WORKOUT VIDEO.
I SHOULD PICK UP VOLUME TWO ON MY WAY HOME...
please
SHHF
SHHF
YOU GOTTA BE KIDDING ME...

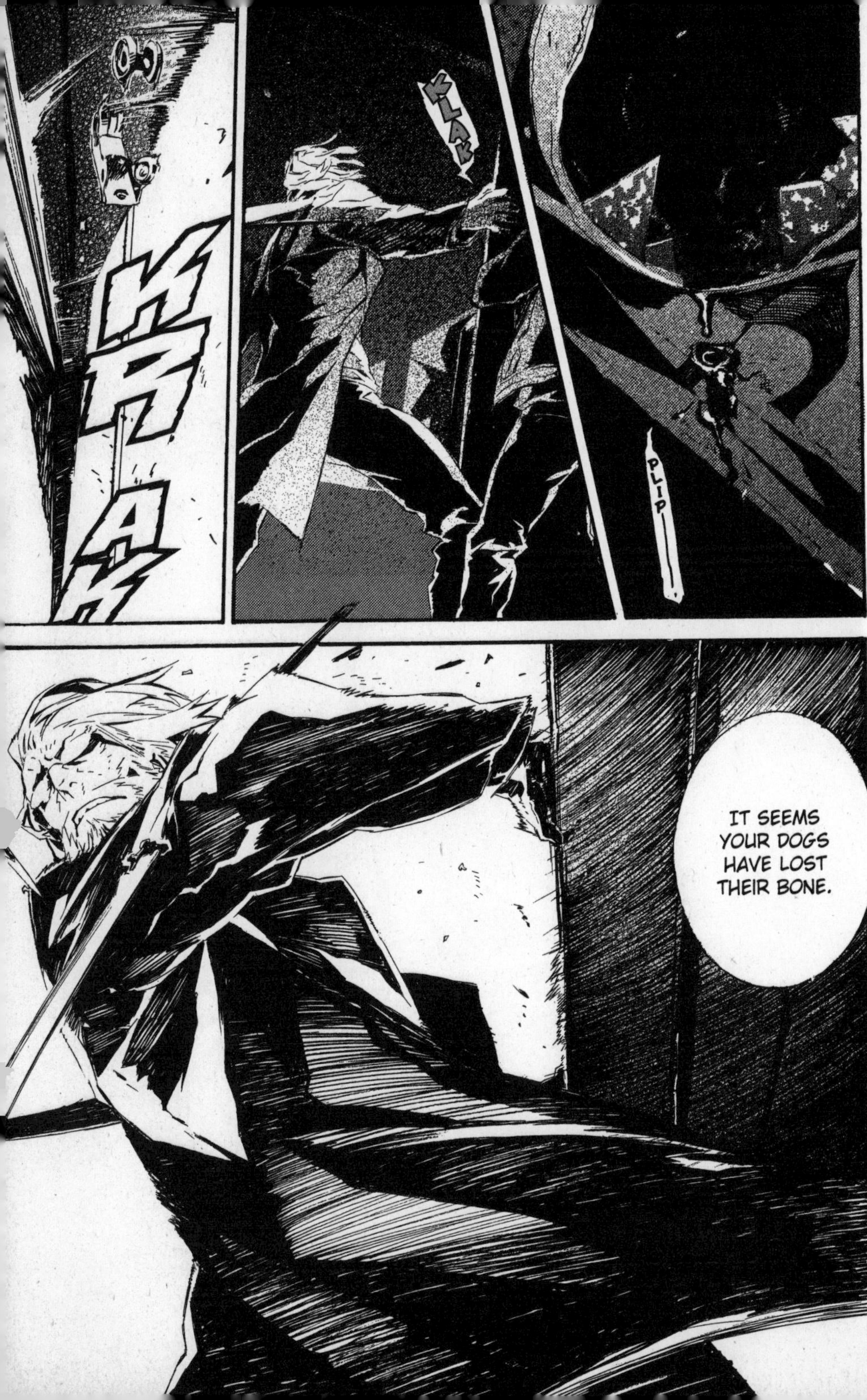
PLIP
KLAK
KRAK
IT SEEMS YOUR DOGS HAVE LOST THEIR BONE.

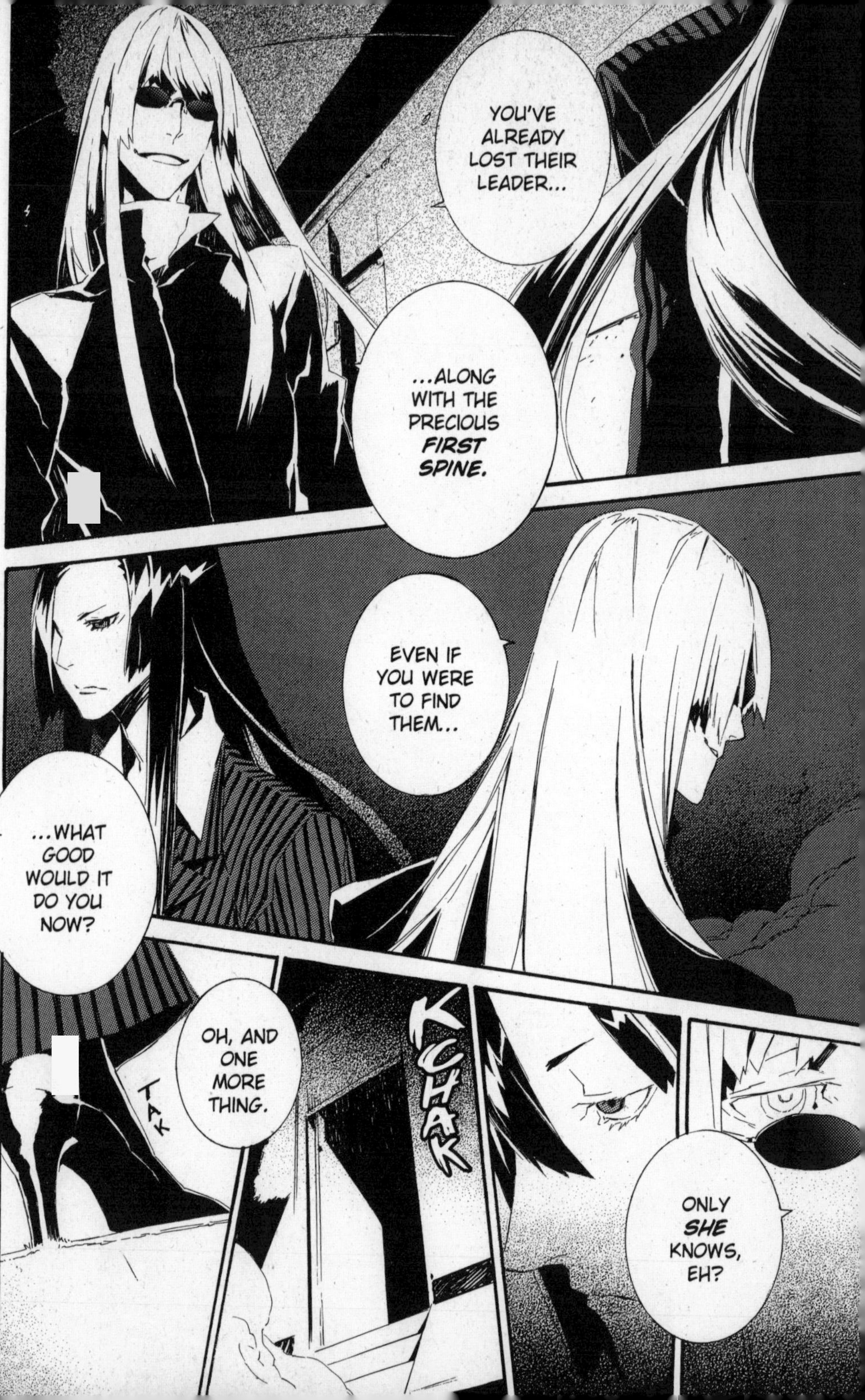
YOU'VE ALREADY LOST THEIR LEADER...
...ALONG WITH THE PRECIOUS FIRST SPINE.
EVEN IF YOU WERE TO FIND THEM...
...WHAT GOOD WOULD IT DO YOU NOW?
ONLY SHE KNOWS, EH?
KCHAK
OH, AND ONE MORE THING.
TAK

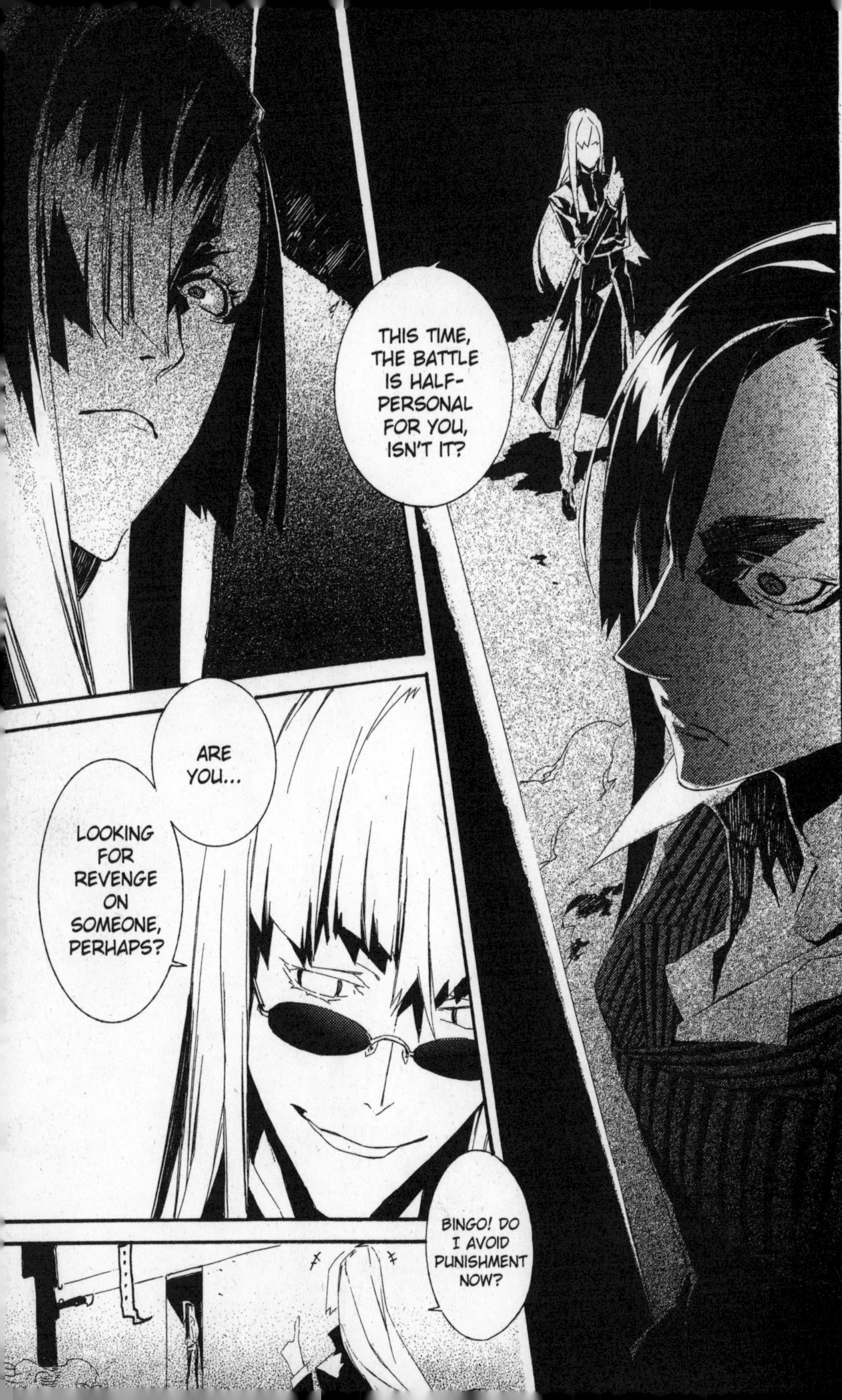
THIS TIME, THE BATTLE IS HALF-PERSONAL FOR YOU, ISN'T IT?
ARE YOU...
LOOKING FOR REVENGE ON SOMEONE, PERHAPS?
BINGO! DO I AVOID PUNISHMENT NOW?

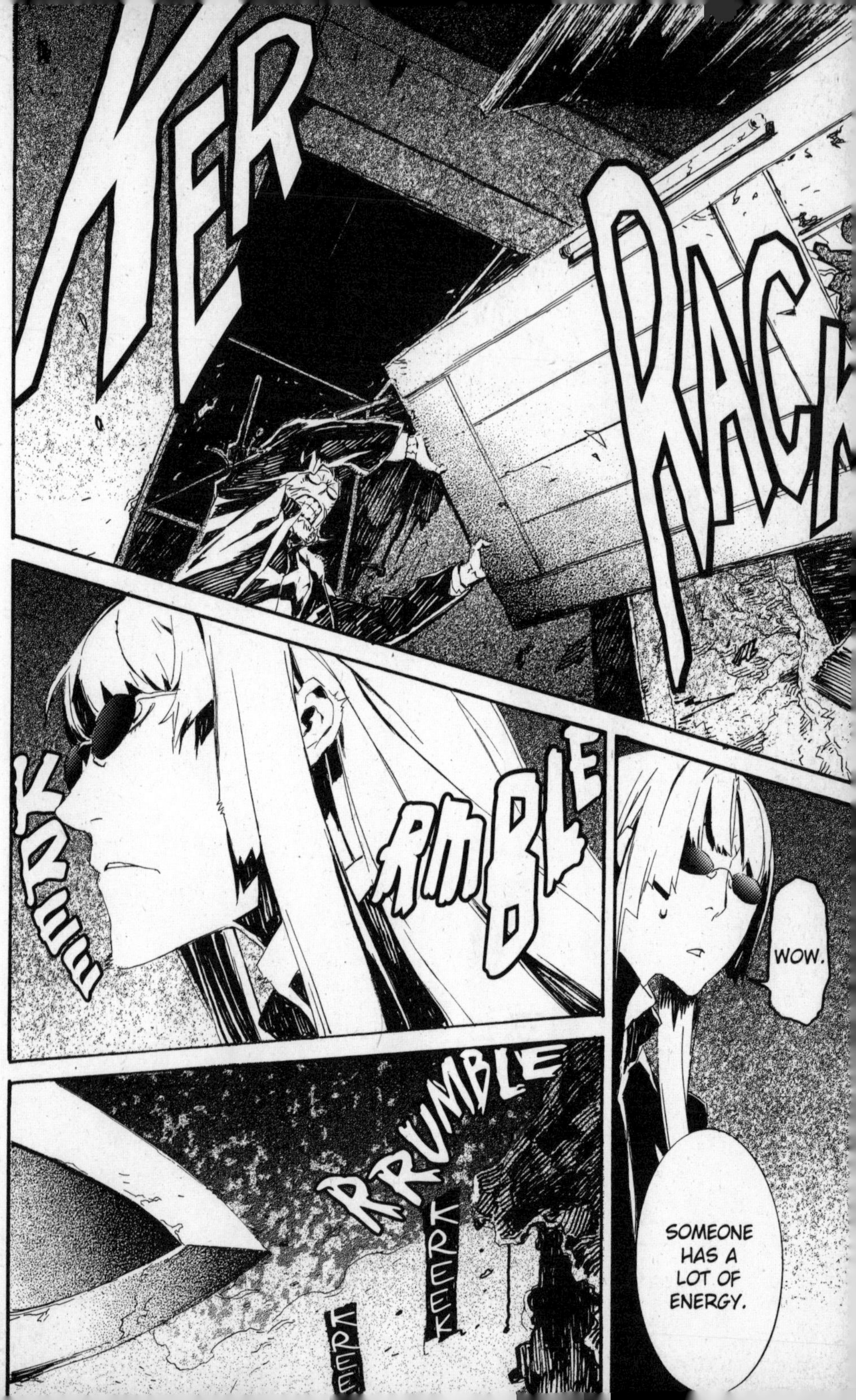
KER
RACK
WOW.
SOMEONE HAS A LOT OF ENERGY.
KRMMM
RMBLE
RRUMBLE
KREEK
KREE

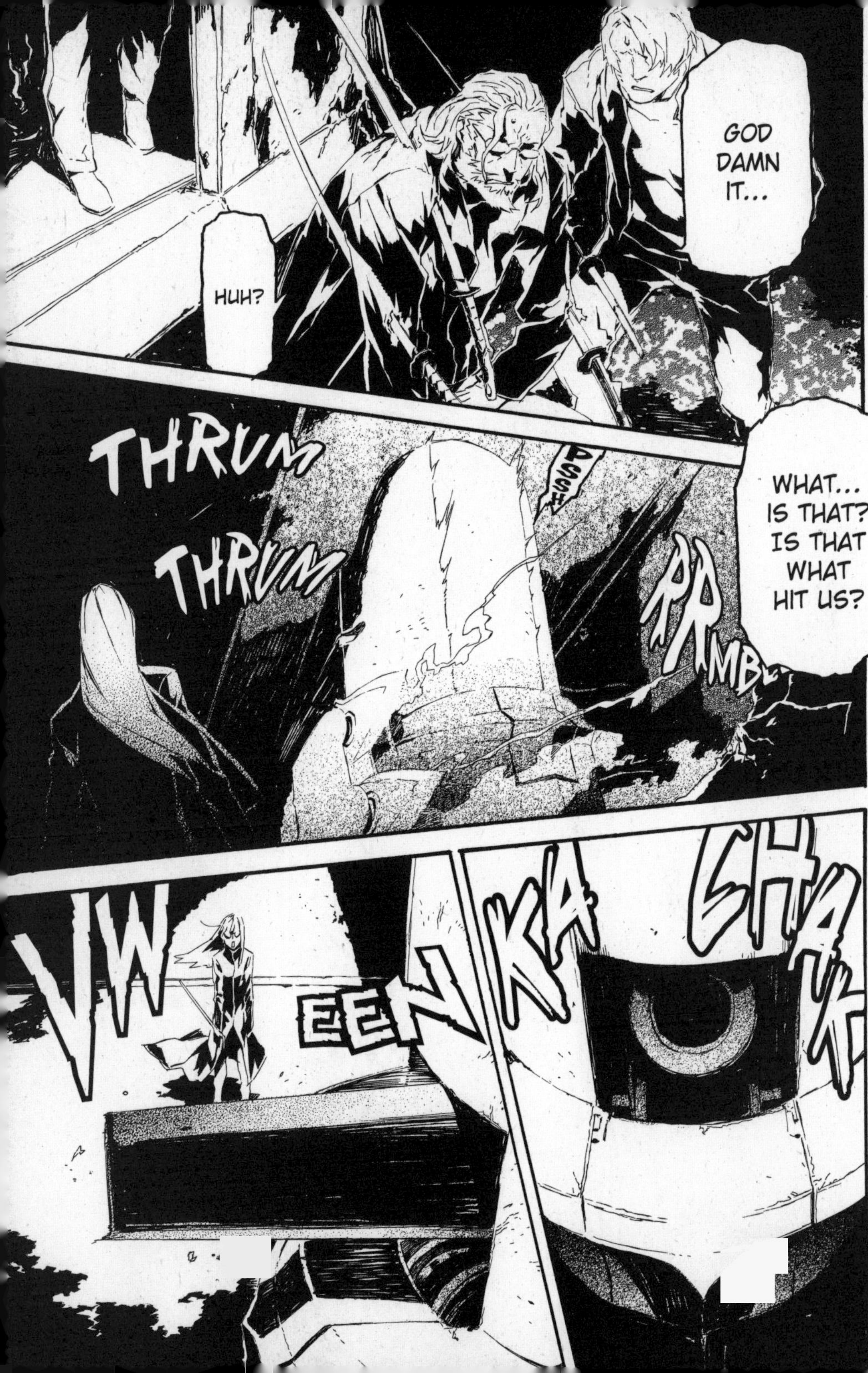
GOD DAMN IT...
HUH?
WHAT... IS THAT? IS THAT WHAT HIT US?
RRMB
PSSH
THRUM
THRUM
KA CHAK
VWEEN

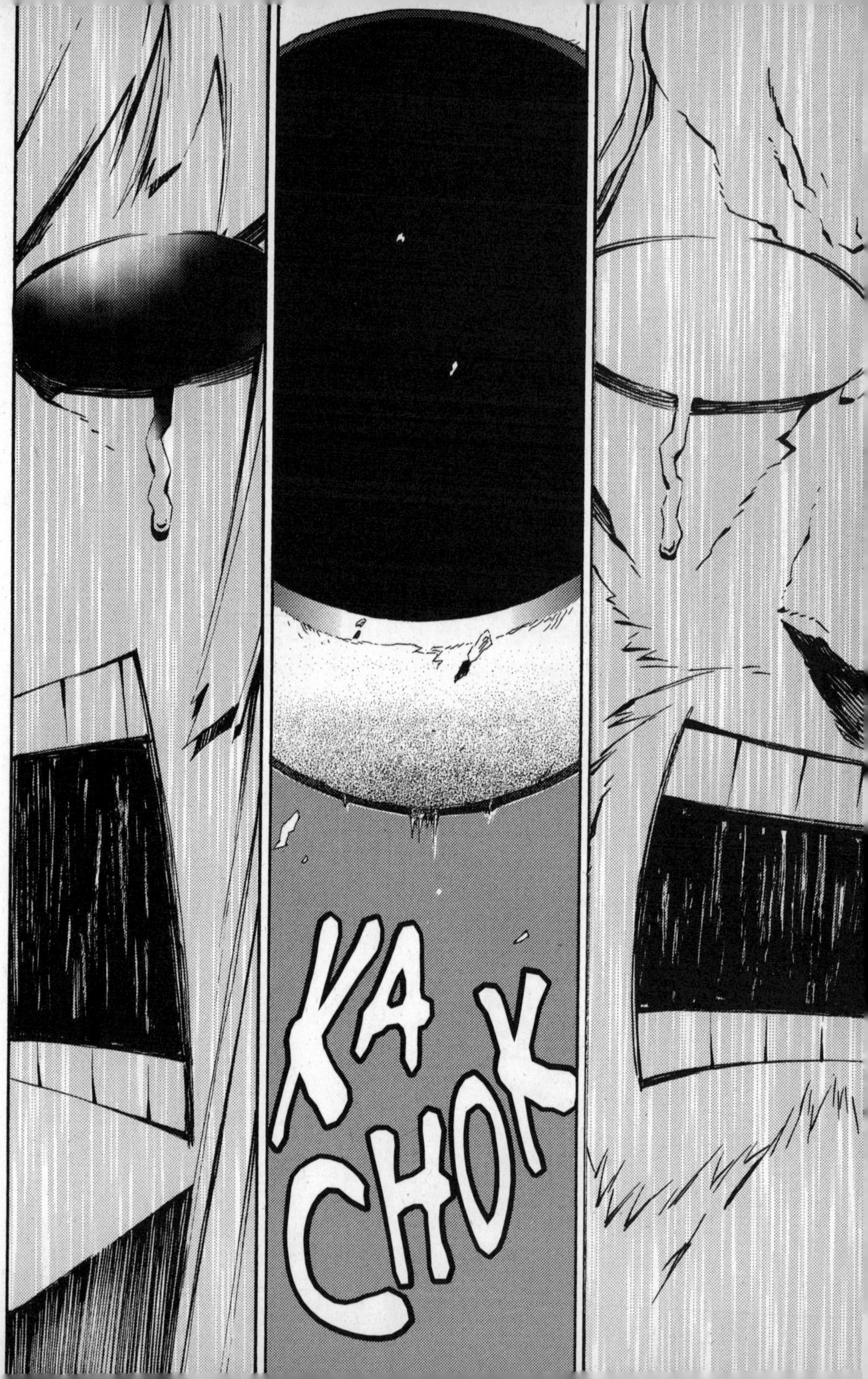
KA CHOK

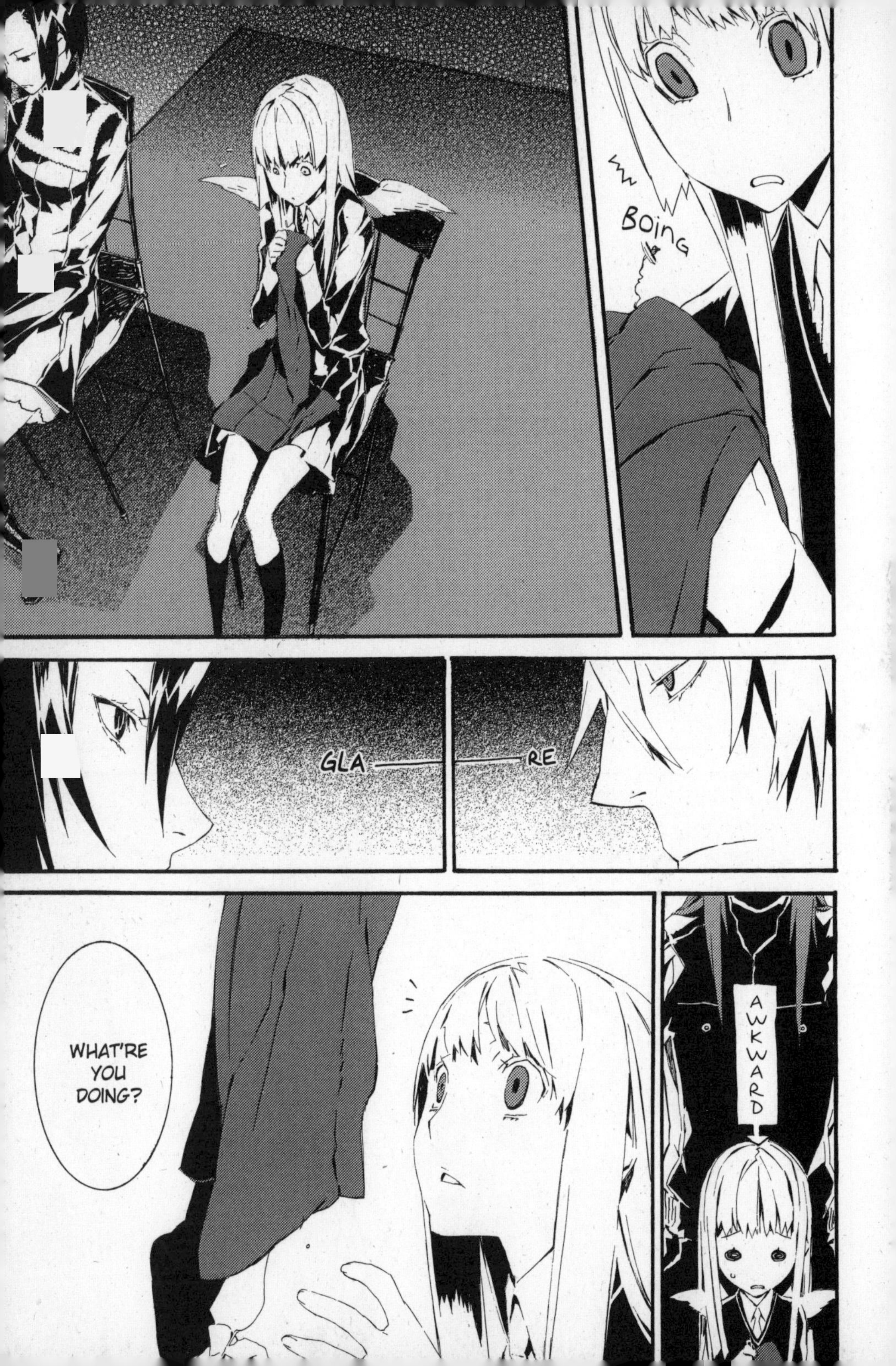
BOING
GLA——RE
AWKWARD
WHAT'RE YOU DOING?

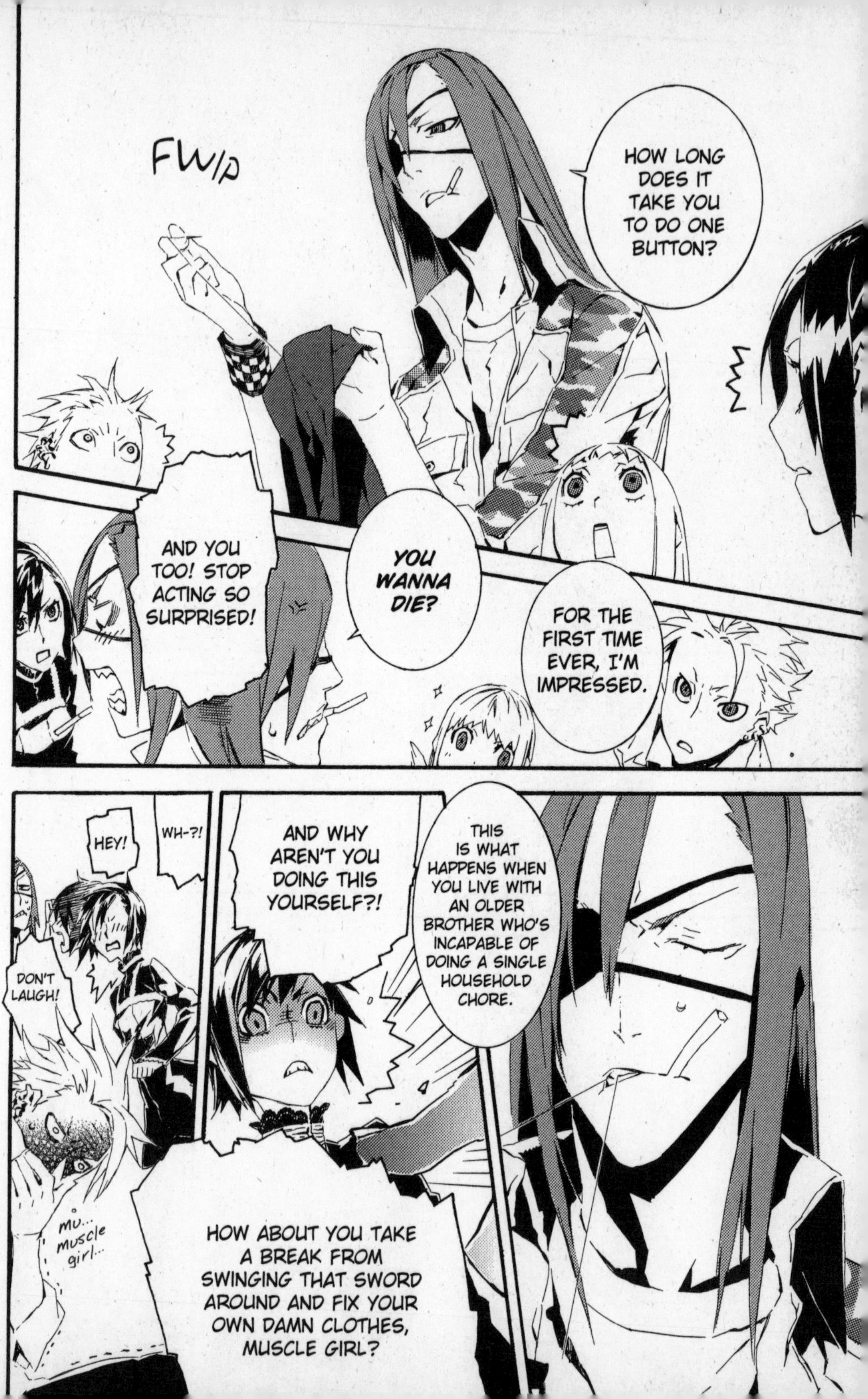
HOW LONG DOES IT TAKE YOU TO DO ONE BUTTON?
FWIP
FOR THE FIRST TIME EVER, I'M IMPRESSED.
YOU WANNA DIE?
AND YOU TOO! STOP ACTING SO SURPRISED!
THIS IS WHAT HAPPENS WHEN YOU LIVE WITH AN OLDER BROTHER WHO'S INCAPABLE OF DOING A SINGLE HOUSEHOLD CHORE.
AND WHY AREN'T YOU DOING THIS YOURSELF?!
HOW ABOUT YOU TAKE A BREAK FROM SWINGING THAT SWORD AROUND AND FIX YOUR OWN DAMN CLOTHES, MUSCLE GIRL?
WH-?!
HEY!
DON'T LAUGH!
mu... muscle girl...

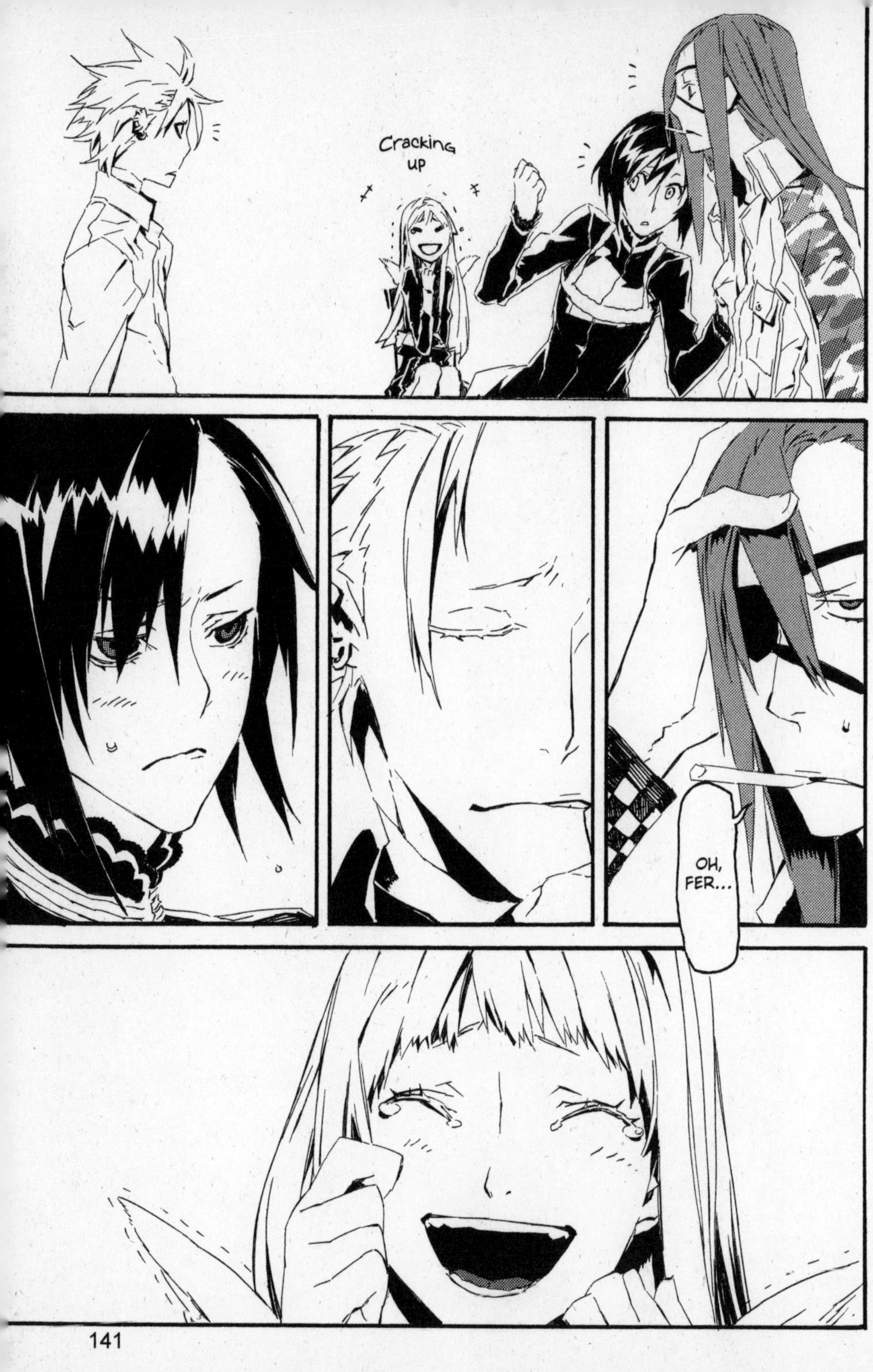
Cracking up
OH, FER...

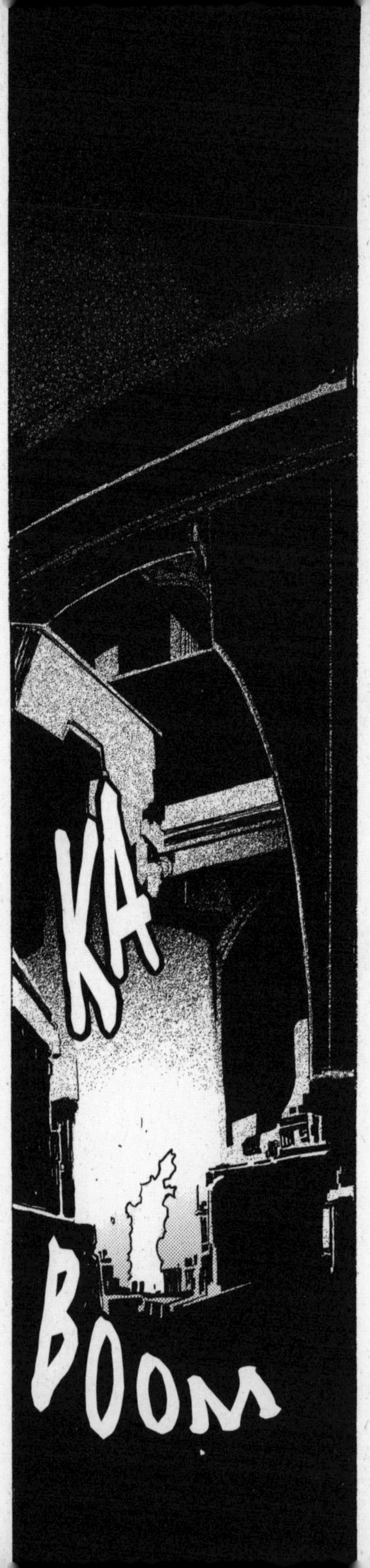
KA-BOOM

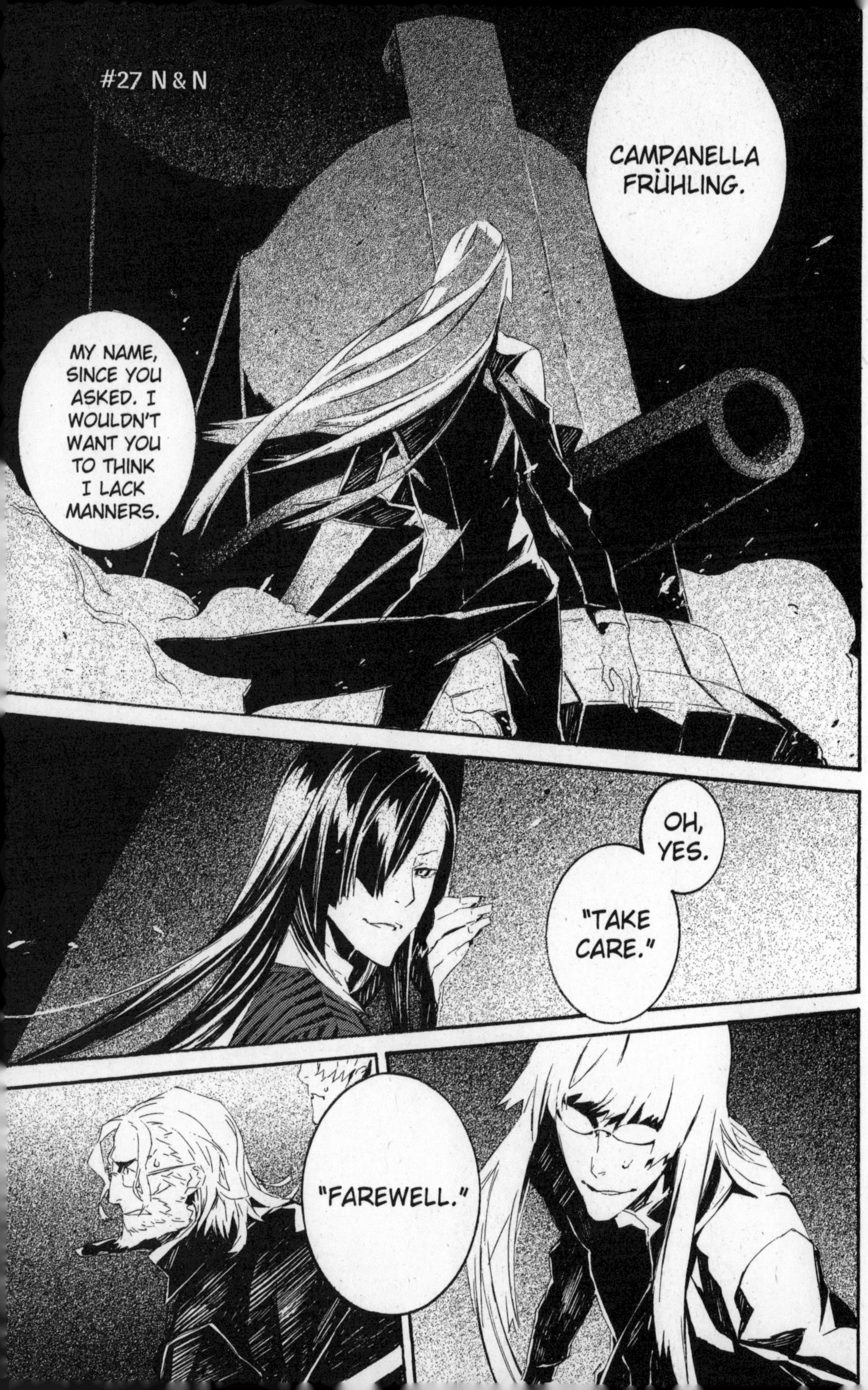
#27 N & N
CAMPANELLA FRÜHLING.
MY NAME, SINCE YOU ASKED. I WOULDN'T WANT YOU TO THINK I LACK MANNERS.
OH, YES.
"TAKE CARE."
"FAREWELL."

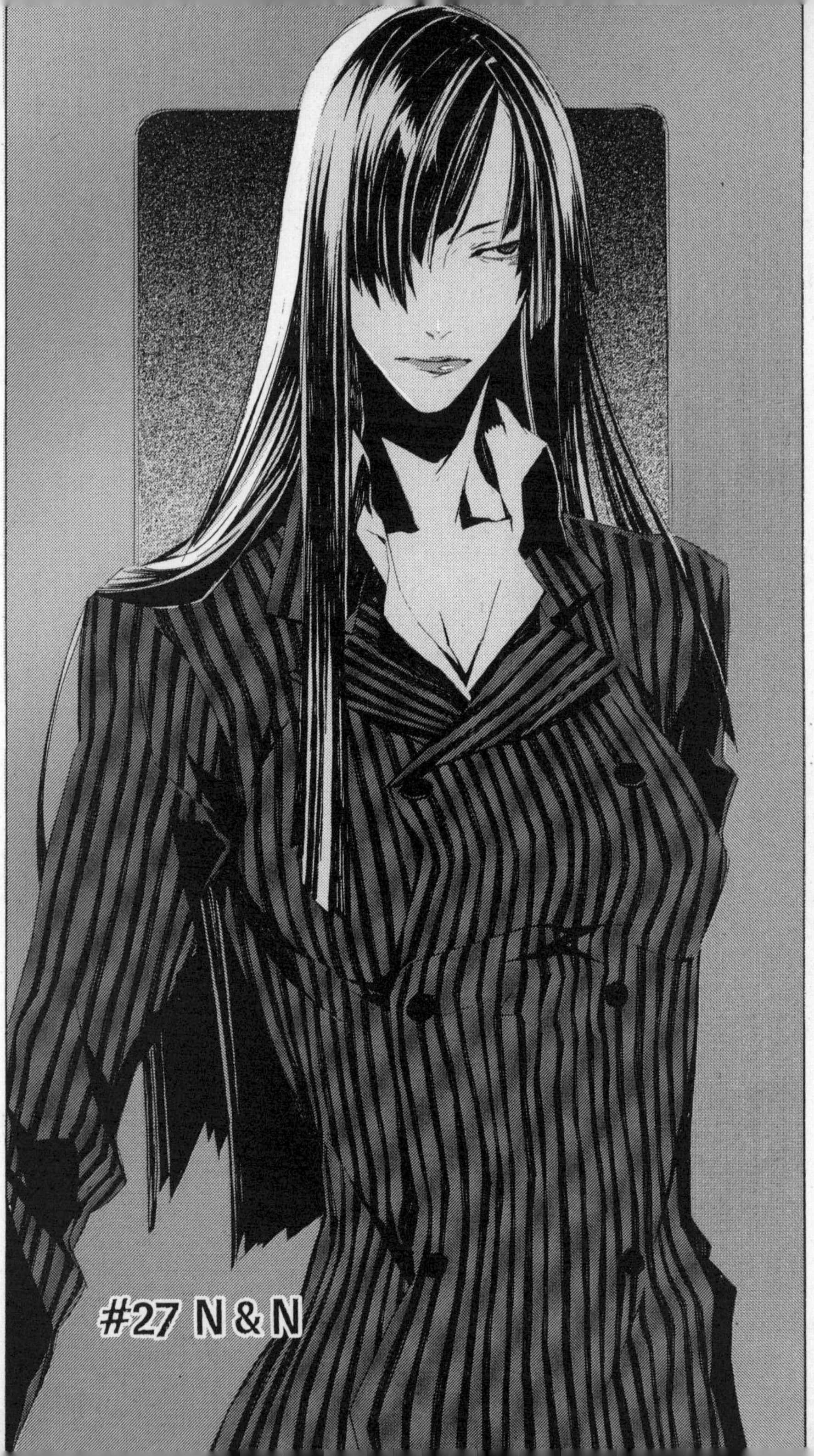
#27 N & N

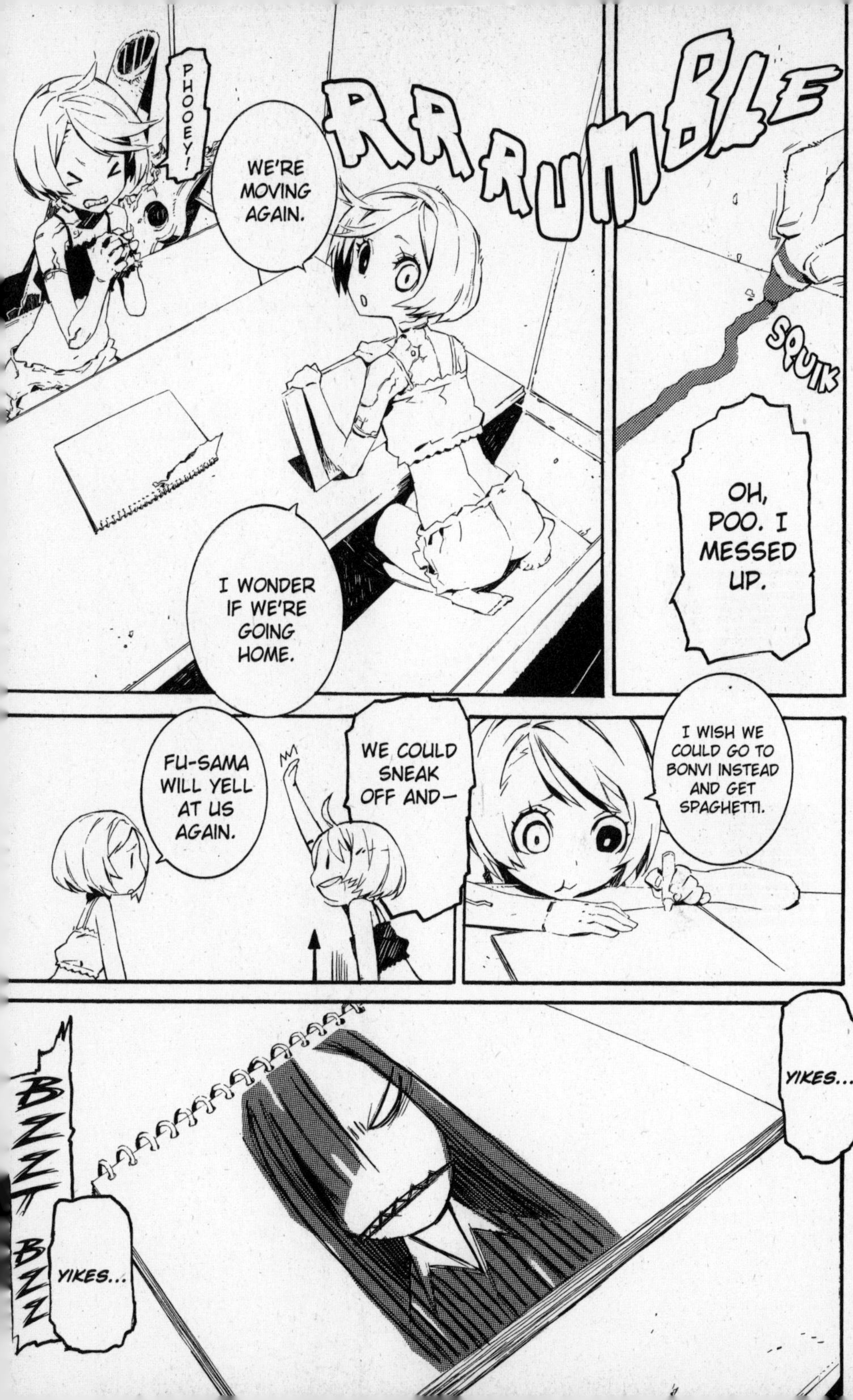
SQUIK
OH, POO. I MESSED UP.
RRRUMBLE
WE'RE MOVING AGAIN.
PHOOEY!
I WONDER IF WE'RE GOING HOME.
I WISH WE COULD GO TO BONVI INSTEAD AND GET SPAGHETTI.
WE COULD SNEAK OFF AND—
FU-SAMA WILL YELL AT US AGAIN.
YIKES...
BZZZT
BZZZ
YIKES...

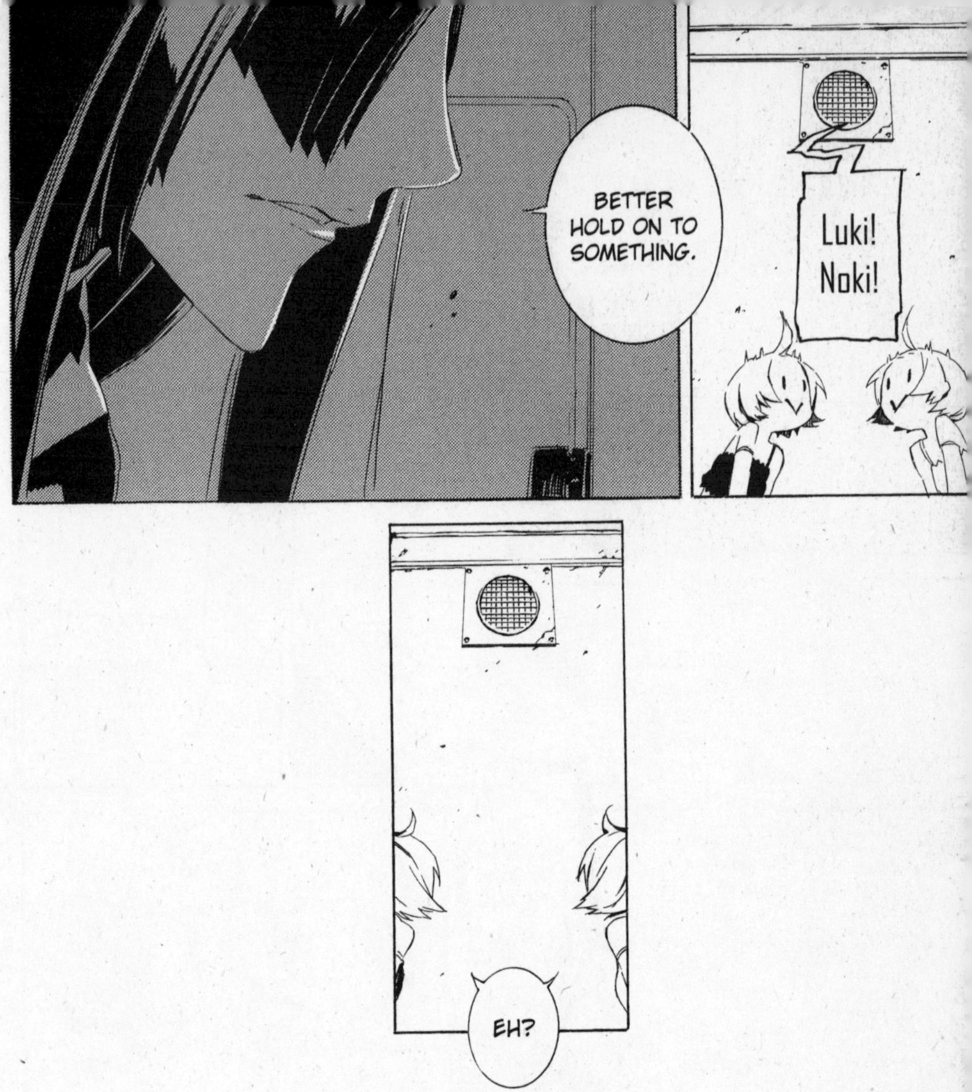
Luki! Noki!
BETTER HOLD ON TO SOMETHING.
EH?

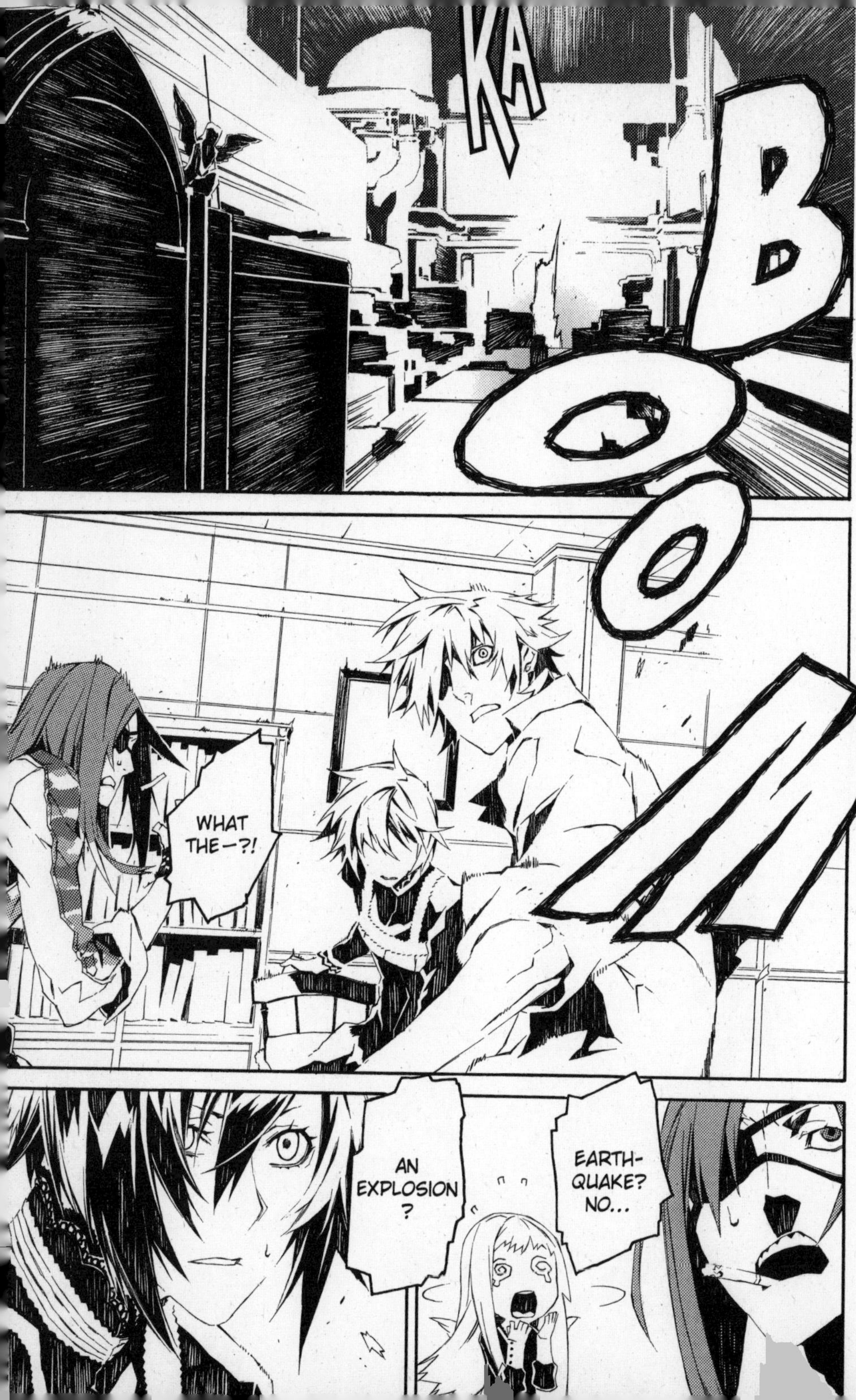
KA
BOOM
WHAT THE—?!
EARTH-QUAKE? NO...
AN EXPLOSION?

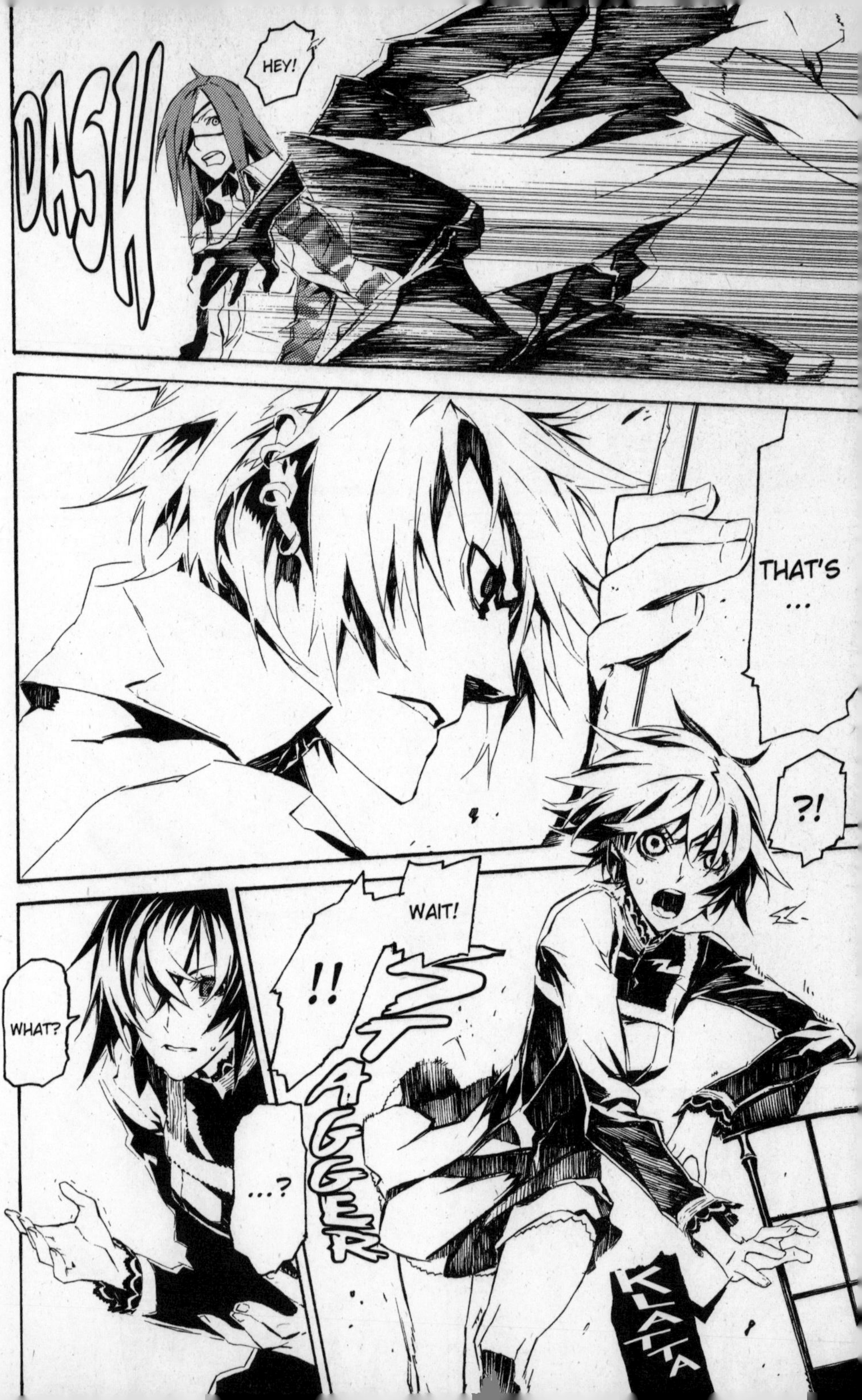
HEY!
DASH
THAT'S ...
?!
WAIT!
!!
STAGGER
KLATTA
WHAT?
...?

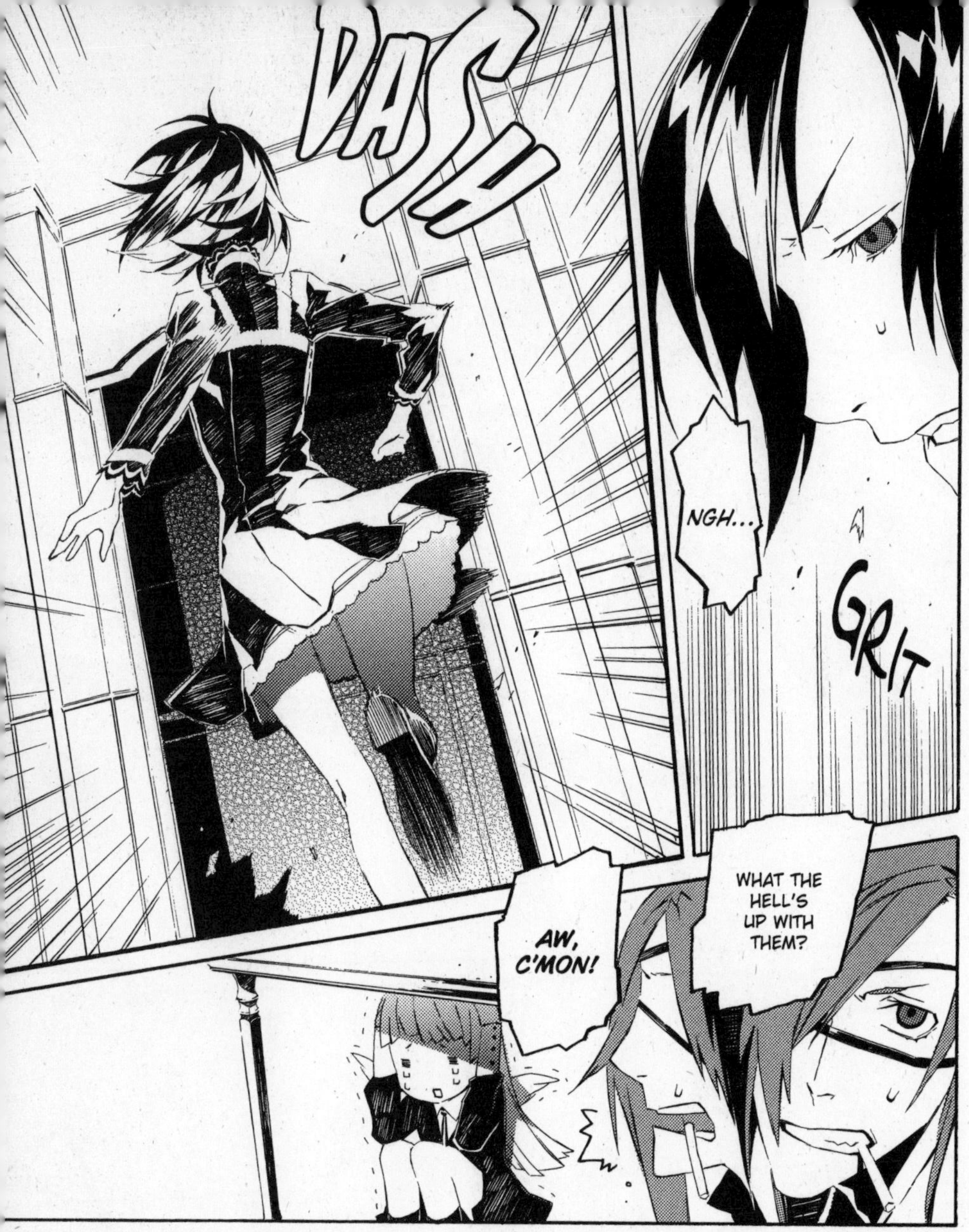
NGH...
GRIT
DASH
WHAT THE HELL'S UP WITH THEM?
AW, C'MON!

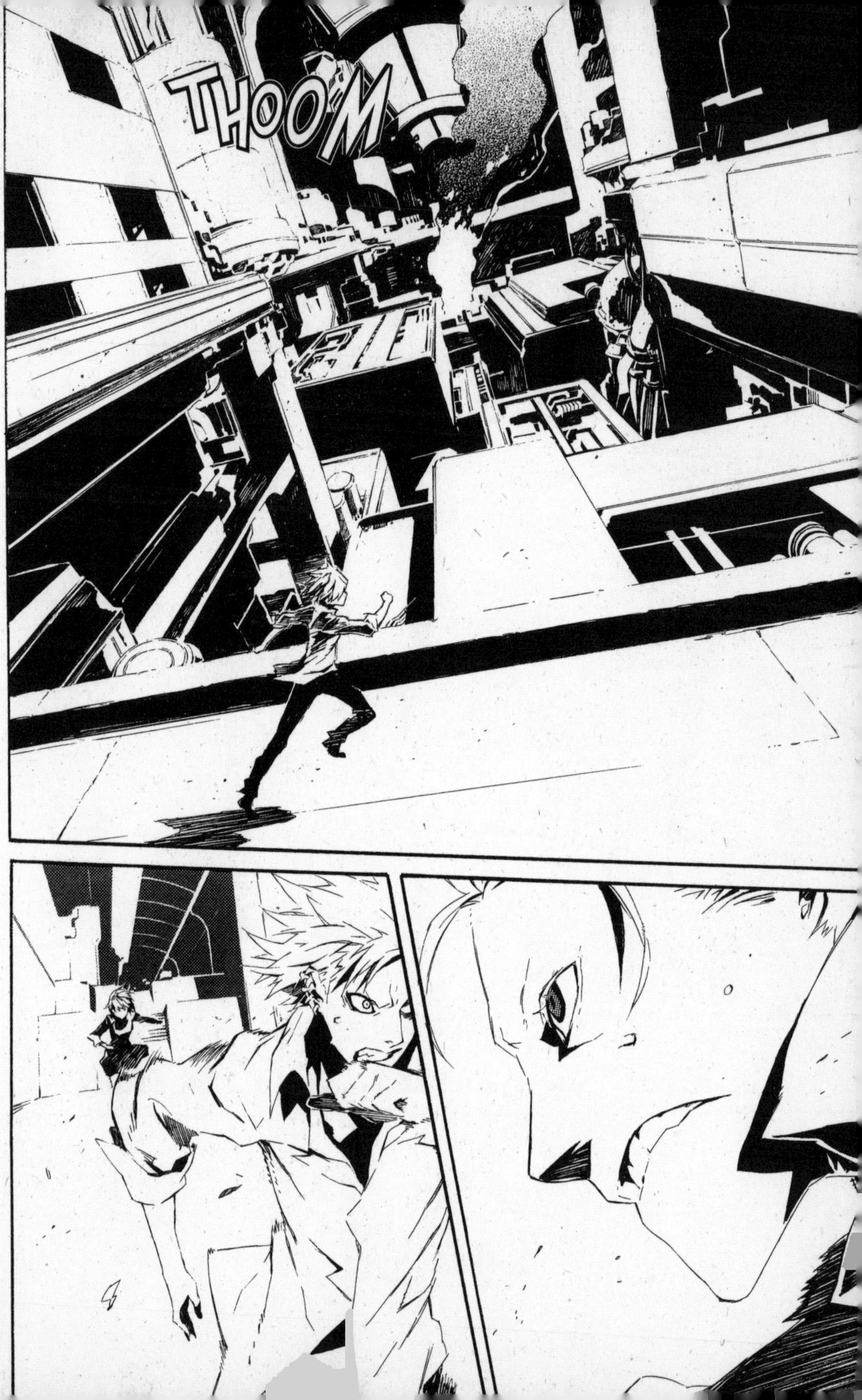
THOOM

TUMP

THUD

SKRITT

AGH!

WHAT'S WRONG WITH ME?

WHAT AM I SO AFRAID OF?

WHAT...

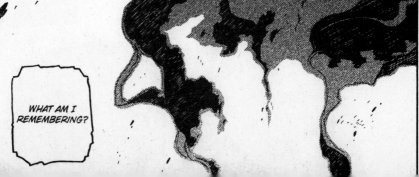

WHAT AM I REMEMBERING?

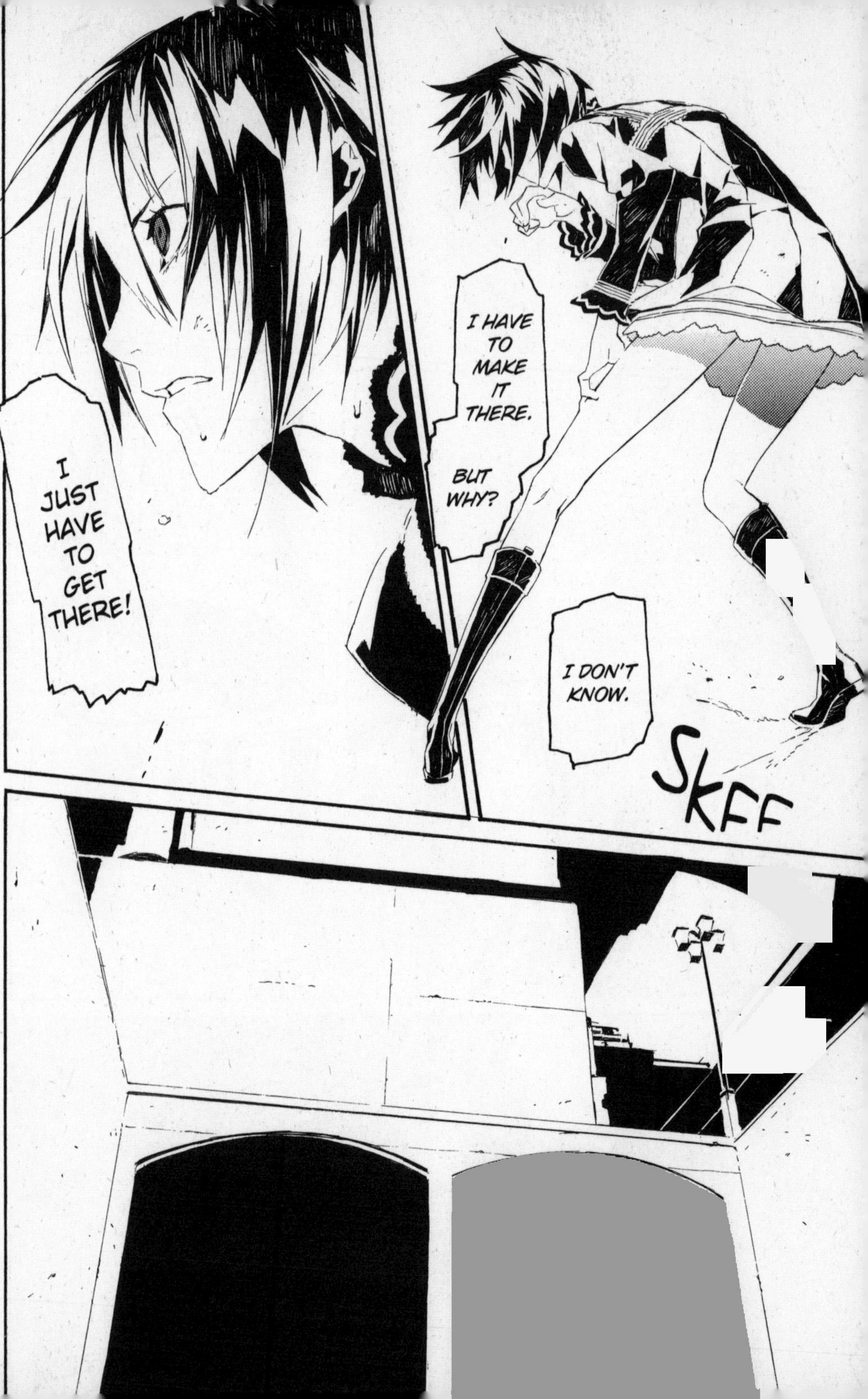
I HAVE TO MAKE IT THERE.
BUT WHY?
I DON'T KNOW.
SKFF
I JUST HAVE TO GET THERE!

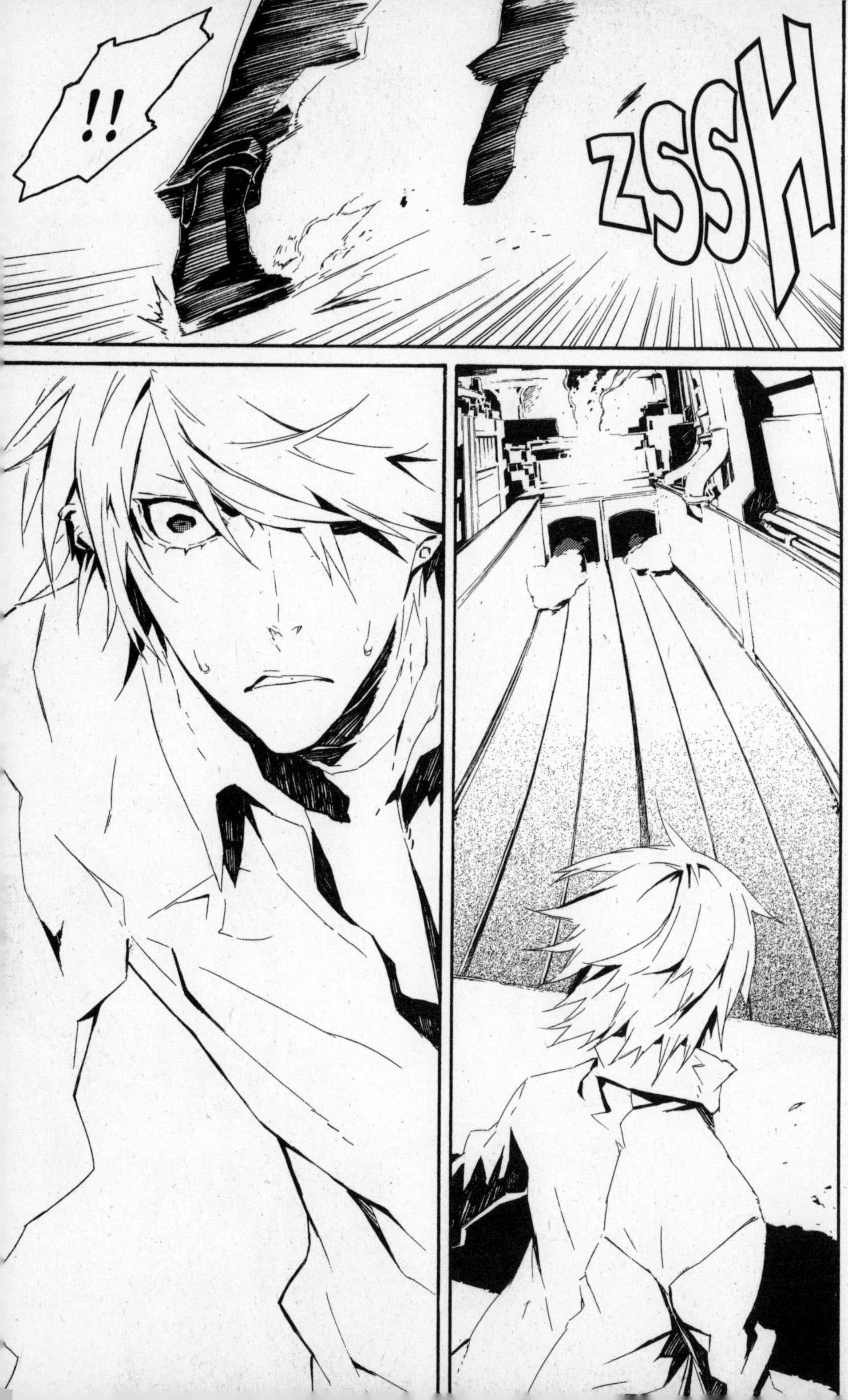
ZSSH
!!

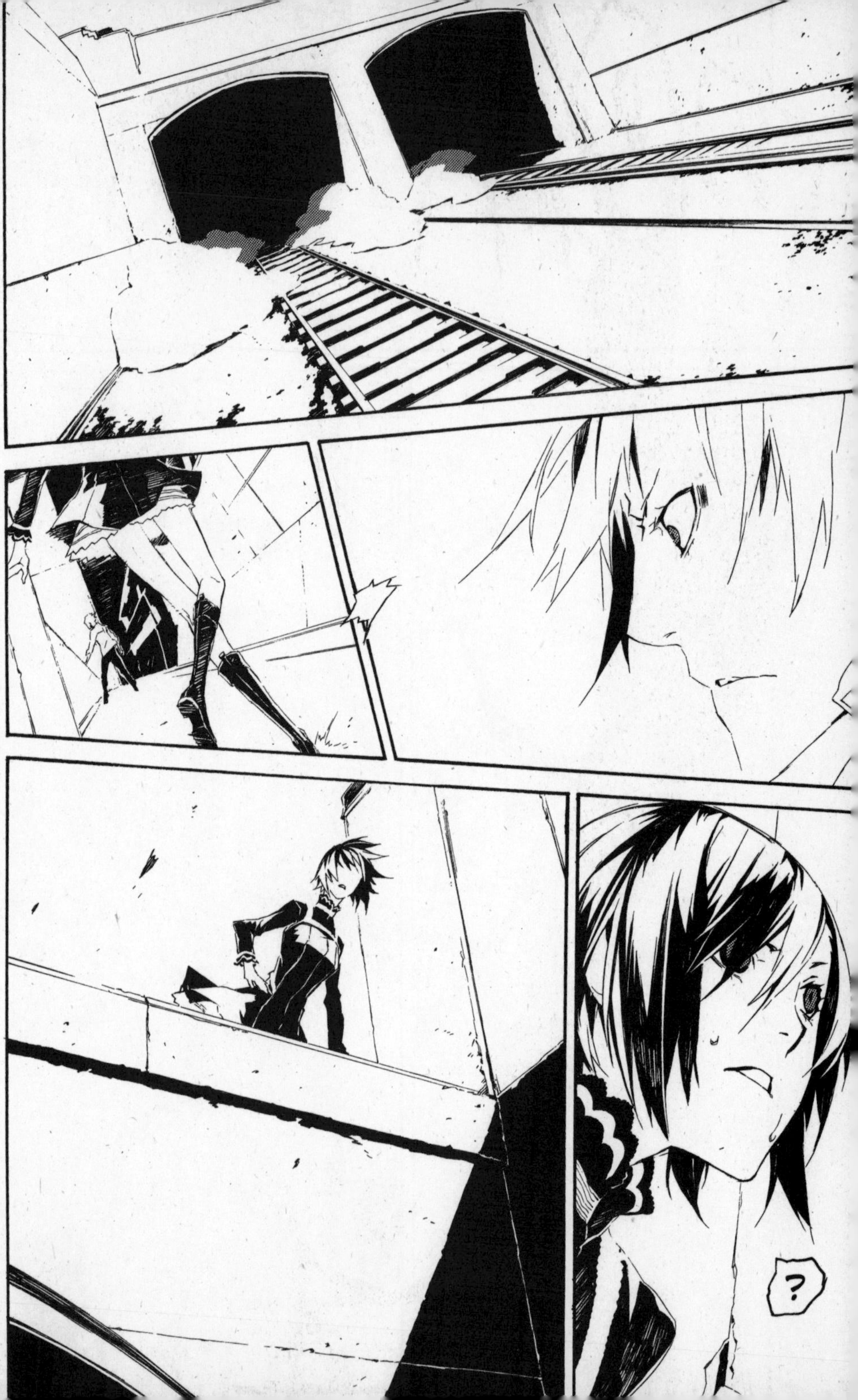
?

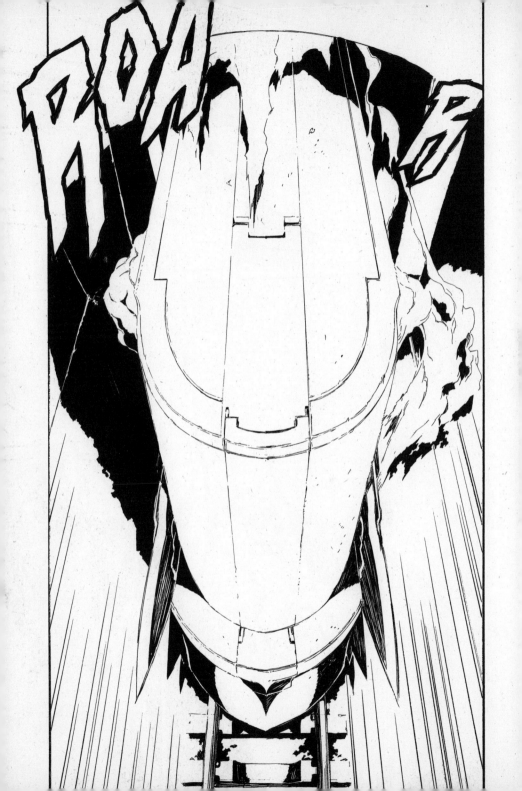

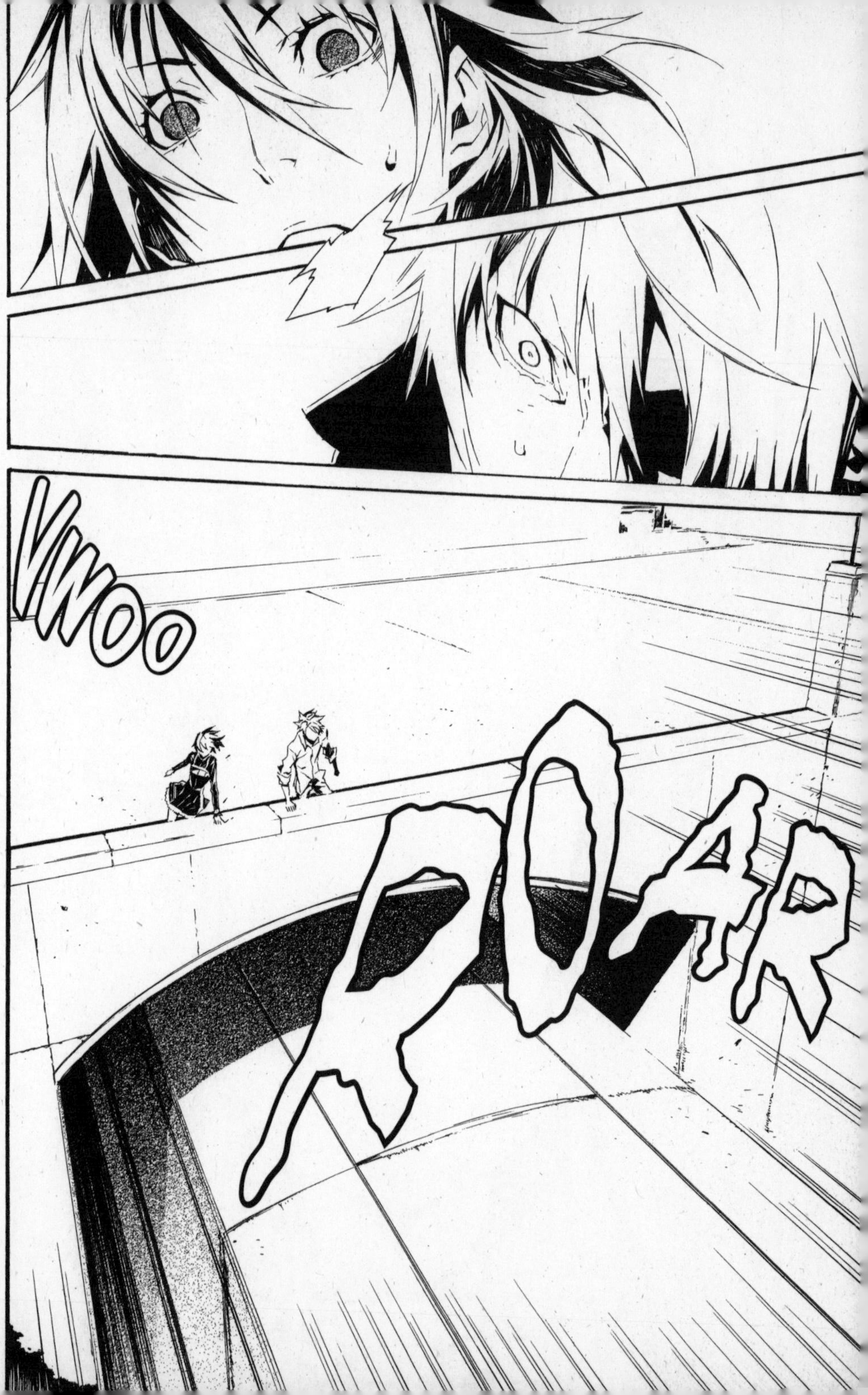
VWOO
DOAR

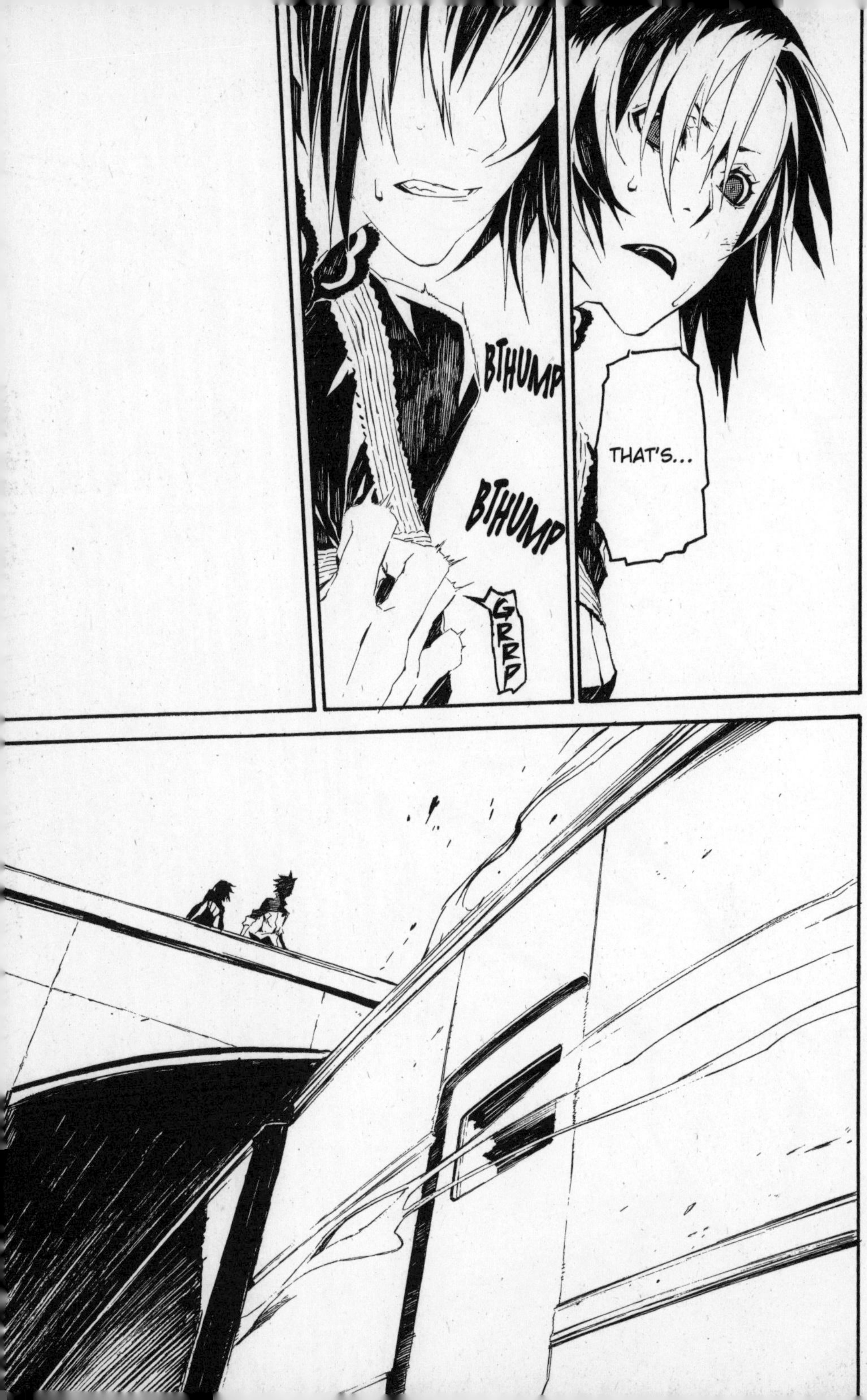
THAT'S...
BTHUMP
BTHUMP
GRRP

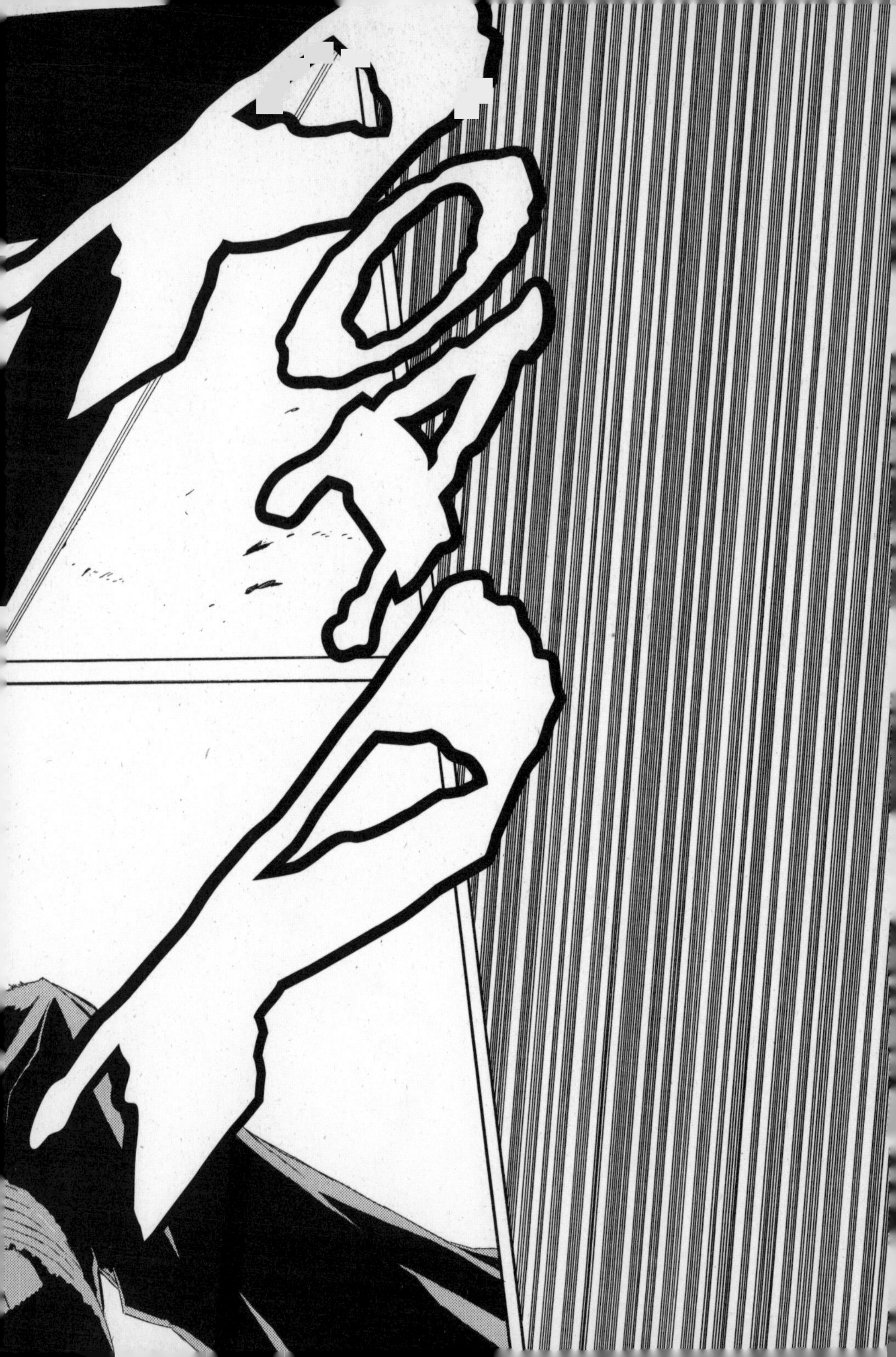

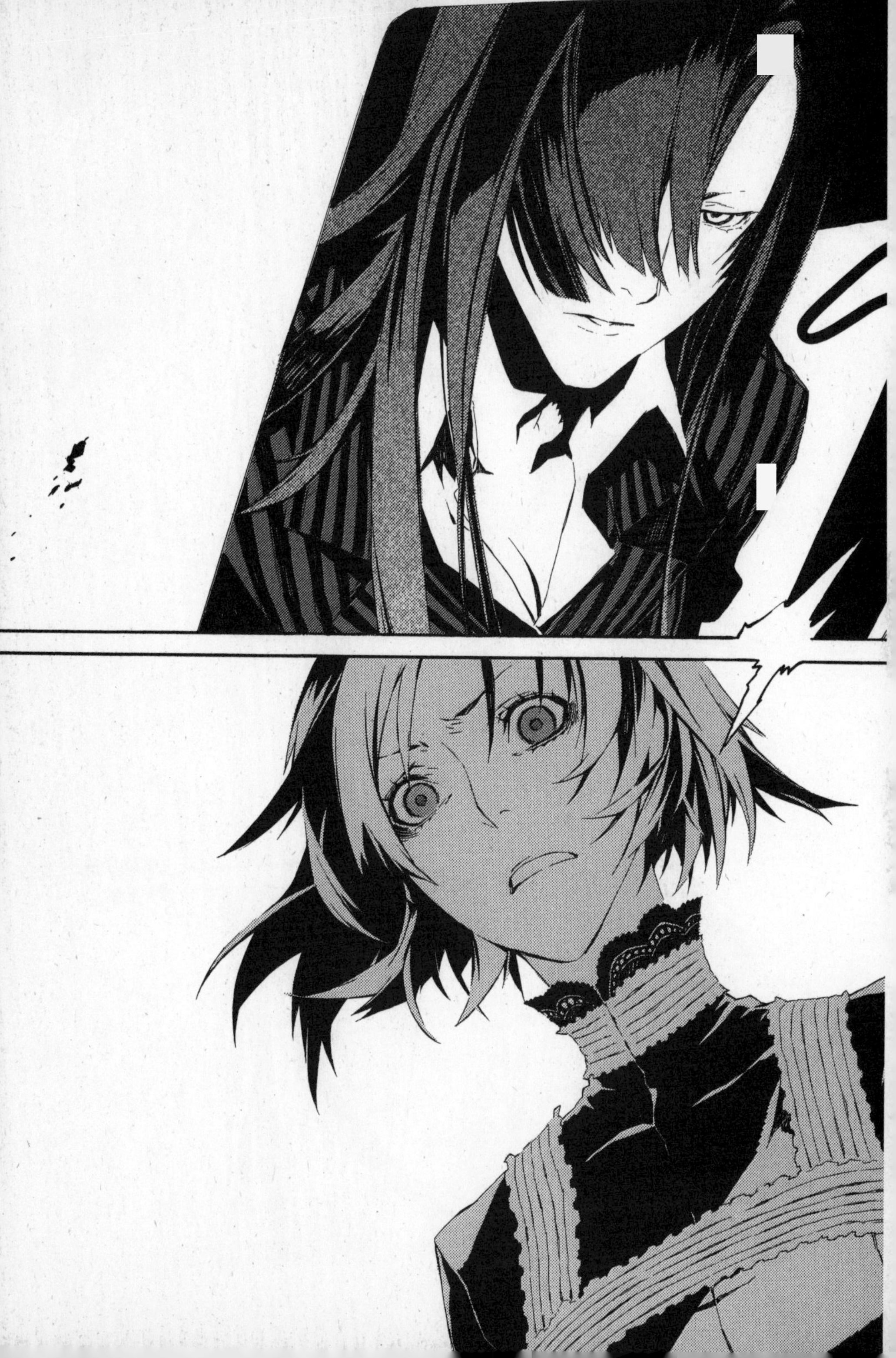

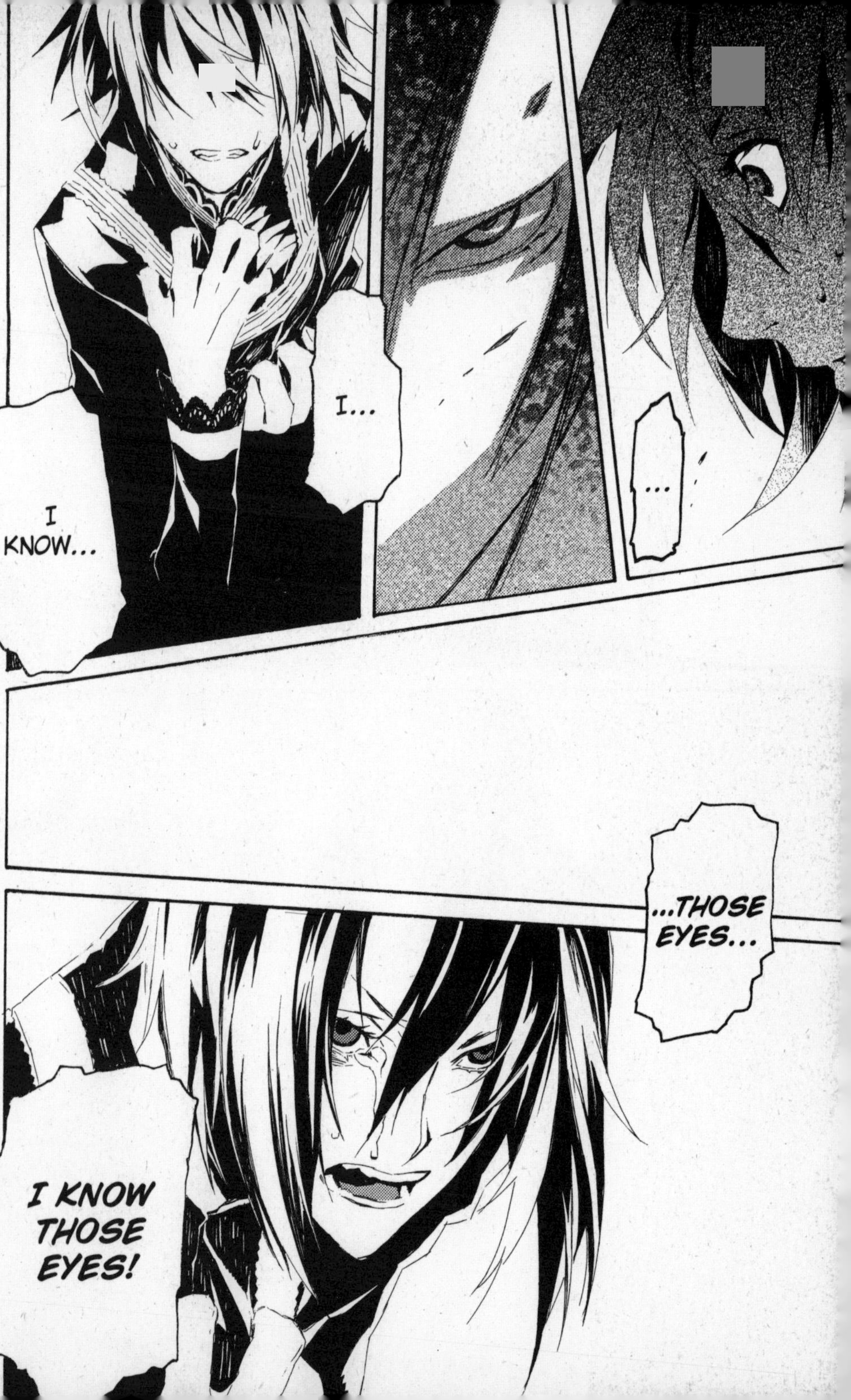
...
I...
I KNOW...
...THOSE EYES...
I KNOW THOSE EYES!

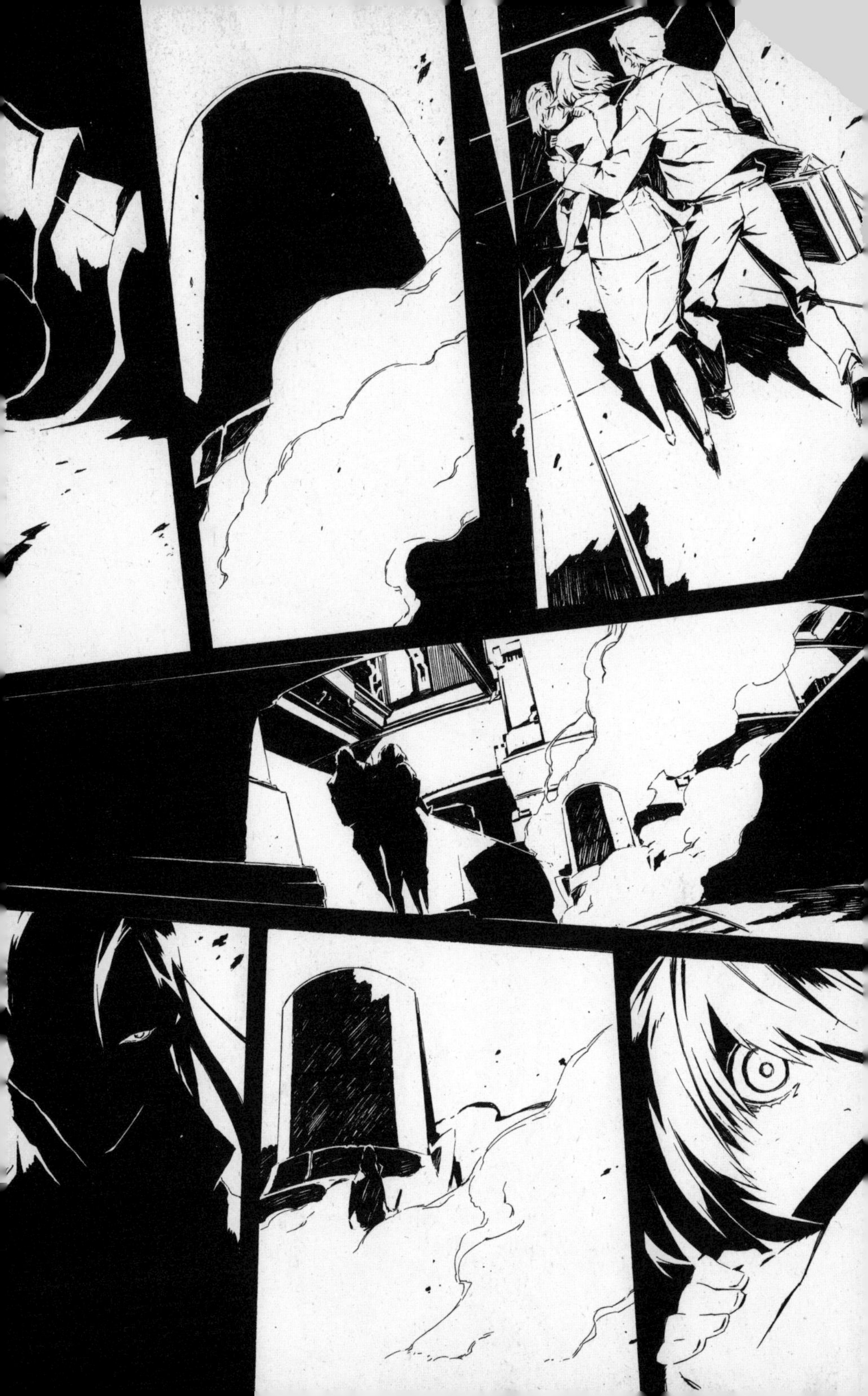

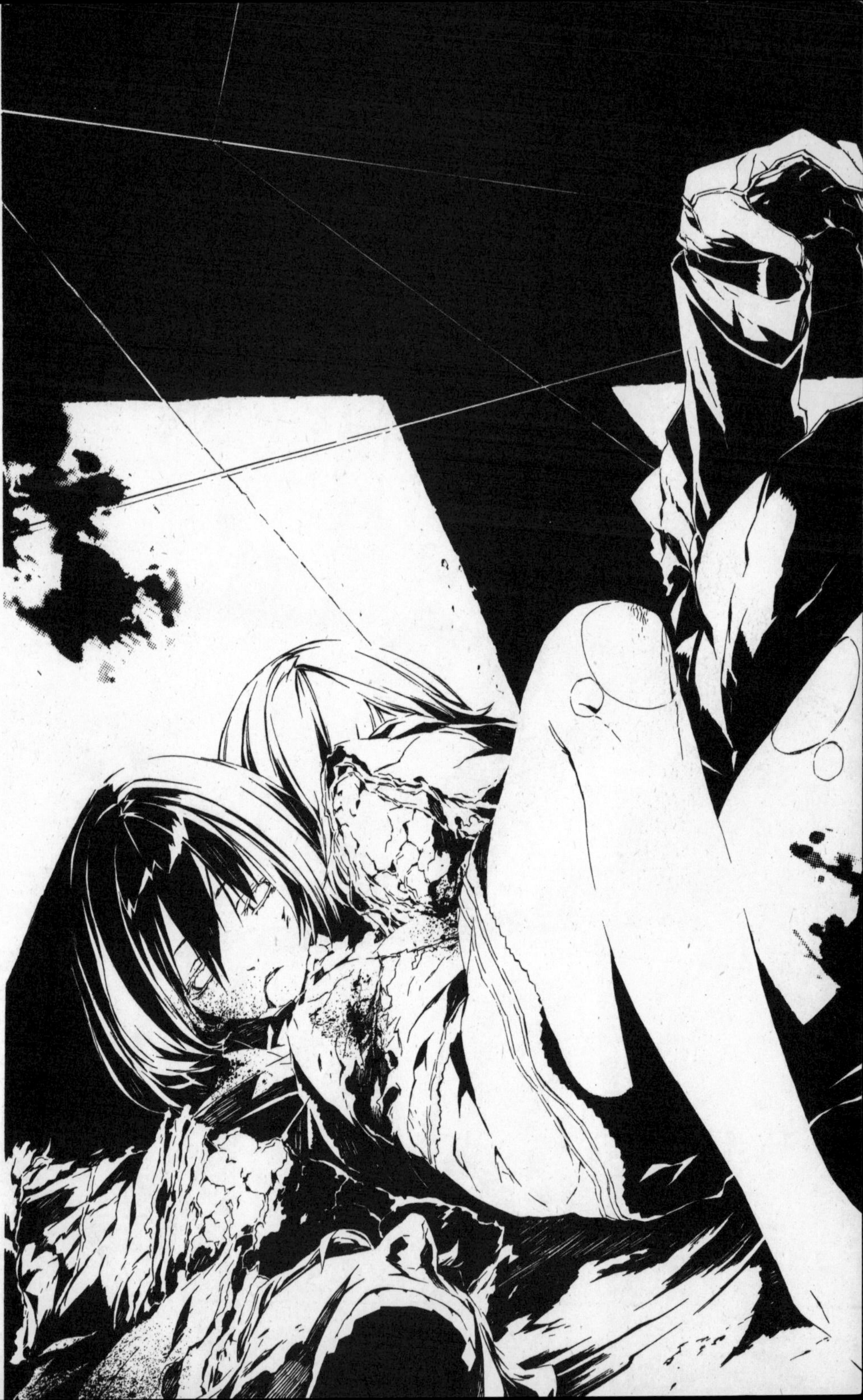

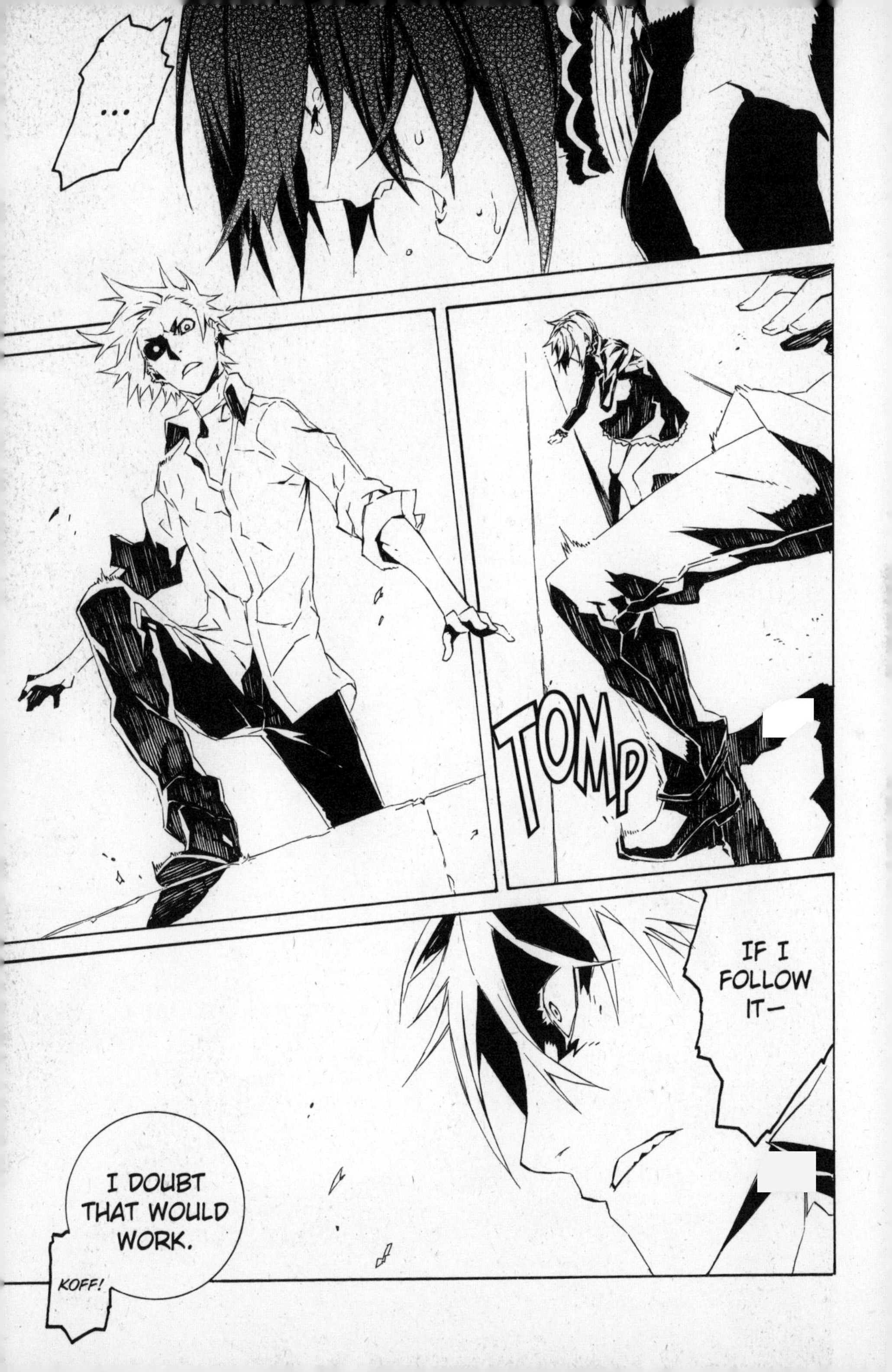
...
TOMP
IF I FOLLOW IT—
I DOUBT THAT WOULD WORK.
KOFF!

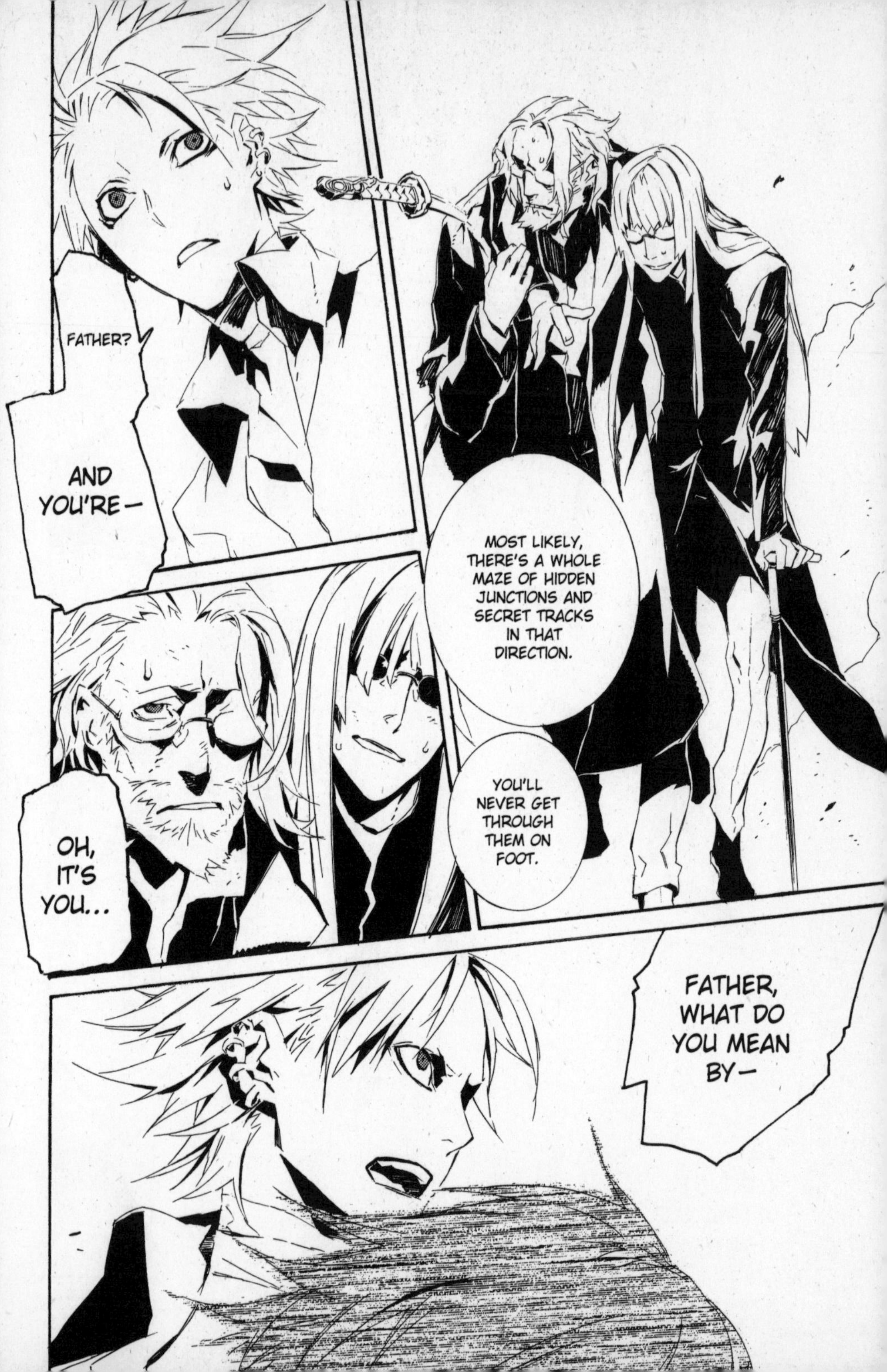
MOST LIKELY, THERE'S A WHOLE MAZE OF HIDDEN JUNCTIONS AND SECRET TRACKS IN THAT DIRECTION.
YOU'LL NEVER GET THROUGH THEM ON FOOT.
FATHER?
AND YOU'RE—
OH, IT'S YOU...
FATHER, WHAT DO YOU MEAN BY—

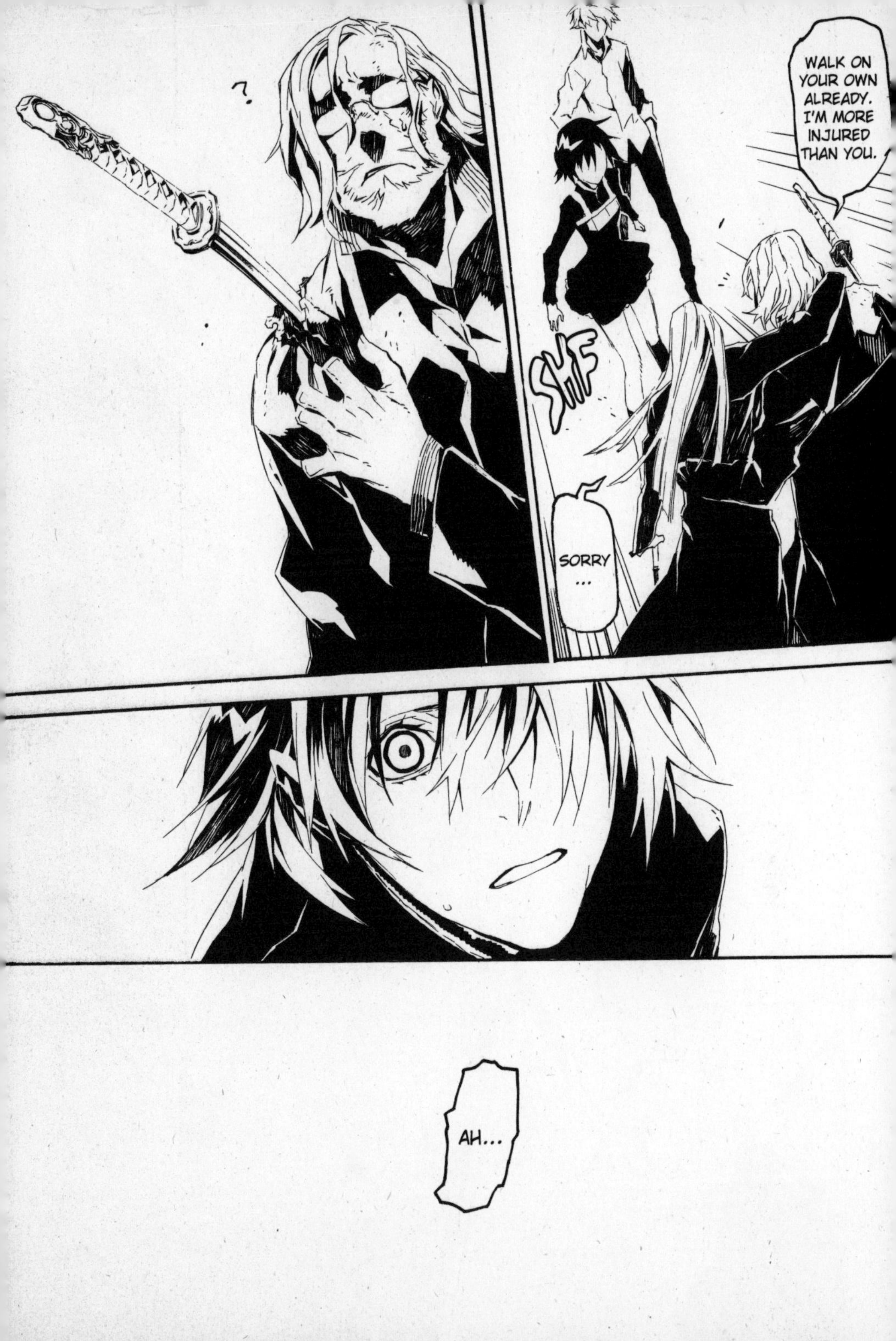
WALK ON YOUR OWN ALREADY. I'M MORE INJURED THAN YOU.
SHF
SORRY ...
?
AH...

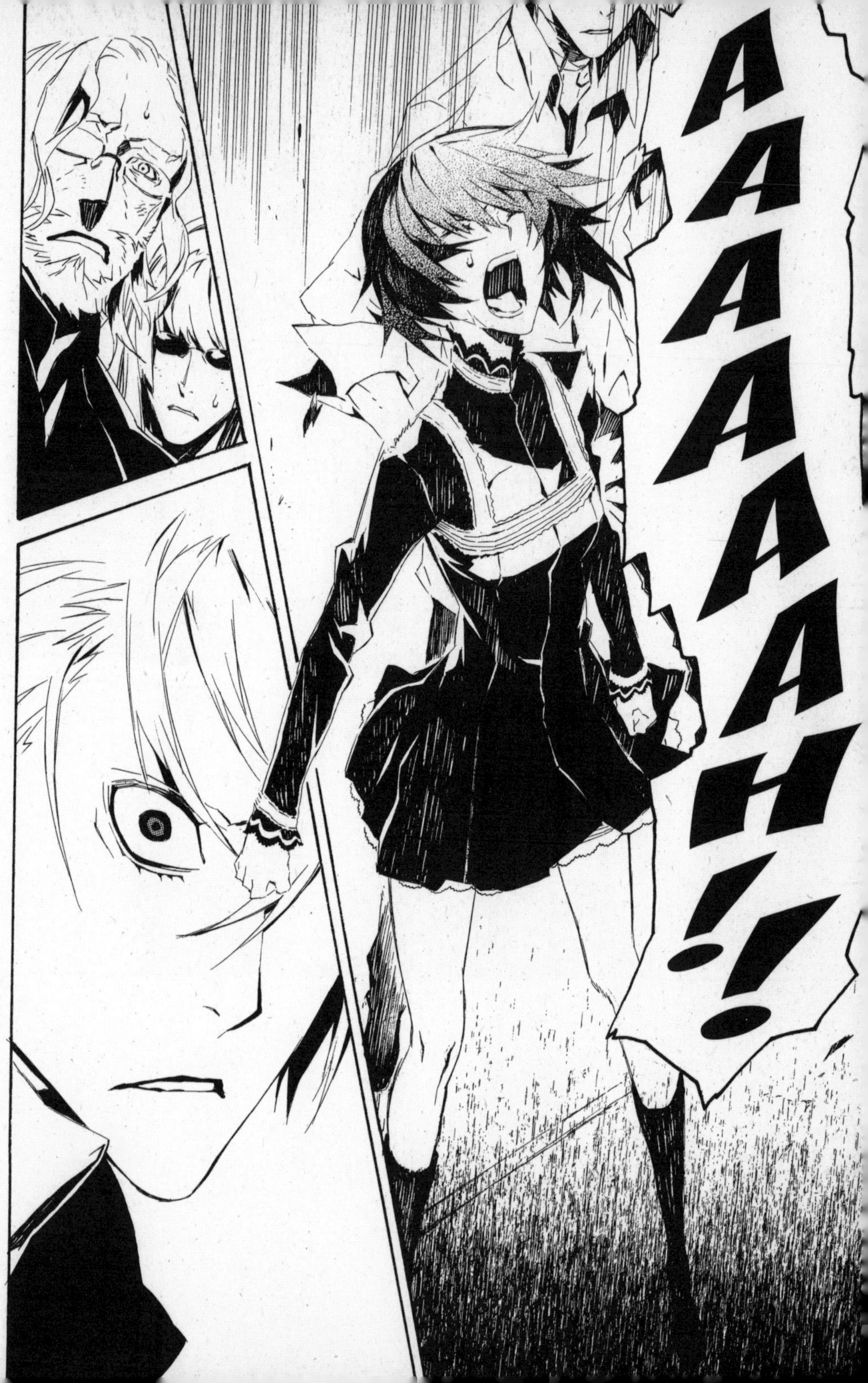
AAAAAAAH!!

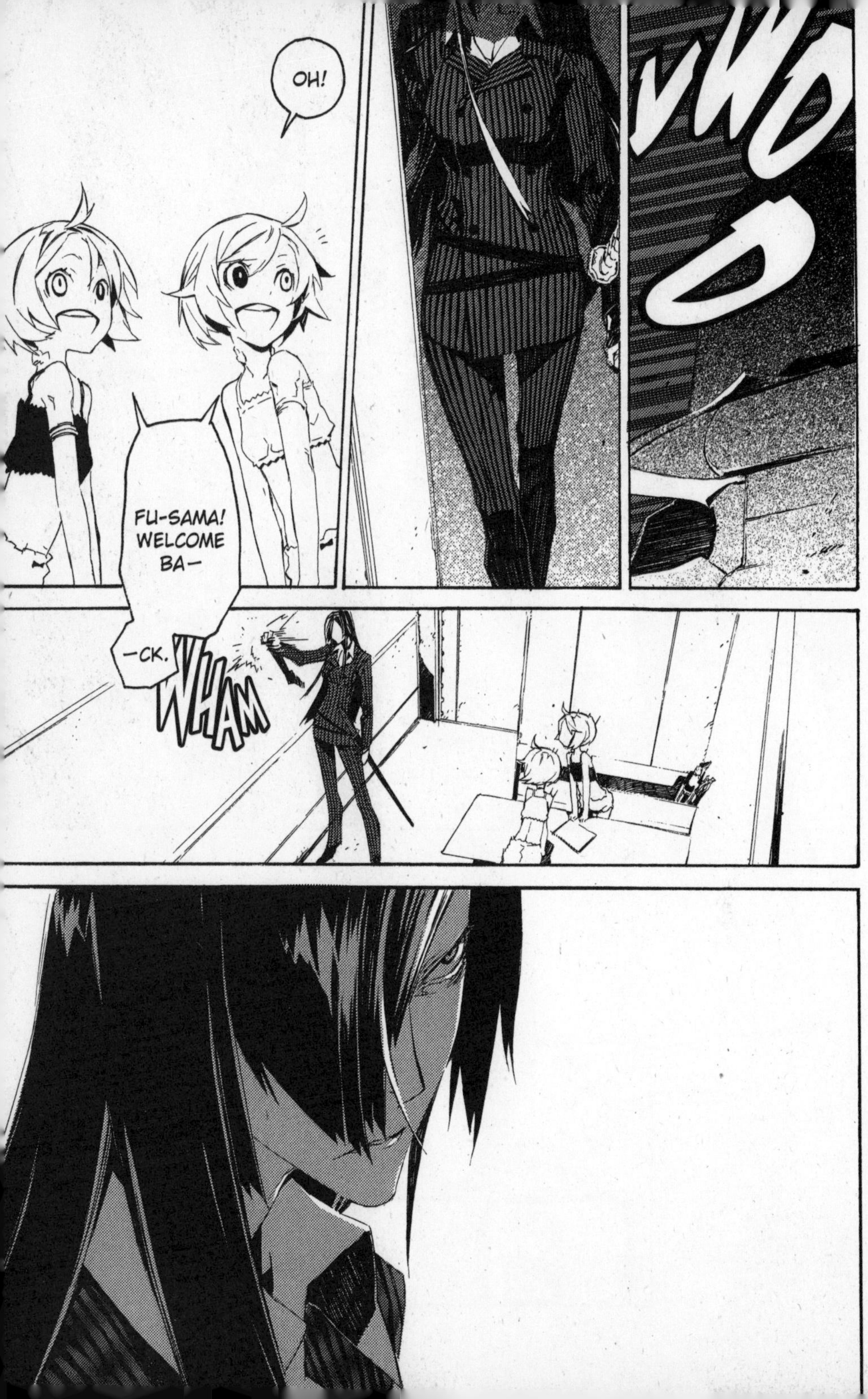
OH!
FU-SAMA! WELCOME BA—
—CK.
WHAM

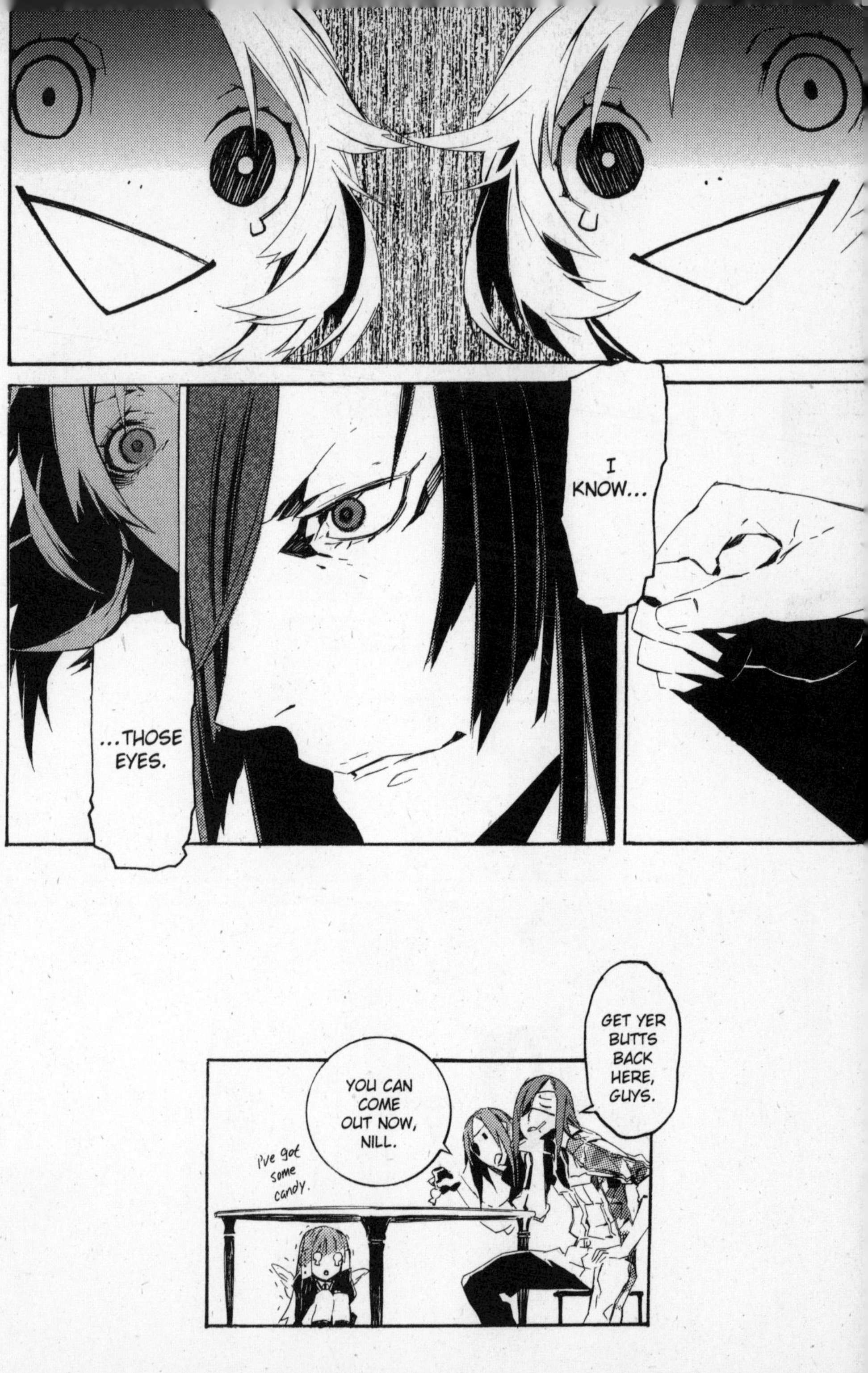
I KNOW...
...THOSE EYES.
GET YER BUTTS BACK HERE, GUYS.
YOU CAN COME OUT NOW, NILL.
I've got some candy.

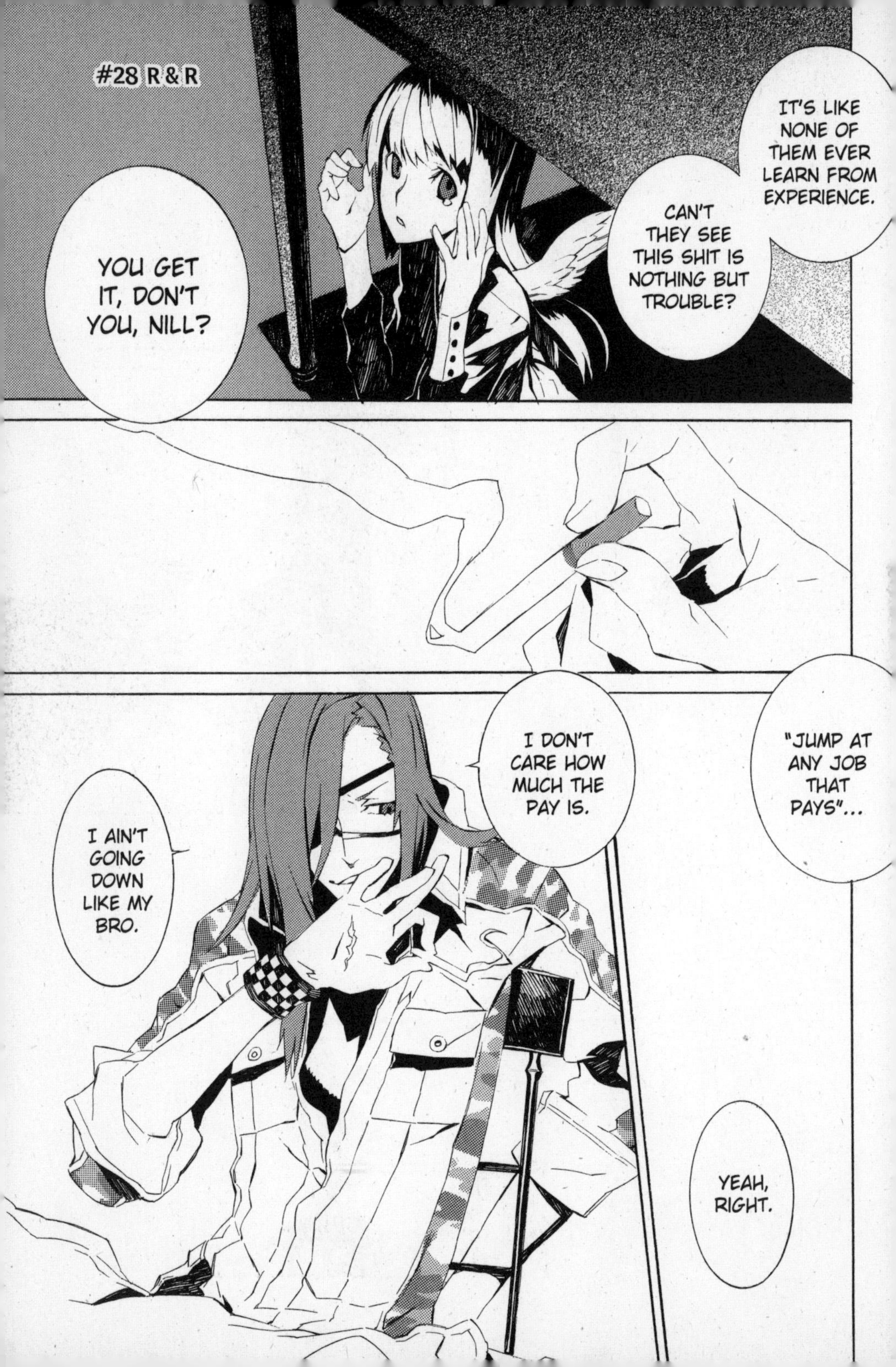
#28 R & R
IT'S LIKE NONE OF THEM EVER LEARN FROM EXPERIENCE.
CAN'T THEY SEE THIS SHIT IS NOTHING BUT TROUBLE?
YOU GET IT, DON'T YOU, NILL?
"JUMP AT ANY JOB THAT PAYS"...
I DON'T CARE HOW MUCH THE PAY IS.
I AIN'T GOING DOWN LIKE MY BRO.
YEAH, RIGHT.

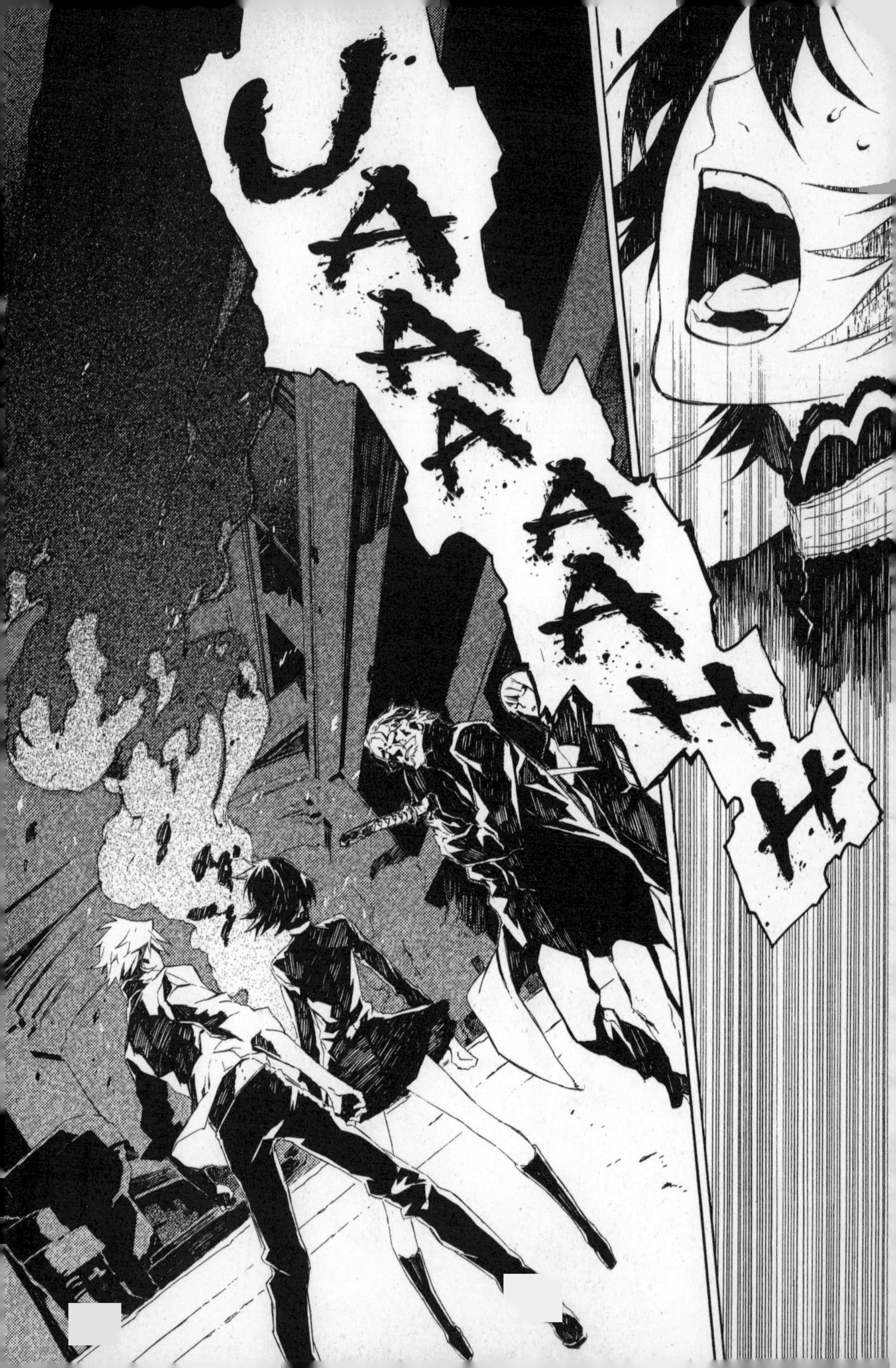
UAAAAAAHH

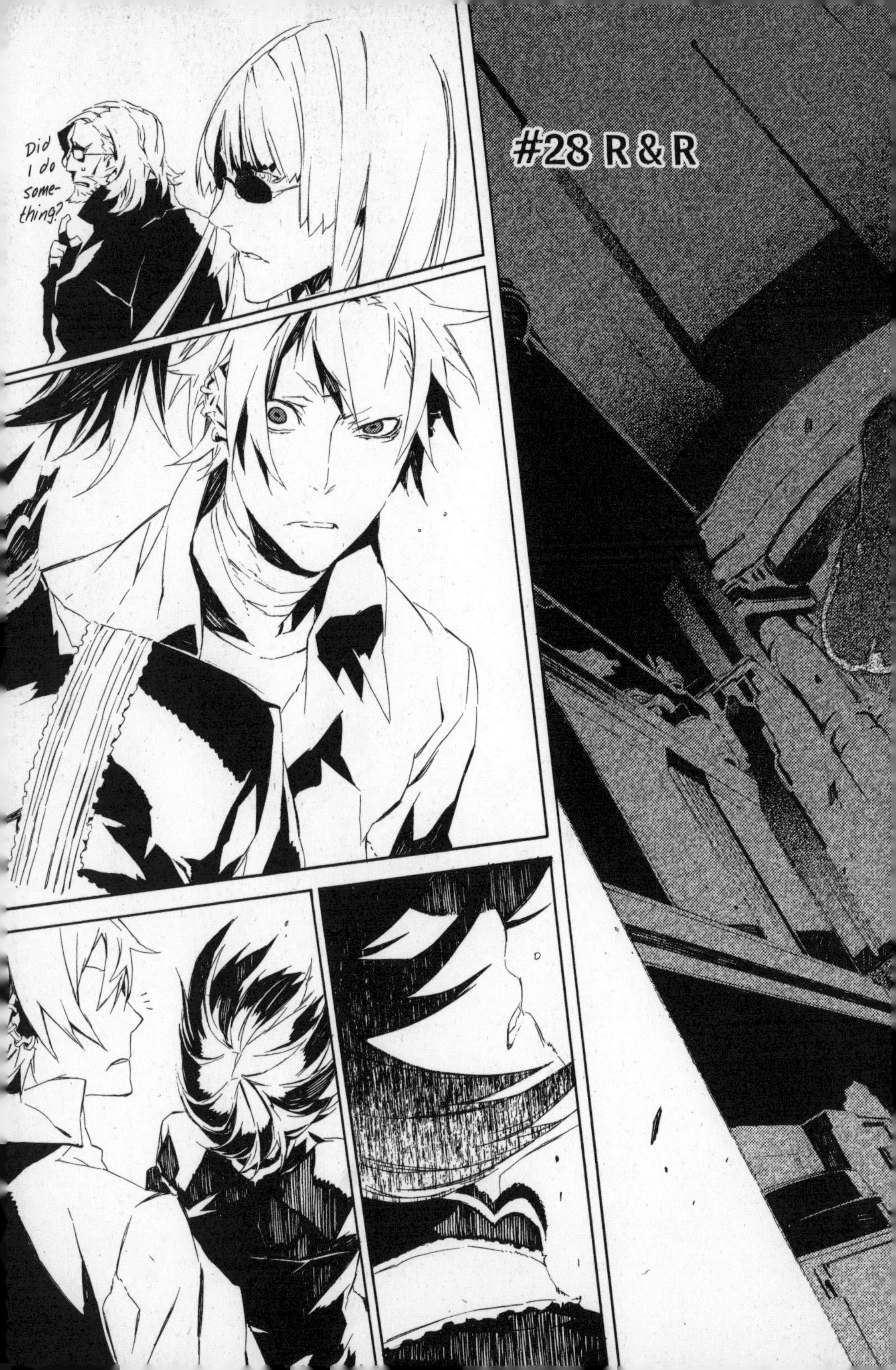
#28 R & R
Did I do some-thing?

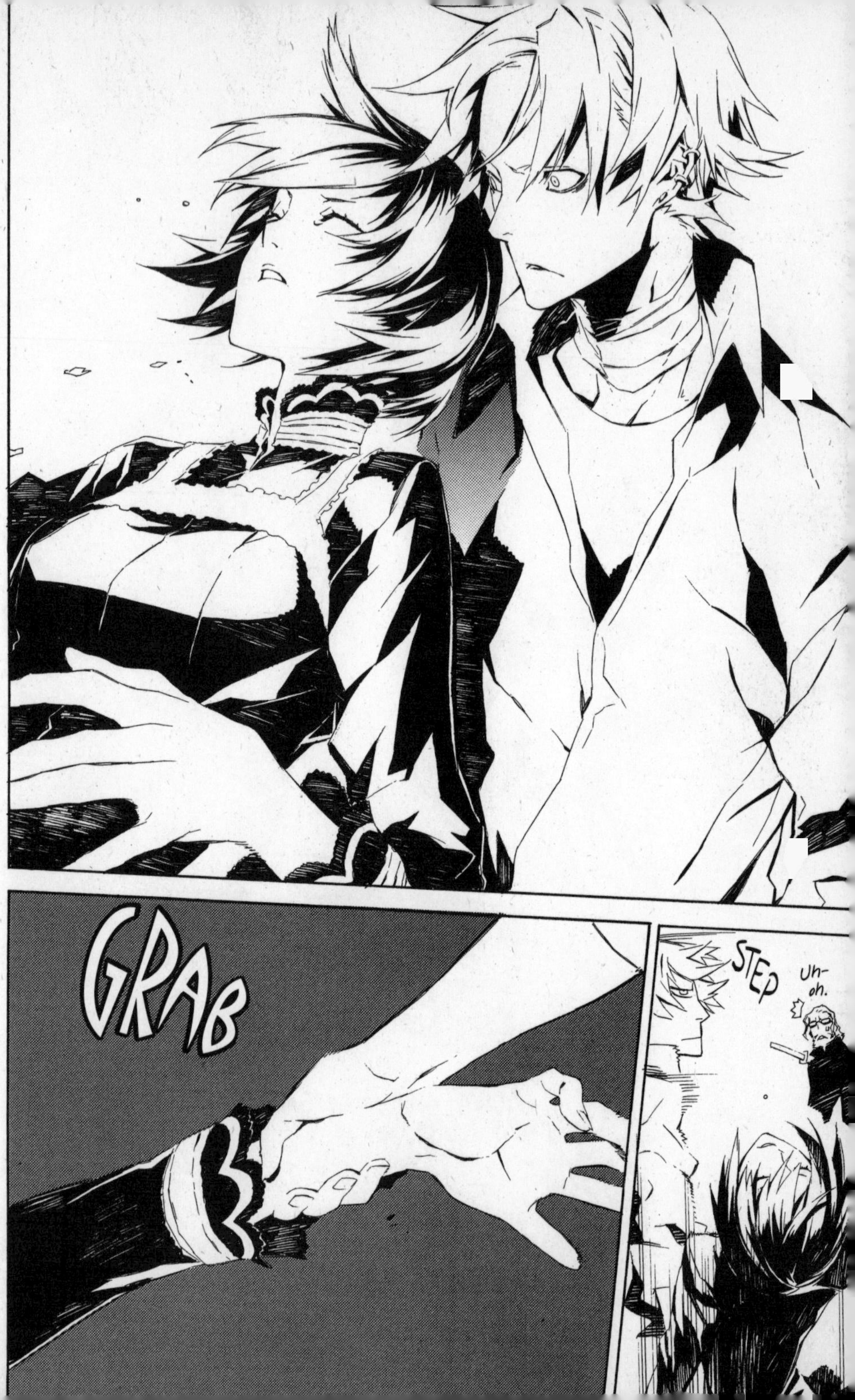
GRAB
STEP
Uh-oh.

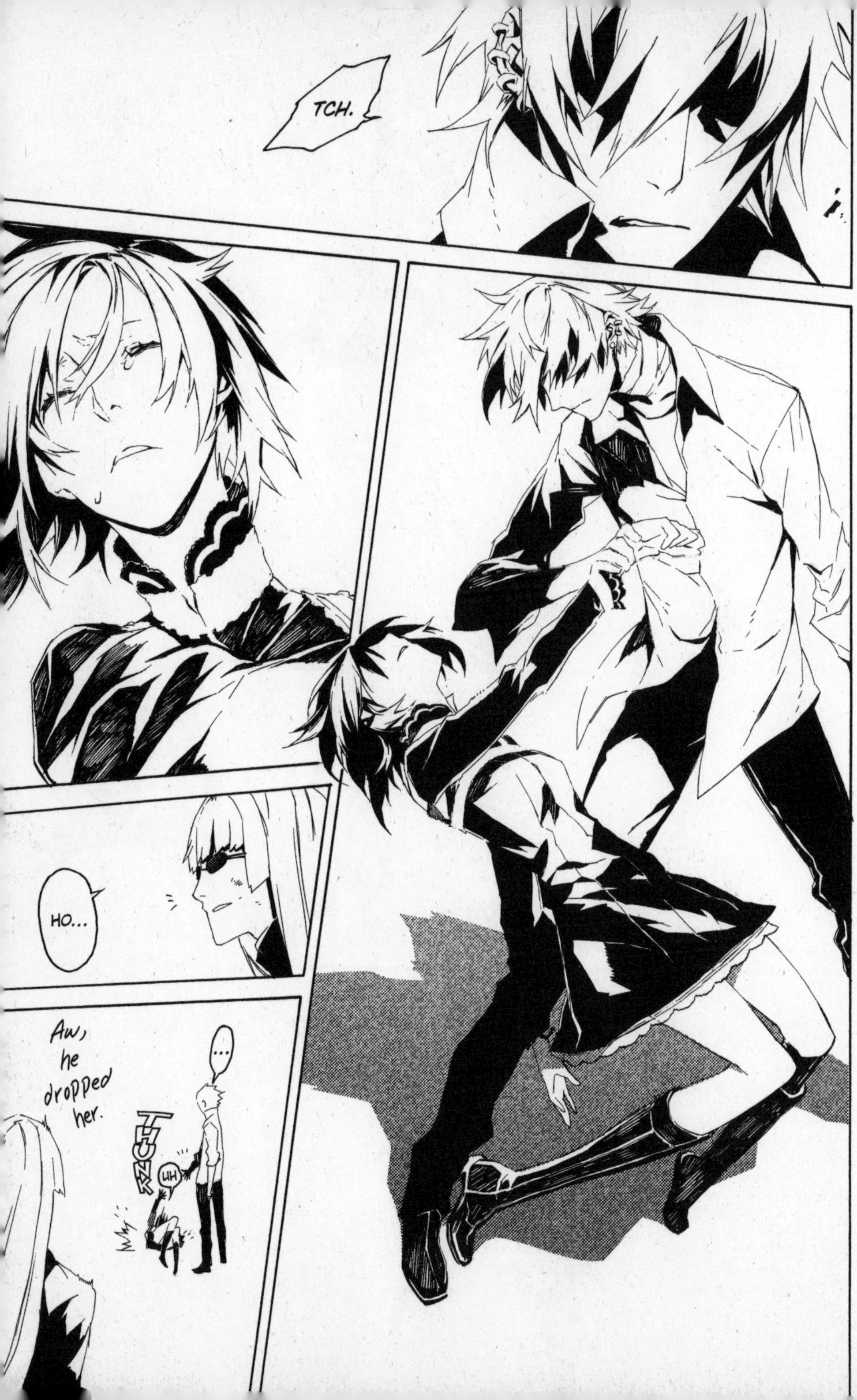
TCH.
HO...
Aw, he dropped her.
...
THUNK
UH

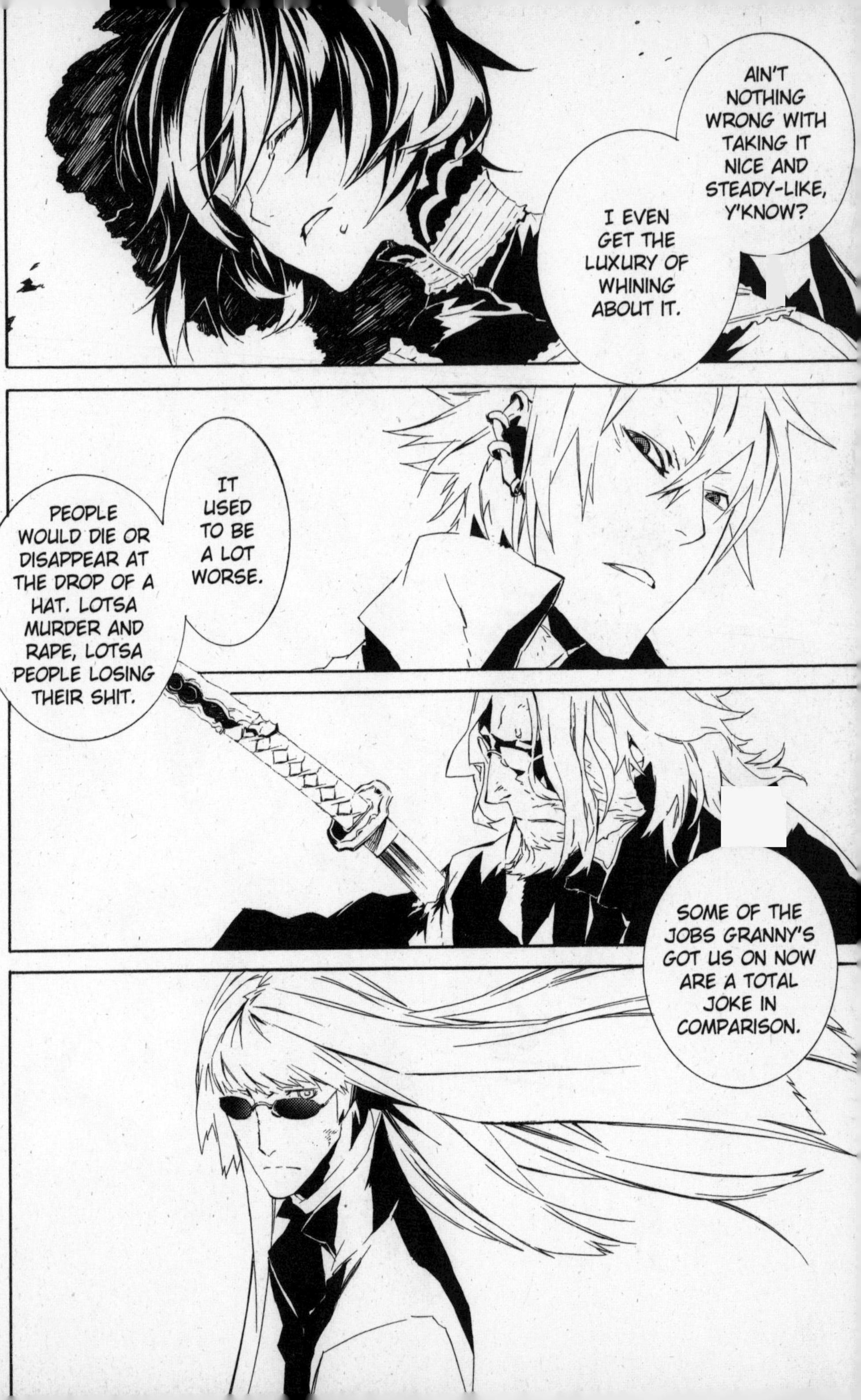
AIN'T NOTHING WRONG WITH TAKING IT NICE AND STEADY-LIKE, Y'KNOW?
I EVEN GET THE LUXURY OF WHINING ABOUT IT.
IT USED TO BE A LOT WORSE.
PEOPLE WOULD DIE OR DISAPPEAR AT THE DROP OF A HAT. LOTSA MURDER AND RAPE, LOTSA PEOPLE LOSING THEIR SHIT.
SOME OF THE JOBS GRANNY'S GOT US ON NOW ARE A TOTAL JOKE IN COMPARISON.

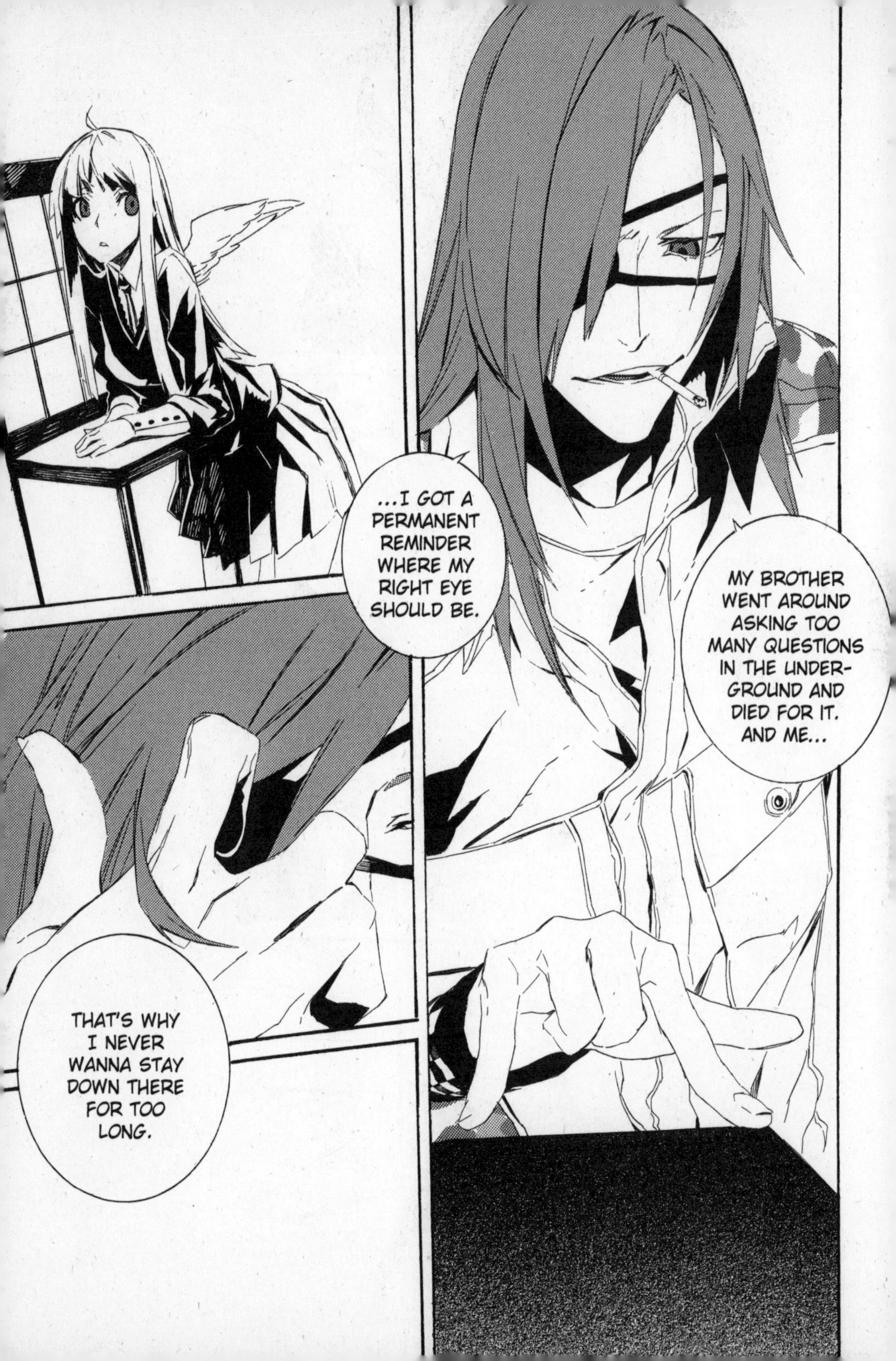
MY BROTHER WENT AROUND ASKING TOO MANY QUESTIONS IN THE UNDER-GROUND AND DIED FOR IT. AND ME...
...I GOT A PERMANENT REMINDER WHERE MY RIGHT EYE SHOULD BE.
THAT'S WHY I NEVER WANNA STAY DOWN THERE FOR TOO LONG.

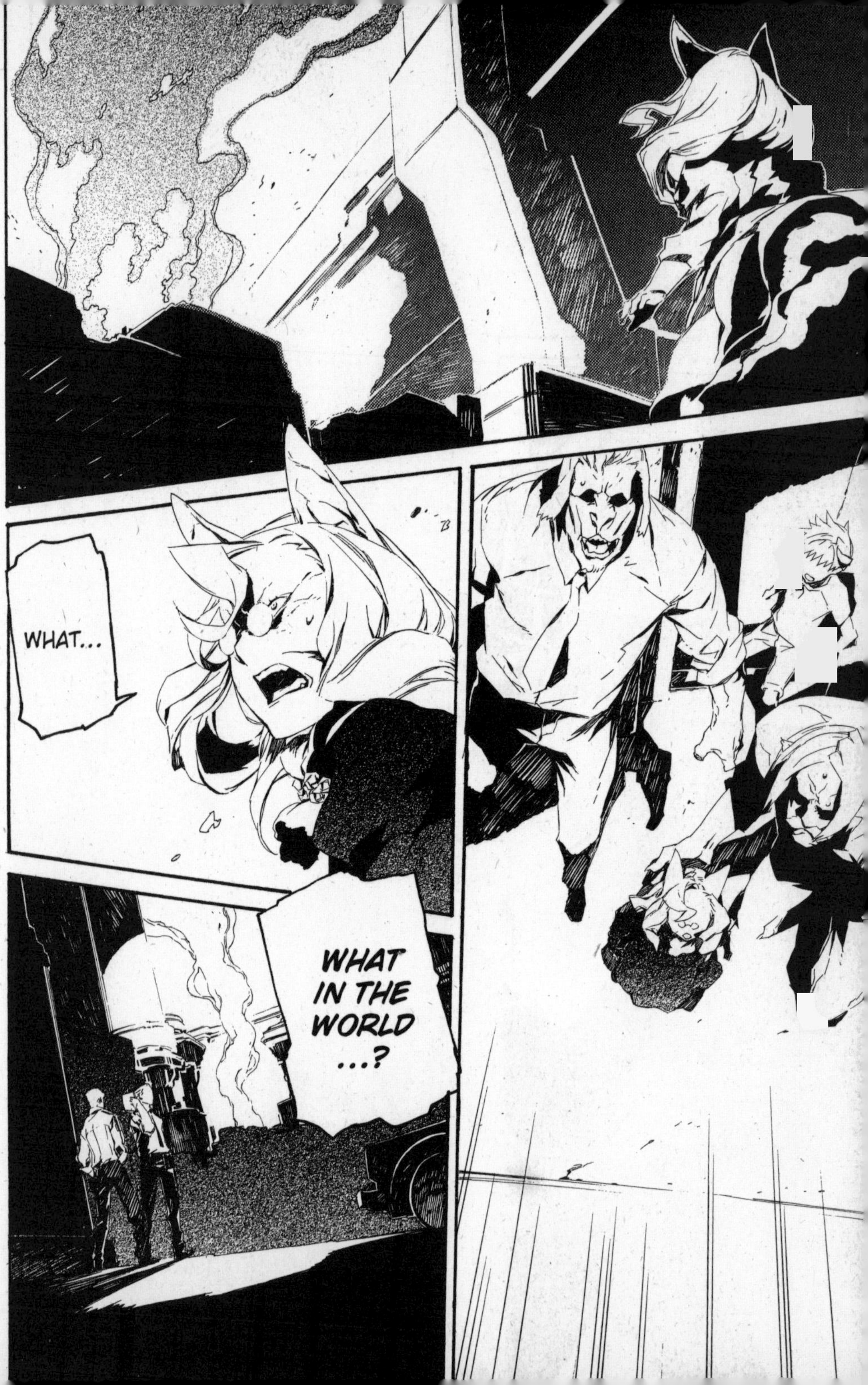
WHAT...
WHAT IN THE WORLD ...?

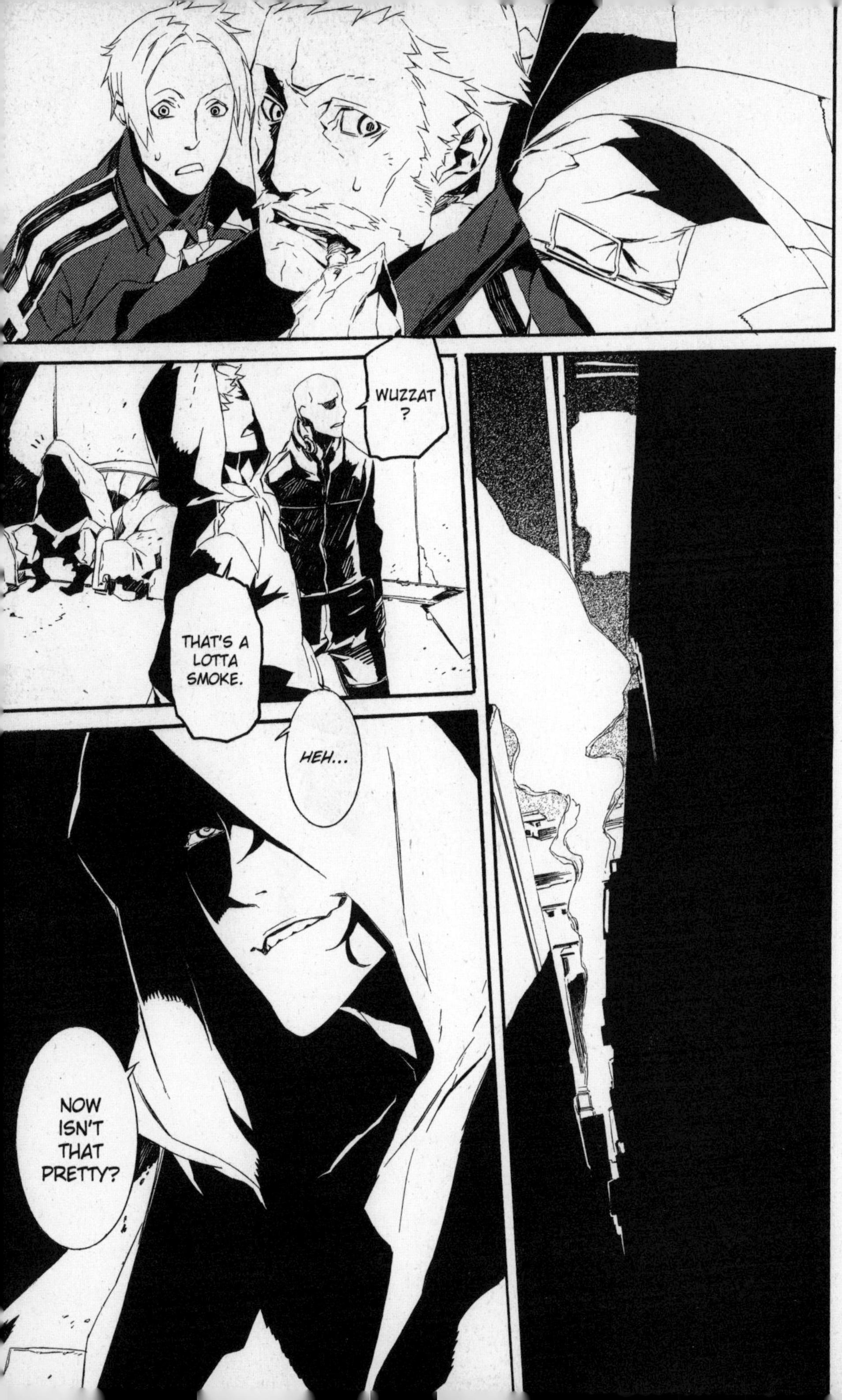
WUZZAT?
THAT'S A LOTTA SMOKE.
HEH...
NOW ISN'T THAT PRETTY?

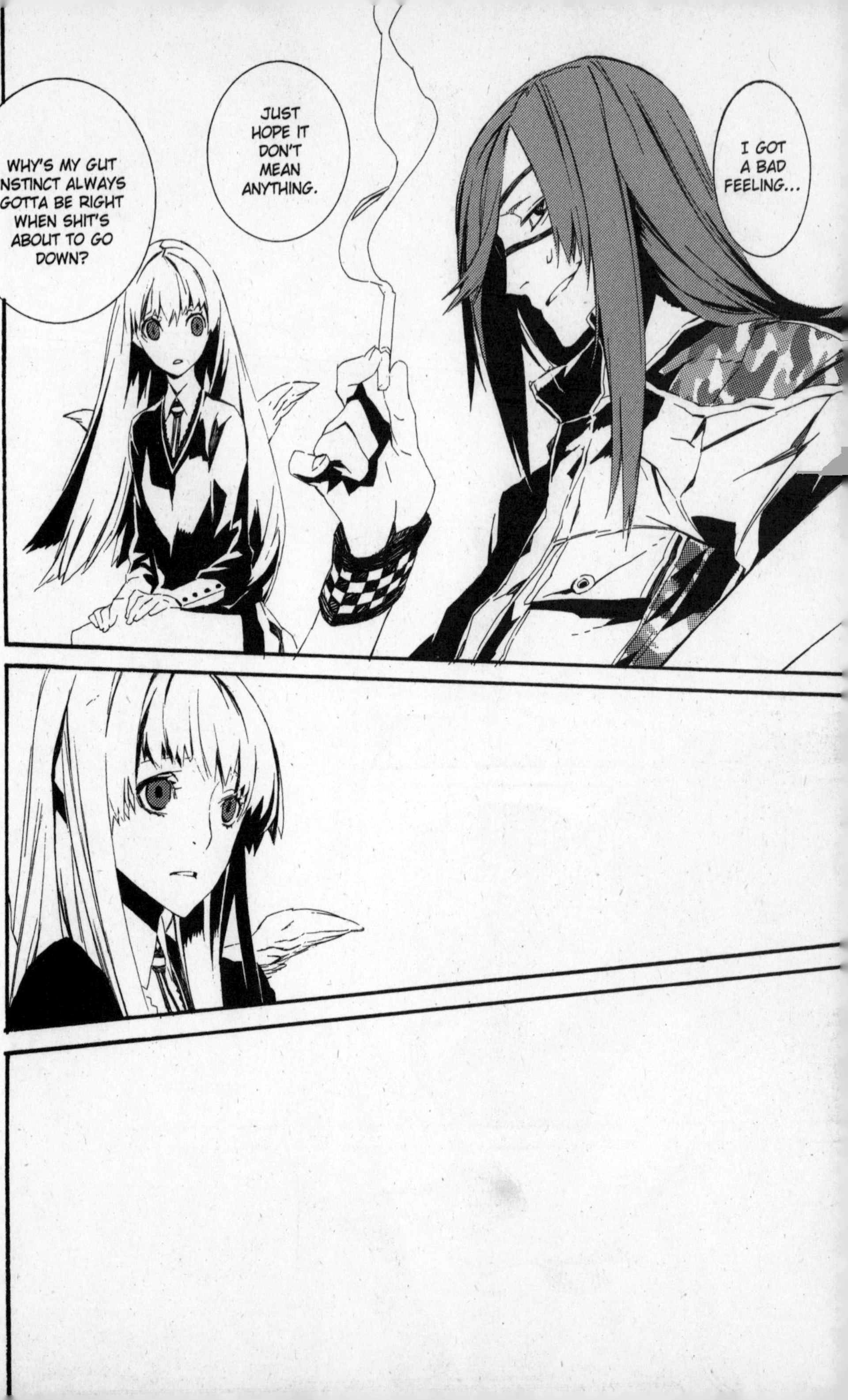
I GOT A BAD FEELING...
JUST HOPE IT DON'T MEAN ANYTHING.
WHY'S MY GUT INSTINCT ALWAYS GOTTA BE RIGHT WHEN SHIT'S ABOUT TO GO DOWN?

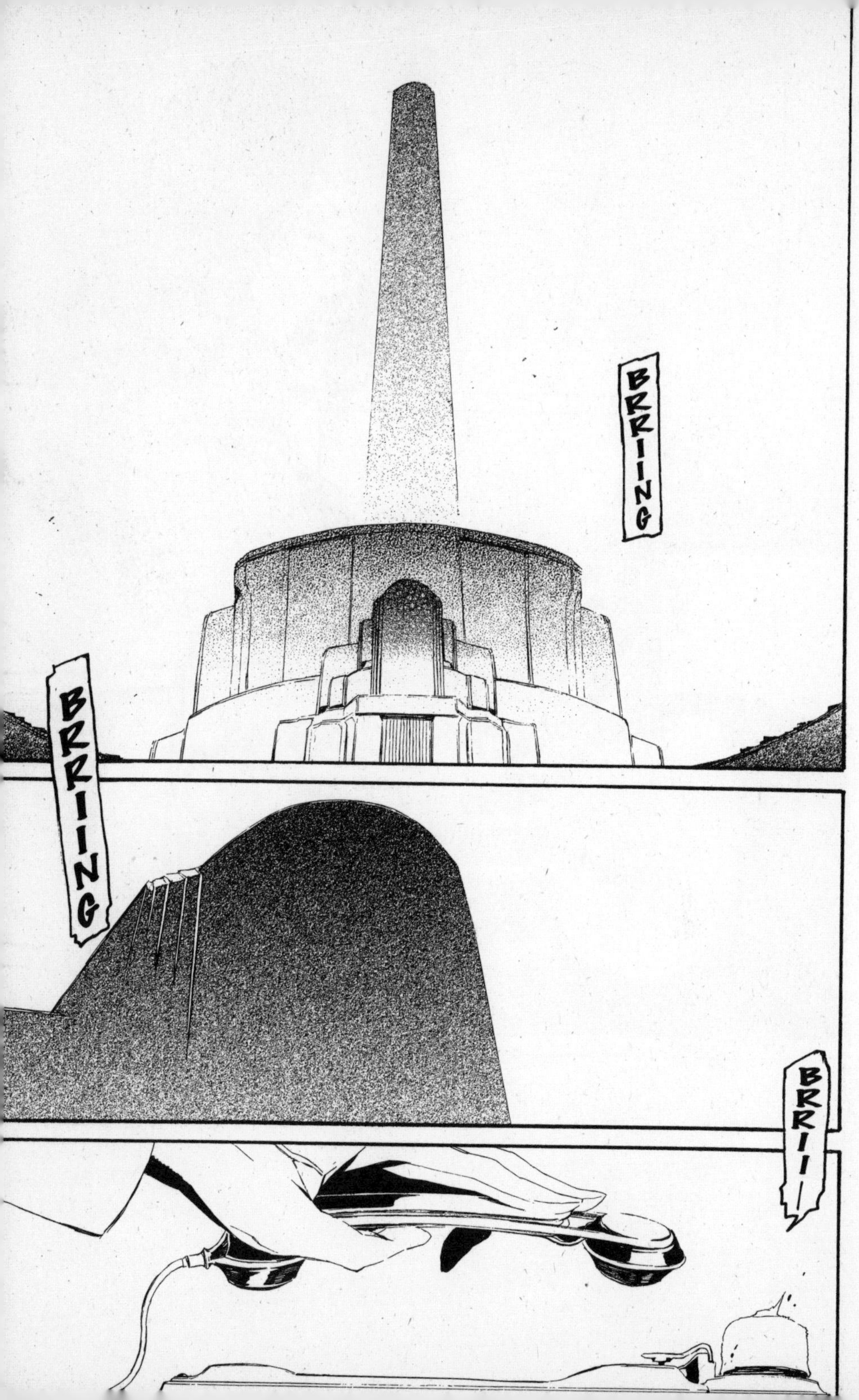
BRRIING
BRRING
BRRII!

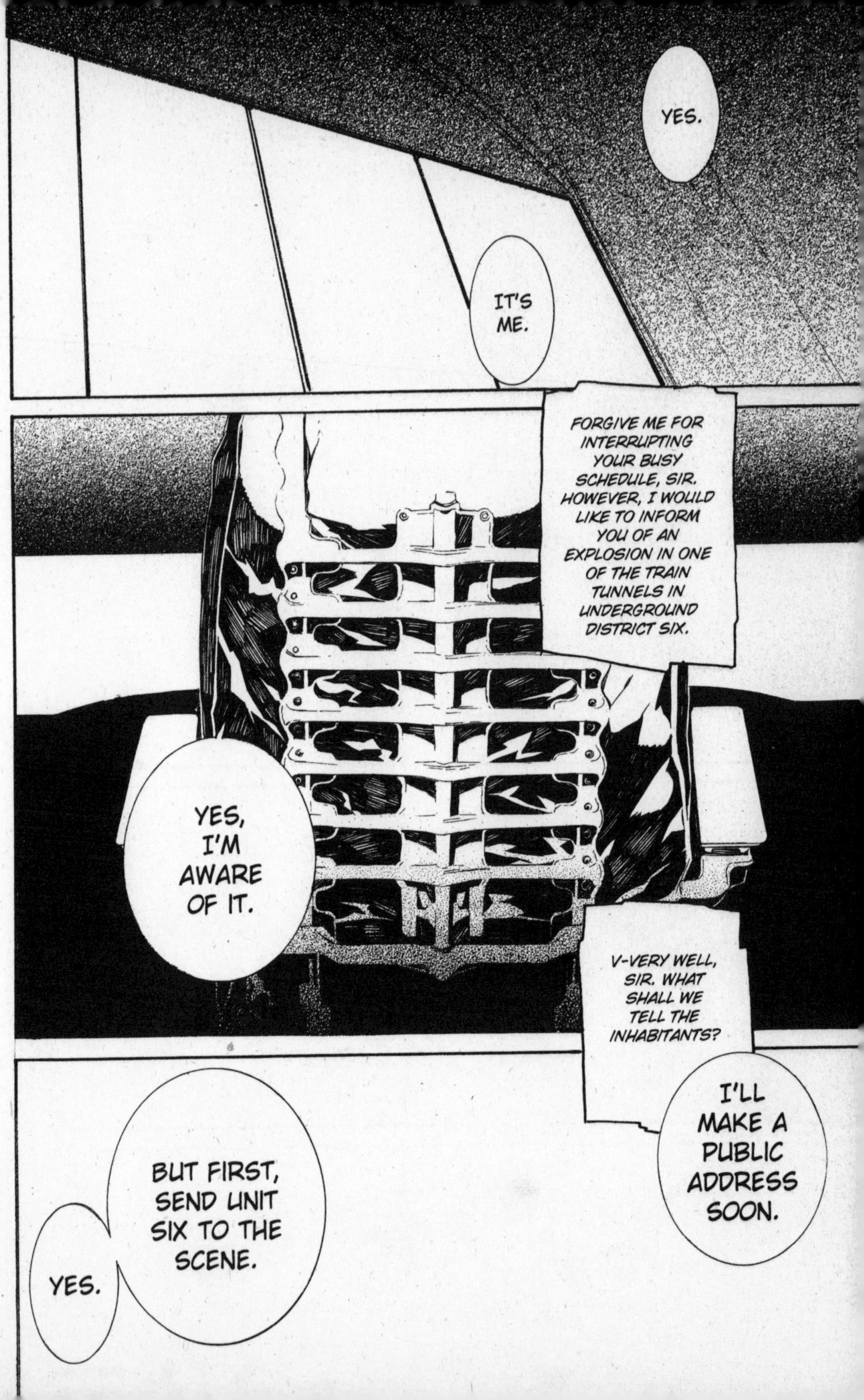
YES.
IT'S ME.
FORGIVE ME FOR INTERRUPTING YOUR BUSY SCHEDULE, SIR. HOWEVER, I WOULD LIKE TO INFORM YOU OF AN EXPLOSION IN ONE OF THE TRAIN TUNNELS IN UNDERGROUND DISTRICT SIX.
YES, I'M AWARE OF IT.
V-VERY WELL, SIR. WHAT SHALL WE TELL THE INHABITANTS?
I'LL MAKE A PUBLIC ADDRESS SOON.
BUT FIRST, SEND UNIT SIX TO THE SCENE.
YES.

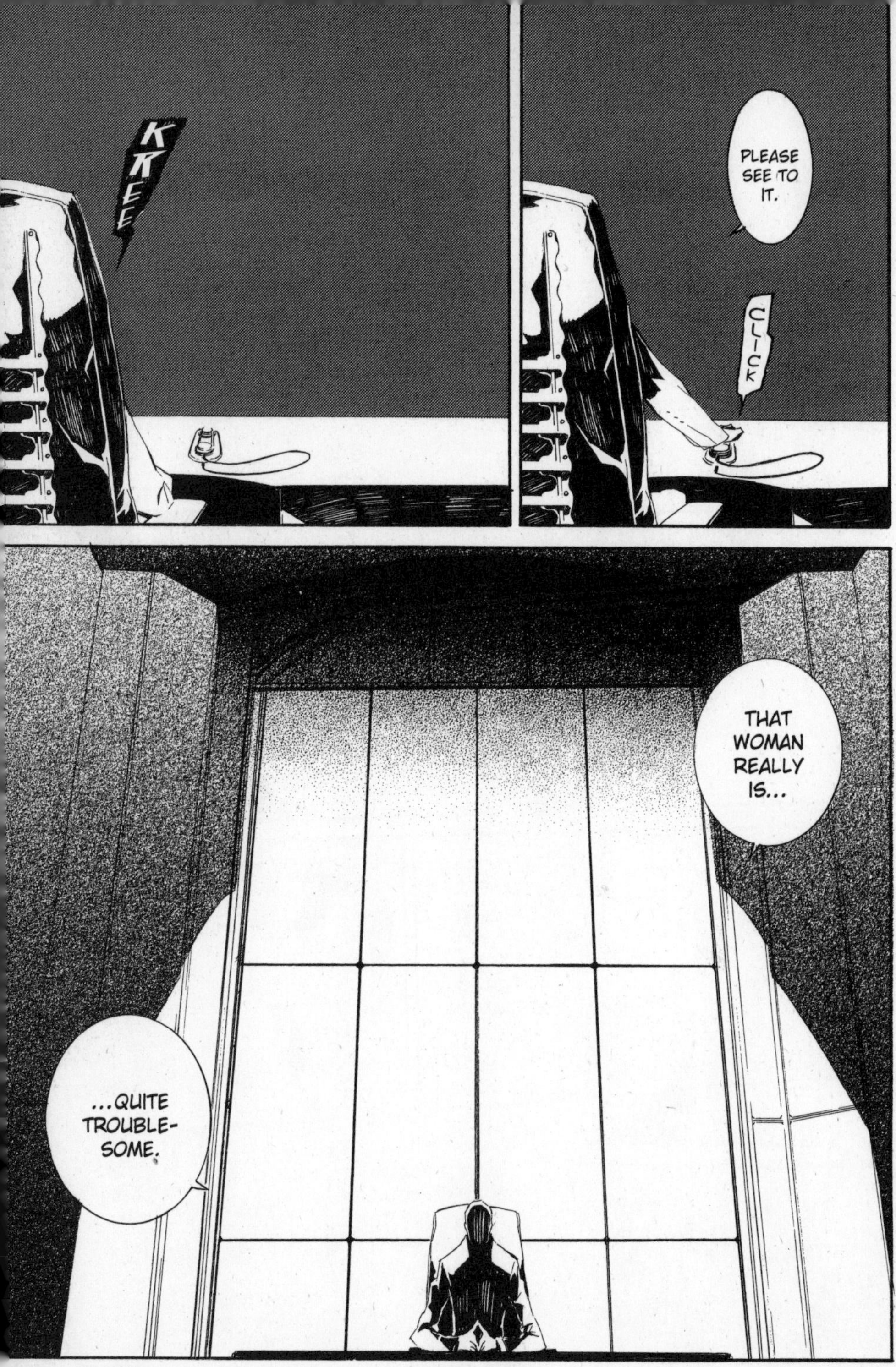
PLEASE SEE TO IT.
CLICK
KREE
THAT WOMAN REALLY IS...
...QUITE TROUBLE-SOME.

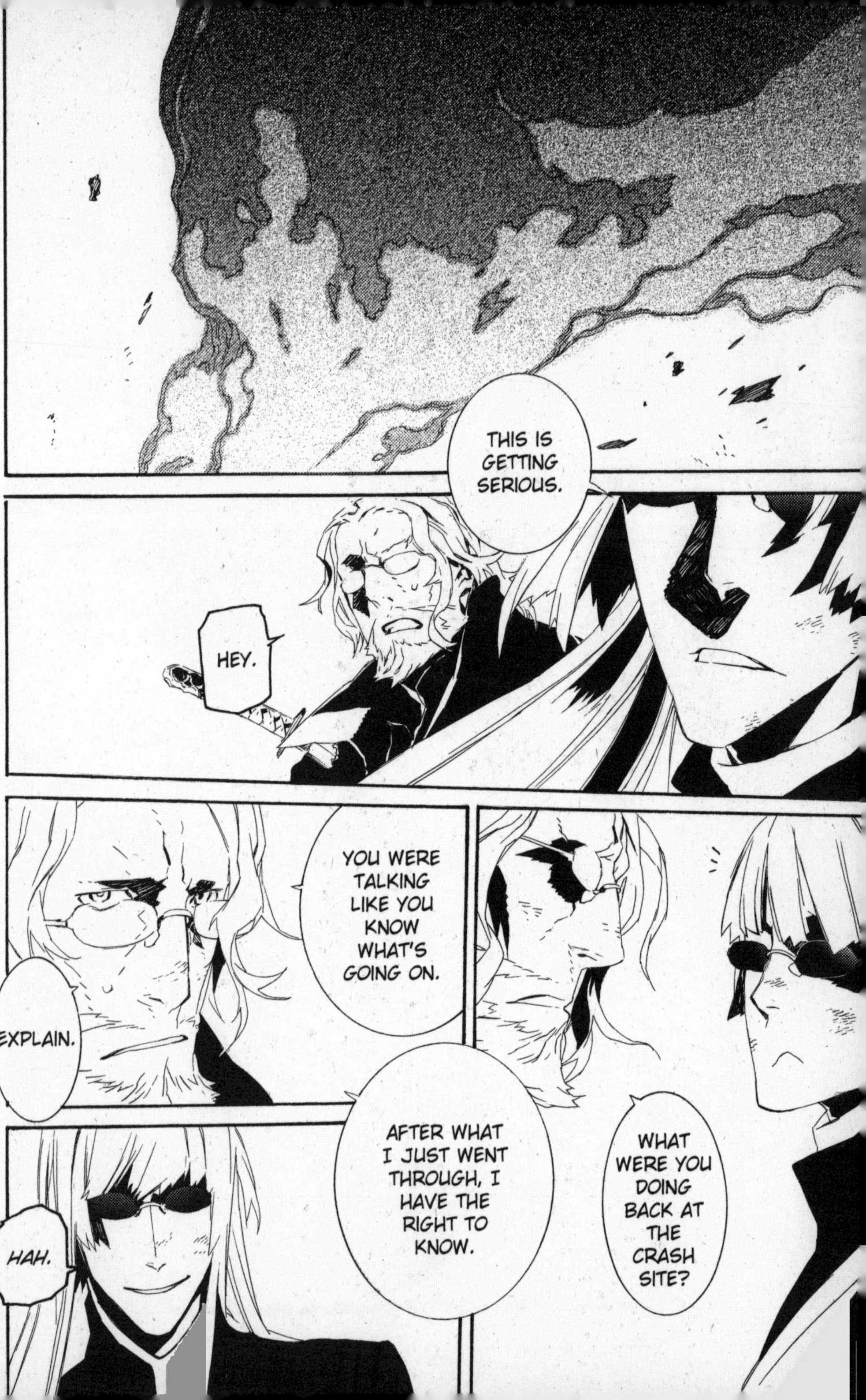
THIS IS GETTING SERIOUS.
HEY.
WHAT WERE YOU DOING BACK AT THE CRASH SITE?
YOU WERE TALKING LIKE YOU KNOW WHAT'S GOING ON.
EXPLAIN.
AFTER WHAT I JUST WENT THROUGH, I HAVE THE RIGHT TO KNOW.
HAH.

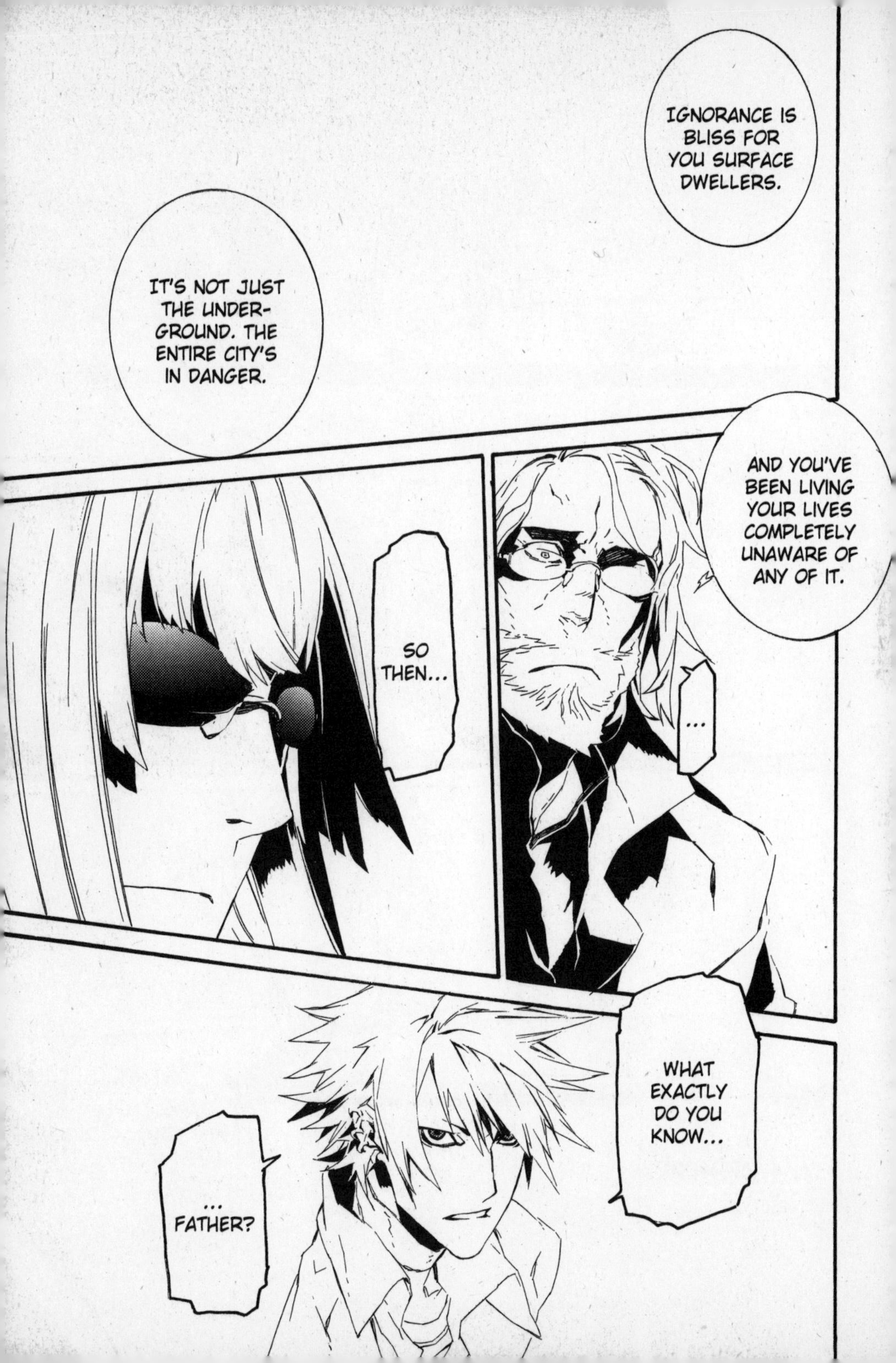
IGNORANCE IS BLISS FOR YOU SURFACE DWELLERS.
IT'S NOT JUST THE UNDER-GROUND. THE ENTIRE CITY'S IN DANGER.
AND YOU'VE BEEN LIVING YOUR LIVES COMPLETELY UNAWARE OF ANY OF IT.
...
SO THEN...
WHAT EXACTLY DO YOU KNOW...
...FATHER?

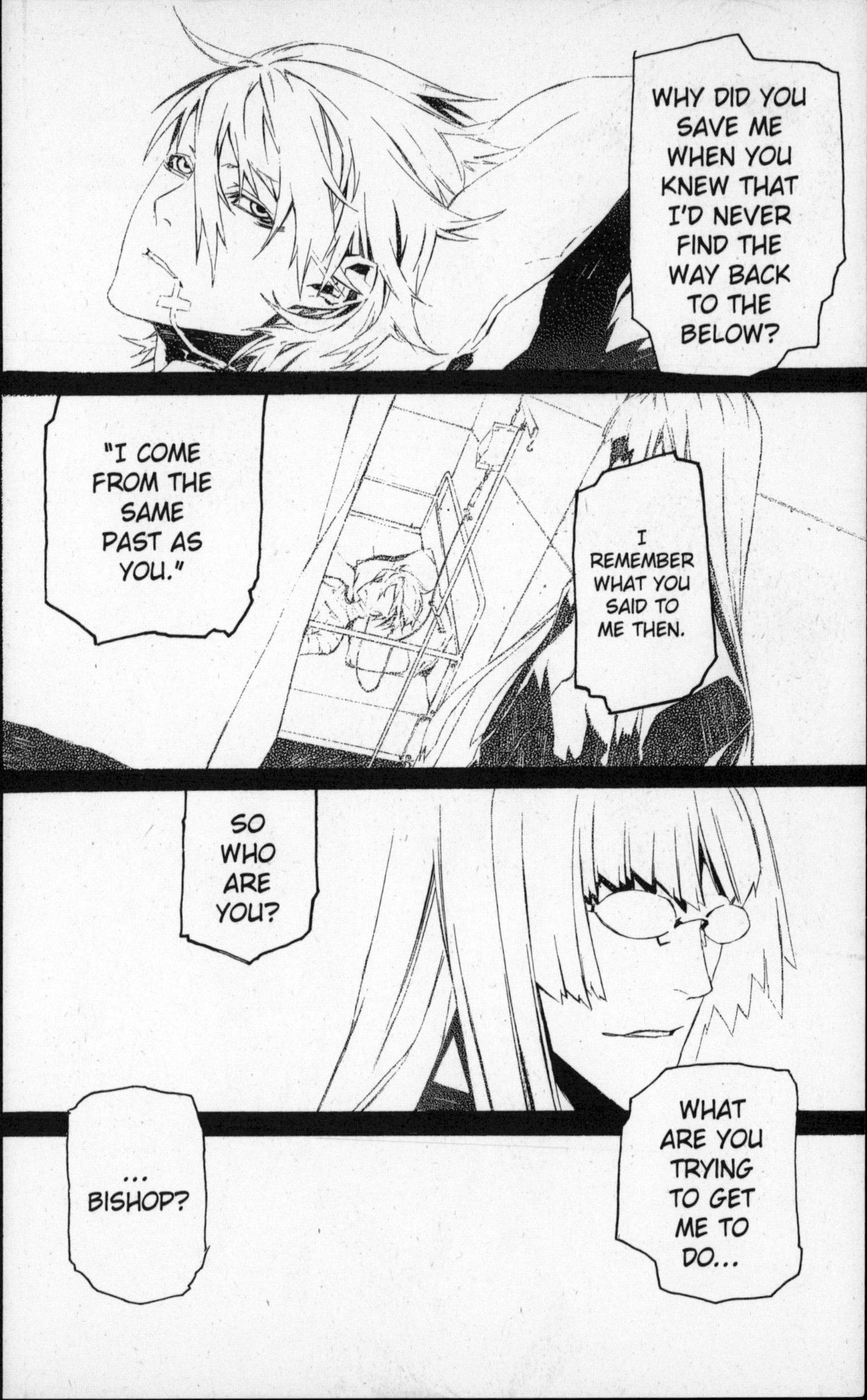
WHY DID YOU SAVE ME WHEN YOU KNEW THAT I'D NEVER FIND THE WAY BACK TO THE BELOW?
I REMEMBER WHAT YOU SAID TO ME THEN.
"I COME FROM THE SAME PAST AS YOU."
SO WHO ARE YOU?
WHAT ARE YOU TRYING TO GET ME TO DO...
...BISHOP?

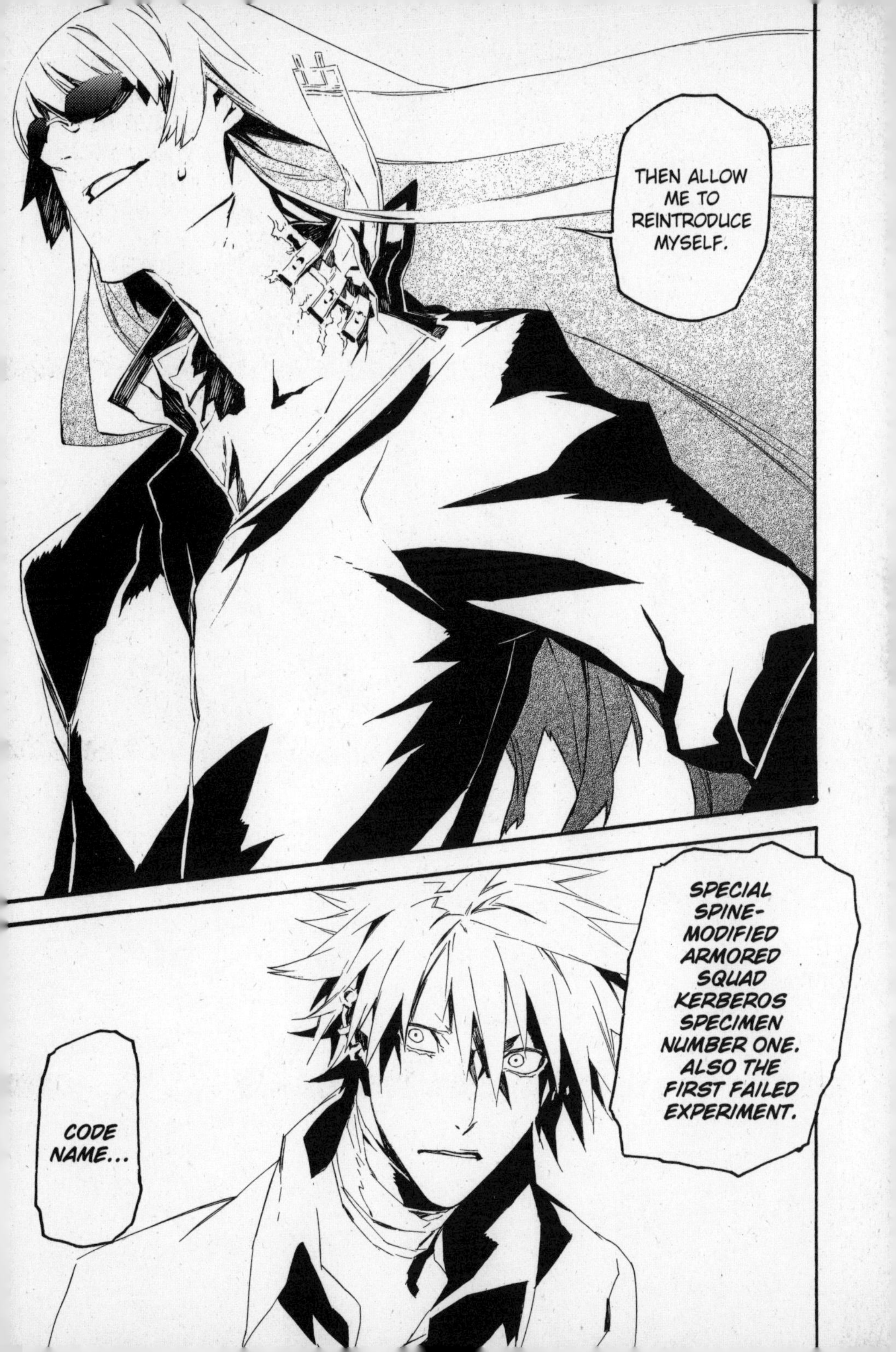
THEN ALLOW ME TO REINTRODUCE MYSELF.
SPECIAL SPINE-MODIFIED ARMORED SQUAD KERBEROS SPECIMEN NUMBER ONE. ALSO THE FIRST FAILED EXPERIMENT.
CODE NAME...

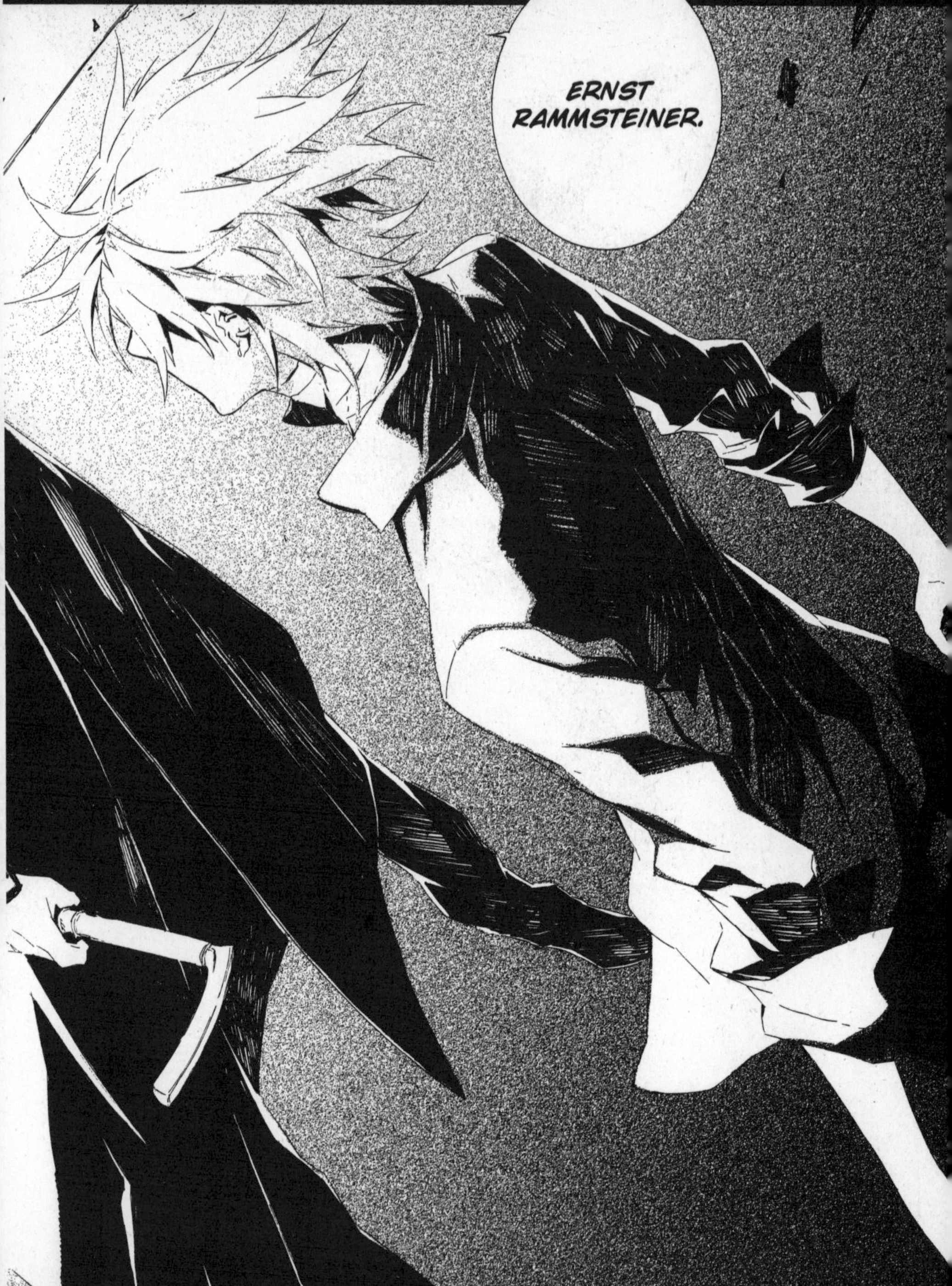
ERNST RAMMSTEINER.

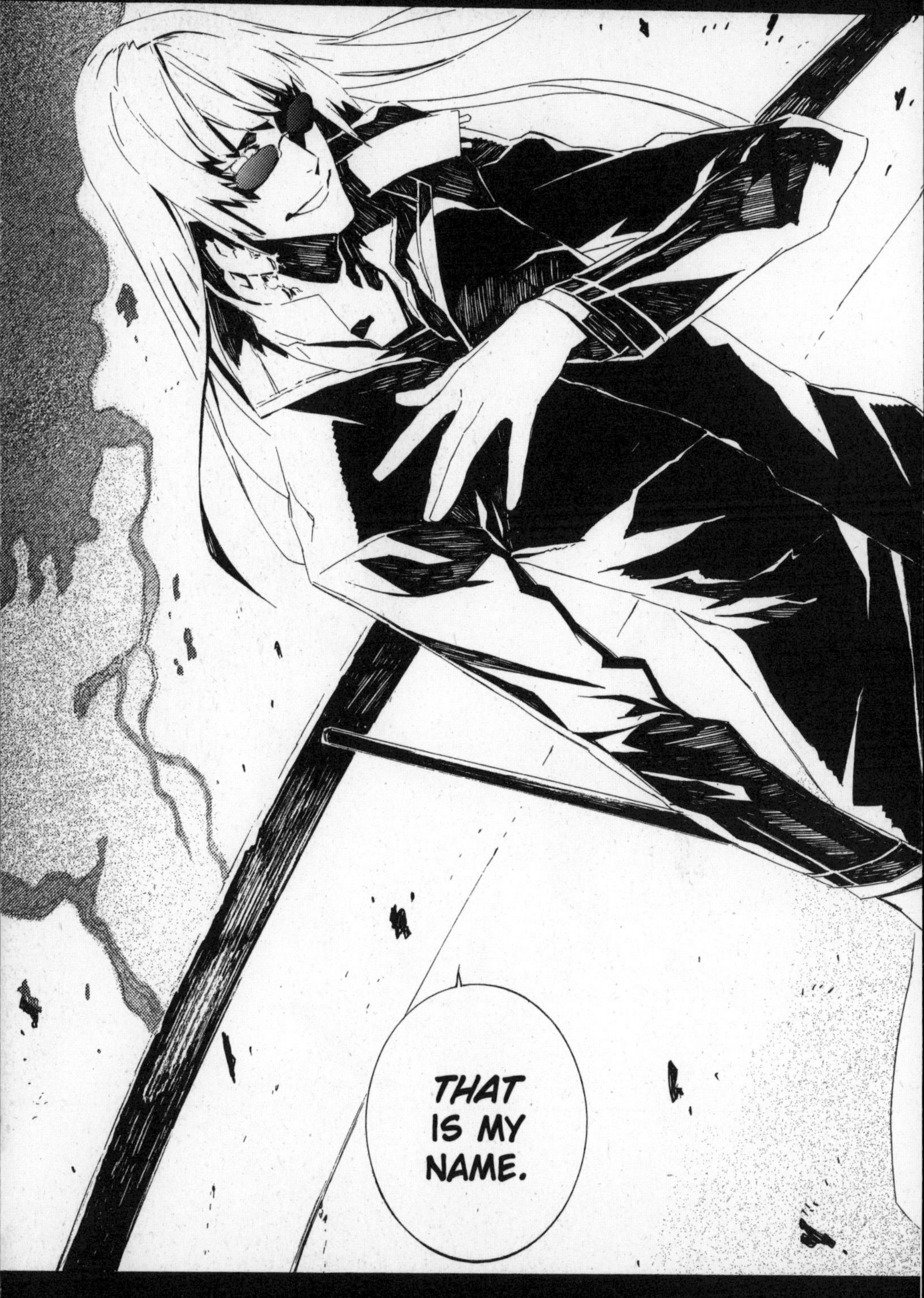
THAT IS MY NAME.

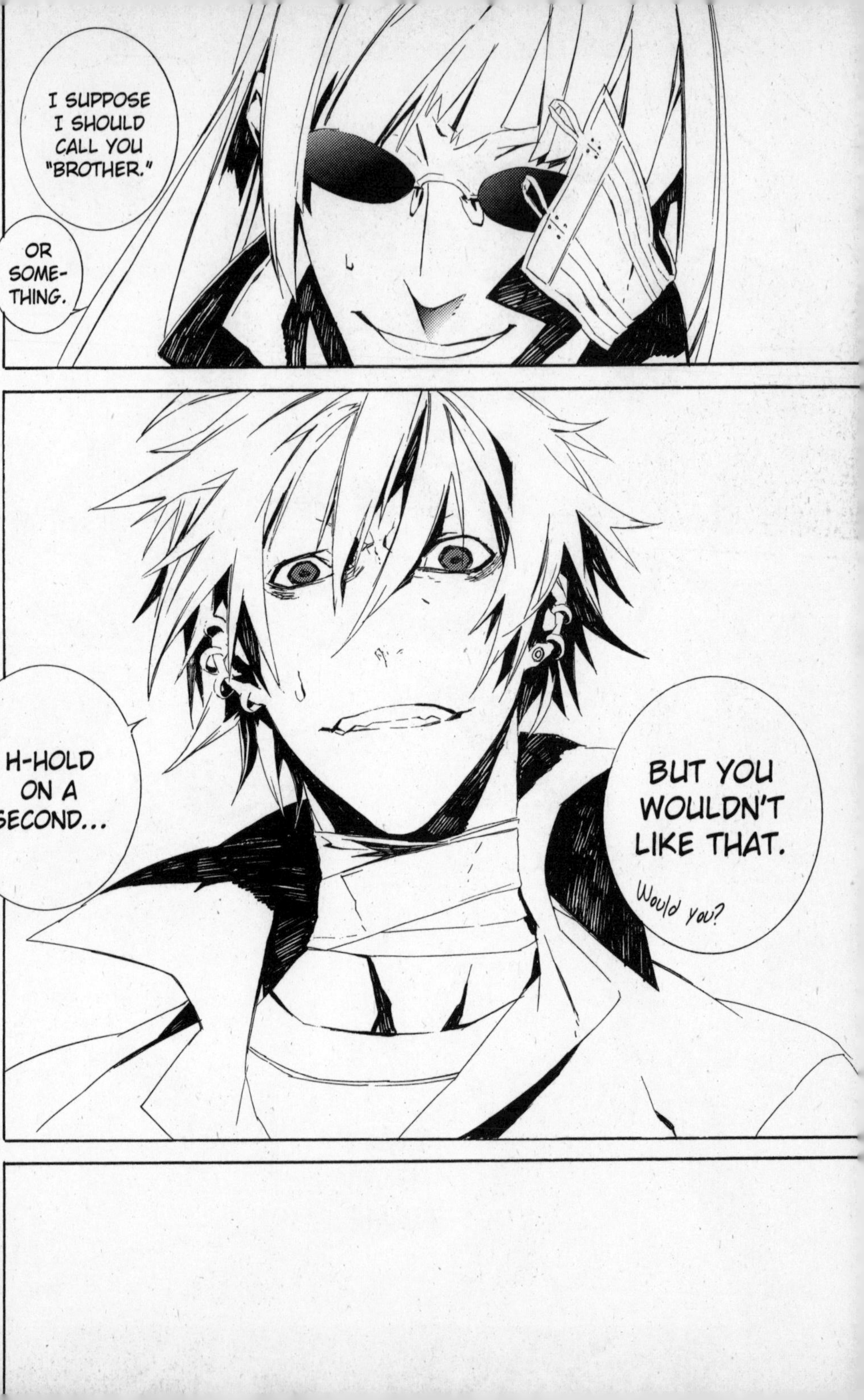
I SUPPOSE I SHOULD CALL YOU "BROTHER."
OR SOME-THING.
BUT YOU WOULDN'T LIKE THAT.
Would you?
H-HOLD ON A SECOND...

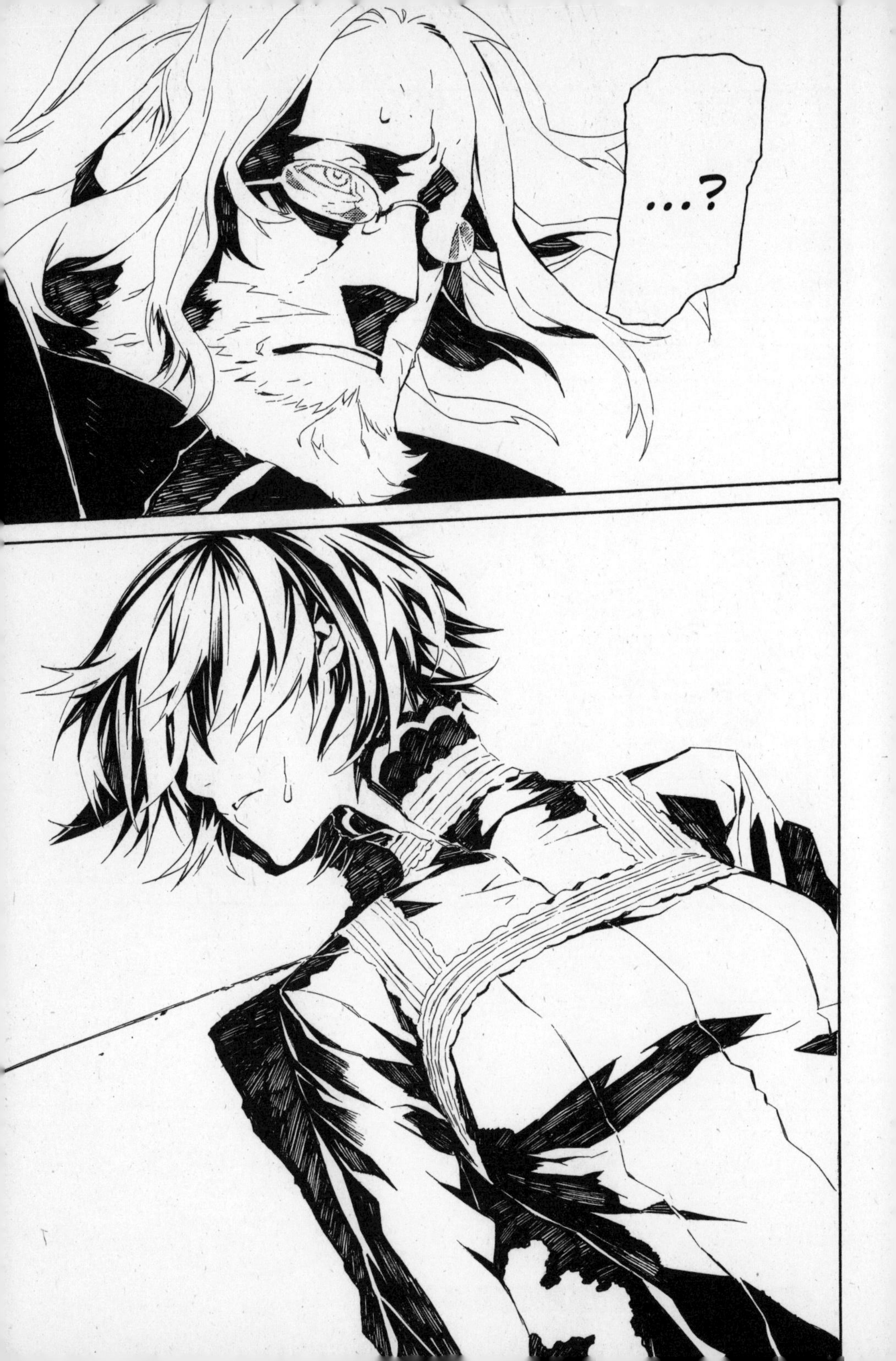
...?

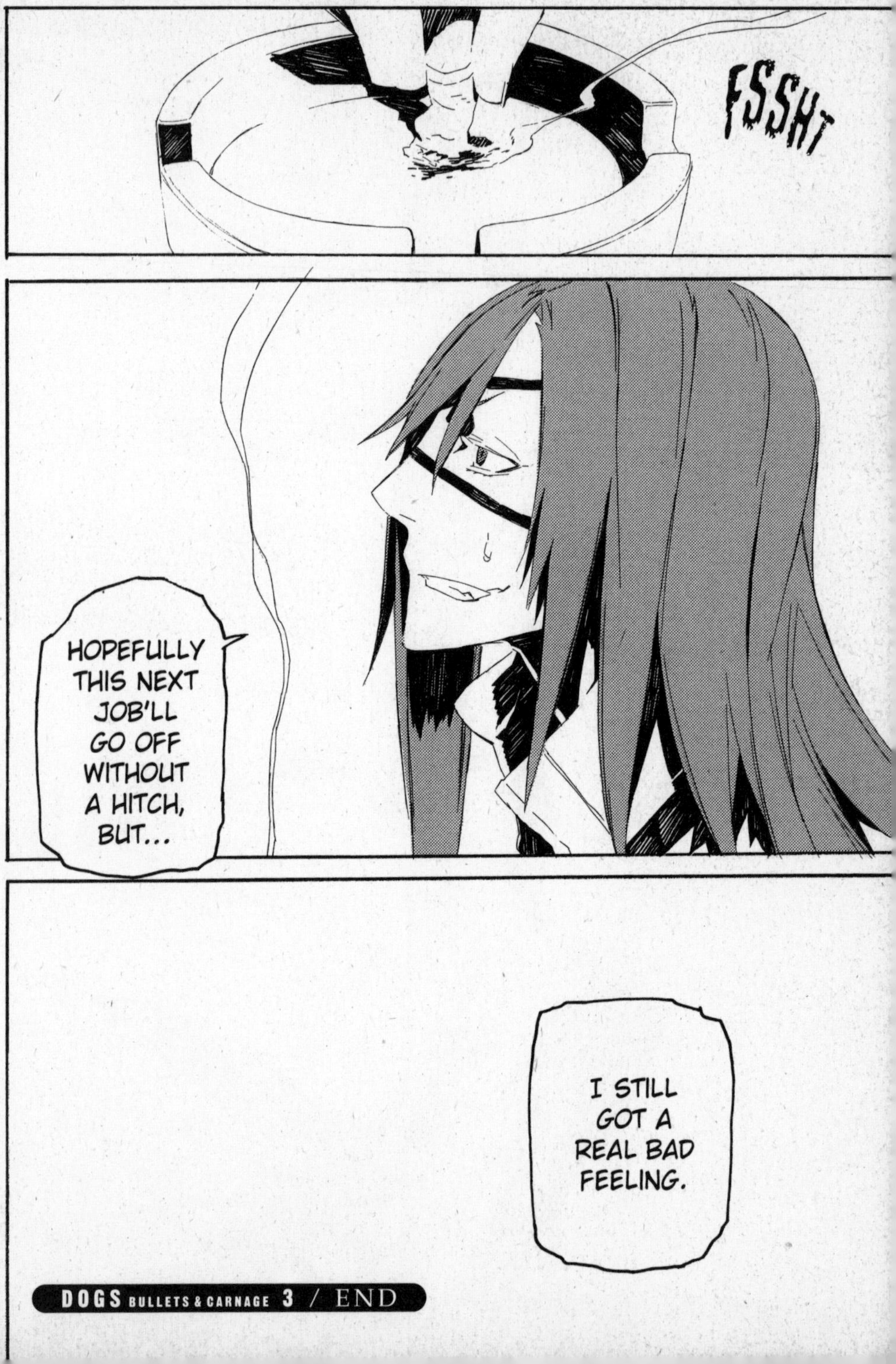
FSSHT
HOPEFULLY THIS NEXT JOB'LL GO OFF WITHOUT A HITCH, BUT...
I STILL GOT A REAL BAD FEELING.
DOGS BULLETS & CARNAGE 3 / END

TO
BE
CONTINUED

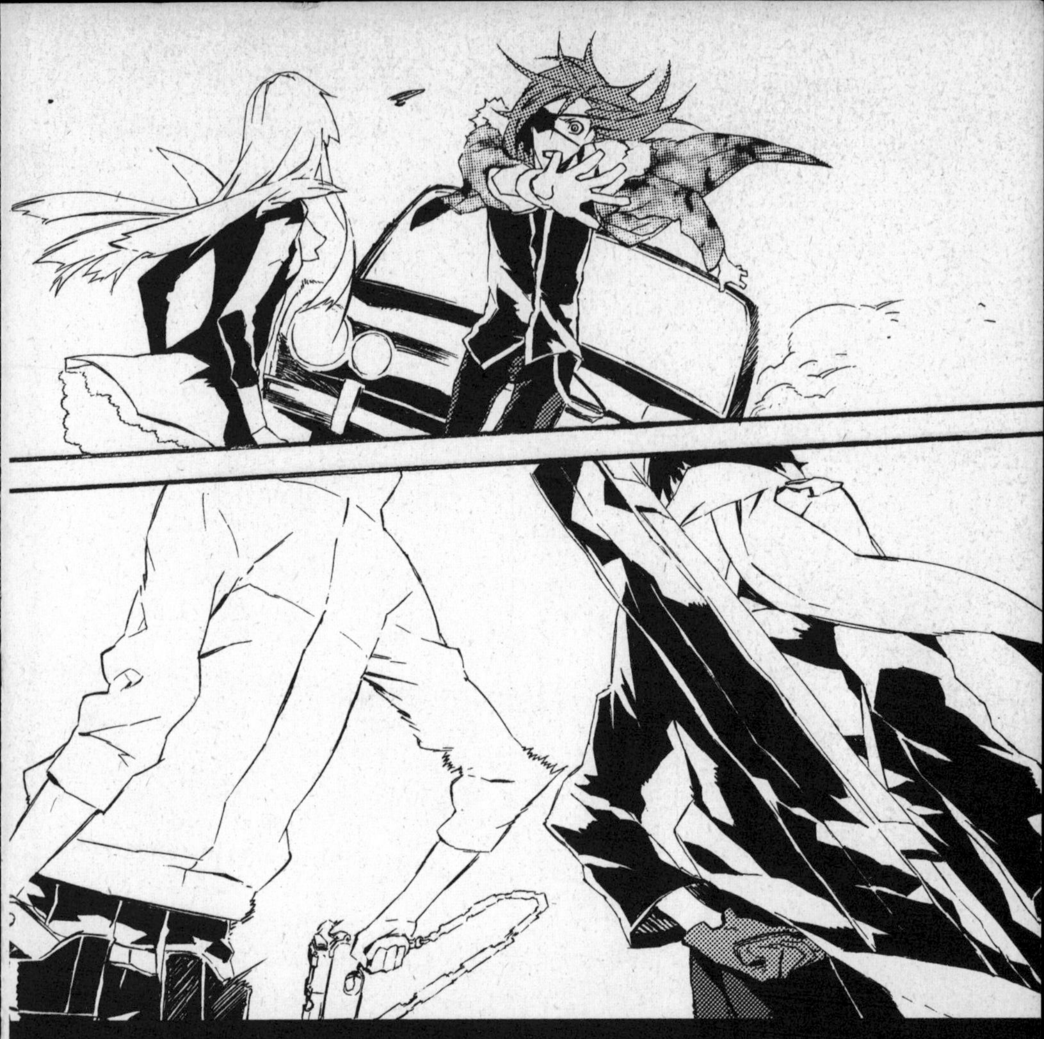

IN THE NEXT VOLUME

As Campanella Frühling's train speeds on, bearing disaster to the Underground and its denizens, Bishop gives Heine more clues to his past. But the aims of Bishop, who wears his own "collar," are unclear: why is he revealing these things now, and why did he save Heine in the first place? Meanwhile, Badou takes on another freelance job from Granny Liza to gather information—and soon discovers it was the information that his brother died pursuing...

Available September 2010

SPECIAL THANKS
Kuroame
U
Henreki

SERIES EDITOR
Satoshi Yamauchi

BOOK EDITOR
Rie Endou

ORIGINAL DESIGN
LIGHTNING

 # ABOUT THE AUTHOR

Shirow Miwa debuted in *UltraJump* magazine in 1999 with the short series *Black Mind*. His next series, *Dogs*, published in the magazine from 2000 to 2001, instantly became a popular success. He returned in 2005 with *Dogs: Bullets & Carnage*, which is currently running in *UltraJump*. Miwa also creates illustrations for books, music videos and magazines, and produces doujinshi (independent comics) under the circle name m.m.m.WORKS. His website is http://mmm-gee.net.

DOGS: BULLETS & CARNAGE
Volume 3

VIZ Signature Edition

Story & Art by
SHIROW MIWA

Translation & Adaptation/Katherine Schilling
Touch-up Art & Lettering/Eric Erbes
Cover & Graphic Design/Sam Elzway
Editor/Leyla Aker

VP, Production/Alvin Lu
VP, Sales & Product Marketing/Gonzalo Ferreyra
VP, Creative/Linda Espinosa
Publisher/Hyoe Narita

DOGS BULLETS & CARNAGE © 2005 by Shirow Miwa.
All rights reserved. First published in Japan in 2005
by SHUEISHA Inc., Tokyo. English translation
rights arranged by SHUEISHA Inc.

The rights of the author(s) of the work(s) in
this publication to be so identified have been
asserted in accordance with the Copyright, Designs
and Patents Act 1988. A CIP catalogue record for
this book is available from the British Library.

The stories, characters and incidents mentioned
in this publication are entirely fictional.

No portion of this book may be reproduced or
transmitted in any form or by any means without
written permission from the copyright holders.

Printed in the U.S.A.

Published by VIZ Media, LLC
P.O. Box 77010
San Francisco, CA 94107

10 9 8 7 6 5 4 3 2
First printing, April 2010
Second printing, May 2010

PARENTAL ADVISORY
DOGS is rated M for Mature and is recommended
for mature readers. This volume contains graphic
violence and mature themes.
ratings.viz.com

VIZ SIGNATURE
www.vizsignature.com

VIZ MEDIA
www.viz.com

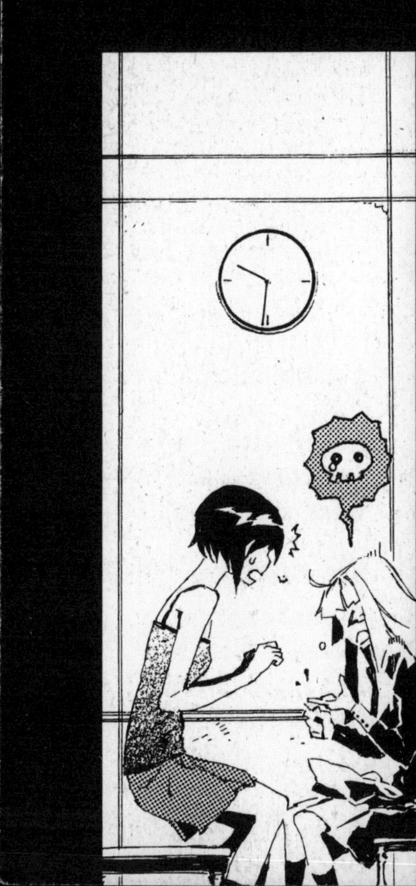

Hey, you're reading the wrong way.

Badou's right—this is actually the end of the book.

To properly enjoy this VIZ graphic novel, please turn it over and begin reading the pages from right to left, starting at the upper right corner of each page and ending at the lower left.

This book has been printed in the Japanese format (right to left) instead of the English format (left to right) in order to preserve the original orientation of the artwork and stay true to the artist's intent. So please flip it over—and have fun.